Two Years Before the Mast

Richard Henry Dana

Infinity Spectrum Books

Published by:
INFINITY SPECTRUM BOOKS
Email: infinityspectrumbooks@gmail.com

First published by Infinity Spectrum Books 2024

Title : **Two Years Before the Mast**
Paperback ISBN **:** 9789361903069
Hardback ISBN: 9789361909528

PREFACE

I am unwilling to present this narrative to the public without a few words in explanation of my reasons for publishing it. Since Mr. Cooper's Pilot and Red Rover, there have been so many stories of sea-life written, that I should really think it unjustifiable in me to add one to the number without being able to give reasons in some measure warranting me in so doing.

With the single exception, as I am quite confident, of Mr. Ames's entertaining, but hasty and desultory work, called "Mariner's Sketches," all the books professing to give life at sea have been written by persons who have gained their experience as naval officers, or passengers, and of these, there are very few which are intended to be taken as narratives of facts.

Now, in the first place, the whole course of life, and daily duties, the discipline, habits and customs of a man-of-war are very different from those of the merchant service; and in the next place, however entertaining and well written these books may be, and however accurately they may give sea-life as it appears to their authors, it must still be plain to every one that a naval officer, who goes to sea as a gentleman, "with his gloves on," (as the phrase is,) and who associated only with his fellow-officers, and hardly speaks to a sailor except through a boatswain's mate, must take a very different view of the whole matter from that which would be taken by a common sailor.

Besides the interest which every one must feel in exhibitions of life in those forms in which he himself has never experienced it; there has been, of late years, a great deal of attention directed toward common seamen, and a strong sympathy awakened in their behalf. Yet I believe that, with the single exception which I have mentioned, there has not been a book written, professing to give their life and experiences, by one who has been of them, and can know what their life really is. A voice from the forecastle has hardly yet been heard.

In the following pages I design to give an accurate and authentic narrative of a little more than two years spent as a common sailor, before the mast, in the American merchant service. It is written out from a journal which I kept at the time, and from notes which

I made of most of the events as they happened; and in it I have adhered closely to fact in every particular, and endeavored to give each thing its true character. In so doing, I have been obliged occasionally to use strong and coarse expressions, and in some instances to give scenes which may be painful to nice feelings; but I have very carefully avoided doing so, whenever I have not felt them essential to giving the true character of a scene. My design is, and it is this which has induced me to publish the book, to present the life of a common sailor at sea as it really is,—the light and the dark together.

There may be in some parts a good deal that is unintelligible to the general reader; but I have found from my own experience, and from what I have heard from others, that plain matters of fact in relation to customs and habits of life new to us, and descriptions of life under new aspects, act upon the inexperienced through the imagination, so that we are hardly aware of our want of technical knowledge. Thousands read the escape of the American frigate through the British channel, and the chase and wreck of the Bristol trader in the Red Rover, and follow the minute nautical manoeuvres with breathless interest, who do not know the name of a rope in the ship; and perhaps with none the less admiration and enthusiasm for their want of acquaintance with the professional detail.

In preparing this narrative I have carefully avoided incorporating into it any impressions but those made upon me by the events as they occurred, leaving to my concluding chapter, to which I shall respectfully call the reader's attention, those views which have been suggested to me by subsequent reflection.

These reasons, and the advice of a few friends, have led me to give this narrative to the press. If it shall interest the general reader, and call more attention to the welfare of seamen, or give any information as to their real condition, which may serve to raise them in the rank of beings, and to promote in any measure their religious and moral improvement, and diminish the hardships of their daily life, the end of its publication will be answered.

R.H.D., Jr.
Boston, July, 1840.

CHAPTER I

DEPARTURE

The fourteenth of August was the day fixed upon for the sailing of the brig Pilgrim on her voyage from Boston round Cape Horn to the western coast of North America. As she was to get under weigh early in the afternoon, I made my appearance on board at twelve o'clock, in full sea-rig, and with my chest, containing an outfit for a two or three year voyage, which I had undertaken from a determination to cure, if possible, by an entire change of life, and by a long absence from books and study, a weakness of the eyes, which had obliged me to give up my pursuits, and which no medical aid seemed likely to cure.

The change from the tight dress coat, silk cap, and kid gloves of an undergraduate at Cambridge, to the loose duck trowsers, checked shirt and tarpaulin hat of a sailor, though somewhat of a transformation, was soon made, and I supposed that I should pass very well for a jack tar. But it is impossible to deceive the practised eye in these matters; and while I supposed myself to be looking as salt as Neptune himself, I was, no doubt, known for a landsman by every one on board as soon as I hove in sight. A sailor has a peculiar cut to his clothes, and a way of wearing them which a green hand can never get. The trowsers, tight round the hips, and thence hanging long and loose round the feet, a superabundance of checked shirt, a low-crowned, well varnished black hat, worn on the back of the head, with half a fathom of black ribbon hanging over the left eye, and a peculiar tie to the black silk neckerchief, with sundry other minutiae, are signs, the want of which betray the beginner at once. Beside the points in my dress which were out of the way, doubtless my complexion and hands were enough to distinguish me from the regular salt, who, with a sun-burnt cheek, wide step, and rolling gait, swings his bronzed and toughened hands athwart-ships, half open, as though just ready to grasp a rope.

"With all my imperfections on my head," I joined the crew, and we hauled out into the stream, and came to anchor for the night. The next day we were employed in preparations for sea, reeving studding-sail gear, crossing royal yards, putting on chafing gear, and taking on board our powder. On the following night, I stood my first watch. I remained awake nearly all the first part of the night from fear that I might not hear when I was called; and when I went on deck, so great were my ideas of the importance of my trust, that I walked regularly fore and aft the whole length of the vessel, looking out over the bows and taffrail at each turn, and was not a little surprised at the coolness of the old salt whom I called to take my place, in stowing himself snugly away under the long boat, for a nap. That was sufficient lookout, he thought, for a fine night, at anchor in a safe harbor.

The next morning was Saturday, and a breeze having sprung up from the southward, we took a pilot on board, hove up our anchor, and began beating down the bay. I took leave of those of my friends who came to see me off, and had barely opportunity to take a last look at the city, and well-known objects, as no time is allowed on board ship for sentiment. As we drew down into the lower harbor, we found the wind ahead in the bay, and were obliged to come to anchor in the roads. We remained there through the day and a part of the night. My watch began at eleven o'clock at night, and I received orders to call the captain if the wind came out from the westward. About midnight the wind became fair, and having called the captain, I was ordered to call all hands. How I accomplished this I do not know, but I am quite sure I did not give the true hoarse, boatswain call of "A-a-ll ha-a-a-nds! up anchor, a-ho-oy!" In a short time every one was in motion, the sails loosed, the yards braced, and we began to heave up the anchor, which was our last hold upon Yankee land. I could take but little part in all these preparations. My little knowledge of a vessel was all at fault. Unintelligible orders were so rapidly given and so immediately executed; there was such a hurrying about, and such an intermingling of strange cries and stranger actions, that I was completely bewildered. There is not so helpless and pitiable an object in the world as a landsman beginning a sailor's life. At length those peculiar, long-drawn sounds, which denote that the crew are heaving the windlass, began, and in a few moments we were under weigh. The noise of the water thrown from the bows began to be heard, the vessel leaned over from the damp night breeze, and rolled with the heavy ground swell, and we had actually begun our long, long journey. This was literally bidding "good night" to my native land.

CHAPTER II

FIRST IMPRESSIONS—"SAIL HO!"

The first day we passed at sea was the Sabbath. As we were just from port, and there was a great deal to be done on board, we were kept at work all day, and at night the watches were set, and everything put into sea order. When we were called aft to be divided into watches, I had a good specimen of the manner of a sea captain. After the division had been made, he gave a short characteristic speech, walking the quarter deck with a cigar in his mouth, and dropping the words out between the puffs.

"Now, my men, we have begun a long voyage. If we get along well together, we shall have a comfortable time; if we don't, we shall have hell afloat.—All you've got to do is to obey your orders and do your duty like men,—then you'll fare well enough;—if you don't, you'll fare hard enough,—I can tell you. If we pull together, you'll find me a clever fellow; if we don't, you'll find me a bloody rascal.—That's all I've got to say.—Go below, the larboard watch!"

I being in the starboard or second mate's watch, had the opportunity of keeping the first watch at sea. S——, a young man, making, like myself, his first voyage, was in the same watch, and as he was the son of a professional man, and had been in a counting-room in Boston, we found that we had many friends and topics in common. We talked these matters over,—Boston, what our friends were probably doing, our voyage, etc., until he went to take his turn at the look-out, and left me to myself. I had now a fine time for reflection. I felt for the first time the perfect silence of the sea. The officer was walking the quarter deck, where I had no right to go, one or two men were talking on the forecastle, whom I had little inclination to join, so that I was left open to the full impression of everything about me. However much I was affected by the beauty of the sea, the bright stars, and the clouds driven swiftly over them, I could not but remember that I was separating myself from all the social and intellectual enjoyments of life. Yet, strange as it may seem, I did then and afterwards take pleasure in these reflections, hoping by them to prevent my becoming insensible to the value of what I was leaving.

But all my dreams were soon put to flight by an order from the officer to trim the yards, as the wind was getting ahead; and I could plainly see by the looks the sailors occasionally cast to windward, and by the dark clouds that were fast coming up, that we had bad weather to prepare for, and had heard the captain say that he expected to be in the Gulf Stream by twelve o'clock. In a few minutes eight bells were struck, the watch called, and we went below. I now began to feel the first discomforts of a sailor's life. The steerage in which I lived was filled with coils of rigging, spare sails, old junk and ship stores, which had not been stowed away. Moreover, there had been no berths built for us to sleep in, and we were not allowed to drive nails to hang our clothes upon. The sea, too, had risen, the vessel was rolling heavily, and everything was pitched about in grand confusion. There was a complete "hurrah's nest," as the sailors say, "everything on top and nothing at hand." A large hawser had been coiled away upon my chest; my hats, boots, mattress and blankets had all fetched away and gone over to leeward, and were jammed and broken under the boxes and coils of rigging. To crown all, we were allowed no light to find anything with, and I was just beginning to feel strong symptoms of sea-sickness, and that listlessness and inactivity which accompany it. Giving up all attempts to collect my things together, I lay down upon the sails, expecting every moment to hear the cry of "all hands, ahoy," which the approaching storm would soon make necessary. I shortly heard the rain-drops falling on deck, thick and fast, and the watch evidently had their hands full of work, for I could hear the loud and repeated orders of the mate, the trampling of feet, the creaking of blocks, and all the accompaniments of a coming storm. In a few minutes the slide of the hatch was thrown back, which let down the noise and tumult of the deck still louder, the loud cry of "All hands, ahoy! tumble up here and take in sail," saluted our ears, and the hatch was quickly shut again. When I got upon deck, a new scene and a new experience were before me. The little brig was close hauled upon the wind, and lying over, as it then seemed to me, nearly upon her beam ends. The heavy head sea was beating against her bows with the noise and force almost of a sledge-hammer, and flying over the deck, drenching us completely through. The topsail halyards had been let go, and the great sails filling out and backing against the masts with a noise like thunder. The wind was whistling through the rigging, loose ropes flying about; loud and, to me, unintelligible orders constantly given and rapidly executed, and the sailors "singing out" at the ropes in their hoarse and peculiar strains. In addition to all this, I had not got my "sea legs on," was dreadfully sick, with hardly strength enough to hold on to anything, and it was "pitch dark." This was my state when I was ordered aloft, for the first time, to reef topsails.

How I got along, I cannot now remember. I "laid out" on the yards and held on with all my strength. I could not have been of much service, for I remember having been sick several times before I left the topsail yard. Soon all was snug aloft, and we were again allowed to go below. This I did not consider much of a favor, for the confusion of everything below, and that inexpressible sickening smell, caused by the shaking up of the bilge-water in the hold, made the steerage but an indifferent refuge from the cold, wet decks. I had often read of the nautical experiences of others, but I felt as though there could be none worse than mine; for in addition to every other evil, I could not but remember that this was only the first night of a two years' voyage. When we were on deck we were not much better off, for we were continually ordered about by the officer, who said that it was good for us to be in motion. Yet anything was better than the horrible state of things below. I remember very well going to the hatchway and putting my head down, when I was oppressed by nausea, and always being relieved immediately. It was as good as an emetic.

This state of things continued for two days.

Wednesday, Aug. 20th. We had the watch on deck from four till eight, this morning. When we came on deck at four o'clock, we found things much changed for the better. The sea and wind had gone down, and the stars were out bright. I experienced a corresponding change in my feelings; yet continued extremely weak from my sickness. I stood in the waist on the weather side, watching the gradual breaking of the day, and the first streaks of the early light. Much has been said of the sun-rise at sea; but it will not compare with the sun-rise on shore. It wants the accompaniments of the songs of birds, the awakening hum of men, and the glancing of the first beams upon trees, hills, spires, and house-tops, to give it life and spirit. But though the actual rise of the sun at sea is not so beautiful, yet nothing will compare with the early breaking of day upon the wide ocean.

There is something in the first grey streaks stretching along the eastern horizon and throwing an indistinct light upon the face of the deep, which combines with the boundlessness and unknown depth of the sea around you, and gives one a feeling of loneliness, of dread, and of melancholy foreboding, which nothing else in nature can give. This gradually passes away as the light grows brighter, and when the sun comes up, the ordinary monotonous sea day begins.

From such reflections as these, I was aroused by the order from the officer, "Forward there! rig the head-pump!" I found that no time was allowed for day-dreaming, but that we must "turn-to" at the first light. Having called up the "idlers," namely carpenter, cook, steward, etc., and rigged the pump, we commenced washing down the decks. This operation, which is performed every morning at sea, takes nearly two hours; and I had hardly strength enough to get through it. After we had finished, swabbed down, and coiled up the rigging, I sat down on the spars, waiting for seven bells, which was the sign for breakfast. The officer, seeing my lazy posture, ordered me to slush the main-mast, from the royal-mast-head, down. The vessel was then rolling a little, and I had taken no sustenance for three days, so that I felt tempted to tell him that I had rather wait till after breakfast; but I knew that I must "take the bull by the horns," and that if I showed any sign of want of spirit or of backwardness, that I should be ruined at once. So I took my bucket of grease and climbed up to the royal-mast-head. Here the rocking of the vessel, which increases the higher you go from the foot of the mast, which is the fulcrum of the lever, and the smell of the grease, which offended my fastidious senses, upset my stomach again, and I was not a little rejoiced when I got upon the comparative terra firma of the deck. In a few minutes seven bells were struck, the log hove, the watch called, and we went to breakfast. Here I cannot but remember the advice of the cook, a simple-hearted African. "Now," says he, "my lad, you are well cleaned out; you haven't got a drop of your 'long-shore swash aboard of you. You must begin on a new tack,—pitch all your sweetmeats overboard, and turn-to upon good hearty salt beef and sea bread, and I'll promise you, you'll have your ribs well sheathed, and be as hearty as any of 'em, afore you are up to the Horn." This would be good advice to give to passengers, when they speak of the little niceties which they have laid in, in case of sea-sickness.

I cannot describe the change which half a pound of cold salt beef and a biscuit or two produced in me. I was a new being. We had a watch below until noon, so that I had some time to myself; and getting a huge piece of strong, cold, salt beef from the cook, I kept gnawing upon it until twelve o'clock. When we went on deck I felt somewhat like a man, and could begin to learn my sea duty with considerable spirit. At about two o'clock we heard the loud cry of "sail ho!" from aloft, and soon saw two sails to windward, going directly athwart our hawse. This was the first time that I had seen a sail at sea. I thought then, and always have since, that it exceeds every other sight in interest and beauty. They passed to leeward of us, and out of hailing distance; but the captain could read the names on their sterns with the glass. They were the ship Helen Mar, of New York, and the brig Mermaid, of Boston. They were both steering westward, and were bound in for our "dear native land."

Thursday, Aug. 21st. This day the sun rose clear, we had a fine wind, and everything was bright and cheerful. I had now got my sea legs on, and was beginning to enter upon the regular duties of a sea-life. About six bells, that is, three o'clock, P.M., we saw a sail on our larboard bow. I was very anxious, like every new sailor, to speak her. She came down to us, backed her main-top-sail, and the two vessels stood "head on," bowing and curvetting at each other like a couple of war-horses reined in by their riders. It was the first vessel that I had seen near, and I was surprised to find how much she rolled and pitched in so quiet a sea. She lunged her head into the sea, and then, her stern settling gradually down, her huge bows rose up, showing the bright copper, and her stern, and bresthooks dripping, like old Neptune's locks, with the brine. Her decks were filled with passengers who had come up at the cry of "sail ho," and who by their dress and features appeared to be Swiss and French emigrants. She hailed us at first in French, but receiving no answer, she tried us in English. She was the ship La Carolina, from Havre, for New York. We desired her to report the brig Pilgrim, from Boston, for the north-west coast of America, five days out. She then filled away and left us to plough on through our waste of waters. This day ended pleasantly; we had got into regular and comfortable weather, and into that routine of sea-life which is only broken by a storm, a sail, or the sight of land.

CHAPTER III

SHIP'S DUTIES—TROPICS

As we had now a long "spell" of fine weather, without any incident to break the monotony of our lives, there can be no better place to describe the duties, regulations, and customs of an American merchantman, of which ours was a fair specimen.

The captain, in the first place, is lord paramount. He stands no watch, comes and goes when he pleases, and is accountable to no one, and must be obeyed in everything, without a question, even from his chief officer. He has the power to turn his officers off duty, and even to break them and make them do duty as sailors in the forecastle. When there are no passengers and no supercargo, as in our vessel, he has no companion but his own dignity, and no pleasures, unless he differs from most of his kind, but the consciousness of possessing supreme power, and, occasionally, the exercise of it.

The prime minister, the official organ, and the active and superintending officer, is the chief mate. He is first lieutenant, boatswain, sailing-master, and quarter-master. The captain tells him what he wishes to have done, and leaves to him the care of overseeing, of allotting the work, and also the responsibility of its being well done. The mate (as he is always called, par excellence) also keeps the log-book, for which he is responsible to the owners and insurers, and has the charge of the stowage, safe keeping, and delivery of the cargo. He is also, ex-officio, the wit of the crew; for the captain does not condescend to joke with the men, and the second mate no one cares for; so that when "the mate" thinks fit to entertain "the people" with a coarse joke or a little practical wit, every one feels bound to laugh.

The second mate's is proverbially a dog's berth. He is neither officer nor man. The men do not respect him as an officer, and he is obliged to go aloft to reef and furl the topsails, and to put his hands into the tar and slush, with the rest. The crew call him the "sailor's waiter," as he has to furnish them with spun-yarn, marline, and all other stuffs that they need in their work, and has charge of the boatswain's locker, which includes serving-boards, marline-spikes, etc. He is expected by the captain to maintain his dignity and to enforce obedience, and still is kept at a great distance from the mate, and obliged to work with the crew. He is one to whom little is given and of whom much is required. His wages are usually double those of a common sailor, and he eats and sleeps in the cabin; but he is obliged to be on deck nearly all the time, and eats at the second table, that is, makes a meal out of what the captain and chief mate leave.

The steward is the captain's servant, and has charge of the pantry, from which every one, even the mate himself, is excluded. These distinctions usually find him an enemy in the mate, who does not like to have any one on board who is not entirely under his control; the crew do not consider him as one of their number, so he is left to the mercy of the captain.

The cook is the patron of the crew, and those who are in his favor can get their wet mittens and stockings dried, or light their pipes at the galley on the night watch. These two worthies, together with the carpenter and sailmaker, if there be one, stand no watch, but, being employed all day, are allowed to "sleep in" at night, unless all hands are called.

The crew are divided into two divisions, as equally as may be, called the watches. Of these the chief mate commands the larboard, and the second mate the starboard. They divide the time between them, being on and off duty, or, as it is called, on deck and below, every other four hours. If, for instance, the chief mate with the larboard watch have the first night-watch from eight to twelve; at the end of the four hours, the starboard watch is called, and the second mate takes the deck, while the larboard watch and the first mate go below until four in the morning, when they come on deck again and remain until eight; having what is called the morning watch. As they will have been on deck eight hours out of the twelve, while those who had the middle watch—from twelve to four, will only have been up four hours, they have what is called a "forenoon watch below," that is, from eight, A.M., till twelve, M. In a man-of-war, and in some merchantmen, this alteration of watches is kept up throughout the twenty-four hours; but our ship, like most merchantmen, had "all hands" from twelve o'clock till dark, except in bad weather, when we had "watch and watch."

An explanation of the "dog watches" may, perhaps, be of use to one who has never been at sea. They are to shift the watches each night, so that the same watch need not be on deck at the same hours. In order to effect this, the watch from four to eight, P.M., is divided into two half, or dog watches, one from four to six, and the other from six to eight. By this means they divide the twenty-four hours into seven watches instead of six, and thus shift the hours every night. As the dog watches come during twilight, after the day's work is done, and before the night watch is set, they are the watches in which everybody is on deck. The captain is up, walking on the weather side of the quarter-deck, the chief mate is on the lee side, and the second mate about the weather gangway. The steward has finished his work in the cabin, and has come up to smoke his pipe with the cook in the galley. The crew are sitting on the windlass or lying on the forecastle, smoking, singing, or telling long yarns. At eight o'clock, eight bells are struck, the log is hove, the watch set, the wheel relieved, the galley shut up, and the other watch goes below.

The morning commences with the watch on deck's "turning-to" at day-break and washing down, scrubbing, and swabbing the decks. This, together with filling the "scuttled butt" with fresh water, and coiling up the rigging, usually occupies the time until seven bells, (half after seven,) when all hands get breakfast. At eight, the day's work begins, and lasts until sun-down, with the exception of an hour for dinner.

Before I end my explanations, it may be well to define a day's work, and to correct a mistake prevalent among landsmen about a sailor's life. Nothing is more common than to hear people say—"Are not sailors very idle at sea?—what can they find to do?" This is a very natural mistake, and being very frequently made, it is one which every sailor feels interested in having corrected. In the first place, then, the discipline of the ship requires every man to be at work upon something when he is on deck, except at night and on Sundays. Except at these times, you will never see a man, on board a well-ordered vessel, standing idle on deck, sitting down, or leaning over the side. It is the officers' duty to keep every one at work, even if there is nothing to be done but to scrape the rust from the chain cables. In no state prison are the convicts more regularly set to work, and more closely watched. No conversation is allowed among the crew at their duty, and though they frequently do talk when aloft, or when near one another, yet they always stop when an officer is nigh.

With regard to the work upon which the men are put, it is a matter which probably would not be understood by one who has not been at sea. When I first left port, and found that we were kept regularly employed for a week or two, I supposed that we were getting the vessel into sea trim, and that it would soon be over, and we should have nothing to do but sail the ship; but I found that it continued so for two years, and at the end of the two years there was as much to be done as ever. As has often been said, a ship is like a lady's watch, always out of repair. When first leaving port, studding-sail gear is to be rove, all the running rigging to be examined, that which is unfit for use to be got down, and new rigging rove in its place: then the standing rigging is to be overhauled, replaced, and repaired, in a thousand different ways; and wherever any of the numberless ropes or the yards are chafing or wearing upon it, there "chafing gear," as it is called, must be put on. This chafing gear consists of worming, parcelling, roundings, battens, and service of all kinds—both rope-yarns, spun-yarn, marline and seizing-stuffs. Taking off, putting on, and mending the chafing gear alone, upon a vessel, would find constant employment for two or three men, during working hours, for a whole voyage.

The next point to be considered is, that all the "small stuffs" which are used on board a ship—such as spun-yarn, marline, seizing-stuff, etc.—are made on board. The owners of a vessel buy up incredible quantities of "old junk," which the sailors unlay, after drawing out the yarns, knot them together, and roll them up in balls. These "rope-yarns" are constantly used for various purposes, but the greater part is manufactured into spun-yarn. For this purpose every vessel is furnished with a "spun-yarn winch;" which is very simple, consisting of a wheel and spindle. This may be heard constantly going on deck in pleasant weather; and we had employment, during a great part of the time, for three hands in drawing and knotting yarns, and making them spun-yarn.

Another method of employing the crew is, "setting up" rigging. Whenever any of the standing rigging becomes slack, (which is continually happening), the seizings and coverings must be taken off, tackles got up, and after the rigging is bowsed well taut, the seizings and coverings replaced; which is a very nice piece of work. There is also such a connection between different parts of a vessel, that one rope can seldom be touched without altering another. You cannot stay a mast aft by the back stays, without slacking up the head stays, etc. If we add to this all the tarring, greasing, oiling, varnishing, painting, scraping, and scrubbing which is required in the course of a long voyage, and also remember this is all to be done in addition to watching at night, steering, reefing, furling, bracing, making and setting sail, and pulling, hauling, and climbing in every direction, one will hardly ask, "What can a sailor find to do at sea?"

If, after all this labor—after exposing their lives and limbs in storms, wet and cold,

"Wherein the cub-drawn bear would couch;
The lion and the belly-pinched wolf
Keep their fur dry;—"

the merchants and captain think that they have not earned their twelve dollars a month, (out of which they clothe themselves,) and their salt beef and hard bread, they keep them picking oakum—ad infinitum. This is the usual resource upon a rainy day, for then it will not do to work upon rigging; and when it is pouring down in floods, instead of letting the sailors stand about in sheltered places, and talk, and keep themselves comfortable, they are separated to different parts of the ship and kept at work picking oakum. I have seen oakum stuff placed about in different parts of the ship, so that the sailors might not be idle in the snatches between the frequent squalls upon crossing the equator. Some officers have been so driven to find work for the crew in a ship ready for sea, that they have set them to pounding the anchors (often done) and scraping the chain cables. The "Philadelphia Catechism" is,

"Six days shalt thou labor and do all thou art able,
And on the seventh—holystone the decks and scrape the cable."

This kind of work, of course, is not kept up off Cape Horn, Cape of Good Hope, and in extreme north and south latitudes; but I have seen the decks washed down and scrubbed, when the water would have frozen if it had been fresh; and all hands kept at work upon the rigging, when we had on our pea-jackets, and our hands so numb that we could hardly hold our marline-spikes.

I have here gone out of my narrative course in order that any who read this may form as correct an idea of a sailor's life and duty as possible. I have done it in this place because, for some time, our life was nothing but the unvarying repetition of these duties, which can be better described together. Before leaving this description, however, I would state, in order to show landsmen how little they know of the nature of a ship, that a ship-carpenter is kept in constant employ during good weather on board vessels which are in, what is called, perfect sea order.

CHAPTER IV

A ROGUE—TROUBLE ON BOARD—"LAND HO!"—POMPERO—CAPE HORN

After speaking the Carolina, on the 21st August, nothing occurred to break the monotony of our life until

Friday, September 5th, when we saw a sail on our weather (starboard) beam. She proved to be a brig under English colors, and passing under our stern, reported herself as forty-nine days from Buenos Ayres, bound to Liverpool. Before she had passed us, "sail ho!" was cried again, and we made another sail, far on our weather bow, and steering athwart our hawse. She passed out of hail, but we made her out to be an hermaphrodite brig, with Brazilian colors in her main rigging. By her course, she must have been bound from Brazil to the south of Europe, probably Portugal.

Sunday, Sept. 7th. Fell in with the north-east trade winds. This morning we caught our first dolphin, which I was very eager to see. I was disappointed in the colors of this fish when dying. They were certainly very beautiful, but not equal to what has been said of them. They are too indistinct. To do the fish justice, there is nothing more beautiful than the dolphin when swimming a few feet below the surface, on a bright day. It is the most elegantly formed, and also the quickest fish, in salt water; and the rays of the sun striking upon it, in its rapid and changing motions, reflected from the water, make it look like a stray beam from a rainbow.

This day was spent like all pleasant Sabbaths at sea. The decks are washed down, the rigging coiled up, and everything put in order; and throughout the day, only one watch is kept on deck at a time. The men are all dressed in their best white duck trowsers, and red or checked shirts, and have nothing to do but to make the necessary changes in the sails. They employ themselves in reading, talking, smoking, and mending their clothes. If the weather is pleasant, they bring their work and their books upon deck, and sit down upon the forecastle and windlass. This is the only day on which these privileges are allowed them. When

Monday comes, they put on their tarry trowsers again, and prepare for six days of labor.

To enhance the value of the Sabbath to the crew, they are allowed on that day a pudding, or, as it is called, a "duff." This is nothing more than flour boiled with water, and eaten with molasses. It is very heavy, dark, and clammy, yet it is looked upon as a luxury, and really forms an agreeable variety with salt beef and pork. Many a rascally captain has made friends of his crew by allowing them duff twice a week on the passage home.

On board some vessels this is made a day of instruction and of religious exercises; but we had a crew of swearers, from the captain to the smallest boy; and a day of rest, and of something like quiet, social enjoyment, was all that we could expect.

We continued running large before the north-east trade winds for several days, until Monday—

September 22d; when, upon coming on deck at seven bells in the morning, we found the other watch aloft throwing water upon the sails; and looking astern, we saw a small clipper-built brig with a black hull heading directly after us. We went to work immediately, and put all the canvas upon the brig which we could get upon her, rigging out oars for studding-sail yards; and continued wetting down the sails by buckets of water whipped up to the mast-head, until about nine o'clock, when there came on a drizzling rain. The vessel continued in pursuit, changing her course as we changed ours, to keep before the wind. The captain, who watched her with his glass, said that she was armed, and full of men, and showed no colors. We continued running dead before the wind, knowing that we sailed better so, and that clippers are fastest on the wind. We had also another advantage. The wind was light, and we spread more canvas than she did, having royals and sky-sails fore and aft, and ten studding-sails; while she, being an hermaphrodite brig, had only a gaff topsail, aft. Early in the morning she was overhauling us a little, but after the rain came on and the wind grew lighter, we began to leave her astern. All hands remained on deck throughout the day, and we got our arms in order; but we were too few to have done anything with her, if she had proved to be what we feared. Fortunately there was no moon, and the night which followed was exceedingly dark, so that by putting out all the lights and altering our course four points, we hoped to get out of her reach. We had no light in the binnacle, but steered by the stars, and kept perfect silence through the night. At daybreak there was no sign of anything in the horizon, and we kept the vessel off to her course.

Wednesday, October 1st. Crossed the equator in long. 24° 24' W. I now, for the first time, felt at liberty, according to the old usage, to call myself a son of Neptune, and was very glad to be able to claim the title without the disagreeable initiation which so many have to go through. After once crossing the line you can never be subjected to the process, but are considered as a son of Neptune, with full powers to play tricks upon others. This ancient custom is now seldom allowed, unless there are passengers on board, in which case there is always a good deal of sport.

It had been obvious to all hands for some time that the second mate, whose name was F——, was an idle, careless fellow, and not much of a sailor, and that the captain was exceedingly dissatisfied with him. The power of the captain in these cases was well known, and we all anticipated a difficulty. F—— (called Mr. by virtue of his office) was but half a sailor, having always been short voyages and remained at home a long time between them. His father was a man of some property, and intended to have given his son a liberal education; but he, being idle and worthless, was sent off to sea, and succeeded no better there; for, unlike many scamps, he had none of the qualities of a sailor—he was "not of the stuff that they make sailor of." He was one of that class of officers who are disliked by their captain and despised by the crew. He used to hold long yarns with the crew, and talk about the captain, and play with the boys, and relax discipline in every way. This kind of conduct always makes the captain suspicious, and is never pleasant, in the end, to the men; they preferring to have an officer active, vigilant, and distant as may be, with kindness. Among other bad practices, he frequently slept on his watch, and having been discovered asleep by the captain, he was told that he would be turned off duty if he did it again. To prevent it in every way possible, the hen-coops were ordered to be knocked up, for the captain never sat down on deck himself, and never permitted an officer to do so.

The second night after crossing the equator, we had the watch from eight till twelve, and it was "my helm" for the last two hours.

There had been light squalls through the night, and the captain told Mr. F——, who commanded our watch, to keep a bright look-out. Soon after I came to the helm, I found that he was quite drowsy, and at last he stretched himself on the companion and went fast asleep. Soon afterwards, the captain came very quietly on deck, and stood by me for some time looking at the compass. The officer at length became aware of the captain's presence, but pretending not to know it, began humming and whistling to himself, to show that he was not asleep, and went forward, without looking behind him, and ordered the main royal to be loosed. On turning round to come aft, he pretended surprise at seeing the master on deck. This would not do. The captain was too "wide awake" for him, and beginning upon him at once, gave him a grand blow-up, in true nautical style—"You're a lazy, good-for-nothing rascal; you're neither man, boy, soger, nor sailor! you're no more than a thing aboard a vessel! you don't earn your salt! you're worse than a Mahon soger!" and other still more choice extracts from the sailor's vocabulary. After the poor fellow had taken the harangue, he was sent into his state-room, and the captain stood the rest of the watch himself.

At seven bells in the morning, all hands were called aft and told that F—— was no longer an officer on board, and that we might choose one of our own number for second mate. It is usual for the captain to make this offer, and it is very good policy, for the crew think themselves the choosers and are flattered by it, but have to obey, nevertheless. Our crew, as is usual, refused to take the responsibility of choosing a man of whom we would never be able to complain, and left it to the captain. He picked out an active and intelligent young sailor, born near the Kennebec, who had been several Canton voyages, and proclaimed him in the following manner: "I choose Jim Hall—he's your second mate. All you've got to do is, to obey him as you would me; and remember that he is Mr. Hall." F—— went forward into the forecastle as a common sailor, and lost the handle to his name, while young fore-mast Jim became Mr. Hall, and took up his quarters in the land of knives and forks and tea-cups.

Sunday, October 5th. It was our morning watch; when, soon after the day began to break, a man on the forecastle called out, "Land ho!" I had never heard the cry before, and did not know what it meant, (and few would suspect what the words were, when hearing the strange sound for the first time,) but I soon found, by the direction of all eyes, that there was land stretching along our weather beam. We immediately took in studding-sails and hauled our wind, running in for the land. This was done to determine our longitude; for by the captain's chronometer we were in 25° W., but by his observations we were much farther, and he had been for some time in doubt whether it was his chronometer or his sextant which was out of order. This land-fall settled the matter, and the former instrument was condemned, and becoming still worse, was never afterwards used.

As we ran in towards the coast, we found that we were directly off the port of Pernambuco, and could see with the telescope the roofs of the houses, and one large church, and the town of Olinda. We ran along by the mouth of the harbor, and saw a full-rigged brig going in. At two, P.M., we again kept off before the wind, leaving the land on our quarter, and at sun-down, it was out of sight. It was here that I first saw one of those singular things called catamarans. They are composed of logs lashed together upon the water; have one large sail, are quite fast, and, strange as it may seem, are trusted as good sea boats. We saw several, with from one to three men in each, boldly putting out to sea, after it had become almost dark. The Indians go out in them after fish, and as the weather is regular in certain seasons, they have no fear. After taking a new departure from Olinda, we kept off on our way to Cape Horn.

We met with nothing remarkable until we were in the latitude of the river La Plata. Here there are violent gales from the south-west, called Pomperos, which are very destructive to the shipping in the river, and are felt for many leagues at sea. They are usually preceded by lightning. The captain told the mates to keep a bright look-out, and if they saw lightning at the south-west, to take in sail at once. We got the first touch of one during my watch on deck. I was walking in the lee gangway, and thought that I saw lightning on the lee bow. I told the second mate, who came over and looked out for some time. It was very black in the south-west, and in about ten minutes we saw a distinct flash. The wind, which had been south-east, had now left us, and it was dead calm. We sprang aloft immediately and furled the royals and top-gallant-sails, and took in the flying jib, hauled up the mainsail and trysail, squared the after yards, and awaited the attack. A huge mist capped with black clouds came driving towards us, extending over that quarter of the horizon, and covering the stars, which shone brightly in the other part of the heavens. It came upon us at once with a blast, and a shower of hail and rain, which almost took our breath from us. The hardiest was obliged to turn his back. We let the halyards run, and fortunately were not taken aback. The little vessel "paid off" from the wind, and ran on for some time directly before it, tearing through the water with everything flying. Having called all hands, we close-reefed the topsails and trysail, furled the courses and job, set the fore-top-mast staysail, and brought her up nearly to her course, with the weather braces hauled in a little, to ease her.

This was the first blow, that I had seen, which could really be called a gale. We had reefed our topsails in the Gulf Stream, and I thought it something serious, but an older sailor would have thought nothing of it. As I had now become used to the vessel and to my duty, I was of some service on a yard, and could knot my reef-point as well as anybody. I obeyed the order to lay*[1]* aloft with the rest, and found the reefing a very exciting scene; for one watch reefed the fore-topsail, and the other the main, and every one did his utmost to get his topsail hoisted first. We had a great advantage over the larboard watch, because the chief mate never goes aloft, while our new second mate used to jump into the rigging as soon as we began to haul out the reef-tackle, and have the weather earing passed before there was a man upon the yard. In this way we were almost always able to raise the cry of "Haul out to leeward" before them, and having knotted our points, would slide down the shrouds and back-stays, and sing out at the topsail halyards to let it be known that we were ahead of them. Reefing is the most exciting part of a sailor's duty. All hands are engaged upon it, and after the halyards are let go, there is no time to be lost—no "sogering," or hanging back, then. If one is not quick enough, another runs over him. The first on the yard goes to the weather earing, the second to the lee, and the next two to the "dog's ears;" while the others lay along into the bunt, just giving each other elbow-room. In reefing, the yard-arms (the extremes of the yards) are the posts of honor; but in furling, the strongest and most experienced stand in the slings, (or, middle of the yard,) to make up the bunt. If the second mate is a smart fellow, he will never let any one take either of these posts from him; but if he is wanting either in seamanship, strength, or activity, some better man will get the bunt and earings from him; which immediately brings him into disrepute.

We remained for the rest of the night, and throughout the next day, under the same close sail, for it continued to blow very fresh; and though we had no more hail, yet there was a soaking rain, and it was quite cold and uncomfortable; the more so, because we were not prepared for cold weather, but had on our thin clothes. We were glad to get a watch below, and put on our thick clothing, boots, and south-westers. Towards sun-down the gale moderated a little, and it began to clear off in the south-west. We shook our reefs out, one by one, and before midnight had top-gallant sails upon her.

We had now made up our minds for Cape Horn and cold weather, and entered upon every necessary preparation.

Tuesday, Nov. 4th. At day-break, saw land upon our larboard quarter. There were two islands, of different size but of the same shape; rather high, beginning low at the water's edge, and running with a curved ascent to the middle. They were so far off as to be of a deep blue color, and in a few hours we sank them in the north-east. These were the Falkland Islands. We had run between them and the main land of Patagonia. At sun-set the second mate, who was at the masthead, said that he saw land on the starboard bow. This must have been the island of Staten Land; and we were now in the region of Cape Horn, with a fine breeze from the northward, top-mast and top-gallant studding-sails set, and every prospect of a speedy and pleasant passage round.

[1] This word "lay," which is in such general use on board ship, being used in giving orders instead of "go"; as "Lay forward!" "Lay aft!" "Lay aloft!" etc., I do not understand to be the neuter verb, lie, mispronounced, but to be the active verb lay, with the objective case understood; as "Lay yourselves forwards!" "Lay yourselves aft!" etc.

CHAPTER V

CAPE HORN—A VISIT

Wednesday, Nov. 5th. The weather was fine during the previous night, and we had a clear view of the Magellan Clouds, and of the Southern Cross. The Magellan Clouds consist of three small nebulae in the southern part of the heavens,—two bright, like the milky-way, and one dark. These are first seen, just above the horizon, soon after crossing the southern tropic. When off Cape Horn, they are nearly overhead. The cross is composed of four stars in that form, and is said to be the brightest constellation in the heavens.

During the first part of this day (Wednesday) the wind was light, but after noon it came on fresh, and we furled the royals. We still kept the studding-sails out, and the captain said he should go round with them, if he could. Just before eight o'clock, (then about sun-down, in that latitude,) the cry of "All hands ahoy!" was sounded down the fore scuttle and the after hatchway, and hurrying upon deck, we found a large black cloud rolling on toward us from the south-west, and blackening the whole heavens. "Here comes the Cape Horn!" said the chief mate; and we had hardly time to haul down and clew up, before it was upon us. In a few moments, a heavier sea was raised than I had ever seen before, and as it was directly ahead, the little brig, which was no better than a bathing machine, plunged into it, and all the forward part of her was under water; the sea pouring in through the bow-ports and hawse-hole and over the knight-heads, threatening to wash everything overboard. In the lee scuppers it was up to a man's waist. We sprang aloft and double reefed the topsails, and furled all the other sails, and made all snug. But this would not do; the brig was laboring and straining against the head sea, and the gale was growing worse and worse. At the same time the sleet and hail were driving with all fury against us. We clewed down, and hauled out the reef-tackles again, and close-reefed the fore-topsail, and furled the main, and hove her to on the starboard tack. Here was an end to our fine prospects. We made up our minds to head winds and cold weather; sent down the royal yards, and unrove the gear, but all the rest of the top hamper remained aloft, even to the sky-sail masts and studding-sail booms.

Throughout the night it stormed violently—rain, hail, snow, and sleet beating down upon the vessel—the wind continuing to break ahead, and the sea running high. At daybreak (about three, A.M.) the deck was covered with snow. The captain sent up the steward with a glass of grog to each of the watch; and all the time that we were off the Cape, grog was given to the morning watch, and to all hands whenever we reefed topsails. The clouds cleared away at sun-rise, and the wind becoming more fair, we again made sail and stood nearly up to our course.

Thursday, Nov. 6th. It continued more pleasant through the first part of the day, but at night we had the same scene over again. This time, we did not heave to, as on the night before, but endeavored to beat to windward under close-reefed top-sails, balance-reefed trysail, and fore top-mast stay-sail. This night it was my turn to steer, or, as the sailors say, my trick at the helm, for two hours. Inexperienced as I was, I made out to steer to the satisfaction of the officer, and neither S—— nor myself gave up our tricks, all the time that we were off the Cape. This was something to boast of, for it requires a good deal of skill and watchfulness to steer a vessel close hauled, in a gale of wind, against a heavy head sea. "Ease her when she pitches," is the word; and a little carelessness in letting her ship a heavy sea, might sweep the decks, or knock masts out of her.

Friday, Nov. 7th. Towards morning the wind went down, and during the whole forenoon we lay tossing about in a dead calm, and in the midst of a thick fog. The calms here are unlike those in most parts of the world, for there is always such a high sea running, and the periods of calm are so short, that it has no time to go down; and vessels, being under no command of sails or rudder, lie like logs upon the water. We were obliged to steady the booms and yards by guys and braces, and to lash everything well below. We now found our top hamper of some use, for though it is liable to be carried away or sprung by the sudden "bringing up" of a vessel when pitching in a chopping sea, yet it is a great help in steadying a vessel when rolling in a long swell; giving it more slowness, ease, and regularity to the motion.

The calm of the morning reminds me of a scene which I forgot to describe at the time of its occurrence, but which I remember from its being the first time that I had heard the near breathing of whales. It was on the night that we passed between the Falkland Islands and Staten Land. We had the watch from twelve to four, and coming upon deck, found the little brig lying perfectly still, surrounded by a thick fog, and the sea as smooth as though oil had been poured upon it; yet now and then a long, low swell rolling over its surface, slightly lifting the vessel, but without breaking the glassy smoothness of the water. We were surrounded far and near by shoals of sluggish whales and grampuses; which the fog prevented our seeing, rising slowly to the surface, or perhaps lying out at length, heaving out those peculiar lazy, deep, and long-drawn breathings which give such an impression of supineness and strength. Some of the watch were asleep, and the others were perfectly still, so that there was nothing to break the illusion, and I stood leaning over the bulwarks, listening to the slow breathing of the mighty creatures—now one breaking the water just alongside, whose black body I almost fancied that I could see through the fog; and again another, which I could just hear in the distance—until the low and regular swell seemed like the heaving of the ocean's mighty bosom to the sound of its heavy and long-drawn respirations.

Towards the evening of this day, (Friday 7th,) the fog cleared off, and we had every appearance of a cold blow; and soon after sun-down it came on. Again it was clew up and haul down, reef and furl, until we had got her down to close-reefed topsails, double-reefed trysail, and reefed forespenser. Snow, hail, and sleet were driving upon us most of the night, and the sea was breaking over the bows and covering the forward part of the little vessel; but as she would lay her course the captain refused to heave her to.

Saturday, Nov. 8th. This day commenced with calm and thick fog, and ended with hail, snow, a violent wind, and close-reefed topsails.

Sunday, Nov. 9th. To-day the sun rose clear and continued so until twelve o'clock, when the captain got an observation. This was very well for Cape Horn, and we thought it a little remarkable that, as we had not had one unpleasant Sunday during the whole voyage, the only tolerable day here should be a Sunday. We got time to clear up the steerage and forecastle, and set things to rights, and to overhaul our wet clothes a little. But this did not last very long. Between five and six—the sun was then nearly three hours high—the cry of "All starbowlines ahoy!" summoned our watch on deck; and immediately all hands were called. A true specimen of Cape Horn was coming upon us. A great cloud of a dark slate-color was driving on us from the south-west; and we did our best to take in sail, (for the light sails had been set during the first part of the day,) before we were in the midst of it. We had got the light sails furled, the courses hauled up, and the topsail reef-tackles hauled out, and were just mounting the fore-rigging, when the storm struck us. In an instant the sea, which had been comparatively quiet, was running higher and higher; and it became almost as dark as night. The hail and sleet were harder than I had yet felt them; seeming to almost pin us down to the rigging. We were longer taking in sail than ever before; for the sails were stiff and wet, the ropes and rigging covered with snow and sleet, and we ourselves cold and nearly blinded with the violence of the storm. By the time we had got down upon deck again, the little brig was plunging madly into a tremendous head sea, which at every drive rushed in through the bow-ports and over the bows, and buried all the forward part of the vessel. At this instant the chief mate, who was standing on the top of the windlass, at the foot of the spenser mast, called out, "Lay out there and furl the jib!" This was no agreeable or safe duty, yet it must be done. An old Swede, (the best sailor on board,) who belonged on the forecastle, sprang out upon the bowsprit. Another one must go: I was near the mate, and sprang forward, threw the down-haul over the windlass, and jumped between the knight-heads out upon the bowsprit. The crew stood abaft the windlass and hauled the jib down, while we got out upon the weather side of the jib-boom, our feet on the foot ropes, holding on by the spar, the great jib flying off to leeward and slatting so as almost to throw us off of the boom. For some time we could do nothing but hold on, and the vessel diving into two huge seas, one after the other, plunged us twice into the water up to our chins. We hardly knew whether we were on or off; when coming up, dripping from the water, we were raised high into the air. John (that was the sailor's name) thought the boom would go, every moment, and called out to the mate to keep the vessel off, and haul down the staysail; but the fury of the wind and the breaking of the seas against the bows defied every attempt to make ourselves heard, and we were obliged to do the best we could in our situation. Fortunately, no other seas so heavy struck her, and we succeeded in furling the jib "after a fashion"; and, coming in over the staysail nettings, were not a little pleased to find that all was snug, and the watch gone below; for we were soaked through, and it was very cold. The weather continued nearly the same through the night.

Monday, Nov. 10th. During a part of this day we were hove to, but the rest of the time were driving on, under close-reefed sails, with a heavy sea, a strong gale, and frequent squalls of hail and snow.

Tuesday, Nov. 11th. The same.

Wednesday, Nov. 12th. The same.

Thursday, Nov. 13th. The same.

We had now got hardened to Cape weather, the vessel was under reduced sail, and everything secured on deck and below, so that we had little to do but steer and to stand our watch. Our clothes were all wet through, and the only change was from wet to more wet. It was in vain to think of reading or working below, for we were too tired, the hatchways were closed down, and everything was wet and uncomfortable, black and dirty, heaving and pitching. We had only to come below when the watch was out, wring out our wet clothes, hang them up, and turn in and sleep as soundly as we could, until the watch was called again. A sailor can sleep anywhere—no sound of wind, water, wood or iron can keep him awake—and we were always fast asleep when three blows on the hatchway, and the unwelcome cry of "All starbowlines ahoy! eight bells there below! do you hear the news?" (the usual formula of calling the watch), roused us up from our berths upon the cold, wet decks. The only time when we could be said to take any pleasure was at night and morning, when we were allowed a tin pot full of hot tea, (or, as the sailors significantly call it, "water bewitched,") sweetened with molasses. This, bad as it was, was still warm and comforting, and, together with our sea biscuit and cold salt beef, made quite a meal. Yet even this meal was attended with some uncertainty. We had to go ourselves to the galley and take our kid of beef and tin pots of tea, and run the risk of losing them before we could get below. Many a kid of beef have I seen rolling in the scuppers, and the bearer lying at his length on the decks. I remember an English lad who was always the life of the crew, but whom we afterwards lost overboard, standing for nearly ten minutes at the galley, with this pot of tea in his hand, waiting for a chance to get down into the forecastle; and seeing what he thought was a "smooth spell," started to go forward. He had just got to the end of the windlass, when a great sea broke over the bows, and for a moment I saw nothing of him but his head and shoulders; and at the next instant, being taken off of his legs, he was carried aft with the sea, until her stern lifting up and sending the water forward, he was left high and dry at the side of the long-boat, still holding on to his tin pot, which had now nothing in it but salt water. But nothing could ever daunt him, or overcome, for a moment, his habitual good humor. Regaining his legs, and shaking his fist at the man at the wheel, he rolled below, saying, as he passed, "A man's no sailor, if he can't take a joke." The ducking was not the worst of such an affair, for, as there was an allowance of tea, you could get no more from the galley; and though sailors would never suffer a man to go without, but would always turn in a little from their own pots to fill up his, yet this was at best but dividing the loss among all hands.

Something of the same kind befell me a few days after. The cook had just made for us a mess of hot "scouse"—that is, biscuit pounded fine, salt beef cut into small pieces, and a few potatoes, boiled up together and seasoned with pepper. This was a rare treat, and I, being the last at the galley, had it put in my charge to carry down for the mess. I got along very well as far as the hatchway, and was just getting down the steps, when a heavy sea, lifting the stern out of water, and passing forward, dropping it down again, threw the steps from their place, and I came down into the steerage a little faster than I meant to, with the kid on top of me, and the whole precious mess scattered over the floor. Whatever your feelings may be, you must make a joke of everything at sea; and if you were to fall from aloft and be caught in the belly of a sail, and thus saved from instant death, it would not do to look at all disturbed, or to make a serious matter of it.

Friday, Nov. 14th. We were now well to the westward of the Cape and were changing our course to the northward as much as we dared, since the strong south-west winds, which prevailed then, carried us in toward Patagonia. At two, P.M., we saw a sail on our larboard beam, and at four we made it out to be a large ship, steering our course, under single-reefed topsails. We at that time had shaken the reefs out of our topsails, as the wind was lighter, and set the main top-gallant sail. As soon as our captain saw what sail she was under, he set the fore top-gallant sail and flying jib; and the old whaler—for such, his boats and short sail showed him to be—felt a little ashamed, and shook the reefs out of his topsails, but could do no more, for he had sent down his top-gallant masts off the Cape. He ran down for us, and answered our hail as the whale-ship, New England, of Poughkeepsie, one hundred and twenty days from New York. Our captain gave our name, and added, ninety-two days from Boston. They then had a little conversation about longitude, in which they found that they could not agree. The ship fell astern, and continued in sight during the night. Toward morning, the wind having become light, we crossed our royal and skysail yards, and at daylight we were seen under a cloud of sail, having royal and skysails fore and aft. The "spouter," as the sailors call a whaleman, had sent up his main top-gallant mast and set the sail, and made signal for us to heave to. About half-past seven their whale-boat came alongside, and Captain Job Terry sprang on board, a man known in every port and by every vessel in the Pacific ocean. "Don't you know Job Terry? I thought everybody knew Job Terry," said a green-hand, who came in the boat, to me, when I asked him about his captain. He was indeed a singular man. He was six feet high, wore thick, cowhide boots, and brown coat and trowsers, and, except a sun-burnt complexion, had not the slightest appearance of a sailor; yet he had been forty years in the whale trade, and, as he said himself, had owned ships, built ships, and sailed ships. His boat's crew were a pretty raw set, just out of the bush, and as the sailor's phrase is, "hadn't got the hayseed out of their hair." Captain Terry convinced our captain that our reckoning was a little out, and, having spent the day on board, put off in his boat at sunset for his ship, which was now six or eight miles astern. He began a "yarn" when he came on board, which lasted, with but little intermission, for four hours. It was all about himself, and the Peruvian government, and the Dublin frigate, and Lord James Townshend, and President Jackson, and the ship Ann M'Kim of Baltimore. It would probably never have come to an end, had not a good breeze sprung up, which sent him off to his own vessel. One of the lads who came in his boat, a thoroughly countrified-looking fellow, seemed to care very little about the vessel, rigging, or anything else, but went round looking at the live stock, and leaned over the pig-sty, and said he wished he was back again tending his father's pigs.

At eight o'clock we altered our course to the northward, bound for Juan Fernandez.

This day we saw the last of the albatrosses, which had been our companions a great part of the time off the Cape. I had been interested in the bird from descriptions which I had read of it, and was not at all disappointed. We caught one or two with a baited hook which we floated astern upon a shingle. Their long, flapping wings, long legs, and large, staring eyes, give them a very peculiar appearance. They look well on the wing; but one of the finest sights that I have ever seen, was an albatross asleep upon the water, during a calm, off Cape Horn, when a heavy sea was running. There being no breeze, the surface of the water was unbroken, but a long, heavy swell was rolling, and we saw the fellow, all white, directly ahead of us, asleep upon the waves, with his head under his wing; now rising on the top of a huge billow, and then falling slowly until he was lost in the hollow between. He was undisturbed for some time, until the noise of our bows, gradually approaching, roused him, when, lifting his head, he stared upon us for a moment, and then spread his wide wings and took his flight.

CHAPTER VI

LOSS OF A MAN—SUPERSTITION

Monday, Nov. 19th. This was a black day in our calendar. At seven o'clock in the morning, it being our watch below, we were aroused from a sound sleep by the cry of "All hands ahoy! a man overboard!" This unwonted cry sent a thrill through the heart of every one, and hurrying on deck we found the vessel hove flat aback, with all her studding-sails set; for the boy who was at the helm left it to throw something overboard, and the carpenter, who was an old sailor, knowing that the wind was light, put the helm down and hove her aback. The watch on deck were lowering away the quarter-boat, and I got on deck just in time to heave myself into her as she was leaving the side; but it was not until out upon the wide Pacific, in our little boat, that I knew whom we had lost. It was George Ballmer, a young English sailor, who was prized by the officers as an active lad and willing seaman, and by the crew as a lively, hearty fellow, and a good shipmate. He was going aloft to fit a strap round the main top-mast-head, for ringtail halyards, and had the strap and block, a coil of halyards and a marline-spike about his neck. He fell from the starboard futtock shrouds, and not knowing how to swim, and being heavily dressed, with all those things round his neck, he probably sank immediately. We pulled astern, in the direction in which he fell, and though we knew that there was no hope of saving him, yet no one wished to speak of returning, and we rowed about for nearly an hour, without the hope of doing anything, but unwilling to acknowledge to ourselves that we must give him up. At length we turned the boat's head and made towards the vessel.

Death is at all times solemn, but never so much so as at sea. A man dies on shore; his body remains with his friends, and "the mourners go about the streets;" but when a man falls overboard at sea and is lost, there is a suddenness in the event, and a difficulty in realizing it, which give to it an air of awful mystery. A man dies on shore—you follow his body to the grave, and a stone marks the spot. You are often prepared for the event. There is always something which helps you to realize it when it happens, and to recall it when it has passed. A man is shot down by your side in battle, and the mangled body remains an object, and a real evidence; but at sea, the man is near you—at your side—you hear his voice, and in an instant he is gone, and nothing but a vacancy shows his loss. Then, too, at sea—to use a homely but expressive phrase—you miss a man so much. A dozen men are shut up together in a little bark, upon the wide, wide sea, and for months and months see no forms and hear no voices but their own, and one is taken suddenly from among them, and they miss him at every turn. It is like losing a limb. There are no new faces or new scenes to fill up the gap. There is always an empty berth in the forecastle, and one man wanting when the small night watch is mustered. There is one less to take the wheel, and one less to lay out with you upon the yard. You miss his form, and the sound of his voice, for habit had made them almost necessary to you, and each of your senses feels the loss.

All these things make such a death peculiarly solemn, and the effect of it remains upon the crew for some time. There is more kindness shown by the officers to the crew, and by the crew to one another. There is more quietness and seriousness. The oath and the loud laugh are gone. The officers are more watchful, and the crew go more carefully aloft. The lost man is seldom mentioned, or is dismissed with a sailor's rude eulogy—"Well, poor George is gone! His cruise is up soon! He knew his work, and did his duty, and was a good shipmate." Then usually follows some allusion to another world, for sailors are almost all believers; but their notions and opinions are unfixed and at loose ends. They say,—"God won't be hard upon the poor fellow," and seldom get beyond the common phrase which seems to imply that their sufferings and hard treatment here will excuse them hereafter,—"To work hard, live hard, die hard, and go to hell after all, would be hard indeed!" Our cook, a simple-hearted old African, who had been through a good deal in his day, and was rather seriously inclined, always going to church twice a day when on shore, and reading his Bible on a Sunday in the galley, talked to the crew about spending their Sabbaths badly, and told them that they might go as suddenly as George had, and be as little prepared.

Yet a sailor's life is at best, but a mixture of a little good with much evil, and a little pleasure with much pain. The beautiful is linked with the revolting, the sublime with the commonplace, and the solemn with the ludicrous.

We had hardly returned on board with our sad report, before an auction was held of the poor man's clothes. The captain had first, however, called all hands aft and asked them if they were satisfied that everything had been done to save the man, and if they thought there was any use in remaining there longer. The crew all said that it was in vain, for the man did not know how to swim, and was very heavily dressed. So we then filled away and kept her off to her course.

The laws regulating navigation make the captain answerable for the effects of a sailor who dies during the voyage, and it is either a law or a universal custom, established for convenience, that the captain should immediately hold an auction of his things, in which they are bid off by the sailors, and the sums which they give are deducted from their wages at the end of the voyage. In this way the trouble and risk of keeping his things through the voyage are avoided, and the clothes are usually sold for more than they would be worth on shore. Accordingly, we had no sooner got the ship before the wind, than his chest was brought up upon the forecastle, and the sale began. The jackets and trowsers in which we had seen him dressed but a few days before, were exposed and bid off while the life was hardly out of his body, and his chest was taken aft and used as a store-chest, so that there was nothing left which could be called his. Sailors have an unwillingness to wear a dead man's clothes during the same voyage, and they seldom do so unless they are in absolute want.

As is usual after a death, many stories were told about George. Some had heard him say that he repented never having learned to swim, and that he knew that he should meet his death by drowning. Another said that he never knew any good to come of a voyage made against the will, and the deceased man shipped and spent his advance and was afterwards very unwilling to go, but not being able to refund, was obliged to sail with us. A boy, too, who had become quite attached to him, said that George talked to him during most of the watch on the night before, about his mother and family at home, and this was the first time that he had mentioned the subject during the voyage.

The night after this event, when I went to the galley to get a light, I found the cook inclined to be talkative, so I sat down on the spars, and gave him an opportunity to hold a yarn. I was the more inclined to do so, as I found that he was full of the superstitions once more common among seamen, and which the recent death had waked up in his mind. He talked about George's having spoken of his friends, and said he believed few men died without having a warning of it, which he supported by a great many stories of dreams, and the unusual behavior of men before death. From this he went on to other superstitions, the Flying Dutchman, etc., and talked rather mysteriously, having something evidently on his mind.

At length he put his head out of the galley and looked carefully about to see if any one was within hearing, and being satisfied on that point, asked me in a low tone—

"I say! you know what countryman 'e carpenter be?"

"Yes," said I; "he's a German."

"What kind of a German?" said the cook.

"He belongs to Bremen," said I.

"Are you sure o' dat?" said he.

I satisfied him on that point by saying that he could speak no language but the German and English.

"I'm plaguy glad o' dat," said the cook. "I was mighty 'fraid he was a Fin. I tell you what, I been plaguy civil to that man all the voyage."

I asked him the reason of this, and found that he was fully possessed with the notion that Fins are wizards, and especially have power over winds and storms. I tried to reason with him about it, but he had the best of all arguments, that from experience, at hand, and was not to be moved. He had been in a vessel at the Sandwich Islands, in which the sail-maker was a Fin, and could do anything he was of a mind to. This sail-maker kept a junk bottle in his berth, which was always just half full of rum, though he got drunk upon it nearly every day. He had seen him sit for hours together, talking to this bottle, which he stood up before him on the table. The same man cut his throat in his berth, and everybody said he was possessed.

He had heard of ships, too, beating up the gulf of Finland against a head wind, and having a ship heave in sight astern, overhaul and pass them, with as fair a wind as could blow, and all studding-sails out, and find she was from Finland.

"Oh ho!" said he; "I've seen too much of them men to want to see 'em 'board a ship. If they can't have their own way, they'll play the d—-l with you."

As I still doubted, he said he would leave it to John, who was the oldest seaman aboard, and would know, if anybody did. John, to be sure, was the oldest, and at the same time the most ignorant, man in the ship; but I consented to have him called. The cook stated the matter to him, and John, as I anticipated, sided with the cook, and said that he himself had been in a ship where they had a head wind for a fortnight, and the captain found out at last that one of the men, whom he had had some hard words with a short time before, was a Fin, and immediately told him if he didn't stop the head wind he would shut him down in the fore peak, and would not give him anything to eat. The Fin held out for a day and a half, when he could not stand it any longer, and did something or other which brought the wind round again, and they let him up.

"There," said the cook, "what do you think o' dat?"

I told him I had no doubt it was true, and that it would have been odd if the wind had not changed in fifteen days, Fin or no Fin.

"Oh," says he, "go 'way! You think, 'cause you been to college, you know better than anybody. You know better than them as 'as seen it with their own eyes. You wait till you've been to sea as long as I have, and you'll know."

CHAPTER VII

JUAN FERNANDEZ—THE PACIFIC

We continued sailing along with a fair wind and fine weather until Tuesday, Nov. 25th, when at daylight we saw the island of Juan Fernandez, directly ahead, rising like a deep blue cloud out of the sea. We were then probably nearly seventy miles from it; and so high and so blue did it appear, that I mistook it for a cloud, resting over the island, and looked for the island under it, until it gradually turned to a deader and greener color, and I could mark the inequalities upon its surface. At length we could distinguish trees and rocks; and by the afternoon, this beautiful island lay fairly before us, and we directed our course to the only harbor. Arriving at the entrance soon after sun-down, we found a Chilian man-of-war brig, the only vessel, coming out. She hailed us, and an officer on board, whom we supposed to be an American, advised us to run in before night, and said that they were bound to Valparaiso. We ran immediately for the anchorage, but, owing to the winds which drew about the mountains and came to us in flaws from every point of the compass, we did not come to an anchor until nearly midnight. We had a boat ahead all the time that we were working in, and those aboard were continually bracing the yards about for every puff that struck us, until about 12 o'clock, when we came-to in 40 fathoms water, and our anchor struck bottom for the first time since we left Boston—one hundred and three days. We were then divided into three watches, and thus stood out the remainder of the night.

I was called on deck to stand my watch at about three in the morning, and I shall never forget the peculiar sensation which I experienced on finding myself once more surrounded by land, feeling the night breeze coming from off shore, and hearing the frogs and crickets. The mountains seemed almost to hang over us, and apparently from the very heart there came out, at regular intervals, a loud echoing sound, which affected me as hardly human. We saw no lights, and could hardly account for the sound, until the mate, who had been there before, told us that it was the "Alerta" of the Spanish soldiers, who were stationed over some convicts confined in caves nearly halfway up the mountain. At the expiration of my watch I went below, feeling not a little anxious for the day, that I might see more nearly, and perhaps tread upon, this romantic, I may almost say, classic island.

When all hands were called it was nearly sunrise, and between that time and breakfast, although quite busy on board in getting up water-casks, etc., I had a good view of the objects about me. The harbor was nearly land-locked, and at the head of it was a landing-place, protected by a small breakwater of stones, upon which two large boats were hauled up, with a sentry standing over them. Near this was a variety of huts or cottages, nearly an hundred in number, the best of them built of mud and white washed, but the greater part only Robinson Crusoe like—of posts and branches of trees. The governor's house, as it is called, was the most conspicuous, being large, with grated windows, plastered walls, and roof of red tiles; yet, like all the rest, only of one story. Near it was a small chapel, distinguished by a cross; and a long, low brown-looking building, surrounded by something like a palisade, from which an old and dingy-looking Chilian flag was flying. This, of course, was dignified by the title of Presidio. A sentinel was stationed at the chapel, another at the governor's house, and a few soldiers armed with bayonets, looking rather ragged, with shoes out at the toes, were strolling about among the houses, or waiting at the landing-place for our boat to come ashore.

The mountains were high, but not so overhanging as they appeared to be by starlight. They seemed to bear off towards the centre of the island, and were green and well wooded, with some large, and, I am told, exceedingly fertile valleys, with mule-tracks leading to different parts of the island.

I cannot forget how my friend S—— and myself got the laugh of the crew upon us for our eagerness to get on shore. The captain having ordered the quarter-boat to be lowered, we both sprang down into the forecastle, filled our jacket pockets with tobacco to barter with the people ashore, and when the officer called for "four hands in the boat," nearly broke our necks in our haste to be first over the side, and had the pleasure of pulling ahead of the brig with a tow-line for a half an hour, and coming on board again to be laughed at by the crew, who had seen our manoeuvre.

After breakfast the second mate was ordered ashore with five hands to fill the water-casks, and to my joy I was among the number. We pulled ashore with the empty casks; and here again fortune favored me, for the water was too thick and muddy to be put into the casks, and the governor had sent men up to the head of the stream to clear it out for us, which gave us nearly two hours of leisure. This leisure we employed in wandering about among the houses, and eating a little fruit which was offered to us. Ground apples, melons, grapes, strawberries of an enormous size, and cherries, abounded here. The latter are said to have been planted by Lord Anson. The soldiers were miserably clad, and asked with some interest whether we had any shoes to sell on board. I doubt very much if they had the means of buying them. They were very eager to get tobacco, for which they gave shells, fruits, etc. Knives also were in demand, but we were forbidden by the governor to let any one have them, as he told us that all the people there, except the soldiers and a few officers, were convicts sent from Valparaiso, and that it was necessary to keep all weapons from their hands. The island, it seems, belongs to Chili, and had been used by the government as a sort of Botany Bay for nearly two years; and the governor—an Englishman who had entered the Chilian navy—with a priest, half a dozen task-masters, and a body of soldiers, were stationed there to keep them in order. This was no easy task; and only a few months before our arrival, a few of them had stolen a boat at night, boarded a brig lying in the harbor, sent the captain and crew ashore in their boat, and gone off to sea. We were informed of this, and loaded our arms and kept strict watch on board through the night, and were careful not to let the convicts get our knives from us when on shore. The worst part of the convicts, I found, were locked up under sentry in caves dug into the side of the mountain, nearly halfway up, with mule-tracks leading to them, whence they were taken by day and set to work under task-masters upon building an aqueduct, a wharf, and other public works; while the rest lived in the houses which they put up for themselves, had their families with them, and seemed to me to be the laziest people on the face of the earth. They did nothing but take a paseo into the woods, a paseo among the houses, a paseo at the landing-place, looking at us and our vessel, and too lazy to speak fast; while the others were driving—or rather, driven—about, at a rapid trot, in single file, with burdens on their shoulders, and followed up by their task-masters, with long rods in their hands, and broadbrimmed straw hats upon their heads. Upon what precise grounds this great distinction was made, I do not know, and I could not very well know, for the governor was the only man who spoke English upon the island, and he was out of my walk.

Having filled our casks, we returned on board, and soon after, the governor, dressed in a uniform like that of an American militia officer, the Padre, in the dress of the grey friars, with hood and all complete, and the Capitan, with big whiskers and dirty regimentals, came on board to dine. While at dinner, a large ship appeared in the offing, and soon afterwards we saw a light whale-boat pulling into the harbor. The ship lay off and on, and a boat came alongside of us, and put on board the captain, a plain young Quaker, dressed all in brown. The ship was the Cortes, whaleman, of New Bedford, and had put in to see if there were any vessels from round the Horn, and to hear the latest news from America. They remained aboard a short time and had a little talk with the crew, when they left us and pulled off to their ship, which, having filled away, was soon out of sight.

A small boat which came from the shore to take away the governor and suite—as they styled themselves—brought, as a present to the crew, a large pail of milk, a few shells, and a block of sandal wood. The milk, which was the first we had tasted since leaving Boston, we soon despatched; a piece of the sandal wood I obtained, and learned that it grew on the hills in the centre of the island. I have always regretted that I did not bring away other specimens of the products of the island, having afterwards lost all that I had with me—the piece of sandal wood, and a small flower which I plucked and brought on board in the crown of my tarpaulin, and carefully pressed between the leaves of a book.

About an hour before sun-down, having stowed our water casks, we commenced getting under weigh, and were not a little while about it; for we were in thirty fathoms water, and in one of the gusts which came off shore had let go our other bow anchor; and as the southerly wind draws round the mountains and comes off in uncertain flaws, we were continually swinging round, and had thus got a very foul hawse. We hove in upon our chain, and after stoppering and unshackling it again and again, and hoisting and hauling down sail, we at length tipped our anchor and stood out to sea. It was bright starlight when we were clear of the bay, and the lofty island lay behind us, in its still beauty, and I gave a parting look, and bid farewell, to the most romantic spot of earth that my eyes had ever seen. I did then, and have ever since, felt an attachment for that island, altogether peculiar. It was partly, no doubt, from its having been the first land that I had seen since leaving home, and still more from the associations which every one has connected with it in their childhood from reading Robinson Crusoe. To this I may add the height and romantic outline of its mountains, the beauty and freshness of its verdure, and the extreme fertility of its soil, and its solitary position in the midst of the wide expanse of the South Pacific, as all concurring to give it its peculiar charm.

When thoughts of this place have occurred to me at different times, I have endeavored to recall more particulars with regard to it. It is situated in about 33° 30' S., and is distant a little more than three hundred miles from Valparaiso, on the coast of Chili, which is in the same latitude. It is about fifteen miles in length and five in breadth. The harbor in which we anchored (called by Lord Anson, Cumberland bay) is the only one in the island; two small bights of land on each side of the main bay (sometimes dignified by the name of bays) being little more than landing-places for boats. The best anchorage is at the western side of the bay, where we lay at about three cables' lengths from the shore, in a little more than thirty fathoms water. This harbor is open to the N.N.E., and in fact nearly from N. to E., but the only dangerous winds being the south-west, on which side are the highest mountains, it is considered very safe. The most remarkable thing perhaps about it is the fish with which it abounds. Two of our crew, who remained on board, caught in a few minutes enough to last us for several days, and one of the men, who was a Marblehead man, said that he never saw or heard of such an abundance. There were cod, breams, silver-fish, and other kinds whose names they did not know, or which I have forgotten.

There is an abundance of the best of water upon the island, small streams running through every valley, and leaping down from the sides of the hills. One stream of considerable size flows through the centre of the lawn upon which the houses are built, and furnishes an easy and abundant supply to the inhabitants. This, by means of a short wooden aqueduct, was brought quite down to our boats. The convicts had also built something in the way of a breakwater, and were to build a landing-place for boats and goods, after which the Chilian government intended to lay port charges.

Of the wood I can only say, that it appeared to be abundant; the island in the month of November, when we were there, being in all the freshness and beauty of spring, appeared covered with trees. These were chiefly aromatic, and the largest was the myrtle. The soil is very loose and rich, and wherever it is broken up, there spring up immediately radishes, turnips, ground apples, and other garden fruits. Goats, we were told, were not abundant, and we saw none, though it was said we might, if we had gone into the interior. We saw a few bullocks winding about in the narrow tracks upon the sides of the mountains, and the settlement was completely overrun with dogs of every nation, kindred, and degree. Hens and chickens were also abundant, and seemed to be taken good care of by the women. The men appeared to be the laziest people upon the face of the earth; and indeed, as far as my observation goes, there are no people to whom the newly-invented Yankee word of "loafer" is more applicable than to the Spanish Americans. These men stood about doing nothing, with their cloaks, little better in texture than an Indian's blanket, but of rich colors, thrown over their shoulders with an air which it is said that a Spanish beggar can always give to his rags; and with great politeness and courtesy in their address, though with holes in their shoes and without a sou in their pockets. The only interruption to the monotony of their day seemed to be when a gust of wind drew round between the mountains and blew off the boughs which they had placed for roofs to their houses, and gave them a few minutes' occupation in running about after them. One of these gusts occurred while we were ashore, and afforded us no little amusement at seeing the men look round, and if they found that their roofs had stood, conclude that they might stand too, while those who saw theirs blown off, after uttering a few Spanish oaths, gathered their cloaks over their shoulders, and started off after them. However, they were not gone long, but soon returned to their habitual occupation of doing nothing.

It is perhaps needless to say that we saw nothing of the interior; but all who have seen it, give very glowing accounts of it. Our captain went with the governor and a few servants upon mules over the mountains, and upon their return, I heard the governor request him to stop at the island on his passage home, and offer him a handsome sum to bring a few deer with him from California, for he said that there were none upon the island, and he was very desirous of having it stocked.

A steady, though light south-westerly wind carried us well off from the island, and when I came on deck for the middle watch I could just distinguish it from its hiding a few low stars in the southern horizon, though my unpracticed eyes would hardly have known it for land. At the close of the watch a few trade-wind clouds which had arisen, though we were hardly yet in their latitude, shut it out from our view, and the next day,

Thursday, Nov. 27th, upon coming on deck in the morning, we were again upon the wide Pacific, and saw no more land until we arrived upon the western coast of the great continent of America.

CHAPTER VIII

"TARRING DOWN"—DAILY LIFE—"GOING AFT"—CALIFORNIA

As we saw neither land nor sail from the time of leaving Juan Fernandez until our arrival in California, nothing of interest occurred except our own doing on board. We caught the south-east trades, and run before them for nearly three weeks, without so much as altering a sail or bracing a yard. The captain took advantage of this fine weather to get the vessel in order for coming upon the coast. The carpenter was employed in fitting up a part of the steerage into a trade-room; for our cargo, we now learned, was not to be landed, but to be sold by retail from on board; and this trade-room was built for the samples and the lighter goods to be kept in, and as a place for the general business. In the mean time we were employed in working upon the rigging. Everything was set up taut, the lower rigging rattled down, or rather rattled up, (according to the modern fashion,) an abundance of spun-yarn and seizing-stuff made, and finally, the whole standing-rigging, fore and aft, was tarred down. This was my first essay at this latter business, and I had enough of it; for nearly all of it came upon my friend S—— and myself. The men were needed at the other work, and M——, the other young man who came out with us, was laid up with the rheumatism in his feet, and the boy was rather too young and small for the business; and as the winds were light and regular, he was kept during most of the daytime at the helm; so that nearly all the tarring came upon us. We put on short duck frocks, and taking a small bucket of tar and a bunch of oakum in our hands we went aloft, one at the main royal-mast-head and the other at the fore, and began tarring down. This is an important operation, and is usually done about once in six months in vessels upon a long voyage. It was done in our vessel several times afterwards, but by the whole crew at once, and finished off in a day; but at this time, as most of it came upon two of us, and we were new at the business, it took us several days. In this operation they always begin at the mast-head and work down, tarring the shrouds, back-stays, standing parts of the lifts, the ties, runners, etc., and go out to the yard-arms, and come in, tarring, as they come, the lifts and foot-ropes. Tarring the stays is more difficult, and is done by an operation which the sailors call "riding down." A long piece of rope—top-gallant-studding-sail halyards, or something of the kind—is taken up to the mast-head from which the stay leads, and rove through a block for a girt-line, or, as the sailors usually call it, a gant-line; with the end of this a bowline is taken round the stay, into which the man gets with his bucket of tar and a bunch of oakum, and the other end being fast on deck, with some one to tend it, he is lowered down gradually, and tars the stay carefully as he goes. There he "sings aloft 'twixt heaven and earth," and if the rope slips, breaks, or is let go, or if the bowline slips, he falls overboard or breaks his neck. This, however, is a thing which never enters into a sailor's calculation. He thinks only of leaving no holydays, (places not tarred,) for in case he should, he would have to go over the whole again; or of dropping no tar upon deck, for then there would be a soft word in his ear from the mate. In this manner I tarred down all the head-stays, but found the rigging about the jib-booms, martingale, and spritsail yard, upon which I was afterwards put, the hardest. Here you have to hang on with your eye-lids and tar with your hands.

This dirty work could not last forever, and on Saturday night we finished it, scraped all the spots from the deck and rails, and, what was of more importance to us, cleaned ourselves thoroughly, rolled up our tarry frocks and trowsers and laid them away for the next occasion, and put on our clean duck clothes, and had a good comfortable sailor's Saturday night. The next day was pleasant, and indeed we had but one unpleasant Sunday during the whole voyage, and that was off Cape Horn, where we could expect nothing better. On Monday we commenced painting, and getting the vessel ready for port. This work, too, is done by the crew, and every sailor who has been long voyages is a little of a painter, in addition to his other accomplishments. We painted her, both inside and out, from the truck to the water's edge. The outside is painted by lowering stages over the side by ropes, and on those we sat, with our brushes and paint-pots by us, and our feet half the time in the water. This must be done, of course, on a smooth day, when the vessel does not roll much. I remember very well being over the side painting in this way, one fine afternoon, our vessel going quietly along at the rate of four or five knots, and a pilot-fish, the sure precursor of the shark, swimming alongside of us.

The captain was leaning over the rail watching him, and we quietly went on with our work. In the midst of our painting, on

Friday, Dec. 19th, we crossed the equator for the second time. I had the feeling which all have when, for the first time, they find themselves living under an entire change of seasons; as, crossing the line under a burning sun in the midst of December, and, as I afterwards was, beating about among ice and snow on the fourth of July.

Thursday, Dec. 25th. This day was Christmas, but it brought us no holiday. The only change was that we had a "plum duff" for dinner, and the crew quarrelled with the steward because he did not give us our usual allowance of molasses to eat with it. He thought the plums would be a substitute for the molasses, but we were not to be cheated out of our rights in this way.

Such are the trifles which produce quarrels on shipboard. In fact, we had been too long from port. We were getting tired of one another, and were in an irritable state, both forward and aft. Our fresh provisions were, of course, gone, and the captain had stopped our rice, so that we had nothing but salt beef and salt pork throughout the week, with the exception of a very small duff on Sunday. This added to the discontent; and a thousand little things, daily and almost hourly occurring, which no one who has not himself been on a long and tedious voyage can conceive of or properly appreciate,—little wars and rumors of wars,—reports of things said in the cabin,—misunderstanding of words and looks,—apparent abuses,—brought us into a state in which everything seemed to go wrong. Every encroachment upon the time allowed for rest, appeared unnecessary. Every shifting of the studding-sails was only to "haze"*[1]* the crew.

In this midst of this state of things, my messmate S—— and myself petitioned the captain for leave to shift our berths from the steerage, where we had previously lived, into the forecastle. This, to our delight, was granted, and we turned in to bunk and mess with the crew forward. We now began to feel like sailors, which we never fully did when we were in the steerage. While there, however useful and active you may be, you are but a mongrel,—and sort of afterguard and "ship's cousin." You are immediately under the eye of the officers, cannot dance, sing, play, smoke, make a noise, or growl, (i.e. complain,) or take any other sailor's pleasure; and you live with the steward, who is usually a go-between; and the crew never feel as though you were one of them. But if you live in the forecastle, you are "as independent as a wood-sawyer's clerk," (nautice',) and are a sailor. You hear sailor's talk, learn their ways, their peculiarities of feeling as well as speaking and acting; and moreover pick up a great deal of curious and useful information in seamanship, ship's customs, foreign countries, etc., from their long yarns and equally long disputes. No man can be a sailor, or know what sailors are, unless he has lived in the forecastle with them—turned in and out with them, eaten of their dish and drank of their cup. After I had been a week there, nothing would have tempted me to go back to my old berth, and never afterwards, even in the worst of weather, when in a close and leaking forecastle off Cape Horn, did I for a moment wish myself in the steerage. Another thing which you learn better in the forecastle than you can anywhere else, is, to make and mend clothes, and this is indispensable to sailors. A large part of their watches below they spend at this work, and here I learned that art which stood me in so good stead afterwards.

But to return to the state of the crew. Upon our coming into the forecastle, there was some difficulty about the uniting of the allowances of bread, by which we thought we were to lose a few pounds. This set us into a ferment. The captain would not condescend to explain, and we went aft in a body, with a Swede, the oldest and best sailor of the crew, for spokesman. The recollection of the scene that followed always brings up a smile, especially the quarter-deck dignity and eloquence of the captain. He was walking the weather side of the quarter-deck, and seeing us coming aft, stopped short in his walk, and, with a voice and look intended to annihilate us, called out, "Well, what do you want now?" Whereupon we stated our grievances as respectfully as we could, but he broke in upon us, saying that we were getting fat and lazy, didn't have enough to do, and that made us find fault. This provoked us, and we began to give word for word. This would never answer. He clenched his fist, stamped and swore, and sent us all forward, saying, with oaths enough interspersed to send the words home,—"Away with you! go forward every one of you! I'll haze you! I'll work you up! You don't have enough to do! You've mistaken your man. I'm F—— T——, all the way from 'down east.' I've been through the mill, ground, and bolted, and come out a regular-built down-east johnny-cake, good when it's hot, but when it's cold, sour and indigestible;—and you'll find me so!" The latter part of the harangue I remember well, for it made a strong impression, and the "down-east johnny-cake" became a by-word for the rest of the voyage. So much for our petition for the redress of grievances. The matter was however set right, for the mate, after allowing the captain due time to cool off, explained it to him, and at night we were all called aft to hear another harangue, in which, of course, the whole blame of the misunderstanding was thrown upon us. We ventured to hint that he would not give us time to explain; but it wouldn't do. We were driven back discomforted. Thus the affair blew over, but the irritation caused by it remained; and we never had peace or a good understanding again so long as the captain and crew remained together.

We continued sailing along in the beautiful temperate climate of the Pacific. The Pacific well deserves its name, for except in the southern part, at Cape Horn, and in the western parts, near the China and Indian oceans, it has few storms, and is never either extremely hot or cold. Between the tropics there is a slight haziness, like a thin gauze, drawn over the sun, which, without obstructing or obscuring the light, tempers the heat which comes down with perpendicular fierceness in the Atlantic and Indian tropics. We sailed well to the westward to have the full advantage of the north-east trades, and when we had reached the latitude of Point Conception, where it is usual to make the land, we were several hundred miles to the westward of it. We immediately changed our course due east, and sailed in that direction for a number of days. At length we began to heave-to after dark, for fear of making the land at night on a coast where there are no light-houses and but indifferent charts, and at daybreak on the morning of

Tuesday, Jan 13th, 1835, we made the land at Point Conception, lat 34° 32' N., long 120° 06' W. The port of Santa Barbara, to which we were bound, lying about sixty miles to the southward of this point, we continued sailing down the coast during the day and following night, and on the next morning,

Jan. 14th, 1835, we came to anchor in the spacious bay of Santa Barbara, after a voyage of one hundred and fifty days from Boston.

[1] Haze is a word of frequent use on board ship, and never, I believe, used elsewhere. It is very expressive to a sailor, and means to punish by hard work. Let an officer once say, "I'll haze you," and your fate is fixed. You will be "worked up," if you are not a better man than he is.

CHAPTER IX

CALIFORNIA—A SOUTH-EASTER

California extends along nearly the whole of the western coast of Mexico, between the gulf of California in the south and the bay of Sir Francis Drake on the north, or between the 22d and 38th degrees of north latitude. It is subdivided into two provinces—Lower or Old California, lying between the gulf and the 32d degree of latitude, or near it; (the division line running, I believe, between the bay of Todos Santos and the port of San Diego;) and New or Upper California, the southernmost port of which is San Diego, in lat. 32° 39', and the northernmost, San Francisco, situated in the large bay discovered by Sir Francis Drake, in lat. 37° 58', and called after him by the English, though the Mexicans call it Yerba Buena. Upper California has the seat of its government at Monterey, where is also the custom-house, the only one on the coast, and at which every vessel intending to trade on the coast must enter its cargo before it can commence its traffic. We were to trade upon this coast exclusively, and therefore expected to go to Monterey at first; but the captain's orders from home were to put in at Santa Barbara, which is the central port of the coast, and wait there for the agent who lives there, and transacts all the business for the firm to which our vessel belonged.

The bay, or, as it was commonly called, the canal of Santa Barbara, is very large, being formed by the main land on one side, (between Point Conception on the north and Point St. Buena Ventura on the south,) which here bends in like a crescent, and three large islands opposite to it and at the distance of twenty miles. This is just sufficient to give it the name of a bay, while at the same time it is so large and so much exposed to the south-east and north-west winds, that it is little better than an open roadstead; and the whole swell of the Pacific ocean rolls in here before a south-easter, and breaks with so heavy a surf in the shallow waters, that it is highly dangerous to lie near to the shore during the south-easter season; that is, between the months of November and April.

This wind (the south-easter) is the bane of the coast of California. Between the months of November and April, (including a part of each,) which is the rainy season in this latitude, you are never safe from it, and accordingly, in the ports which are open to it, vessels are obliged, during these months, to lie at anchor at a distance of three miles from the shore, with slip-ropes on their cables, ready to slip and go to sea at a moment's warning. The only ports which are safe from this wind are San Francisco and Monterey in the north, and San Diego in the south.

As it was January when we arrived, and the middle of the south-easter season, we accordingly came to anchor at the distance of three miles from the shore, in eleven fathoms water, and bent a slip-rope and buoys to our cables, cast off the yard-arm gaskets from the sails, and stopped them all with rope-yarns. After we had done this, the boat went ashore with the captain, and returned with orders to the mate to send a boat ashore for him at sundown. I did not go in the first boat, and was glad to find that there was another going before night; for after so long a voyage as ours had been, a few hours is long to pass in sight and out of reach of land. We spent the day on board in the usual avocations; but as this was the first time we had been without the captain, we felt a little more freedom, and looked about us to see what sort of a country we had got into, and were to spend a year or two of our lives in.

In the first place, it was a beautiful day, and so warm that we had on straw hats, duck trowsers, and all the summer gear; and as this was mid-winter, it spoke well for the climate; and we afterwards found that the thermometer never fell to the freezing-point throughout the winter, and that there was very little difference between the seasons, except that during a long period of rainy and south-easterly weather, thick clothes were not uncomfortable.

The large bay lay about us, nearly smooth, as there was hardly a breath of wind stirring, though the boat's crew who went ashore told us that the long ground swell broke into a heavy surf upon the beach. There was only one vessel in the port—a long, sharp brig of about 300 tons, with raking masts and very square yards, and English colors at her peak. We afterwards learned that she was built at Guayaquil, and named the Ayacucho, after the place where the battle was fought that gave Peru her independence, and was now owned by a Scotchman named Wilson, who commanded her, and was engaged in the trade between Callao, the Sandwich

Islands, and California. She was a fast sailer, as we frequently afterwards perceived, and had a crew of Sandwich Islanders on board. Beside this vessel there was no object to break the surface of the bay. Two points ran out as the horns of the crescent, one of which—the one to the westward—was low and sandy, and is that to which vessels are obliged to give a wide berth when running out for a south-easter; the other is high, bold, and well wooded, and, we were told, has a mission upon it, called St. Buenaventura, from which the point is named. In the middle of this crescent, directly opposite the anchoring ground, lie the mission and town of Santa Barbara, on a low, flat plain, but little above the level of the sea, covered with grass, though entirely without trees, and surrounded on three sides by an amphitheatre of mountains, which slant off to the distance of fifteen or twenty miles. The mission stands a little back of the town, and is a large building, or rather a collection of buildings, in the centre of which is a high tower, with a belfry of five bells; and the whole, being plastered, makes quite a show at a distance, and is the mark by which vessels come to anchor. The town lies a little nearer to the beach—about half a mile from it—and is composed of one-story houses built of brown clay—some of them plastered—with red tiles on the roofs. I should judge that there were about an hundred of them; and in the midst of them stands the Presidio, or fort, built of the same materials, and apparently but little stronger. The town is certainly finely situated, with a bay in front, and an amphitheatre of hills behind. The only thing which diminishes its beauty is, that the hills have no large trees upon them, they having been all burnt by a great fire which swept them off about a dozen years before, and they had not yet grown up again. The fire was described to me by an inhabitant, as having been a very terrible and magnificent sight. The air of the whole valley was so heated that the people were obliged to leave the town and take up their quarters for several days upon the beach.

Just before sun-down the mate ordered a boat's crew ashore, and I went as one of the number. We passed under the stern of the English brig, and had a long pull ashore. I shall never forget the impression which our first landing on the beach of California made upon me. The sun had just gone down; it was getting dusky; the damp night wind was beginning to blow, and the heavy swell of the Pacific was setting in, and breaking in loud and high "combers" upon the beach. We lay on our oars in the swell, just outside of the surf, waiting for a good chance to run in, when a boat, which had put off from the Ayacucho just after us, came alongside of us, with a crew of dusky Sandwich Islanders, talking and halooing in their outlandish tongue. They knew that we were novices in this kind of boating, and waited to see us go in. The second mate, however, who steered our boat, determined to have the advantage of their experience, and would not go in first. Finding, at length, how matters stood, they gave a shout, and taking advantage of a great comber which came swelling in, rearing its head, and lifting up the stern of our boat nearly perpendicular, and again dropping it in the trough, they gave three or four long and strong pulls, and went in on top of the great wave, throwing their oars overboard, and as far from the boat as they could throw them, and jumping out the instant that the boat touched the beach, and then seizing hold of her and running her up high and dry upon the sand. We saw, at once, how it was to be done, and also the necessity of keeping the boat "stern on" to the sea; for the instant the sea should strike upon her broad-side or quarter, she would be driven up broad-side-on, and capsized. We pulled strongly in, and as soon as we felt that the sea had got hold of us and was carrying us in with the speed of a race-horse, we threw the oars as far from the boat as we could, and took hold of the gunwale, ready to spring out and seize her when she struck, the officer using his utmost strength to keep her stern on. We were shot up upon the beach like an arrow from a bow, and seizing the boat, ran her up high and dry, and soon picked up our oars, and stood by her, ready for the captain to come down.

Finding that the captain did not come immediately, we put our oars in the boat, and leaving one to watch it, walked about the beach to see what we could, of the place. The beach is nearly a mile in length between the two points, and of smooth sand. We had taken the only good landing-place, which is in the middle; it being more stony toward the ends. It is about twenty yards in width from high-water mark to a slight bank at which the soil begins, and so hard that it is a favorite place for running horses. It was growing dark, so that we could just distinguish the dim outlines of the two vessels in the offing; and the great seas were rolling in, in regular lines, growing larger and larger as they approached the shore, and hanging over the beach upon which they were to break, when their tops would curl over and turn white with foam, and, beginning at one extreme of the line, break rapidly to the other, as a long card-house falls when the children knock down the cards at one end. The Sandwich Islanders, in the mean time, had turned their boat round, and ran her down into the water, and were loading her with hides and tallow. As this was the work in which we were soon to be engaged, we looked on with some curiosity. They ran the boat into the water so far that every large sea might float her, and two of them, with their trowsers rolled up, stood by the bows, one on each side, keeping her in her right position. This was hard work; for beside the force they had to use upon the boat, the large seas nearly took them off their legs. The others were running from the boat to the bank, upon which, out of the reach of the water, was a pile of dry bullocks' hides, doubled lengthwise in the middle, and nearly as stiff as boards. These they took upon their heads, one or two at a time, and carried down to the boat, where one of their number stowed them away. They were obliged to carry them on their heads, to keep them out of the water, and we observed that they had on thick woolen caps. "Look here, Bill, and see what you're coming to!" said one of our men to another who stood by the boat. "Well, D——," said the second mate to me, "this does not look much like Cambridge college, does it? This is what I call 'head work.'" To tell the truth, it did not look very encouraging.

After they had got through with the hides, they laid hold of the bags of tallow, (the bags are made of hide, and are about the size of a common meal bag,) and lifting each upon the shoulders of two men, one at each end, walked off with them to the boat, and prepared to go aboard. Here, too, was something for us to learn. The man who steered, shipped his oar and stood up in the stern, and those that pulled the after oars sat upon their benches, with their oars shipped, ready to strike out as soon as she was afloat. The two men at the bows kept their places; and when, at length, a large sea came in and floated her, seized hold of the gunwale, and ran out with her till they were up to their armpits, and then tumbled over the gunwale into the bows, dripping with water. The men at the oars struck out, but it wouldn't do; the sea swept back and left them nearly high and dry. The two fellows jumped out again; and the next time they succeeded better, and, with the help of a deal of outlandish hallooing and bawling, got her well off. We watched them till they were out of the breakers, and saw them steering for their vessel, which was now hidden in the darkness.

The sand of the beach began to be cold to our bare feet; the frogs set up their croaking in the marshes, and one solitary owl, from the end of the distant point, gave out his melancholy note, mellowed by the distance, and we began to think that it was high time for "the old man," as the captain is generally called, to come down. In a few minutes we heard something coming towards us. It was a man on horseback. He came up on the full gallop, reined up near us, addressed a few words to us, and receiving no answer, wheeled around and galloped off again. He was nearly as dark as an Indian, with a large Spanish hat, blanket cloak or surreppa, and leather leggins, with a long knife stuck in them. "This is the seventh city that ever I was in, and no Christian one neither," said Bill Brown. "Stand by!" said Tom, "you haven't seen the worst of it yet." In the midst of this conversation the captain appeared; and we winded the boat round, shoved her down, and prepared to go off. The captain, who had been on the coast before and "knew the ropes," took the steering oar, and we went off in the same way as the other boat. I, being the youngest, had the pleasure of standing at the bow, and getting wet through. We went off well, though the seas were high. Some of them lifted us up, and sliding from under us, seemed to let us drop through the air like a flat plank upon the body of the water. In a few minutes we were in the low, regular swell, and pulled for a light, which, as we came up, we found had been run up to our trysail gaff.

Coming aboard, we hoisted up all the boats, and diving down into the forecastle, changed our wet clothes, and got our supper. After supper the sailors lighted their pipes, (cigars, those of us who had them,) and we had to tell all we had seen ashore. Then followed conjectures about the people ashore, the length of the voyage, carrying hides, etc., until eight bells, when all hands were called aft, and the "anchor watch" set. We were to stand two in a watch, and as the nights were pretty long, two hours were to make a watch. The second mate was to keep the deck until eight o'clock, and all hands were to be called at daybreak, and the word was passed to keep a bright look-out, and to call the mate if it should come on to blow from the south-east. We had also orders to strike the bells every half-hour through the night, as at sea. My watchmate was John, the Swedish sailor, and we stood from twelve to two, he walking the larboard side, and I the starboard. At daylight all hands were called, and we went through the usual process of washing down, swabbing, etc., and got breakfast at eight o'clock. In the course of the forenoon, a boat went aboard of the Ayacucho and brought off a quarter of beef, which made us a fresh bite for dinner. This we were glad enough to have, and the mate told us that we should live upon fresh beef while we were on the coast, as it was cheaper here than the salt. While at dinner, the cook called, "Sail ho!" and coming on deck, we saw two sails coming round the point. One was a large ship under top-gallant sails, and the other a small hermaphrodite brig. They both backed their topsails and sent boats aboard of us. The ship's colors had puzzled us, and we found that she was from Genoa, with an assorted cargo, and was trading on the coast. She filled away again, and stood out; being bound up the coast to San Francisco. The crew of the brig's boat were Sandwich Islanders, but one of them, who spoke a little English, told us that she was the Loriotte, Captain Nye, from Oahu, and was engaged in this trade. She was a lump of a thing—what the sailors call a butter-box. This vessel, as well as the Ayacucho, and others which we afterwards saw engaged in the same trade, have English or Americans for officers, and two or three before the mast to do the work upon the rigging, and to rely upon for seamanship, while the rest of the crew are Sandwich Islanders, who are active, and very useful in boating.

The three captains went ashore after dinner, and came off again at night. When in port, everything is attended to by the chief mate; the captain, unless he is also supercargo, has little to do, and is usually ashore much of his time. This we thought would be pleasanter for us, as the mate was a good-natured man and not very strict. So it was for a time, but we were worse off in the end; for wherever the captain is a severe, energetic man, and the mate is wanting in both these qualities, there will always be trouble. And trouble we had already begun to anticipate. The captain had several times found fault with the mate, in presence of the crew; and hints had been dropped that all was not right between them. When this is the case, and the captain suspects that his officer is too easy and familiar with the crew, then he begins to interfere in all the duties, and to draw the reins tauter, and the crew have to suffer.

CHAPTER X

A SOUTH-EASTER—PASSAGE UP THE COAST

This night, after sundown, it looked black at the southward and eastward, and we were told to keep a bright look-out. Expecting to be called up, we turned in early. Waking up about midnight, I found a man who had just come down from his watch, striking a light. He said that it was beginning to puff up from the south-east, and that the sea was rolling in, and he had called the captain; and as he threw himself down on his chest with all his clothes on, I knew that he expected to be called. I felt the vessel pitching at her anchor, and the chain surging and snapping, and lay awake, expecting an instant summons. In a few minutes it came—three knocks on the scuttle, and "All hands ahoy! bear-a-hand up and make sail." We sprang up for our clothes, and were about halfway dressed, when the mate called out, down the scuttle, "Tumble up here, men! tumble up! before she drags her anchor." We were on deck in an instant. "Lay aloft and loose the topsails!" shouted the captain, as soon as the first man showed himself. Springing into the rigging, I saw that the Ayacucho's topsails were loosed, and heard her crew singing-out at the sheets as they were hauling them home. This had probably started our captain; as "old Wilson" (the captain of the Ayacucho) had been many years on the coast, and knew the signs of the weather. We soon had the topsails loosed; and one hand remaining, as usual, in each top, to overhaul the rigging and light the sail out, the rest of us laid down to man the sheets. While sheeting home, we saw the Ayacucho standing athwart our bows, sharp upon the wind, cutting through the head sea like a knife, with her raking masts and sharp bows running up like the head of a greyhound. It was a beautiful sight. She was like a bird which had been frightened and had spread her wings in flight. After the topsails had been sheeted home, the head yards braced aback, the fore-top-mast staysail hoisted, and the buoys streamed, and all ready forward, for slipping, we went aft and manned the slip-rope which came through the stern port with a turn round the timber-heads. "All ready forward?" asked the captain. "Aye, aye, sir; all ready," answered the mate. "Let go!" "All gone, sir;" and the iron cable grated over the windlass and through the hawse-hole, and the little vessel's head swinging off from the wind under the force of her backed head sails, brought the strain upon the slip-rope. "Let go aft!" Instantly all was gone, and we were under weigh. As soon as she was well off from the wind, we filled away the head yards, braced all up sharp, set the foresail and trysail, and left our anchorage well astern, giving the point a good berth. "Nye's off too," said the captain to the mate; and looking astern, we could just see the little hermaphrodite brig under sail standing after us.

It now began to blow fresh; the rain fell fast, and it grew very black; but the captain would not take in sail until we were well clear of the point. As soon as we left this on our quarter, and were standing out to sea, the order was given, and we sprang aloft, double reefed each topsail, furled the foresail, and double reefed the trysail, and were soon under easy sail. In those cases of slipping for south-easters, there is nothing to be done, after you have got clear of the coast, but to lie-to under easy sail, and wait for the gale to be over, which seldom lasts more than two days, and is often over in twelve hours; but the wind never comes back to the southward until there has been a good deal of rain fallen. "Go below the watch," said the mate; but here was a dispute which watch it should be, which the mate soon however settled by sending his watch below, saying that we should have our turn the next time we got under weigh. We remained on deck till the expiration of the watch, the wind blowing very fresh and the rain coming down in torrents. When the watch came up, we wore ship, and stood on the other tack, in towards land. When we came up again, which was at four in the morning, it was very dark, and there was not much wind, but it was raining as I thought I had never seen it rain before. We had on oil-cloth suits and south-wester caps, and had nothing to do but to stand bolt upright and let it pour down upon us. There are no umbrellas, and no sheds to go under, at sea.

While we were standing about on deck, we saw the little brig drifting by us, hove to under her fore topsail double reefed; and she glided by like a phantom. Not a word was spoken, and we saw no one on deck but the man at the wheel. Toward morning the captain put his head out of the companion-way and told the second mate, who commanded our watch, to look out for a change of wind, which usually followed a calm and heavy rain; and it was well that he did; for in a few minutes it fell dead calm, the vessel lost her steerage-way, and the rain ceased. We hauled up the trysail and courses, squared the after yards, and waited for the change, which came in a few minutes, with a vengeance, from the north-west, the opposite point of the compass. Owing to our precautions, we were not taken aback, but ran before the wind with square yards. The captain coming on deck, we braced up a little and stood back for our anchorage. With the change of wind came a change of weather, and in two hours the wind moderated into the light steady breeze, which blows down the coast the greater part of the year, and, from its regularity, might be called a trade-wind. The sun came up bright, and we set royals, skysails, and studding-sails, and were under fair way for Santa Barbara. The little Loriotte was astern of us, nearly out of sight; but we saw nothing of the Ayacucho. In a short time she appeared, standing out from Santa Rosa Island, under the lee of which she had been hove to, all night. Our captain was anxious to get in before her, for it would be a great credit to us, on the coast, to beat the Ayacucho, which had been called the best sailer in the North Pacific, in which she had been known as a trader for six years or more. We had an advantage over her in light winds, from our royals and skysails which we carried both at the fore and main, and also in our studding-sails; for Captain Wilson carried nothing above top-gallant-sails, and always unbent his studding-sails when on the coast. As the wind was light and fair, we held our own, for some time, when we were both obliged to brace up and come upon a taut bowline, after rounding the point; and here he had us on fair ground, and walked away from us, as you would haul in a line. He afterwards said that we sailed well enough with the wind free, but that give him a taut bowline, and he would beat us, if we had all the canvas of the Royal George.

The Ayacucho got to the anchoring ground about half an hour before us, and was furling her sails when we came up to it. This picking up your cables is a very nice piece of work. It requires some seamanship to do it, and come to at your former moorings, without letting go another anchor. Captain Wilson was remarkable, among the sailors on the coast, for his skill in doing this; and our captain never let go a second anchor during all the time that I was with him. Coming a little to windward of our buoy, we clewed up the light sails, backed our main topsail, and lowered a boat, which pulled off, and made fast a spare hawser to the buoy on the end of the slip-rope. We brought the other end to the captain, and hove in upon it until we came to the slip-rope, which we took to the windlass, and walked her up to her chain, the captain helping her by backing and filling the sails. The chain is then passed through the hawse-hole and round the windlass, and bitted, the slip-rope taken round outside and brought into the stern port, and she is safe in her old berth. After we had got through, the mate told us that this was a small touch of California, the like of which we must expect to have through the winter.

After we had furled the sails and got dinner, we saw the Loriotte nearing, and she had her anchor before night. At sun-down we went ashore again, and found the Loriotte's boat waiting on the beach. The Sandwich Islander who could speak English, told us that he had been up to the town; that our agent, Mr. R——, and some other passengers, were going to Monterey with us, and that we were to sail the same night. In a few minutes Captain T——, with two gentlemen and one female, came down, and we got ready to go off. They had a good deal of baggage, which we put into the bows of the boat, and then two of us took the señora in our arms, and waded with her through the water, and put her down safely in the stern. She appeared much amused with the transaction, and her husband was perfectly satisfied, thinking any arrangement good which saved his wetting his feet. I pulled the after oar, so that I heard the conversation, and learned that one of the men, who, as well as I could see in the darkness, was a young-looking man, in the European dress, and covered up in a large cloak, was the agent of the firm to which our vessel belonged; and the other, who was dressed in the Spanish dress of the country, was a brother of our captain, who had been many years a trader on the coast, and had married the lady who was in the boat. She was a delicate, dark-complexioned young woman, and of one of the best families in California. I also found that we were to sail the same night. As soon as we got on board, the boats were hoisted up, the sails loosed, the windlass manned, the slip-ropes and gear cast off; and after about twenty minutes of heaving at the windlass, making sail, and bracing yards, we were well under weigh, and going with a fair wind up the coast to Monterey. The Loriotte got under weigh at the same time, and was also bound up to Monterey, but as she took a different course from us, keeping the land aboard, while we kept well out to sea, we soon lost sight of her. We had a fair wind, which is something unusual when going up, as the prevailing wind is the north, which blows directly down the coast; whence the northern are called the windward, and the southern the leeward ports.

CHAPTER XI

PASSAGE UP THE COAST—MONTEREY

We got clear of the islands before sunrise the next morning, and by twelve o'clock were out of the canal, and off Point Conception, the place where we first made the land upon our arrival. This is the largest point on the coast, and is uninhabited headland, stretching out into the Pacific, and has the reputation of being very windy. Any vessel does well which gets by it without a gale, especially in the winter season. We were going along with studding-sails set on both sides, when, as we came round the point, we had to haul our wind, and take in the lee studding-sails. As the brig came more upon the wind, she felt it more, and we doused the sky-sails, but kept the weather studding-sails on her, bracing the yards forward so that the swinging-boom nearly touched the sprit-sail yard. She now lay over to it, the wind was freshening, and the captain was evidently "dragging on to her." His brother and Mr. R——, looking a little squally, said something to him, but he only answered that he knew the vessel and what she would carry. He was evidently showing off his vessel, and letting them know how he could carry sail. He stood up to windward, holding on by the backstays, and looking up at the sticks, to see how much they would bear; when a puff came which settled the matter. Then it was "haul down," and "clew up," royals, flying-jib, and studding-sails, all at once. There was what the sailors call a "mess"—everything let go, nothing hauled in, and everything flying. The poor Spanish woman came to the companion-way, looking as pale as a ghost, and nearly frightened to death. The mate and some men forward were trying to haul in the lower studding-sail, which had blown over the sprit-sail yard-arm and round the guys; while the topmast-studding-sail boom, after buckling up and springing out again like a piece of whalebone, broke off at the boom-iron. I sprang aloft to take in the main top-gallant studding-sail, but before I got into the top, the tack parted, and away went the sail, swinging forward of the top-gallant-sail, and tearing and slatting itself to pieces. The halyards were at this moment let go by the run; and such a piece of work I never had before, in taking in a sail. After great exertions I got it, or the remains of it, into the top, and was making it fast, when the captain, looking up, called out to me, "Lay aloft there, D——, and furl that main royal." Leaving the studding-sail, I went up to the cross trees; and here it looked rather squally. The foot of the top-gallant-mast was working between the cross and trussel trees, and the royal-mast lay over at a fearful angle with the mast below, while everything was working, and cracking, strained to the utmost.

There's nothing for Jack to do but to obey orders, and I went up upon the yard; and there was a worse "mess," if possible, than I had left below. The braces had been let go, and the yard was swinging about like a turnpike-gate, and the whole sail having blown over to leeward, the lee leach was over the yard-arm, and the sky-sail was all adrift and flying over my head. I looked down, but it was in vain to attempt to make myself heard, for every one was busy below, and the wind roared, and sails were flapping in every direction. Fortunately, it was noon and broad daylight, and the man at the wheel, who had his eyes aloft, soon saw my difficulty, and after numberless signs and gestures, got some one to haul the necessary ropes taut. During this interval I took a look below. Everything was in confusion on deck; the little vessel was tearing through the water as if she were mad, the seas flying over her, and the masts leaning over at an angle of forty-five degrees from the vertical. At the other royal-mast-head was S——, working away at the sail, which was blowing from him as fast as he could gather it in. The top-gallant-sail below me was soon clewed up, which relieved the mast, and in a short time I got my sail furled, and went below; but I lost overboard a new tarpaulin hat, which troubled me more than anything else. We worked for about half an hour with might and main; and in an hour from the time the squall struck us, from having all our flying kites abroad, we came down to double-reefed top-sails and the storm-sails.

The wind had hauled ahead during the squall, and we were standing directly in for the point. So, as soon as we had got all snug, we wore round and stood off again, and had the pleasant prospect of beating up to Monterey, a distance of an hundred miles, against a violent head wind. Before night it began to rain; and we had five days of rainy, stormy weather, under close sail all the time, and were blown several hundred miles off the coast. In the midst of this, we discovered that our fore topmast was sprung, (which no doubt happened in the squall,) and were obliged to send down the fore top-gallant-mast and carry as little sail as possible forward. Our four passengers were dreadfully sick, so that we saw little or nothing of them during the five days. On the sixth day it cleared off, and the sun came out bright, but the wind and sea were still very high. It was quite like being at sea again: no land for hundreds of miles, and the captain taking the sun every day at noon. Our passengers now made their appearance, and I had for the first time the opportunity of seeing what a miserable and forlorn creature a sea-sick passenger is. Since I had got over my own sickness, the third day from Boston, I had seen nothing but hale, hearty men, with their sea legs on, and able to go anywhere, (for we had no passengers;) and I will own there was a pleasant feeling of superiority in being able to walk the deck, and eat, and go about, and comparing one's self with two poor, miserable, pale creatures, staggering and shuffling about decks, or holding on and looking up with giddy heads, to see us climbing to the mast-heads, or sitting quietly at work on the ends of the lofty yards. A well man at sea has little sympathy with one who is seasick; he is too apt to be conscious of a comparison favorable to his own manhood. After a few days we made the land at Point Pinos, (pines,) which is the headland at the entrance of the bay of Monterey. As we drew in, and ran down the shore, we could distinguish well the face of the country, and found it better wooded than that to the southward of Point Conception. In fact, as I afterwards discovered, Point Conception may be made the dividing line between two different faces of the country. As you go to the northward of the point, the country becomes more wooded, has a richer appearance, and is better supplied with water. This is the case with Monterey, and still more so with San Francisco; while to the southward of the point, as at Santa Barbara, San Pedro, and particularly San Diego, there is very little wood, and the country has a naked, level appearance, though it is still very fertile.

The bay of Monterey is very wide at the entrance, being about twenty-four miles between the two points, Año Nuevo at the north, and Pinos at the south, but narrows gradually as you approach the town, which is situated in a bend, or large cove, at the south-eastern extremity, and about eighteen miles from the points, which makes the whole depth of the bay. The shores are extremely well wooded, (the pine abounding upon them,) and as it was now the rainy season, everything was as green as nature could make it,—the grass, the leaves, and all; the birds were singing in the woods, and great numbers of wild-fowl were flying over our heads. Here we could lie safe from the south-easters. We came to anchor within two cable lengths of the shore, and the town lay directly before us, making a very pretty appearance; its houses being plastered, which gives a much better effect than those of Santa Barbara, which are of a mud-color. The red tiles, too, on the roofs, contrasted well with the white plastered sides and with the extreme greenness of the lawn upon which the houses—about an hundred in number—were dotted about, here and there, irregularly. There are in this place, and in every other town which I saw in California, no streets, or fences, (except here and there a small patch was fenced in for a garden,) so that the houses are placed at random upon the green, which, as they are of one story and of the cottage form, gives them a pretty effect when seen from a little distance.

It was a fine Saturday afternoon when we came to anchor, the sun about an hour high, and everything looking pleasantly. The Mexican flag was flying from the little square Presidio, and the drums and trumpets of the soldiers, who were out on parade, sounded over the water, and gave great life to the scene. Every one was delighted with the appearance of things. We felt as though we had got into a Christian (which in the sailor's vocabulary means civilized) country. The first impression which California had made upon us was very disagreeable:—the open roadstead of Santa Barbara; anchoring three miles from the shore; running out to sea before every south-easter; landing in a high surf; with a little dark-looking town, a mile from the beach; and not a sound to be heard, or anything to be seen, but Sandwich Islanders, hides, and tallow-bags. Add to this the gale off Point Conception, and no one can be at a loss to account for our agreeable disappointment in Monterey. Beside all this, we soon learned, which was of no small importance to us, that there was little or no surf here, and this afternoon the beach was as smooth as a duck-pond.

We landed the agent and passengers, and found several persons waiting for them on the beach, among whom were some, who, though dressed in the costume of the country, spoke English; and who, we afterwards learned, were English and Americans who had married and settled in the country.

I also connected with our arrival here another circumstance which more nearly concerns myself; viz, my first act of what the sailors will allow to be seamanship—sending down a royal-yard. I had seen it done once or twice at sea, and an old sailor, whose favor I had taken some pains to gain, had taught me carefully everything which was necessary to be done, and in its proper order, and advised me to take the first opportunity when we were in port, and try it. I told the second mate, with whom I had been pretty thick when he was before the mast, that I would do it, and got him to ask the mate to send me up the first time they were struck. Accordingly I was called upon, and went up, repeating the operations over in my mind, taking care to get everything in its order, for the slightest mistake spoils the whole. Fortunately, I got through without any word from the officer, and heard the "well done" of the mate, when the yard reached the deck, with as much satisfaction as I ever felt at Cambridge on seeing a "bene" at the foot of a Latin exercise.

CHAPTER XII

LIFE AT MONTEREY

The next day being Sunday, which is the liberty-day among merchantmen, when it is usual to let a part of the crew go ashore, the sailors had depended upon a day on land, and were already disputing who should ask to go, when, upon being called in the morning, we were turned-to upon the rigging, and found that the topmast, which had been sprung, was to come down, and a new one to go up, and top-gallant and royal-masts, and the rigging to be set up. This was too bad. If there is anything that irritates sailors and makes them feel hardly used, it is being deprived of their Sabbath. Not that they would always, or indeed generally, spend it religiously, but it is their only day of rest. Then, too, they are often necessarily deprived of it by storms, and unavoidable duties of all kinds, that to take it from them when lying quietly and safely in port, without any urgent reason, bears the more hardly. The only reason in this case was, that the captain had determined to have the custom-house officers on board on Monday, and wished to have his brig in order. Jack is a slave aboard ship; but still he has many opportunities of thwarting and balking his master. When there is danger, or necessity, or when he is well used, no one can work faster than he; but the instant he feels that he is kept at work for nothing, no sloth could make less headway. He must not refuse his duty, or be in any way disobedient, but all the work that an officer gets out of him, he may be welcome to. Every man who has been three months at sea knows how to "work Tom Cox's traverse"—"three turns round the long-boat, and a pull at the scuttled-butt." This morning everything went in this way. "Sogering" was the order of the day. Send a man below to get a block, and he would capsize everything before finding it, then not bring it up till an officer had called him twice, and take as much time to put things in order again. Marline-spikes were not to be found; knives wanted a prodigious deal of sharpening, and, generally, three or four were waiting round the grindstone at a time. When a man got to the mast-head, he would come slowly down again to get something which he had forgotten; and after the tackles were got up, six men would pull less than three who pulled "with a will." When the mate was out of sight, nothing was done. It was all uphill work; and at eight o'clock, when we went to breakfast, things were nearly where they were when we began.

During our short meal, the matter was discussed. One proposed refusing to work; but that was mutiny, and of course was rejected at once. I remember, too, that one of the men quoted "Father Taylor," (as they call the seamen's preacher at Boston,) who told them that if they were ordered to work on Sunday, they must not refuse their duty, and the blame would not come upon them. After breakfast, it leaked out, through the officers, that if we would get through our work soon, we might have a boat in the afternoon and go fishing. This bait was well thrown, and took with several who were fond of fishing; and all began to find that as we had one thing to do, and were not to be kept at work for the day, the sooner we did it, the better.

Accordingly, things took a new aspect; and before two o'clock this work, which was in a fair way to last two days, was done; and five of us went a fishing in the jolly-boat, in the direction of Point Pinos; but leave to go ashore was refused. Here we saw the Loriotte, which sailed with us from Santa Barbara, coming slowly in with a light sea-breeze, which sets in towards afternoon, having been becalmed off the point all the first part of the day. We took several fish of various kinds, among which cod and perch abounded, and F——, (the ci-devant second mate,) who was of our number, brought up with his hook a large and beautiful pearl-oyster shell. We afterwards learned that this place was celebrated for shells, and that a small schooner had made a good voyage, by carrying a cargo of them to the United States.

We returned by sun-down, and found the Loriotte at anchor, within a cable's length of the Pilgrim. The next day we were "turned-to" early, and began taking off the hatches, overhauling the cargo, and getting everything ready for inspection. At eight, the officers of the customs, five in number, came on board, and began overhauling the cargo, manifest, etc.

The Mexican revenue laws are very strict, and require the whole cargo to be landed, examined, and taken on board again; but our agent, Mr. R——, had succeeded in compounding with them for the two last vessels, and saving the trouble of taking the cargo ashore. The officers were dressed in the costume which we found prevailed through the country. A broad-brimmed hat, usually of a black or dark-brown color, with a gilt or figured band round the crown, and lined inside with silk; a short jacket of silk or figured calico, (the European skirted body-coat is never worn;) the shirt open in the neck; rich waistcoat, if any; pantaloons wide, straight, and long, usually of velvet, velveteen, or broadcloth; or else short breeches and white stockings. They wear the deer-skin shoe, which is of a dark-brown color, and, (being made by Indians,) usually a good deal ornamented. They have no suspenders, but always wear a sash round the waist, which is generally red, and varying in quality with the means of the wearer. Add to this the never-failing cloak, and you have the dress of the Californian. This last garment, the cloak, is always a mark of the rank and wealth of the owner. The "gente de razón," or aristocracy, wear cloaks of black or dark blue broadcloth, with as much velvet and trimmings as may be; and from this they go down to the blanket of the Indian; the middle classes wearing something like a large table-cloth, with a hole in the middle for the head to go through. This is often as coarse as a blanket, but being beautifully woven with various colors, is quite showy at a distance. Among the Mexicans there is no working class; (the Indians being slaves and doing all the hard work;) and every rich man looks like a grandee, and every poor scamp like a broken-down gentleman. I have often seen a man with a fine figure, and courteous manners, dressed in broadcloth and velvet, with a noble horse completely covered with trappings; without a real in his pocket, and absolutely suffering for something to eat.

CHAPTER XIII

TRADING—A BRITISH SAILOR

The next day, the cargo having been entered in due form, we began trading. The trade-room was fitted up in the steerage, and furnished out with the lighter goods, and with specimens of the rest of the cargo; and M——, a young man who came out from Boston with us, before the mast, was taken out of the forecastle, and made supercargo's clerk. He was well qualified for the business, having been clerk in a counting-house in Boston. He had been troubled for some time with the rheumatism, which unfitted him for the wet and exposed duty of a sailor on the coast. For a week or ten days all was life on board. The people came off to look and to buy—men, women, and children; and we were continually going in the boats, carrying goods and passengers,—for they have no boats of their own. Everything must dress itself and come aboard and see the new vessel, if it were only to buy a paper of pins. The agent and his clerk managed the sales, while we were busy in the hold or in the boats. Our cargo was an assorted one; that is, it consisted of everything under the sun. We had spirits of all kinds, (sold by the cask,) teas, coffee, sugars, spices, raisins, molasses, hardware, crockery-ware, tinware, cutlery, clothing of all kinds, boots and shoes from Lynn, calicoes and cottons from Lowell, crepes, silks; also shawls, scarfs, necklaces, jewelry, and combs for the ladies; furniture; and in fact, everything that can be imagined, from Chinese fire-works to English cart-wheels—of which we had a dozen pairs with their iron rims on.

The Californians are an idle, thriftless people, and can make nothing for themselves. The country abounds in grapes, yet they buy bad wines made in Boston and brought round by us, at an immense price, and retail it among themselves at a real (12½ cents) by the small wine-glass. Their hides, too, which they value at two dollars in money, they give for something which costs seventy-five cents in Boston; and buy shoes (like as not, made of their own hides, and which have been carried twice around Cape Horn) at three or four dollars, and "chicken-skin" boots at fifteen dollars apiece. Things sell, on an average, at an advance of nearly three hundred per cent upon the Boston prices. This is partly owing to the heavy duties which the government, in their wisdom, with the intent, no doubt, of keeping the silver in the country, has laid upon imports. These duties, and the enormous expenses of so long a voyage, keep all merchants, but those of heavy capital, from engaging in the trade. Nearly two-thirds of all the articles imported into the country from round Cape Horn, for the last six years, have been by the single house of Bryant, Sturgis & Co., to whom our vessel belonged, and who have a permanent agent on the coast.

This kind of business was new to us, and we liked it very well for a few days, though we were hard at work every minute from daylight to dark; and sometimes even later.

By being thus continually engaged in transporting passengers with their goods, to and fro, we gained considerable knowledge of the character, dress, and language of the people. The dress of the men was as I have before described it. The women wore gowns of various texture—silks, crape, calicoes, etc.,—made after the European style, except that the sleeves were short, leaving the arm bare, and that they were loose about the waist, having no corsets. They wore shoes of kid, or satin; sashes or belts of bright colors; and almost always a necklace and ear-rings. Bonnets they had none. I only saw one on the coast, and that belonged to the wife of an American sea-captain who had settled in San Diego, and had imported the chaotic mass of straw and ribbon, as a choice present to his new wife. They wear their hair (which is almost invariably black, or a very dark brown) long in their necks, sometimes loose, and sometimes in long braids; though the married women often do it up on a high comb. Their only protection against the sun and weather is a large mantle which they put over their heads, drawing it close round their faces, when they go out of doors, which is generally only in pleasant weather. When in the house, or sitting out in front of it, which they often do in fine weather, they usually wear a small scarf or neckerchief of a rich pattern. A band, also, about the top of the head, with a cross, star, or other ornament in front, is common. Their complexions are various, depending—as well as their dress and manner—upon their rank; or, in other words, upon the amount of Spanish blood they can lay claim to. Those who are of pure Spanish blood, having never intermarried with the aborigines, have clear brunette complexions, and sometimes, even as fair as those of English women. There are but few of these families in California; being mostly those in official stations, or who, on the expiration of their offices, have settled here upon property which they have acquired; and others who have been banished for state offences. These form the aristocracy; inter-marrying, and keeping up an exclusive system in every respect. They can be told by their complexions, dress, manner, and also by their speech; for, calling themselves Castilians, they are very ambitious of speaking the pure Castilian language, which is spoken in a somewhat corrupted dialect by the lower classes. From this upper class, they go down by regular shades, growing more and more dark and muddy, until you come to the pure Indian, who runs about with nothing upon him but a small piece of cloth, kept up by a wide leather strap drawn round his waist. Generally speaking, each person's caste is decided by the quality of the blood, which shows itself, too plainly to be concealed, at first sight. Yet the least drop of Spanish blood, if it be only of quadroon or octoroon, is sufficient to raise them from the rank of slaves, and entitle them to a suit of clothes—boots, hat, cloak, spurs, long knife, and all complete, though coarse and dirty as may be,—and to call themselves Españolos, and to hold property, if they can get any.

The fondness for dress among the women is excessive, and is often the ruin of many of them. A present of a fine mantle, or of a necklace or pair of ear-rings, gains the favor of the greater part of them. Nothing is more common than to see a woman living in a house of only two rooms, and the ground for a floor, dressed in spangled satin shoes, silk gown, high comb, and gilt, if not gold, ear-rings and necklace. If their husbands do not dress them well enough, they will soon receive presents from others. They used to spend whole days on board our vessels, examining the fine clothes and ornaments, and frequently made purchases at a rate which would have made a seamstress or waiting-maid in Boston open her eyes.

Next to the love of dress, I was most struck with the fineness of the voices and beauty of the intonations of both sexes. Every common ruffian-looking fellow, with a slouched hat, blanket cloak, dirty under-dress, and soiled leather leggins, appeared to me to be speaking elegant Spanish. It was a pleasure, simply to listen to the sound of the language, before I could attach any meaning to it. They have a good deal of the Creole drawl, but it is varied with an occasional extreme rapidity of utterance, in which they seem to skip from consonant to consonant, until, lighting upon a broad, open vowel, they rest upon that to restore the balance of sound. The women carry this peculiarity of speaking to a much greater extreme than the men, who have more evenness and stateliness of utterance. A common bullock-driver, on horseback, delivering a message, seemed to speak like an ambassador at an audience. In fact, they sometimes appeared to me to be a people on whom a curse had fallen, and stripped them of everything but their pride, their manners, and their voices.

Another thing that surprised me was the quantity of silver that was in circulation. I certainly never saw so much silver at one time in my life, as during the week that we were at Monterey. The truth is, they have no credit system, no banks, and no way of investing money but in cattle. They have no circulating medium but silver and hides—which the sailors call "California bank notes." Everything that they buy they must pay for in one or the other of these things. The hides they bring down dried and doubled, in clumsy ox-carts, or upon mules' backs, and the money they carry tied up in a handkerchief;—fifty, eighty, or an hundred dollars and half dollars.

I had never studied Spanish while at college, and could not speak a word, when at Juan Fernandez; but during the latter part of the passage out, I borrowed a grammar and dictionary from the cabin, and by a continual use of these, and a careful attention to every word that I heard spoken, I soon got a vocabulary together, and began talking for myself. As I soon knew more Spanish than any of the crew, (who indeed knew none at all,) and had been at college and knew Latin, I got the name of a great linguist, and was always sent for by the captain and officers to get provisions, or to carry letters and messages to different parts of the town. I was often sent to get something which I could not tell the name of to save my life; but I liked the business, and accordingly never pleaded ignorance. Sometimes I managed to jump below and take a look at my dictionary before going ashore; or else I overhauled some English resident on my way, and got the word from him; and then, by signs, and the help of my Latin and French, contrived to get along. This was a good exercise for me, and no doubt taught me more than I should have learned by months of study and reading; it also gave me opportunities of seeing the customs, characters, and domestic arrangements of the people; beside being a great relief from the monotony of a day spent on board ship.

Monterey, as far as my observation goes, is decidedly the pleasantest and most civilized-looking place in California. In the centre of it is an open square, surrounded by four lines of one-story plastered buildings, with half a dozen cannon in the centre; some mounted, and others not. This is the "Presidio," or fort. Every town has a presidio in its centre; or rather, every presidio has a town built around it; for the forts were first built by the Mexican government, and then the people built near them for protection. The presidio here was entirely open and unfortified. There were several officers with long titles, and about eighty soldiers, but they were poorly paid, fed, clothed, and disciplined. The governor-general, or, as he is commonly called, the "general," lives here; which makes it the seat of government. He is appointed by the central government at Mexico, and is the chief civil and military officer. In addition to him, each town has a commandant, who is the chief military officer, and has charge of the fort, and of all transactions with foreigners and foreign vessels; and two or three alcaldes and corregidores, elected by the inhabitants, who are the civil officers. Courts and jurisprudence they have no knowledge of. Small municipal matters are regulated by the alcaldes and corregidores; and everything relating to the general government, to the military, and to foreigners, by the commandants, acting under the governor-general. Capital cases are decided by him, upon personal inspection, if he is near; or upon minutes sent by the proper officers, if the offender is at a distant place. No Protestant has any civil rights, nor can he hold any property, or, indeed, remain more than a few weeks on shore, unless he belong to some vessel. Consequently, the Americans and English who intend to remain here become Catholics, to a man; the current phrase among them being,—"A man must leave his conscience at Cape Horn."

But to return to Monterey. The houses here, as everywhere else in California, are of one story, built of clay made into large bricks, about a foot and a half square and three or four inches thick, and hardened in the sun. These are cemented together by mortar of the same material, and the whole are of a common dirt-color. The floors are generally of earth, the windows grated and without glass; and the doors, which are seldom shut, open directly into the common room; there being no entries. Some of the more wealthy inhabitants have glass to their windows and board floors; and in Monterey nearly all the houses are plastered on the outside. The better houses, too, have red tiles upon the roofs. The common ones have two or three rooms which open into each other, and are furnished with a bed or two, a few chairs and tables, a looking-glass, a crucifix of some material or other, and small daubs of paintings enclosed in glass, and representing some miracle or martyrdom. They have no chimneys or fire-places in the houses, the climate being such as to make a fire unnecessary; and all their cooking is done in a small cook-house, separated from the house. The Indians, as I have said before, do all the hard work, two or three being attached to each house; and the poorest persons are able to keep one, at least, for they have only to feed them and give them a small piece of coarse cloth and a belt, for the males; and a coarse gown, without shoes or stockings, for the females.

In Monterey there are a number of English and Americans (English or "Ingles" all are called who speak the English language) who have married Californians, become united to the Catholic church, and acquired considerable property. Having more industry, frugality, and enterprise than the natives, they soon get nearly all the trade into their hands. They usually keep shops, in which they retail the goods purchased in larger quantities from our vessels, and also send a good deal into the interior, taking hides in pay, which they again barter with our vessels. In every town on the coast there are foreigners engaged in this kind of trade, while I recollect but two shops kept by natives. The people are generally suspicious of foreigners, and they would not be allowed to remain, were it not that they become good Catholics, and by marrying natives, and bringing up their children as Catholics and Mexicans, and not teaching them the English language, they quiet suspicion, and even become popular and leading men. The chief alcaldes in Monterey and Santa Barbara were both Yankees by birth.

The men in Monterey appeared to me to be always on horseback. Horses are as abundant here as dogs and chickens were in Juan Fernandez. There are no stables to keep them in, but they are allowed to run wild and graze wherever they please, being branded, and having long leather ropes, called "lassos," attached to their necks and dragging along behind them, by which they can be easily taken. The men usually catch one in the morning, throw a saddle and bridle upon him, and use him for the day, and let him go at night, catching another the next day. When they go on long journeys, they ride one horse down, and catch another, throw the saddle and bridle upon him, and after riding him down, take a third, and so on to the end of the journey. There are probably no better riders in the world. They get upon a horse when only four or five years old, their little legs not long enough to come half way over his sides; and may almost be said to keep on him until they have grown to him. The stirrups are covered or boxed up in front, to prevent their catching when riding through the woods; and the saddles are large and heavy, strapped very tight upon the horse, and have large pommels, or loggerheads, in front, round which the "lasso" is coiled when not in use. They can hardly go from one house to another without getting on a horse, there being generally several standing tied to the door-posts of the little cottages. When they wish to show their activity, they make no use of their stirrups in mounting, but striking the horse, spring into the saddle as he starts, and sticking their long spurs into him, go off on the full run. Their spurs are cruel things, having four or five rowels, each an inch in length, dull and rusty. The flanks of the horses are often sore from them, and I have seen men come in from chasing bullocks with their horses' hind legs and quarters covered with blood. They frequently give exhibitions of their horsemanship, in races, bull-baitings, etc.; but as we were not ashore during any holyday, we saw nothing of it. Monterey is also a great place for cock-fighting, gambling of all sorts, fandangos, and every kind of amusement and knavery. Trappers and hunters, who occasionally arrive here from over the Rocky mountains, with their valuable skins and furs, are often entertained with every sort of amusement and dissipation, until they have wasted their time and their money, and go back, stripped of everything.

Nothing but the character of the people prevents Monterey from becoming a great town. The soil is as rich as man could wish; climate as good as any in the world; water abundant, and situation extremely beautiful. The harbor, too, is a good one, being subject only to one bad wind, the north; and though the holding-ground is not the best, yet I heard of but one vessel's being driven ashore here. That was a Mexican brig, which went ashore a few months before our arrival, and was a total wreck, all the crew but one being drowned. Yet this was from the carelessness or ignorance of the captain, who paid out all his small cable before he let go his other anchor. The ship Lagoda, of Boston, was there at the time, and rode out the gale in safety, without dragging at all, or finding it necessary to strike her top-gallant masts.

The only vessel in port with us was the little Loriotte. I frequently went on board her, and became very well acquainted with her Sandwich Island crew. One of them could speak a little English, and from him I learned a good deal about them. They were well formed and active, with black eyes, intelligent countenances, dark-olive, or, I should rather say, copper complexions and coarse black hair, but not woolly like the negroes. They appeared to be talking continually. In the forecastle there was a complete Babel. Their language is extremely guttural, and not pleasant at first, but improves as you hear it more, and is said to have great capacity. They use a good deal of gesticulation, and are exceedingly animated, saying with their might what their tongues find to say. They are complete water-dogs, therefore very good in boating. It is for this reason that there are so many of them on the coast of California; they being very good hands in the surf. They are also quick and active in the rigging, and good hands in warm weather; but those who have been with them round Cape Horn, and in high latitudes, say that they are useless in cold weather. In their dress they are precisely like our sailors. In addition to these Islanders, the vessel had two English sailors, who acted as boatswains over the Islanders, and took care of the rigging. One of them I shall always remember as the best specimen of the thoroughbred English sailor that I ever saw. He had been to sea from a boy, having served a regular apprenticeship of seven years, as all English sailors are obliged to do, and was then about four or five and twenty. He was tall; but you only perceived it when he was standing by the side of others, for the great breadth of his shoulders and chest made him appear but little above the middle height. His chest was as deep as it was wide; his arm like that of Hercules; and his hand "the fist of a tar—every hair a rope-yarn." With all this he had one of the pleasantest smiles I ever saw. His cheeks were of a handsome brown; his teeth brilliantly white; and his hair, of a raven black, waved in loose curls all over his head, and fine, open forehead; and his eyes he might have sold to a duchess at the price of diamonds, for their brilliancy. As for their color, they were like the Irishman's pig, which would not stay to be counted, every change of position and light seemed to give them a new hue; but their prevailing color was black, or nearly so. Take him with his well-varnished black tarpaulin stuck upon the back of his head; his long locks coming down almost into his eyes; his white duck trowsers and shirt; blue jacket; and black kerchief, tied loosely round his neck; and he was a fine specimen of manly beauty. On his broad chest he had stamped with India ink "Parting moments;"—a ship ready to sail; a boat on the beach; and a girl and her sailor lover taking their farewell. Underneath were printed the initials of his own name, and two other letters, standing for some name which he knew better than I did. This was very well done, having been executed by a man who made it his business to print with India ink, for sailors, at Havre. On one of his broad arms, he had the crucifixion, and on the other the sign of the "foul anchor."

He was very fond of reading, and we lent him most of the books which we had in the forecastle, which he read and returned to us the next time we fell in with him. He had a good deal of information, and his captain said he was a perfect seaman, and worth his weight in gold on board a vessel, in fair weather and in foul. His strength must have been great, and he had the sight of a vulture. It is strange that one should be so minute in the description of an unknown, outcast sailor, whom one may never see again, and whom no one may care to hear about; but so it is. Some people we see under no remarkable circumstances, but whom, for some reason or other, we never forget. He called himself Bill Jackson; and I know no one of all my accidental acquaintances to whom I would more gladly give a shake of the hand than to him. Whoever falls in with him will find a handsome, hearty fellow, and a good shipmate.

Sunday came again while we were at Monterey, but as before, it brought us no holyday. The people on shore dressed themselves and came off in greater numbers than ever, and we were employed all day in boating and breaking out cargo, so that we had hardly time to eat. Our cidevant second mate, who was determined to get liberty if it was to be had, dressed himself in a long coat and black hat, and polished his shoes, and went aft and asked to go ashore. He could not have done a more imprudent thing; for he knew that no liberty would be given; and besides, sailors, however sure they may be of having liberty granted them always go aft in their working clothes, to appear as though they had no reason to expect anything, and then wash, dress, and shave, after they get their liberty. But this poor fellow was always getting into hot water, and if there was a wrong way of doing a thing, was sure to hit upon it. We looked to see him go aft, knowing pretty well what his reception would be. The captain was walking the quarter-deck, smoking his morning cigar, and F—— went as far as the break of the deck, and there waited for him to notice him. The captain took two or three turns, and then walking directly up to him, surveyed him from head to foot, and lifting up his forefinger, said a word or two, in a tone too low for us to hear, but which had a magical effect upon poor F——. He walked forward, sprang into the forecastle, and in a moment more made his appearance in his common clothes, and went quietly to work again. What the captain said to him, we never could get him to tell, but it certainly changed him outwardly and inwardly in a most surprising manner.

CHAPTER XIV

SANTA BARBARA—HIDE-DROGHING—HARBOR DUTIES—DISCONTENT—SAN PEDRO

After a few days, finding the trade beginning to slacken, we hove our anchor up, set our topsails, ran the stars and stripes up to the peak, fired a gun, which was returned from the Presidio, and left the little town astern, running out of the bay, and bearing down the coast again, for Santa Barbara. As we were now going to leeward, we had a fair wind and a plenty of it. After doubling Point Pinos, we bore up, set studding-sails alow and aloft, and were walking off at the rate of eight or nine knots, promising to traverse in twenty-four hours the distance which we were nearly three weeks in traversing on the passage up. We passed Point Conception at a flying rate, the wind blowing so that it would have seemed half a gale to us, if we had been going the other way and close hauled. As we drew near the islands off Santa Barbara, it died away a little but we came-to at our old anchoring-ground in less than thirty hours from the time of leaving Monterey.

Here everything was pretty much as we left it—the large bay without a vessel in it; the surf roaring and rolling in upon the beach; the white mission; the dark town and the high, treeless mountains. Here, too, we had our south-easter tacks aboard again,—slip-ropes, buoy-ropes, sails furled with reefs in them, and rope-yarns for gaskets. We lay here about a fortnight, employed in landing goods and taking off hides, occasionally, when the surf was not high; but there did not appear to be one-half the business doing here that there was in Monterey. In fact, so far as we were concerned, the town might almost as well have been in the middle of the Cordilleras. We lay at a distance of three miles from the beach, and the town was nearly a mile farther; so that we saw little or nothing of it. Occasionally we landed a few goods, which were taken away by Indians in large, clumsy ox-carts, with the yoke on the ox's neck instead of under it, and with small solid wheels. A few hides were brought down, which we carried off in the California style. This we had now got pretty well accustomed to;

and hardened to also; for it does require a little hardening even to the toughest.

The hides are always brought down dry, or they would not be received. When they are taken from the animal, they have holes cut in the ends, and are staked out, and thus dried in the sun without shrinking. They are then doubled once, lengthwise, with the hair side usually in, and sent down, upon mules or in carts, and piled above highwater mark; and then we rake them upon our heads, one at a time, or two, if they are small, and wade out with them and throw them into the boat, which as there are no wharves, we are usually kept anchored by a small kedge, or keelek, just outside of the surf. We all provided ourselves with thick Scotch caps, which would be soft to the head, and at the same time protect it; for we soon found that however it might look or feel at first the "head-work" was the only system for California. For besides that the seas, breaking high, often obliged us to carry the hides so, in order to keep them dry, we found that, as they were very large and heavy, and nearly as stiff as boards, it was the only way that we could carry them with any convenience to ourselves. Some of the crew tried other expedients, saying that they looked too much like West India negroes; but they all came to it at last. The great art is in getting them on the head. We had to take them from the ground, and as they were often very heavy, and as wide as the arms could stretch and easily taken by the wind, we used to have some trouble with them. I have often been laughed at myself, and joined in laughing at others, pitching themselves down in the sand, trying to swing a large hide upon their heads, or nearly blown over with one in a little gust of wind. The captain made it harder for us, by telling us that it was "California fashion" to carry two on the head at a time; and as he insisted upon it, and we did not wish to be outdone by other vessels, we carried two for the first few months; but after falling in with a few other "hide-droghers," and finding that they carried only one at a time we "knocked off" the extra one, and thus made our duty somewhat easier.

After we had got our heads used to the weight, and had learned the true California style of tossing a hide, we could carry off two or three hundred in a short time, without much trouble; but it was always wet work, and, if the beach was stony, bad for our feet; for we, of course, always went barefooted on this duty, as no shoes could stand such constant wetting with salt water. Then, too, we had a long pull of three miles, with a loaded boat, which often took a couple of hours.

We had now got well settled down into our harbor duties, which, as they are a good deal different from those at sea, it may be well enough to describe. In the first place, all hands are called at daylight, or rather—especially if the days are short—before daylight, as soon as the first grey of the morning. The cook makes his fire in the galley; the steward goes about his work in the cabin; and the crew rig the head pump, and wash down the decks. The chief mate is always on deck, but takes no active part, all the duty coming upon the second mate, who has to roll up his trowsers and paddle about decks barefooted, like the rest of the crew. The washing, swabbing, squilgeeing, etc., lasts, or is made to last, until eight o'clock, when breakfast is ordered, fore and aft. After breakfast, for which half an hour is allowed, the boats are lowered down, and made fast astern, or out to the swinging booms, by ges-warps, and the crew are turned-to upon their day's work. This is various, and its character depends upon circumstances. There is always more or less of boating, in small boats; and if heavy goods are to be taken ashore, or hides are brought down to the beach for us, then all hands are sent ashore with an officer in the long boat. Then there is always a good deal to be done in the hold: goods to be broken out; and cargo to be shifted, to make room for hides, or to keep the trim of the vessel. In addition to this, the usual work upon the rigging must be done. There is a good deal of the latter kind of work which can only be done when the vessel is in port;—and then everything must be kept taut and in good order; spun-yarn made; chafing gear repaired; and all the other ordinary work. The great difference between sea and harbor duty is in the division of time. Instead of having a watch on deck and a watch below, as at sea, all hands are at work together, except at meal times, from daylight till dark; and at night an "anchor-watch" is kept, which consists of only two at a time; the whole crew taking turns. An hour is allowed for dinner, and at dark, the decks are cleared up; the boats hoisted; supper ordered; and at eight, the lights put out, except in the binnacle, where the glass stands; and the anchor-watch is set. Thus, when at anchor, the crew have more time at night, (standing watch only about two hours,) but have no time to themselves in the day; so that reading, mending clothes, etc., has to be put off until Sunday, which is usually given. Some religious captains give their crews Saturday afternoons to do their washing and mending in, so that they may have their Sundays free. This is a good arrangement, and does much toward creating the preference sailors usually show for religious vessels. We were well satisfied if we got Sunday to ourselves, for, if any hides came down on that day, as was often the case when they were brought from a distance, we were obliged to bring them off, which usually took half a day; and as we now lived on fresh beef, and ate one bullock a week, the animal was almost always brought down on Sunday, and we had to go ashore, kill it, dress it, and bring it aboard, which was another interruption. Then, too, our common day's work was protracted and made more fatiguing by hides coming down late in the afternoon, which sometimes kept us at work in the surf by star-light, with the prospect of pulling on board, and stowing them all away, before supper.

But all these little vexations and labors would have been nothing,—they would have been passed by as the common evils of a sea-life, which every sailor, who is a man, will go through without complaint,—were it not for the uncertainty, or worse than uncertainty, which hung over the nature and length of our voyage. Here we were, in a little vessel, with a small crew, on a half-civilized coast, at the ends of the earth, and with a prospect of remaining an indefinite period, two or three years at the least. When we left Boston we supposed that it was to be a voyage of eighteen months, or two years, at most; but upon arriving on the coast, we learned something more of the trade, and found that in the scarcity of hides, which was yearly greater and greater, it would take us a year, at least, to collect our own cargo, beside the passage out and home; and that we were also to collect a cargo for a large ship belonging to the same firm, which was soon to come on the coast, and to which we were to act as tender. We had heard rumors of such a ship to follow us, which had leaked out from the captain and mate, but we passed them by as mere "yarns," till our arrival, when they were confirmed by the letters which we brought from the owners to their agent. The ship California, belonging to the same firm, had been nearly two years on the coast; had collected a full cargo, and was now at San Diego, from which port she was expected to sail in a few weeks for Boston; and we were to collect all the hides we could, and deposit them at San Diego, when the new ship, which would carry forty thousand, was to be filled and sent home; and then we were to begin anew, and collect our own cargo. Here was a gloomy prospect before us, indeed. The California had been twenty months on the coast, and the Lagoda, a smaller ship, carrying only thirty-one or thirty-two thousand, had been two years getting her cargo; and we were to collect a cargo of forty thousand beside our own, which would be twelve or fifteen thousand; and hides were said to be growing scarcer. Then, too, this ship, which had been to us a worse phantom than any flying Dutchman, was no phantom, or ideal thing, but had been reduced to a certainty; so much so that a name was given her, and it was said that she was to be the Alert, a well-known India-man, which was expected in Boston in a few months, when we sailed. There could be no doubt, and all looked black enough. Hints were thrown out about three years and four years;—the older sailors said they never should see Boston again, but should lay their bones in California; and a cloud seemed to hang over the whole voyage. Besides, we were not provided for so long a voyage, and clothes, and all sailors' necessaries, were excessively dear—three or four hundred per cent. advance upon the Boston prices. This was bad enough for them; but still worse was it for me, who did not mean to be a sailor for life; having intended only to be gone eighteen months or two years. Three or four years would make me a sailor in every respect, mind and habits, as well as body—nolens volens; and would put all my companions so far ahead of me that college and a profession would be in vain to think of; and I made up my mind that, feel as I might, a sailor I must be, and to be master of a vessel, must be the height of my ambition.

Beside the length of the voyage, and the hard and exposed life, we were at the ends of the earth; on a coast almost solitary; in a country where there is neither law nor gospel, and where sailors are at their captain's mercy, there being no American consul, or any one to whom a complaint could be made. We lost all interest in the voyage; cared nothing about the cargo, which we were only collecting for others; began to patch our clothes; and felt as though we were fixed beyond all hope of change.

In addition to, and perhaps partly as a consequence of, this state of things, there was trouble brewing on board the vessel. Our mate (as the first mate is always called, par excellence) was a worthy man;—a more honest, upright, and kind-hearted man I never saw;

but he was too good for the mate of a merchantman. He was not the man to call a sailor a "son of a b—-h," and knock him down with a handspike. He wanted the energy and spirit for such a voyage as ours, and for such a captain. Captain T—— was a vigorous, energetic fellow. As sailors say, "he hadn't a lazy bone in him." He was made of steel and whalebone. He was a man to "toe the mark," and to make every one else step up to it. During all the time that I was with him, I never saw him sit down on deck. He was always active and driving; severe in his discipline, and expected the same of his officers. The mate not being enough of a driver for him, and being perhaps too easy with the crew, he was dissatisfied with him, became suspicious that discipline was getting relaxed, and began to interfere in everything. He drew the reins tauter; and as, in all quarrels between officers, the sailors side with the one who treats them best, he became suspicious of the crew. He saw that everything went wrong—that nothing was done "with a will;" and in his attempt to remedy the difficulty by severity, he made everything worse. We were in every respect unfortunately situated. Captain, officers, and crew, entirely unfitted for one another; and every circumstance and event was like a two-edged sword, and cut both ways. The length of the voyage, which made us dissatisfied, made the captain, at the same time, feel the necessity of order and strict discipline; and the nature of the country, which caused us to feel that we had nowhere to go for redress, but were entirely at the mercy of a hard master, made the captain feel, on the other hand, that he must depend entirely upon his own resources. Severity created discontent, and signs of discontent provoked severity. Then, too, ill-treatment and dissatisfaction are no "linimenta laborum;" and many a time have I heard the sailors say that they should not mind the length of the voyage, and the hardships, if they were only kindly treated, and if they could feel that something was done to make things lighter and easier. We felt as though our situation was a call upon our superiors to give us occasional relaxations, and to make our yoke easier. But the contrary policy was pursued. We were kept at work all day when in port; which, together with a watch at night, made us glad to turn-in as soon as we got below. Thus we got no time for reading, or—which was of more importance to us—for washing and mending our clothes. And then, when we were at sea, sailing from port to port, instead of giving us "watch and watch," as was the custom on board every other vessel on the coast, we were all kept on deck and at work, rain or shine, making spun-yarn and rope, and at other work in good weather, and picking oakum, when it was too wet for anything else. All hands were called to "come up and see it rain," and kept on deck hour after hour in a drenching rain, standing round the deck so far apart as to prevent our talking with one another, with our tarpaulins and oil-cloth jackets on, picking old rope to pieces, or laying up gaskets and robands. This was often done, too, when we were lying in port with two anchors down, and no necessity for more than one man on deck as a look-out. This is what is called "hazing" a crew, and "working their old iron up."

While lying at Santa Barbara, we encountered another south-easter; and, like the first, it came on in the night; the great black clouds coming round from the southward, covering the mountain, and hanging down over the town, appearing almost to rest upon the roofs of the houses. We made sail, slipped our cable, cleared the point, and beat about, for four days, in the offing, under close sail, with continual rain and high seas and winds. No wonder, thought we, they have no rain in the other seasons, for enough seemed to have fallen in those four days to last through a common summer. On the fifth day it cleared up, after a few hours, as is usual, of rain coming down like a four hours' shower-bath, and we found ourselves drifted nearly ten leagues from the anchorage; and having light head winds, we did not return until the sixth day. Having recovered our anchor, we made preparations for getting under weigh to go down to leeward. We had hoped to go directly to San Diego, and thus fall in with the California before she sailed for Boston; but our orders were to stop at an intermediate port called San Pedro, and as we were to lie there a week or two, and the California was to sail in a few days, we lost the opportunity. Just before sailing, the captain took on board a short, red-haired, round-shouldered, vulgar-looking fellow, who had lost one eye, and squinted with the other, and introducing him as Mr. Russell, told us that he was an officer on board. This was too bad. We had lost overboard, on the passage, one of the best of our number, another had been taken from us and appointed clerk, and thus weakened and reduced, instead of shipping some hands to make our work easier, he had put another officer over us, to watch and drive us. We had now four officers, and only six in the forecastle. This was bringing her too much down by the stern for our comfort.

Leaving Santa Barbara, we coasted along down, the country appearing level or moderately uneven, and, for the most part, sandy and treeless; until, doubling a high, sandy point, we let go our anchor at a distance of three or three and a half miles from shore. It was like a vessel, bound to Halifax, coming to anchor on the Grand Banks; for the shore being low, appeared to be at a greater distance than it actually was, and we thought we might as well have staid at Santa Barbara, and sent our boat down for the hides. The land was of a clayey consistency, and, as far as the eye could reach, entirely bare of trees and even shrubs; and there was no sign of a town,—not even a house to be seen. What brought us into such a place, we could not conceive. No sooner had we come to anchor, than the slip-rope, and the other preparations for south-easters, were got ready; and there was reason enough for it, for we lay exposed to every wind that could blow, except the north-west, and that came over a flat country with a range of more than a league of water. As soon as everything was snug on board, the boat was lowered, and we pulled ashore, our new officer, who had been several times in the port before, taking the place of steersman. As we drew in, we found the tide low, and the rocks and stones, covered with kelp and sea-weed, lying bare for the distance of nearly an eighth of a mile. Picking our way barefooted over these, we came to what is called the landing-place, at high-water mark. The soil was as it appeared at first, loose and clayey, and except the stalks of the mustard plant, there was no vegetation. Just in front of the landing, and immediately over it, was a small hill, which, from its being not more than thirty or forty feet high, we had not perceived from our anchorage. Over this hill we saw three men coming down, dressed partly like sailors and partly like Californians; one of them having on a pair of untanned leather trowsers and a red baize shirt. When they came down to us, we found that they were Englishmen, and they told us that they had belonged to a small Mexican brig which had been driven ashore here in a south-easter, and now lived in a small house just over the hill. Going up this hill with them, we saw, just behind it, a small, low building, with one room, containing a fire-place, cooking apparatus, etc., and the rest of it unfinished, and used as a place to store hides and goods. This, they told us, was built by some traders in the Pueblo, (a town about thirty miles in the interior, to which this was the port,) and used by them as a storehouse, and also as a lodging place when they came down to trade with the vessels. These three men were employed by them to keep the house in order, and to look out for the things stored in it. They said that they had been there nearly a year; had nothing to do most of the time, living upon beef, hard bread, and frijoles (a peculiar kind of bean very abundant in California). The nearest house, they told us, was a Rancho, or cattle-farm, about three miles off; and one of them went up, at the request of our officer, to order a horse to be sent down, with which the agent, who was on board, might go up to the Pueblo. From one of them, who was an intelligent English sailor, I learned a good deal, in a few minutes' conversation, about the place, its trade, and the news from the southern ports. San Diego, he said, was about eighty miles to the leeward of San Pedro; that they had heard from there, by a Mexican who came up on horseback, that the California had sailed for Boston, and that the Lagoda, which had been in San Pedro only a few weeks before, was taking in her cargo for Boston. The Ayacucho was also there, loading for Callao, and the little Loriotte, which had run directly down from Monterey, where we left her. San Diego, he told me, was a small, snug place, having very little trade, but decidedly the best harbor on the coast, being completely land-locked, and the water as smooth as a duck-pond. This was the depot for all the vessels engaged in the trade; each one having a large house there, built of rough boards, in which they stowed their hides, as fast as they collected them in their trips up and down the coast, and when they had procured a full cargo, spent a few weeks there, taking it in, smoking ship, supplying wood and water, and making other preparations for the voyage home. The Lagoda was now about this business. When we should be about it, was more than I could tell; two years, at least, I thought to myself.

I also learned, to my surprise, that the desolate-looking place we were in was the best place on the whole coast for hides. It was the only port for a distance of eighty miles, and about thirty miles in the interior was a fine plane country, filled with herds of cattle, in the centre of which was the Pueblo de los Angelos—the largest town in California—and several of the wealthiest missions; to all of which San Pedro was the sea-port.

Having made our arrangements for a horse to take the agent to the Pueblo the next day, we picked our way again over the green, slippery rocks, and pulled aboard. By the time we reached the vessel, which was so far off that we could hardly see her, in the increasing darkness, the boats were hoisted up, and the crew at supper. Going down into the forecastle, eating our supper, and lighting our cigars and pipes, we had, as usual, to tell all we had seen or heard ashore. We all agreed that it was the worst place we had seen yet, especially for getting off hides, and our lying off at so great a distance looked as though it was bad for south-easters. After a few disputes as to whether we should have to carry our goods up the hill, or not, we talked of San Diego, the probability of seeing the Lagoda before she sailed, etc., etc.

The next day we pulled the agent ashore, and he went up to visit the Pueblo and the neighboring missions; and in a few days, as the result of his labors, large ox-carts, and droves of mules, loaded with hides, were seen coming over the flat country. We loaded our long-boat with goods of all kinds, light and heavy, and pulled ashore. After landing and rolling them over the stones upon the beach, we stopped, waiting for the carts to come down the hill and take them; but the captain soon settled the matter by ordering us to carry them all up to the top, saying that, that was "California fashion." So what the oxen would not do, we were obliged to do. The hill was low, but steep, and the earth, being clayey and wet with the recent rains, was but bad holding-ground for our feet. The heavy barrels and casks we rolled up with some difficulty, getting behind and putting our shoulders to them; now and then our feet slipping, added to the danger of the casks rolling back upon us. But the greatest trouble was with the large boxes of sugar. These, we had to place upon oars, and lifting them up rest the oars upon our shoulders, and creep slowly up the hill with the gait of a funeral procession. After an hour or two of hard work, we got them all up, and found the carts standing full of hides, which we had to unload, and also to load again with our own goods; the lazy Indians, who came down with them, squatting down on their hams, looking on, doing nothing, and when we asked them to help us, only shaking their heads, or drawling out "no quiero."

Having loaded the carts, we started up the Indians, who went off, one on each side of the oxen, with long sticks, sharpened at the end, to punch them with. This is one of the means of saving labor in California;—two Indians to two oxen. Now, the hides were to be got down; and for this purpose, we brought the boat round to a place where the hill was steeper, and threw them down, letting them slide over the slope. Many of them lodged, and we had to let ourselves down and set them agoing again; and in this way got covered with dust, and our clothes torn. After we had got them all down, we were obliged to take them on our heads, and walk over the stones, and through the water, to the boat. The water and the stones together would wear out a pair of shoes a day, and as shoes were very scarce and very dear, we were compelled to go barefooted. At night, we went on board, having had the hardest and most disagreeable day's work that we had yet experienced. For several days, we were employed in this manner, until we had landed forty or fifty tons of goods, and brought on board about two thousand hides; when the trade began to slacken, and we were kept at work, on board, during the latter part of the week, either in the hold or upon the rigging. On Thursday night, there was a violent blow from the northward, but as this was off-shore, we had only to let go our other anchor and hold on. We were called up at night to send down the royal-yards. It was as dark as a pocket, and the vessel pitching at her anchors, I went up to the fore, and my friend S——, to the main, and we soon had them down "ship-shape and Bristol fashion," for, as we had now got used to our duty aloft, everything above the cross-trees was left to us, who were the youngest of the crew, except one boy.

CHAPTER XV

A FLOGGING—A NIGHT ON SHORE—THE STATE OF THINGS ON BOARD—SAN DIEGO

For several days the captain seemed very much out of humor. Nothing went right, or fast enough for him. He quarrelled with the cook, and threatened to flog him for throwing wood on deck; and had a dispute with the mate about reeving a Spanish burton; the mate saying that he was right, and had been taught how to do it by a man who was a sailor! This, the captain took in dudgeon, and they were at sword's points at once. But his displeasure was chiefly turned against a large, heavy-moulded fellow from the Middle States, who was called Sam. This man hesitated in his speech, and was rather slow in his motions, but was a pretty good sailor, and always seemed to do his best; but the captain took a dislike to him, thought he was surly, and lazy; and "if you once give a dog a bad name"—as the sailor-phrase is—"he may as well jump overboard." The captain found fault with everything this man did, and hazed him for dropping a marline-spike from the main-yard, where he was at work. This, of course, was an accident, but it was set down against him. The captain was on board all day Friday, and everything went on hard and disagreeably. "The more you drive a man, the less he will do," was as true with us as with any other people. We worked late Friday night, and were turned-to early Saturday morning. About ten o'clock the captain ordered our new officer, Russell, who by this time had become thoroughly disliked by all the crew, to get the gig ready to take him ashore. John, the Swede, was sitting in the boat alongside, and Russell and myself were standing by the main hatchway, waiting for the captain, who was down in the hold, where the crew were at work, when we heard his voice raised in violent dispute with somebody, whether it was with the mate, or one of the crew, I could not tell; and then came blows and scuffling. I ran to the side and beckoned to John, who came up, and we leaned down the hatchway; and though we could see no one, yet we knew that the captain had the advantage, for his voice was loud and clear—

"You see your condition! You see your condition! Will you ever give me any more of your jaw?" No answer; and then came wrestling and heaving, as though the man was trying to turn him. "You may as well keep still, for I have got you," said the captain. Then came the question, "Will you ever give me any more of your jaw?"

"I never gave you any, sir," said Sam; for it was his voice that we heard, though low and half choked.

"That's not what I ask you. Will you ever be impudent to me again?"

"I never have been, sir," said Sam.

"Answer my question, or I'll make a spread eagle of you! I'll flog you, by G—d."

"I'm no negro slave," said Sam.

"Then I'll make you one," said the captain; and he came to the hatchway, and sprang on deck, threw off his coat, and rolling up his sleeves, called out to the mate—"Seize that man up, Mr. A——! Seize him up! Make a spread eagle of him! I'll teach you all who is master aboard!"

The crew and officers followed the captain up the hatchway, and after repeated orders the mate laid hold of Sam, who made no resistance, and carried him to the gangway.

"What are you going to flog that man for, sir?" said John, the Swede, to the captain.

Upon hearing this, the captain turned upon him, but knowing him to be quick and resolute, he ordered the steward to bring the irons, and calling upon Russell to help him, went up to John.

"Let me alone," said John. "I'm willing to be put in irons. You need not use any force;" and putting out his hands, the captain slipped the irons on, and sent him aft to the quarter-deck. Sam by this time was seized up, as it is called, that is, placed against the shrouds, with his wrists made fast to the shrouds, his jacket off, and his back exposed. The captain stood on the break of the deck, a few feet from him, and a little raised, so as to have a good swing at him, and held in his hand the bight of a thick, strong rope. The officers stood round, and the crew grouped together in the waist. All these preparations made me feel sick and almost faint, angry and excited as I was. A man—a human being, made in God's likeness—fastened up and flogged like a beast! A man, too, whom

I had lived with and eaten with for months, and knew almost as well as a brother. The first and almost uncontrollable impulse was resistance. But what was to be done? The time for it had gone by. The two best men were fast, and there were only two beside myself, and a small boy of ten or twelve years of age. And then there were (beside the captain) three officers, steward, agent and clerk. But beside the numbers, what is there for sailors to do? If they resist, it is mutiny; and if they succeed, and take the vessel, it is piracy. If they ever yield again, their punishment must come; and if they do not yield, they are pirates for life. If a sailor resist his commander, he resists the law, and piracy or submission are his only alternatives. Bad as it was, it must be borne. It is what a sailor ships for. Swinging the rope over his head, and bending his body so as to give it full force, the captain brought it down upon the poor fellow's back. Once, twice—six times. "Will you ever give me any more of your jaw?" The man writhed with pain, but said not a word. Three times more. This was too much, and he muttered something which I could not hear; this brought as many more as the man could stand; when the captain ordered him to be cut down, and to go forward.

"Now for you," said the captain, making up to John and taking his irons off. As soon as he was loose, he ran forward to the forecastle. "Bring that man aft," shouted the captain. The second mate, who had been a shipmate of John's, stood still in the waist, and the mate walked slowly forward; but our third officer, anxious to show his zeal, sprang forward over the windlass, and laid hold of John; but he soon threw him from him. At this moment I would have given worlds for the power to help the poor fellow; but it was all in vain. The captain stood on the quarter-deck, bare-headed, his eyes flashing with rage, and his face as red as blood, swinging the rope, and calling out to his officers, "Drag him aft!—Lay hold of him! I'll sweeten him!" etc., etc. The mate now went forward and told John quietly to go aft; and he, seeing resistance in vain, threw the blackguard third mate from him; said he would go aft of himself; that they should not drag him; and went up to the gangway and held out his hands; but as soon as the captain began to make him fast, the indignity was too much, and he began to resist; but the mate and Russell holding him, he was soon seized up. When he was made fast, he turned to the captain, who stood turning up his sleeves and getting ready for the blow, and asked him what he was to be flogged for. "Have I ever refused my duty, sir? Have you ever known me to hang back, or to be insolent, or not to know my work?"

"No," said the captain, "it is not that that I flog you for; I flog you for your interference—for asking questions."

"Can't a man ask a question here without being flogged?"

"No," shouted the captain; "nobody shall open his mouth aboard this vessel, but myself;" and began laying the blows upon his back, swinging half round between each blow, to give it full effect. As he went on, his passion increased, and he danced about the deck, calling out as he swung the rope,—"If you want to know what I flog you for, I'll tell you. It's because I like to do it!—because I like to do it!—It suits me! That's what I do it for!"

The man writhed under the pain, until he could endure it no longer, when he called out, with an exclamation more common among foreigners than with us—"Oh, Jesus Christ! Oh, Jesus Christ!"

"Don't call on Jesus Christ," shouted the captain; "he can't help you. Call on Captain T——, he's the man! He can help you! Jesus Christ can't help you now!"

At these words, which I never shall forget, my blood ran cold. I could look on no longer. Disgusted, sick, and horror-struck, I turned away and leaned over the rail, and looked down into the water. A few rapid thoughts of my own situation, and of the prospect of future revenge, crossed my mind; but the falling of the blows and the cries of the man called me back at once. At length they ceased, and turning round, I found that the mate, at a signal from the captain had cut him down. Almost doubled up with pain, the man walked slowly forward, and went down into the forecastle. Every one else stood still at his post, while the captain, swelling with rage and with the importance of his achievement, walked the quarter-deck, and at each turn, as he came forward, calling out to us,—"You see your condition! You see where I've got you all, and you know what to expect!"—"You've been mistaken in me—you didn't know what I was! Now you know what I am!"—"I'll make you toe the mark, every soul of you, or I'll flog you all, fore and aft, from the boy, up!"—"You've got a driver over you! Yes, a slave-driver—a negro-driver! I'll see who'll tell me he isn't a negro slave!"

With this and the like matter, equally calculated to quiet us, and to allay any apprehensions of future trouble, he entertained us for about ten minutes, when he went below. Soon after, John came aft, with his bare back covered with stripes and wales in every direction, and dreadfully swollen, and asked the steward to ask the captain to let him have some salve, or balsam, to put upon it. "No," said the captain, who heard him from below; "tell him to put his shirt on; that's the best thing for him; and pull me ashore in the boat. Nobody is going to lay-up on board this vessel." He then called to Mr. Russell to take those men and two others in the boat, and pull him ashore. I went for one. The two men could hardly bend their backs, and the captain called to them to "give way," "give way!" but finding they did their best, he let them alone. The agent was in the stern sheets, but during the whole pull—a league or more—not a word was spoken. We landed; the captain, agent, and officer went up to the house, and left us with the boat. I, and the man with me, staid near the boat, while John and Sam walked slowly away, and sat down on the rocks. They talked some time together, but at length separated, each sitting alone. I had some fears of John. He was a foreigner, and violently tempered, and under suffering; and he had his knife with him, and the captain was to come down alone to the boat. But nothing happened; and we went quietly on board. The captain was probably armed, and if either of them had lifted a hand against him, they would have had nothing before them but flight, and starvation in the woods of California, or capture by the soldiers and Indian blood-hounds, whom the offer of twenty dollars would have set upon them.

After the day's work was done, we went down into the forecastle, and ate our plain supper; but not a word was spoken. It was Saturday night; but there was no song—no "sweethearts and wives." A gloom was over everything. The two men lay in their berths, groaning with pain, and we all turned in, but for myself, not to sleep. A sound coming now and then from the berths of the two men showed that they were awake, as awake they must have been, for they could hardly lie in one posture a moment; the dim, swinging lamp of the forecastle shed its light over the dark hole in which we lived; and many and various reflections and purposes coursed through my mind. I thought of our situation, living under a tyranny; of the character of the country we were in; of the length of the voyage, and of the uncertainty attending our return to

America; and then, if we should return, of the prospect of obtaining justice and satisfaction for these poor men; and vowed that if God should ever give me the means, I would do something to redress the grievances and relieve the sufferings of that poor class of beings, of whom I then was one.

The next day was Sunday. We worked as usual, washing decks, etc., until breakfast-time. After breakfast, we pulled the captain ashore, and finding some hides there which had been brought down the night before, he ordered me to stay ashore and watch them, saying that the boat would come again before night. They left me, and I spent a quiet day on the hill, eating dinner with the three men at the little house. Unfortunately, they had no books, and after talking with them and walking about, I began to grow tired of doing nothing. The little brig, the home of so much hardship and suffering, lay in the offing, almost as far as one could see; and the only other thing which broke the surface of the great bay was a small, desolate-looking island, steep and conical, of a clayey soil, and without the sign of vegetable life upon it; yet which had a peculiar and melancholy interest to me, for on the top of it were buried the remains of an Englishman, the commander of a small merchant brig, who died while lying in this port. It was always a solemn and interesting spot to me. There it stood, desolate, and in the midst of desolation; and there were the remains of one who died and was buried alone and friendless. Had it been a common burying-place, it would have been nothing. The single body corresponded well with the solitary character of everything around. It was the only thing in California from which I could ever extract anything like poetry. Then, too, the man died far from home; without a friend near him; by poison, it was suspected, and no one to inquire into it; and without proper funeral rites; the mate, (as I was told,) glad to have him out of the way, hurrying him up the hill and into the ground, without a word or a prayer.

I looked anxiously for a boat, during the latter part of the afternoon, but none came; until toward sundown, when I saw a speck on the water, and as it drew near, I found it was the gig, with the captain. The hides, then, were not to go off. The captain came up the hill, with a man, bringing my monkey jacket and a blanket. He looked pretty black, but inquired whether I had enough to eat; told me to make a house out of the hides, and keep myself warm, as I should have to sleep there among them, and to keep good watch over them. I got a moment to speak to the man who brought my jacket.

"How do things go aboard?" said I.

"Bad enough," said he; "hard work and not a kind word spoken."

"What," said I, "have you been at work all day?"

"Yes! no more Sunday for us. Everything has been moved in the hold, from stem to stern, and from the waterways to the keelson."

I went up to the house to supper. We had frijoles, (the perpetual food of the Californians, but which, when well cooked, are the best bean in the world,) coffee made of burnt wheat, and hard bread. After our meal, the three men sat down by the light of a tallow candle, with a pack of greasy Spanish cards, to the favorite game of "treinta uno," a sort of Spanish "everlasting." I left them and went out to take up my bivouack among the hides. It was now dark; the vessel was hidden from sight, and except the three men in the house, there was not a living soul within a league. The coati (a wild animal of a nature and appearance between that of the fox and the wolf) set up their sharp, quick bark, and two owls, at the end of two distant points running out into the bay, on different sides of the hills where I lay, kept up their alternate, dismal notes. I had heard the sound before at night, but did not know what it was, until one of the men, who came down to look at my quarters, told me it was the owl. Mellowed by the distance, and heard alone, at night, I thought it was the most melancholy, boding sound I had ever heard. Through nearly all the night they kept it up, answering one another slowly, at regular intervals. This was relieved by the noisy coati, some of which came quite near to my quarters, and were not very pleasant neighbors. The next morning, before sunrise, the long-boat came ashore, and the hides were taken off.

We lay at San Pedro about a week, engaged in taking off hides and in other labors, which had now become our regular duties. I spent one more day on the hill, watching a quantity of hides and goods, and this time succeeded in finding a part of a volume of Scott's Pirate, in a corner of the house; but it failed me at a most interesting moment, and I betook myself to my acquaintances on shore, and from them learned a good deal about the customs of the country, the harbors, etc. This, they told me, was a worse harbor than Santa Barbara, for south-easters; the bearing of the headland being a point and a half more to windward, and it being so shallow that the sea broke often as far out as where we lay at anchor. The gale from which we slipped at Santa Barbara, had been so bad a one here, that the whole bay, for a league out, was filled with the foam of the breakers, and seas actually broke over the Dead Man's island. The Lagoda was lying there, and slipped at the first alarm, and in such haste that she was obliged to leave her launch behind her at anchor. The little boat rode it out for several hours, pitching at her anchor, and standing with her stern up almost perpendicularly. The men told me that they watched her till towards night, when she snapped her cable and drove up over the breakers, high and dry upon the beach.

On board the Pilgrim, everything went on regularly, each one trying to get along as smoothly as possible; but the comfort of the voyage was evidently at an end. "That is a long lane which has no turning"—-"Every dog must have his day, and mine will come by-and-by"—and the like proverbs, were occasionally quoted; but no one spoke of any probable end to the voyage, or of Boston, or anything of the kind; or if he did, it was only to draw out the perpetual, surly reply from his shipmate—"Boston, is it? You may thank your stars if you ever see that place. You had better have your back sheathed, and your head coppered, and your feet shod, and make out your log for California for life!" or else something of this kind—"Before you get to Boston the hides will wear the hair off your head, and you'll take up all your wages in clothes, and won't have enough left to buy a wig with!"

The flogging was seldom if ever alluded to by us, in the forecastle. If any one was inclined to talk about it, the others, with a delicacy which I hardly expected to find among them, always stopped him, or turned the subject. But the behavior of the two men who were flogged toward one another showed a delicacy and a sense of honor, which would have been worthy of admiration in the highest walks of life. Sam knew that the other had suffered solely on his account, and in all his complaints, he said that if he alone had been flogged, it would have been nothing; but that he never could see that man without thinking what had been the means of bringing that disgrace upon him; and John never, by word or deed, let anything escape him to remind the other that it was by interfering to save his shipmate, that he had suffered.

Having got all our spare room filled with hides, we hove up our anchor and made sail for San Diego. In no operation can the disposition of a crew be discovered better than in getting under weigh.

Where things are "done with a will," every one is like a cat aloft: sails are loosed in an instant; each one lays out his strength on his handspike, and the windlass goes briskly round with the loud cry of "Yo heave ho! Heave and pawl! Heave hearty ho!" But with us, at this time, it was all dragging work. No one went aloft beyond his ordinary gait, and the chain came slowly in over the windlass. The mate, between the knight-heads, exhausted all his official rhetoric, in calls of "Heave with a will!"—"Heave hearty, men!—heave hearty!"—"Heave and raise the dead!"—"Heave, and away!" etc., etc.; but it would not do. Nobody broke his back or his handspike by his efforts. And when the cat-tackle-fall was strung along, and all hands—cook, steward, and all—laid hold, to cat the anchor, instead of the lively song of "Cheerily, men!" in which all hands join in the chorus, we pulled a long, heavy, silent pull, and—as sailors say a song is as good as ten men—the anchor came to the cat-head pretty slowly. "Give us 'Cheerily!'" said the mate; but there was no "cheerily" for us, and we did without it. The captain walked the quarterdeck, and said not a word. He must have seen the change, but there was nothing which he could notice officially.

We sailed leisurely down the coast before a light fair wind, keeping the land well aboard, and saw two other missions, looking like blocks of white plaster, shining in the distance; one of which, situated on the top of a high hill, was San Juan Campestrano, under which vessels sometimes come to anchor, in the summer season, and take off hides. The most distant one was St. Louis Rey, which the third mate said was only fifteen miles from San Diego. At sunset on the second day, we had a large and well wooded headland directly before us, behind which lay the little harbor of San Diego. We were becalmed off this point all night, but the next morning, which was Saturday, the 14th of March, having a good breeze, we stood round the point, and hauling our wind, brought the little harbor, which is rather the outlet of a small river, right before us. Every one was anxious to get a view of the new place. A chain of high hills, beginning at the point, (which was on our larboard hand, coming in,) protected the harbor on the north and west, and ran off into the interior as far as the eye could reach. On the other sides, the land was low, and green, but without trees. The entrance is so narrow as to admit but one vessel at a time, the current swift, and the channel runs so near to a low stony point that the ship's sides appeared almost to touch it. There was no town in sight, but on the smooth sand beach, abreast, and within a cable's length of which three vessels lay moored, were four large houses, built of rough boards, and looking like the great barns in which ice is stored on the borders of the large ponds near Boston; with piles of hides standing round them, and men in red shirts and large straw hats, walking in and out of the doors. These were the hide-houses. Of the vessels: one, a short, clumsy, little hermaphrodite brig, we recognized as our old acquaintance, the Loriotte; another, with sharp bows and raking masts, newly painted and tarred, and glittering in the morning sun, with the blood-red banner and cross of St. George at her peak, was the handsome Ayacucho. The third was a large ship, with top-gallant-masts housed, and sails unbent, and looking as rusty and worn as two years' "hide-droghing" could make her. This was the Lagoda. As we drew near, carried rapidly along by the current, we overhauled our chain, and clewed up the topsails. "Let go the anchor!" said the captain but either there was not chain enough forward of the windlass, or the anchor went down foul, or we had too much headway on, for it did not bring us up. "Pay out chain!" shouted the captain; and we gave it to her; but it would not do. Before the other anchor could be let go, we drifted down, broadside on, and went smash into the Lagoda. Her crew were at breakfast in the forecastle, and the cook, seeing us coming, rushed out of his galley, and called up the officers and men.

Fortunately no great harm was done. Her jib-boom ran between our fore and main masts, carrying away some of our rigging, and breaking down the rail. She lost her martingale. This brought us up, and as they paid out chain, we swung clear of them, and let go the other anchor; but this had as bad luck as the first, for, before any one perceived it, we were drifting on to the Loriotte. The captain now gave out his orders rapidly and fiercely, sheeting home the topsails, and backing and filling the sails, in hope of starting or clearing the anchors; but it was all in vain, and he sat down on the rail, taking it very leisurely, and calling out to Captain Nye, that he was coming to pay him a visit. We drifted fairly into the Loriotte, her larboard bow into our starboard quarter, carrying away a part of our starboard quarter railing, and breaking off her larboard bumpkin, and one or two stanchions above the deck. We saw our handsome sailor, Jackson, on the forecastle, with the Sandwich Islanders, working away to get us clear. After paying out chain, we swung clear, but our anchors were no doubt afoul of hers. We manned the windlass, and hove, and hove away, but to no purpose. Sometimes we got a little upon the cable, but a good surge would take it all back again. We now began to drift down toward the Ayacucho, when her boat put off and brought her commander, Captain Wilson, on board. He was a short, active, well-built man, between fifty and sixty years of age; and being nearly twenty years older than our captain, and a thorough seaman, he did not hesitate to give his advice, and from giving advice, he gradually came to taking the command; ordering us when to heave and when to pawl, and backing and filling the topsails, setting and taking in jib and trysail, whenever he thought best. Our captain gave a few orders, but as Wilson generally countermanded them, saying, in an easy, fatherly kind of way, "Oh no! Captain T——, you don't want the jib on her," or "it isn't time yet to heave!" he soon gave it up. We had no objections to this state of things, for Wilson was a kind old man, and had an encouraging and pleasant way of speaking to us, which made everything go easily. After two or three hours of constant labor at the windlass, heaving and "Yo ho!"-ing with all our might, we brought up an anchor, with the Loriotte's small bower fast to it, Having cleared this and let it go, and cleared our hawse, we soon got our other anchor, which had dragged half over the harbor. "Now," said Wilson, "I'll find you a good berth;" and setting both the topsails, he carried us down, and brought us to anchor, in handsome style, directly abreast of the hide-house which we were to use. Having done this, he took his leave, while we furled the sails, and got our breakfast, which was welcome to us, for we had worked hard, and it was nearly twelve o'clock. After breakfast, and until night, we were employed in getting out the boats and mooring ship.

After supper, two of us took the captain on board the Lagoda. As he came alongside, he gave his name, and the mate, in the gangway, called out to the captain down the companion-way—"Captain T—— has come aboard, sir!" "Has he brought his brig with him?" said the rough old fellow, in a tone which made itself heard fore and aft. This mortified our captain a little, and it became a standing joke among us for the rest of the voyage. The captain went down into the cabin, and we walked forward and put our heads down the forecastle, where we found the men at supper, "Come down, shipmates! Come down!" said they, as soon as they saw us; and we went down, and found a large, high forecastle, well lighted; and a crew of twelve or fourteen men, eating out of their kids and pans, and drinking their tea, and talking and laughing, all as independent and easy as so many "wood-sawyer's clerks." This looked like comfort and enjoyment, compared with the dark little forecastle, and scanty, discontented crew of the brig. It was Saturday night; they had got through with their work for the week; and being snugly moored, had nothing to do until Monday, again. After two years' hard service, they had seen the worst, and all, of California;—had got their cargo nearly stowed, and expected to sail in a week or two, for Boston. We spent an hour or more with them, talking over California matters, until the word was passed—"Pilgrims, away!" and we went back with our captain. They were a hardy, but intelligent crew; a little roughened, and their clothes patched and old, from California wear; all able seamen, and between the ages of twenty and thirty-five. They inquired about our vessel, the usage, etc., and were not a little surprised at the story of the flogging. They said there were often difficulties in vessels on the coast, and sometimes knock-downs and fightings, but they had never heard before of a regular seizing-up and flogging. "Spread-eagles" were a new kind of bird in California.

Sunday, they said, was always given in San Diego, both at the hide-houses and on board the vessels, a large number usually going up to the town, on liberty. We learned a good deal from them about curing and stowing of hides, etc. and they were anxious to have the latest news (seven months old) from Boston. One of their first inquiries was for Father Taylor, the seamen's preacher in Boston. Then followed the usual strain of conversation, inquiries, stories, and jokes, which, one must always hear in a ship's forecastle, but which are perhaps, after all, no worse, nor, indeed, more gross, than that of many well-dressed gentlemen at their clubs.

CHAPTER XVI

LIBERTY-DAY ON SHORE

The next day being Sunday, after washing and clearing decks, and getting breakfast, the mate came forward with leave for one watch to go ashore, on liberty. We drew lots, and it fell to the larboard, which I was in. Instantly all was preparation. Buckets of fresh water, (which we were allowed in port,) and soap, were put in use; go-ashore jackets and trowsers got out and brushed; pumps, neckerchiefs, and hats overhauled; one lending to another; so that among the whole each one got a good fit-out. A boat was called to pull the "liberty men" ashore, and we sat down in the stern sheets, "as big as pay passengers," and jumping ashore, set out on our walk for the town, which was nearly three miles off.

It is a pity that some other arrangement is not made in merchant vessels, with regard to the liberty-day. When in port, the crews are kept at work all the week, and the only day they are allowed for rest or pleasure is the Sabbath; and unless they go ashore on that day, they cannot go at all. I have heard of a religious captain who gave his crew liberty on Saturdays, after twelve o'clock. This would be a good plan, if shipmasters would bring themselves to give their crews so much time. For young sailors especially, many of whom have been brought up with a regard for the sacredness of the day, this strong temptation to break it, is exceedingly injurious. As it is, it can hardly be expected that a crew, on a long and hard voyage, will refuse a few hours of freedom from toil and the restraints of a vessel, and an opportunity to tread the ground and see the sights of society and humanity, because it is on a Sunday. It is too much like escaping from prison, or being drawn out of a pit, on the Sabbath day.

I shall never forget the delightful sensation of being in the open air, with the birds singing around me, and escaped from the confinement, labor, and strict rule of a vessel—of being once more in my life, though only for a day, my own master. A sailor's liberty is but for a day; yet while it lasts it is perfect. He is under no one's eye, and can do whatever, and go wherever, he pleases. This day, for the first time, I may truly say, in my whole life, I felt the meaning of a term which I had often heard—the sweets of liberty.

My friend S—— was with me, and turning our backs upon the vessels, we walked slowly along, talking of the pleasure of being our own masters, of the times past, and when we were free in the midst of friends, in America, and of the prospect of our return; and planning where we would go, and what we would do, when we reached home. It was wonderful how the prospect brightened, and how short and tolerable the voyage appeared, when viewed in this new light. Things looked differently from what they did when we talked them over in the little dark forecastle, the night after the flogging at San Pedro. It is not the least of the advantages of allowing sailors occasionally a day of liberty, that it gives them a spring, and makes them feel cheerful and independent, and leads them insensibly to look on the bright side of everything for some time after.

S—— and myself determined to keep as much together as possible, though we knew that it would not do to cut our shipmates; for, knowing our birth and education, they were a little suspicious that we would try to put on the gentleman when we got ashore, and would be ashamed of their company; and this won't do with Jack. When the voyage is at an end, you may do as you please, but so long as you belong to the same vessel, you must be a shipmate to him on shore, or he will not be a shipmate to you on board. Being forewarned of this before I went to sea, I took no "long togs" with me, and being dressed like the rest, in white duck trowsers, blue jacket and straw hat, which would prevent my going in better company, and showing no disposition to avoid them, I set all suspicion at rest. Our crew fell in with some who belonged to the other vessels, and, sailor-like, steered for the first grog-shop. This was a small mud building, of only one room, in which were liquors, dry and West India goods, shoes, bread, fruits, and everything which is vendible in California. It was kept by a yankee, a one-eyed man, who belonged formerly to Fall River, came out to the Pacific in a whale-ship, left her at the Sandwich Islands, and came to California and set up a "Pulperia." S—— and I followed in our shipmates' wake, knowing that to refuse to drink with them would be the highest affront, but determining to slip away at the first opportunity. It is the universal custom with sailors for each one, in his turn, to treat the whole, calling for a glass all round, and obliging every one who is present, even the keeper of the shop, to take a glass with him. When we first came in, there was some dispute between our crew and the others, whether the new comers or the old California rangers should treat first; but it being settled in favor of the latter, each of the crews of the other vessels treated all round in their turn, and as there were a good many present, (including some "loafers" who had dropped in, knowing what was going on, to take advantage of Jack's hospitality,) and the liquor was a real (12½ cents) a glass, it made somewhat of a hole in their lockers. It was now our ship's turn, and S—— and I, anxious to get away, stepped up to call for glasses; but we soon found that we must go in order—the oldest first, for the old sailors did not choose to be preceded by a couple of youngsters; and bon gré mal gré, we had to wait our turn, with the twofold apprehension of being too late for our horses, and of getting corned; for drink you must, every time; and if you drink with one and not with another, it is always taken as an insult.

Having at length gone through our turns and acquitted ourselves of all obligations, we slipped out, and went about among the houses, endeavoring to get horses for the day, so that we might ride round and see the country. At first we had but little success, all that we could get out of the lazy fellows, in reply to our questions, being the eternal drawling "Quien sabe?" ("who knows?") which is an answer to all questions. After several efforts, we at length fell in with a little Sandwich Island boy, who belonged to Captain Wilson of the Ayacucho, and was well acquainted in the place; and he, knowing where to go, soon procured us two horses, ready saddled and bridled, each with a lasso coiled over the pommel. These we were to have all day, with the privilege of riding them down to the beach at night, for a dollar, which we had to pay in advance. Horses are the cheapest thing in California; the very best not being worth more than ten dollars apiece, and very good ones being often sold for three, and four. In taking a day's ride, you pay for the use of the saddle, and for the labor and trouble of catching the horses. If you bring the saddle back safe, they care but little what becomes of the horse. Mounted on our horses, which were spirited beasts, and which, by the way, in this country, are always steered by pressing the contrary rein against the neck, and not by pulling on the bit,—we started off on a fine run over the country. The first place we went to was the old ruinous presidio, which stands on a rising ground near the village, which it overlooks. It is built in the form of an open square, like all the other presidios, and was in a most ruinous state, with the exception of one side, in which the commandant lived, with his family. There were only two guns, one of which was spiked, and the other had no carriage. Twelve, half clothed, and half starved looking fellows, composed the garrison; and they, it was said, had not a musket apiece. The small settlement lay directly below the fort, composed of about forty dark brown looking huts, or houses, and two larger ones, plastered, which belonged to two of the "gente de razón." This town is not more than half as large as Monterey, or Santa Barbara, and has little or no business. From the presidio, we rode off in the direction of the mission, which we were told was three miles distant. The country was rather sandy, and there was nothing for miles which could be called a tree, but the grass grew green and rank, and there were many bushes and thickets, and the soil is said to be good. After a pleasant ride of a couple of miles, we saw the white walls of the mission, and fording a small river, we came directly before it. The mission is built of mud, or rather of the unburnt bricks of the country, and plastered. There was something decidedly striking in its appearance: a number of irregular buildings, connected with one another, and disposed in the form of a hollow square, with a church at one end, rising above the rest, with a tower containing five belfries, in each of which hung a large bell, and with immense rusty iron crosses at the tops. Just outside of the buildings, and under the walls, stood twenty or thirty small huts, built of straw and of the branches of trees, grouped together, in which a few Indians lived, under the protection and in the service of the mission.

Entering a gate-way, we drove into the open square, in which the stillness of death reigned. On one side was the church; on another, a range of high buildings with grated windows; a third was a range of smaller buildings, or offices; and the fourth seemed to be little more than a high connecting wall. Not a living creature could we see. We rode twice round the square, in the hope of waking up some one; and in one circuit, saw a tall monk, with shaven head, sandals, and the dress of the Grey Friars, pass rapidly through a gallery, but he disappeared without noticing us. After two circuits, we stopped our horses, and saw, at last, a man show himself in front of one of the small buildings. We rode up to him, and found him dressed in the common dress of the country, with a silver chain round his neck, supporting a large bunch of keys. From this, we took him to be the steward of the mission, and addressing him as "Mayordomo," received a low bow and an invitation to walk into his room. Making our horses fast, we went in. It was a plain room, containing a table, three or four chairs, a small picture or two of some saint, or miracle, or martyrdom, and a few dishes and glasses. "Hay algunas cosa de comer?" said I. "Si Señor!" said he. "Que gusta usted?" Mentioning frijoles, which I knew they must have if they had nothing else, and beef and bread, and a hint for wine, if they had any, he went off to another building, across the court, and returned in a few moments, with a couple of Indian boys, bearing dishes and a decanter of wine. The dishes contained baked meats, frijoles stewed with peppers and onions, boiled eggs, and California flour baked into a kind of macaroni. These, together with the wine, made the most sumptuous meal we had eaten since we left Boston; and, compared with the fare we had lived upon for seven months, it was a regal banquet. After despatching our meal, we took out some money and asked him how much we were to pay. He shook his head, and crossed himself, saying that it was charity:—that the Lord gave it to us. Knowing the amount of this to be that he did not sell it, but was willing to receive a present, we gave him ten or twelve reals, which he pocketed with admirable nonchalance, saying, "Dios se lo pague." Taking leave of him, we rode out to the Indians' huts. The little children were running about among the huts, stark naked, and the men were not much better; but the women had generally coarse gowns, of a sort of tow cloth. The men are employed, most of the time, in tending the cattle of the mission, and in working in the garden, which is a very large one, including several acres, and filled, it is said, with the best fruits of the climate. The language of these people, which is spoken by all the Indians of California, is the most brutish and inhuman language, without any exception, that I ever heard, or that could well be conceived of. It is a complete slabber. The words fall off of the ends of their tongues, and a continual slabbering sound is made in the cheeks, outside of the teeth. It cannot have been the language of Montezuma and the independent Mexicans.

Here, among the huts, we saw the oldest man that I had ever seen; and, indeed, I never supposed that a person could retain life and exhibit such marks of age. He was sitting out in the sun, leaning against the side of a hut; and his legs and arms, which were bare, were of a dark red color, the skin withered and shrunk up like burnt leather, and the limbs not larger round than those of a boy of five years. He had a few grey hairs, which were tied together at the back of his head; and he was so feeble that, when we came up to him, he raised his hands slowly to his face, and taking hold of his lids with his fingers, lifted them up to look at us; and being satisfied, let them drop again. All command over the lid seemed to have gone. I asked his age, but could get no answer but "Quien sabe?" and they probably did not know the age.

Leaving the mission, we returned to village, going nearly all the way on a full run. The California horses have no medium gait, which is pleasant, between walking and running; for as there are no streets and parades, they have no need of the genteel trot, and their riders usually keep them at the top of their speed until they are fired, and then let them rest themselves by walking. The fine air of the afternoon; the rapid rate of the animals, who seemed almost to fly over the ground; and the excitement and novelty of the motion to us, who had been so long confined on shipboard, were exhilarating beyond expression, and we felt willing to ride all day long. Coming into the village, we found things looking very lively. The Indians, who always have a holyday on Sunday, were engaged at playing a kind of running game of ball, on a level piece of ground, near the houses. The old ones sat down in a ring, looking on, while the young ones—men, boys and girls—were chasing the ball, and throwing it with all their might. Some of the girls ran like greyhounds. At every accident, or remarkable feat, the old people set up a deafening screaming and clapping of hands. Several blue jackets were reeling about among the houses, which showed that the pulperias had been well patronized. One or two of the sailors had got on horseback, but being rather indifferent horsemen, and the Spaniards having given them vicious horses, they were soon thrown, much to the amusement of the people. A half dozen Sandwich Islanders, from the hide-houses and the two brigs, who are bold riders, were dashing about on the full gallop, hallooing and laughing like so many wild men.

It was now nearly sundown, and S—— and myself went into a house and sat quietly down to rest ourselves before going down to the beach. Several people were soon collected to see "los Ingles marineros," and one of them—a young woman—took a great fancy to my pocket handkerchief, which was a large silk one that I had before going to sea, and a handsomer one than they had been in the habit of seeing. Of course, I gave it to her; which brought us into high favor; and we had a present of some pears and other fruits, which we took down to the beach with us. When we came to leave the house, we found that our horses, which we left tied at the door, were both gone. We had paid for them to ride down to the beach, but they were not to be found. We went to the man of whom we hired them, but he only shrugged his shoulders, and to our question, "Where are the horses?" only answered—"Quien sabe?" but as he was very easy, and made no inquiries for the saddles, we saw that he knew very well where they were. After a little trouble, determined not to walk down,—a distance of three miles—we procured two, at four reals apiece, with an Indian boy to run on behind and bring them back. Determined to have "the go" out of the horses, for our trouble, we went down at full speed, and were on the beach in fifteen minutes. Wishing to make our liberty last as long as possible, we rode up and down among the hide-houses, amusing ourselves with seeing the men, as they came down, (it was now dusk,) some on horseback and others on foot. The Sandwich Islanders rode down, and were in "high snuff." We inquired for our shipmates, and were told that two of them had started on horseback and had been thrown or had fallen off, and were seen heading for the beach, but steering pretty wild, and by the looks of things, would not be down much before midnight.

The Indian boys having arrived, we gave them our horses, and having seen them safely off, hailed for a boat and went aboard. Thus ended our first liberty-day on shore. We were well tired, but had had a good time, and were more willing to go back to our old duties. About midnight, we were waked up by our two watchmates, who had come aboard in high dispute. It seems they had started to come down on the same horse, double-backed; and each was accusing the other of being the cause of his fall. They soon, however, turned-in and fell asleep, and probably forgot all about it, for the next morning the dispute was not renewed.

CHAPTER XVII

SAN DIEGO—A DESERTION—SAN PEDRO AGAIN—BEATING THE COAST

The next sound we heard was "All hands ahoy!" and looking up the scuttle, saw that it was just daylight. Our liberty had now truly taken flight, and with it we laid away our pumps, stockings, blue jackets, neckerchiefs, and other go-ashore paraphernalia, and putting on old duck trowsers, red shirts, and Scotch caps, began taking out and landing our hides. For three days we were hard at work, from the grey of the morning until starlight, with the exception of a short time allowed for meals, in this duty. For landing and taking on board hides, San Diego is decidedly the best place in California. The harbor is small and land-locked; there is no surf; the vessels lie within a cable's length of the beach; and the beach itself is smooth, hard sand, without rocks or stones. For these reasons, it is used by all the vessels in the trade, as a depot; and, indeed, it would be impossible, when loading with the cured hides for the passage home, to take them on board at any of the open ports, without getting them wet in the surf, which would spoil them. We took possession of one of the hide-houses, which belonged to our firm, and had been used by the California. It was built to hold forty thousand hides, and we had the pleasing prospect of filling it before we could leave the coast; and toward this, our thirty-five hundred, which we brought down with us, would do but little. There was not a man on board who did not go a dozen times into the house, and look round, and make some calculation of the time it would require.

The hides, as they come rough and uncured from the vessels, are piled up outside of the houses, whence they are taken and carried through a regular process of pickling, drying, cleaning, etc., and stowed away in the house, ready to be put on board. This process is necessary in order that they may keep, during a long voyage, and in warm latitudes. For the purpose of curing and taking care of these hides, an officer and a part of the crew of each vessel are usually left ashore and it was for this business, we found, that our new officer had joined us. As soon as the hides were landed, he took charge of the house, and the captain intended to leave two or three of us with him, hiring Sandwich Islanders to take our places on board; but he could not get any Sandwich Islanders to go, though he offered them fifteen dollars a month; for the report of the flogging had got among them, and he was called "aole maikai," (no good,) and that was an end of the business. They were, however, willing to work on shore, and four of them were hired and put with Mr. Russell to cure the hides.

After landing our hides, we next sent ashore all our spare spars and rigging; all the stores which we did not want to use in the course of one trip to windward; and, in fact, everything which we could spare, so as to make room for hides: among other things, the pig-sty, and with it "old Bess." This was an old sow that we had brought from Boston, and which lived to get around Cape Horn, where all the other pigs died from cold and wet. Report said that she had been a Canton voyage before. She had been the pet of the cook during the whole passage, and he had fed her with the best of everything, and taught her to know his voice, and to do a number of strange tricks for his amusement. Tom Cringle says that no one can fathom a negro's affection for a pig; and I believe he is right, for it almost broke our poor darky's heart when he heard that Bess was to be taken ashore, and that he was to have the care of her no more during the whole voyage. He had depended upon her as a solace, during the long trips up and down the coast. "Obey orders, if you break owners!" said he. "Break hearts," he meant to have said; and lent a hand to get her over the side, trying to make it as easy for her as possible. We got a whip up on the main-yard, and hooking it to a strap around her body, swayed away; and giving a wink to one another, ran her chock up to the yard. "'Vast there! 'vast!" said the mate; "none of your skylarking! Lower away!" But he evidently enjoyed the joke. The pig squealed like the "crack of doom," and tears stood in the poor darky's eyes; and he muttered something about having no pity on a dumb beast. "Dumb beast!" said Jack; "if she's what you call a dumb beast, then my eyes a'n't mates." This produced a laugh from all but the cook. He was too intent upon seeing her safe in the boat. He watched her all the way ashore, where, upon her landing, she was received by a whole troop of her kind, who had been sent ashore from the other vessels, and had multiplied and formed a large commonwealth. From the door of his galley, the cook used to watch them in their manoeuvres, setting up a shout and clapping his hands whenever Bess came off victorious in the struggles for pieces of raw hide and half-picked bones which were lying about the beach. During the day, he saved all the nice things, and made a bucket of swill, and asked us to take it ashore in the gig, and looked quite disconcerted when the mate told him that he would pitch the swill overboard, and him after it, if he saw any of it go into the boats. We told him that he thought more about the pig than he did about his wife, who lived down in Robinson's Alley; and, indeed, he could hardly have been more attentive, for he actually, on several nights, after dark, when he thought he would not be seen, sculled himself ashore in a boat with a bucket of nice swill, and returned like Leander from crossing the Hellespont.

The next Sunday the other half of our crew went ashore on liberty, and left us on board, to enjoy the first quiet Sunday which we had had upon the coast. Here were no hides to come off, and no south-easters to fear. We washed and mended our clothes in the morning, and spent the rest of the day in reading and writing. Several of us wrote letters to send home by the Lagoda. At twelve o'clock the Ayacucho dropped her fore topsail, which was a signal for her sailing. She unmoored and warped down into the bight, from which she got under way. During this operation, her crew were a long time heaving at the windlass, and I listened for nearly an hour to the musical notes of a Sandwich Islander, called Mahannah, who "sang out" for them. Sailors, when heaving at a windlass, in order that they may heave together, always have one to sing out; which is done in a peculiar, high and long-drawn note, varying with the motion of the windlass. This requires a high voice, strong lungs, and much practice, to be done well. This fellow had a very peculiar, wild sort of note, breaking occasionally into a falsetto. The sailors thought it was too high, and not enough of the boatswain hoarseness about it; but to me it had a great charm. The harbor was perfectly still, and his voice rang among the hills, as though it could have been heard for miles. Toward sundown, a good breeze having sprung up, she got under weigh, and with her long, sharp head cutting elegantly through the water, on a taut bowline, she stood directly out of the harbor, and bore away to the southward. She was bound to Callao, and thence to the Sandwich Islands, and expected to be on the coast again in eight or ten months.

At the close of the week we were ready to sail, but were delayed a day or two by the running away of F——, the man who had been our second mate, and was turned forward. From the time that he was "broken," he had had a dog's berth on board the vessel, and determined to run away at the first opportunity. Having shipped for an officer when he was not half a seaman, he found little pity with the crew, and was not man enough to hold his ground among them. The captain called him a "soger,"[1] and promised to "ride him down as he would the main tack;" and when officers are once determined to "ride a man down," it is a gone case with him. He had had several difficulties with the captain, and asked leave to go home in the Lagoda; but this was refused him. One night he was insolent to an officer on the beach, and refused to come aboard in the boat. He was reported to the captain; and as he came aboard,—it being past the proper hour,—he was called aft, and told that he was to have a flogging. Immediately, he fell down on the deck, calling out—"Don't flog me, Captain T——; don't flog me!" and the captain, angry with him, and disgusted with his cowardice, gave him a few blows over the back with a rope's end and sent him forward. He was not much hurt, but a good deal frightened, and made up his mind to run away that very night. This was managed better than anything he ever did in his life, and seemed really to show some spirit and forethought. He gave his bedding and mattress to one of the Lagoda's crew, who took it aboard his vessel as something which he had bought, and promised to keep it for him. He then unpacked his chest, putting all his valuable clothes into a large canvas bag, and told one of us, who had the watch, to call him at midnight. Coming on deck, at midnight, and finding no officer on deck, and all still aft, he lowered his bag into a boat, got softly down into it, cast off the painter, and let it drop silently with the tide until he was out of hearing, when he sculled ashore.

The next morning, when all hands were mustered, there was a great stir to find F——. Of course, we would tell nothing, and all they could discover was, that he had left an empty chest behind him, and that he went off in a boat; for they saw it lying up high and dry on the beach. After breakfast, the captain went up to the town, and offered a reward of twenty dollars for him; and for a couple of days, the soldiers, Indians, and all others who had nothing to do, were scouring the country for him, on horseback, but without effect; for he was safely concealed, all the time, within fifty rods of the hide-houses. As soon as he had landed, he went directly to the Lagoda's hide-house, and a part of her crew, who were living there on shore, promised to conceal him and his traps until the Pilgrim should sail, and then to intercede with Captain Bradshaw to take him on board the ship. Just behind the hide-houses, among the thickets and underwood, was a small cave, the entrance to which was known only to two men on the beach, and which was so well concealed that, though, when I afterwards came to live on shore, it was shown to me two or three times, I was never able to find it alone. To this cave he was carried before daybreak in the morning, and supplied with bread and water, and there remained until he saw us under weigh and well round the point.

Friday, March 27th. The captain, having given up all hope of finding F——, and being unwilling to delay any longer, gave orders for unmooring the ship, and we made sail, dropping slowly down with the tide and light wind. We left letters with Captain Bradshaw to take to Boston, and had the satisfaction of hearing him say that he should be back again before we left the coast. The wind, which was very light, died away soon after we doubled the point, and we lay becalmed for two days, not moving three miles the whole time, and a part of the second day were almost within sight of the vessels. On the third day, about noon, a cool sea-breeze came rippling and darkening the surface of the water, and by sundown we were off San Juan's, which is about forty miles from San Diego, and is called half way to San Pedro, where we were now bound. Our crew was now considerably weakened. One man we had lost overboard; another had been taken aft as clerk; and a third had run away; so that, beside S—— and myself, there were only three able seamen and one boy of twelve years of age. With this diminished and discontented crew, and in a small vessel, we were now to battle the watch through a couple of years of hard service; yet there was not one who was not glad that F—— had escaped; for, shiftless and good for nothing as he was, no one could wish to see him dragging on a miserable life, cowed down and disheartened; and we were all rejoiced to hear, upon our return to San Diego, about two months afterwards, that he had been immediately taken aboard the Lagoda, and went home in her, on regular seaman's wages.

After a slow passage of five days, we arrived, on Wednesday, the first of April, at our old anchoring ground at San Pedro. The bay was as deserted, and looked as dreary, as before, and formed no pleasing contrast with the security and snugness of San Diego, and the activity and interest which the loading and unloading of four vessels gave to that scene. In a few days the hides began to come slowly down, and we got into the old business of rolling goods up the hill, pitching hides down, and pulling our long league off and on. Nothing of note occurred while we were lying here, except that an attempt was made to repair the small Mexican brig which had been cast away in a south-easter, and which now lay up, high and dry, over one reef of rocks and two sand-banks. Our carpenter surveyed her, and pronounced her capable of refitting, and in a few days the owners came down from the Pueblo, and, waiting for the high spring tides, with the help of our cables, kedges, and crew, got her off and afloat, after several trials. The three men at the house on shore, who had formerly been a part of her crew, now joined her, and seemed glad enough at the prospect of getting off the coast.

On board our own vessel, things went on in the common monotonous way. The excitement which immediately followed the flogging scene had passed off, but the effect of it upon the crew, and especially upon the two men themselves, remained. The different manner in which these men were affected, corresponding to their different characters, was not a little remarkable. John was a foreigner and high-tempered, and, though mortified, as any one would be at having had the worst of an encounter, yet his chief feeling seemed to be anger; and he talked much of satisfaction and revenge, if he ever got back to Boston. But with the other, it was very different. He was an American, and had had some education; and this thing coming upon him, seemed completely to break him down. He had a feeling of the degradation that had been inflicted upon him, which the other man was incapable of. Before that, he had a good deal of fun, and mused us often with queer negro stories,—(he was from a slave state); but afterwards he seldom smiled; seemed to lose all life and elasticity; and appeared to have but one wish, and that was for the voyage to be at an end. I have often known him to draw a long sigh when he was alone, and he took but little part or interest in John's plans of satisfaction and retaliation.

After a stay of about a fortnight, during which we slipped for one south-easter, and were at sea two days, we got under weigh for Santa Barbara. It was now the middle of April, and the south-easter season was nearly over; and the light, regular trade-winds, which blow down the coast, began to set steadily in, during the latter part of each day. Against these, we beat slowly up to Santa Barbara—a distance of about ninety miles—in three days. There we found, lying at anchor, the large Genoese ship which we saw in the same place, on the first day of our coming upon the coast. She had been up to San Francisco, or, as it is called, "chock up to windward," had stopped at Monterey on her way down, and was shortly to proceed to San Pedro and San Diego, and thence, taking in her cargo, to sail for Valparaiso and Cadiz. She was a large, clumsy ship, and with her topmasts stayed forward, and high poop-deck, looked like an old woman with a crippled back. It was now the close of Lent, and on Good Friday she had all her yards a'cock-bill, which is customary among Catholic vessels. Some also have an effigy of Judas, which the crew amuse themselves with keel-hauling and hanging by the neck from the yard-arms.

[1] Soger (soldier) is the worst term of reproach that can be applied to a sailor. It signifies a skulk, a sherk,—one who is always trying to get clear of work, and is out of the way, or hanging back, when duty is to be done. "Marine" is the term applied more particularly to a man who is ignorant and clumsy about seaman's work—a green-horn—a land-lubber. To make a sailor shoulder a handspike, and walk fore and aft the deck, like a sentry, is the most ignominious punishment that could be put upon him. Such a punishment inflicted upon an able seaman in a vessel of war, would break his spirit down more than a flogging.

CHAPTER XVIII

EASTER SUNDAY—"SAIL HO!"—WHALES—SAN JUAN—ROMANCE OF HIDE-DROGHING—SAN DIEGO AGAIN

The next Sunday was Easter Sunday, and as there had been no liberty at San Pedro, it was our turn to go ashore and misspend another Sabbath. Soon after breakfast, a large boat, filled with men in blue jackets, scarlet caps, and various colored underclothes, bound ashore on liberty, left the Italian ship, and passed under our stern; the men singing beautiful Italian boat-songs, all the way, in fine, full chorus. Among the songs I recognized the favorite "O Pescator dell' onda." It brought back to my mind pianofortes, drawing-rooms, young ladies singing, and a thousand other things which as little befitted me, in my situation, to be thinking upon. Supposing that the whole day would be too long a time to spend ashore, as there was no place to which we could take a ride, we remained quietly on board until after dinner. We were then pulled ashore in the stern of the boat, and, with orders to be on the beach at sundown, we took our way for the town. There, everything wore the appearance of a holyday. The people were all dressed in their best; the men riding about on horseback among the houses, and the women sitting on carpets before the doors. Under the piazza of a "pulperia," two men were seated, decked out with knots of ribbons and bouquets, and playing the violin and the Spanish guitar. These are the only instruments, with the exception of the drums and trumpets at Monterey that I ever heard in California; and I suspect they play upon no others, for at a great fandango at which I was afterwards present, and where they mustered all the music they could find, there were three violins and two guitars, and no other instrument. As it was now too near the middle of the day to see any dancing and hearing that a bull was expected down from the country, to be baited in the presidio square, in the course of an hour or two we took a stroll among the houses. Inquiring for an American who, we had been told, had married in the place, and kept a shop, we were directed to a long, low building, at the end of which was a door, with a sign over it, in Spanish. Entering the shop, we found no one in it, and the whole had an empty, deserted appearance. In a few minutes the man made his appearance, and apologized for having nothing to entertain us with, saying that he had had a fandango at his house the night before, and the people had eaten and drunk up everything.

"Oh yes!" said I, "Easter holydays?"

"No!" said he, with a singular expression to his face; "I had a little daughter die the other day, and that's the custom of the country."

Here I felt a little strangely, not knowing what to say, or whether to offer consolation or no, and was beginning to retire, when he opened a side door and told us to walk in. Here I was no less astonished; for I found a large room, filled with young girls, from three or four years of age up to fifteen and sixteen, dressed all in white, with wreaths of flowers on their heads, and bouquets in their hands. Following our conductor through all these girls, who were playing about in high spirits, we came to a table, at the end of the room, covered with a white cloth, on which lay a coffin, about three feet long, with the body of his child. The coffin was lined on the outside with white cloth, and on the inside with white satin, and was strewed with flowers. Through an open door we saw, in another room, a few elderly people in common dresses; while the benches and tables thrown up in a corner, and the stained walls, gave evident signs of the last night's "high go." Feeling, like Garrick, between tragedy and comedy, an uncertainty of purpose and a little awkwardness, I asked the man when the funeral would take place, and being told that it would move toward the mission in about an hour, took my leave.

To pass away the time, we took horses and rode down to the beach, and there found three or four Italian sailors, mounted, and riding up and down, on the hard sand, at a furious rate. We joined them, and found it fine sport. The beach gave us a stretch of a mile or more, and the horses flew over the smooth, hard sand, apparently invigorated and excited by the salt sea-breeze, and by the continual roar and dashing of the breakers. From the beach we returned to the town, and finding that the funeral procession had moved, rode on and overtook it, about half-way to the mission. Here was as peculiar a sight as we had seen before in the house; the one looking as much like a funeral procession as the other did like a house of mourning. The little coffin was borne by eight girls, who were continually relieved by others, running forward from the procession and taking their places. Behind it came a straggling company of girls, dressed as before, in white and flowers, and including, I should suppose by their numbers, nearly all the girls between five and fifteen in the place. They played along on the way, frequently stopping and running all together to talk to some one, or to pick up a flower, and then running on again to overtake the coffin. There were a few elderly women in common colors; and a herd of young men and boys, some on foot and others mounted, followed them, or walked or rode by their side, frequently interrupting them by jokes and questions. But the most singular thing of all was, that two men walked, one on each side of the coffin, carrying muskets in their hands, which they continually loaded, and fired into the air. Whether this was to keep off the evil spirits or not, I do not know. It was the only interpretation that I could put upon it.

As we drew near the mission, we saw the great gate thrown open, and the pádre standing on the steps, with a crucifix in hand. The mission is a large and deserted-looking place, the out-buildings going to ruin, and everything giving one the impression of decayed grandeur. A large stone fountain threw out pure water, from four mouths, into a basin, before the church door; and we were on the point of riding up to let our horses drink, when it occurred to us that it might be consecrated, and we forbore. Just at this moment, the bells set up their harsh, discordant clang; and the procession moved into the court. I was anxious to follow, and see the ceremony, but the horse of one of my companions had become frightened, and was tearing off toward the town; and having thrown his rider, and got one of his feet caught in the saddle, which had slipped, was fast dragging and ripping it to pieces. Knowing that my shipmate could not speak a word of Spanish, and fearing that he would get into difficulty, I was obliged to leave the ceremony and ride after him. I soon overtook him, trudging along, swearing at the horse, and carrying the remains of the saddle, which he had picked up on the road. Going to the owner of the horse, we made a settlement with him, and found him surprisingly liberal. All parts of the saddle were brought back, and, being capable of repair, he was satisfied with six reáls. We thought it would have been a few dollars. We pointed to the horse, which was now half way up one of the mountains; but he shook his head, saying, "No importe!" and giving us to understand that he had plenty more.

Having returned to the town, we saw a great crowd collected in the square before the principal pulperia, and riding up, found that all these people—men, women, and children—had been drawn together by a couple of bantam cocks. The cocks were in full tilt, springing into one another, and the people were as eager, laughing and shouting, as though the combatants had been men. There had been a disappointment about the bull; he had broken his bail, and taken himself off, and it was too late to get another; so the people were obliged to put up with a cock-fight. One of the bantams having been knocked in the head, and had an eye put out, he gave in, and two monstrous prize-cocks were brought on. These were the object of the whole affair; the two bantams having been merely served up as a first course, to collect the people together. Two fellows came into the ring holding the cocks in their arms, and stroking them, and running about on all fours, encouraging and setting them on. Bets ran high, and, like most other contests, it remained for some time undecided. They both showed great pluck, and fought probably better and longer than their masters would have done. Whether, in the end, it was the white or the red that beat, I do not recollect; but, whichever it was, he strutted off with the true veni-vidi-vici look, leaving the other lying panting on his beam-ends.

This matter having been settled, we heard some talk about "caballos" and "carrera" and seeing the people all streaming off in one direction, we followed, and came upon a level piece of ground, just out of the town, which was used as a race-course. Here the crowd soon became thick again; the ground was marked off; the judges stationed; and the horses led up to one end. Two fine-looking old gentlemen—Don Carlos and Don Domingo, so called—held the stakes, and all was now ready. We waited some time, during which we could just see the horses twisting round and turning, until, at length, there was a shout along the lines, and on they came—heads stretched out and eyes starting;—working all over, both man and beast. The steeds came by us like a couple of chain-shot—neck and neck; and now we could see nothing but their backs, and their hind hoofs flying in the air. As fast as the horses passed, the crowd broke up behind them, and ran to the goal. When we got there, we found the horses returning on a slow walk, having run far beyond the mark, and heard that the long, bony one had come in head and shoulders before the other. The riders were light-built men; had handkerchiefs tied round their heads; and were bare-armed and bare-legged. The horses were noble-looking beasts, not so sleek and combed as our Boston stable-horses, but with fine limbs, and spirited eyes. After this had been settled, and fully talked over, the crowd scattered again and flocked back to the town.

Returning to the large pulperia, we found the violin and guitar screaming and twanging away under the piazza, where they had been all day. As it was now sundown, there began to be some dancing. The Italian sailors danced, and one of our crew exhibited himself in a sort of West India shuffle, much to the amusement of the bystanders, who cried out, "Bravo!" "Otra vez!" and "Vivan los marineros!" but the dancing did not become general, as the women and the "gente de razón" had not yet made their appearance. We wished very much to stay and see the style of dancing; but, although we had had our own way during the day, yet we were, after all, but 'foremast Jacks; and having been ordered to be on the beach by sundown, did not venture to be more than an hour behind the time; so we took our way down. We found the boat just pulling ashore through the breakers, which were running high, there having been a heavy fog outside, which, from some cause or other, always brings on, or precedes a heavy sea. Liberty-men are privileged from the time they leave the vessel until they step on board again; so we took our places in the stern sheets, and were congratulating ourselves upon getting off dry, when a great comber broke fore and aft the boat, and wet us through and through, filling the boat half full of water. Having lost her buoyancy by the weight of the water, she dropped heavily into every sea that struck her, and by the time we had pulled out of the surf into deep water, she was but just afloat, and we were up to our knees. By the help of a small bucket and our hats, we bailed her out, got on board, hoisted the boats, eat our supper, changed our clothes, gave (as is usual) the whole history of our day's adventures to those who had staid on board, and having taken a night-smoke, turned-in. Thus ended our second day's liberty on shore.

On Monday morning, as an offset to our day's sport, we were all set to work "tarring down" the rigging. Some got girt-lines up for riding down the stays and back-stays, and others tarred the shrouds, lifts, etc., laying out on the yards, and coming down the rigging. We overhauled our bags and took out our old tarry trowsers and frocks, which we had used when we tarred down before, and were all at work in the rigging by sunrise. After breakfast, we had the satisfaction of seeing the Italian ship's boat go ashore, filled with men, gaily dressed, as on the day before, and singing their barcarollas. The Easter holydays are kept up on shore during three days; and being a Catholic vessel, the crew had the advantage of them. For two successive days, while perched up in the rigging, covered with tar and engaged in our disagreeable work, we saw these fellows going ashore in the morning, and coming off again at night, in high spirits. So much for being Protestants. There's no danger of Catholicism's spreading in New England; Yankees can't afford the time to be Catholics. American shipmasters get nearly three weeks more labor out of their crews, in the course of a year, than the masters of vessels from Catholic countries. Yankees don't keep Christmas, and ship-masters at sea never know when Thanksgiving comes, so Jack has no festival at all.

About noon, a man aloft called out "Sail ho!" and looking round, we saw the head sails of a vessel coming round the point. As she drew round, she showed the broadside of a full-rigged brig, with the Yankee ensign at her peak. We ran up our stars and stripes, and, knowing that there was no American brig on the coast but ourselves, expected to have news from home. She rounded-to and let go her anchor, but the dark faces on her yards, when they furled the sails, and the Babel on deck, soon made known that she was from the Islands. Immediately afterwards, a boat's crew came aboard, bringing her skipper, and from them we learned that she was from Oahu, and was engaged in the same trade with the Ayacucho, Loriotte, etc., between the coast, the Sandwich Islands, and the leeward coast of Peru and Chili. Her captain and officers were Americans, and also a part of her crew; the rest were Islanders. She was called the Catalina, and, like all the others vessels in that trade, except the Ayacucho, her papers and colors were from Uncle Sam. They, of course, brought us no news, and we were doubly disappointed, for we had thought, at first, it might be the ship which we were expecting from Boston.

After lying here about a fortnight, and collecting all the hides the place afforded, we set sail again for San Pedro. There we found the brig which we had assisted in getting off lying at anchor, with a mixed crew of Americans, English, Sandwich Islanders, Spaniards, and Spanish Indians; and, though much smaller than we, yet she had three times the number of men; and she needed them, for her officers were Californians. No vessels in the world go so poorly manned as American and English; and none do so well. A Yankee brig of that size would have had a crew of four men, and would have worked round and round her. The Italian ship had a crew of thirty men; nearly three times as many as the Alert, which was afterwards on the coast, and was of the same size; yet the Alert would get under weigh and come-to in half the time, and get two anchors, while they were all talking at once—jabbering like a parcel of "Yahoos," and running about decks to find their cat-block.

There was only one point in which they had the advantage over us, and that was in lightening their labors in the boats by their songs. The Americans are a time and money saving people, but have not yet, as a nation, learned that music may be "turned to account." We pulled the long distances to and from the shore, with our loaded boats, without a word spoken, and with discontented looks, while they not only lightened the labor of rowing, but actually made it pleasant and cheerful, by their music. So true is it, that—

"For the tired slave, song lifts the languid oar,
And bids it aptly fall, with chime
That beautifies the fairest shore,
And mitigates the harshest clime."

We lay about a week in San Pedro, and got under weigh for San Diego, intending to stop at San Juan, as the south-easter season was nearly over, and there was little or no danger.

This being the spring season, San Pedro, as well as all the other open ports upon the coast, was filled with whales, that had come in to make their annual visit upon soundings. For the first few days that we were here and at Santa Barbara, we watched them with great interest—calling out "there she blows!" every time we saw the spout of one breaking the surface of the water; but they soon became so common that we took little notice of them. They often "broke" very near us; and one thick, foggy night, during a dead calm, while I was standing anchor-watch, one of them rose so near, that he struck our cable, and made all surge again. He did not seem to like the encounter much himself, for he sheered off, and spouted at a good distance. We once came very near running one down in the gig, and should probably have been knocked to pieces and blown sky-high. We had been on board the little Spanish brig, and were returning, stretching out well at our oars, the little boat going like a swallow; our backs were forward, (as is always the case in pulling,) and the captain, who was steering, was not looking ahead, when, all at once, we heard the spout of a whale directly ahead. "Back water! back water, for your lives!" shouted the captain; and we backed our blades in the water and brought the boat to in a smother of foam. Turning our heads, we saw a great, rough, hump-backed whale, slowly crossing our fore foot, within three or four yards of the boat's stem. Had we not backed water just as we did, we should inevitably have gone smash upon him, striking him with our stem just about amidships. He took no notice of us, but passed slowly on, and dived a few yards beyond us, throwing his tail high in the air. He was so near that we had a perfect view of him and as may be supposed, had no desire to see him nearer. He was a disgusting creature; with a skin rough, hairy, and of an iron-grey color. This kind differs much from the sperm, in color and skin, and is said to be fiercer. We saw a few sperm whales; but most of the whales that come upon the coast are fin-backs, hump-backs, and right-whales, which are more difficult to take, and are said not to give oil enough to pay for the trouble. For this reason whale-ships do not come upon the coast after them. Our captain, together with Captain Nye of the Loriotte, who had been in a whale-ship, thought of making an attempt upon one of them with two boats' crews, but as we had only two harpoons and no proper lines, they gave it up.

During the months of March, April, and May, these whales appear in great numbers in the open ports of Santa Barbara, San Pedro, etc., and hover off the coast, while a few find their way into the close harbors of San Diego and Monterey. They are all off again before midsummer, and make their appearance on the "off-shore ground." We saw some fine "schools" of sperm whales, which are easily distinguished by their spout, blowing away, a few miles to windward, on our passage to San Juan.

Coasting along on the quiet shore of the Pacific, we came to anchor, in twenty fathoms' water, almost out at sea, as it were, and directly abreast of a steep hill which overhung the water, and was twice as high as our royal-mast-head. We had heard much of this place, from the Lagoda's crew, who said it was the worst place in California. The shore is rocky, and directly exposed to the south-east, so that vessels are obliged to slip and run for their lives on the first sign of a gale; and late as it was in the season, we got up our slip-rope and gear, though we meant to stay only twenty-four hours. We pulled the agent ashore, and were ordered to wait for him, while he took a circuitous way round the hill to the mission, which was hidden behind it. We were glad of the opportunity to examine this singular place, and hauling the boat up and making her well fast, took different directions up and down the beach, to explore it.

San Juan is the only romantic spot in California. The country here for several miles is high table-land, running boldly to the shore, and breaking off in a steep hill, at the foot of which the waters of the Pacific are constantly dashing. For several miles the water washes the very base of the hill, or breaks upon ledges and fragments of rocks which run out into the sea. Just where we landed was a small cove, or "bight," which gave us, at high tide, a few square feet of sand-beach between the sea and the bottom of the hill. This was the only landing-place. Directly before us, rose the perpendicular height of four or five hundred feet. How we were to get hides down, or goods up, upon the table-land on which the mission was situated, was more than we could tell. The agent had taken a long circuit, and yet had frequently to jump over breaks, and climb up steep places, in the ascent. No animal but a man or monkey could get up it. However, that was not our look-out; and knowing that the agent would be gone an hour or more, we strolled about, picking up shells, and following the sea where it tumbled in, roaring and spouting, among the crevices of the great rocks. What a sight, thought I, must this be in a south-easter! The rocks were as large as those of Nahant or Newport, but, to my eye, more grand and broken. Beside, there was a grandeur in everything around, which gave almost a solemnity to the scene: a silence and solitariness which affected everything! Not a human being but ourselves for miles; and no sound heard but the pulsations of the great Pacific! and the great steep hill rising like a wall, and cutting us off from all the world, but the "world of waters!" I separated myself from the rest and sat down on a rock, just where the sea ran in and formed a fine spouting horn. Compared with the plain, dull sand-beach of the rest of the coast, this grandeur was as refreshing as a great rock in a weary land. It was almost the first time that I had been positively alone—free from the sense that human beings were at my elbow, if not talking with me—since I had left home. My better nature returned strong upon me. Everything was in accordance with my state of feeling, and I experienced a glow of pleasure at finding that what of poetry and romance I ever had in me, had not been entirely deadened by the laborious and frittering life I had led. Nearly an hour did I sit, almost lost in the luxury of this entire new scene of the play in which I had been so long acting, when I was aroused by the distant shouts of my companions, and saw that they were collecting together, as the agent had made his appearance, on his way back to our boat.

We pulled aboard, and found the long-boat hoisted out, and nearly laden with goods; and after dinner, we all went on shore in the quarter-boat, with the long-boat in tow. As we drew in, we found an ox-cart and a couple of men standing directly on the brow of the hill; and having landed, the captain took his way round the hill, ordering me and one other to follow him. We followed, picking our way out, and jumping and scrambling up, walking over briers and prickly pears, until we came to the top. Here the country stretched out for miles as far as the eye could reach, on a level, table surface; and the only habitation in sight was the small white mission of San Juan Capistrano, with a few Indian huts about it, standing in a small hollow, about a mile from where we were. Reaching the brow of the hill where the cart stood, we found several piles of hides, and Indians sitting round them. One or two other carts were coming slowly on from the mission, and the captain told us to begin and throw the hides down. This, then, was the way they were to be got down: thrown down, one at a time, a distance of four hundred feet! This was doing the business on a great scale. Standing on the edge of the hill and looking down the perpendicular height, the sailors,

—"That walk upon the beach,
Appeared like mice; and our tall anchoring bark

Diminished to her cock; her cock a buoy
Almost too small for sight."

Down this height we pitched the hides, throwing them as far out into the air as we could; and as they were all large, stiff, and doubled, like the cover of a book, the wind took them, and they swayed and eddied about, plunging and rising in the air, like a kite when it has broken its string. As it was now low tide, there was no danger of their falling into the water, and as fast as they came to ground, the men below picked them up, and taking them on their heads, walked off with them to the boat. It was really a picturesque sight: the great height; the scaling of the hides; and the continual walking to and fro of the men, who looked like mites, on the beach! This was the romance of hide-droghing!

Some of the hides lodged in cavities which were under the bank and out of our sight, being directly under us; but by sending others down in the same direction, we succeeded in dislodging them. Had they remained there, the captain said he should have sent on board for a couple of pairs of long halyards, and got some one to have gone down for them. It was said that one of the crew of an English brig went down in the same way, a few years before. We looked over, and thought it would not be a welcome task, especially for a few paltry hides; but no one knows what he can do until he is called upon; for, six months afterwards, I went down the same place by a pair of top-gallant studding-sail halyards, to save a half a dozen hides which had lodged there.

Having thrown them all down, we took our way back again, and found the boat loaded and ready to start. We pulled off; took the hides all aboard; hoisted in the boats; hove up our anchor; made sail; and before sundown, were on our way to San Diego.

Friday, May 8th, 1835. Arrived at San Diego. Here we found the little harbor deserted. The Lagoda, Ayacucho, Loriotte, and all, had left the coast, and we were nearly alone. All the hide-houses on the beach, but ours, were shut up, and the Sandwich Islanders, a dozen or twenty in number, who had worked for the other vessels and been paid off when they sailed, were living on the beach, keeping up a grand carnival. A Russian discovery-ship which had been in this port a few years before, had built a large oven for baking bread, and went away, leaving it standing. This, the Sandwich Islanders took possession of, and had kept, ever since, undisturbed. It was big enough to hold six or eight men—that is, it was as large as a ship's forecastle; had a door at the side, and a vent-hole at top. They covered it with Oahu mats, for a carpet; stopped up the vent-hole in bad weather, and made it their head-quarters. It was now inhabited by as many as a dozen or twenty men, who lived there in complete idleness—drinking, playing cards, and carousing in every way. They bought a bullock once a week, which kept them in meat, and one of them went up to the town every day to get fruit, liquor, and provisions. Besides this, they had bought a cask of ship-bread, and a barrel of flour from the Lagoda, before she sailed. There they lived, having a grand time, and caring for nobody. Captain T—— was anxious to get three or four of them to come on board the Pilgrim, as we were so much diminished in numbers; and went up to the oven and spent an hour or two trying to negotiate with them. One of them,—a finely built, active, strong and intelligent fellow,— who was a sort of king among them, acted as spokesman. He was called Mannini,—or rather, out of compliment to his known importance and influence, Mr. Mannini—and was known all over California. Through him, the captain offered them fifteen dollars a month, and one month's pay in advance; but it was like throwing pearls before swine, or rather, carrying coals to Newcastle. So long as they had money, they would not work for fifty dollars a month, and when their money was gone, they would work for ten.

"What do you do here, Mr. Mannini?"*[1]* said the captain.

"Oh, we play cards, get drunk, smoke—do anything we're a mind to."

"Don't you want to come aboard and work?"

"Aole! aole make make makou i ka hana. Now, got plenty money; no good, work. Mamule, money pau—all gone. Ah! very good, work!—maikai, hana hana nui!"

"But you'll spend all your money in this way," said the captain.

"Aye! me know that. By-'em-by money pau—all gone; then Kanaka work plenty." This was a hopeless case, and the captain left them, to wait patiently until their money was gone.

We discharged our hides and tallow, and in about a week were ready to set sail again for the windward. We unmoored, and got everything ready, when the captain made another attempt upon the oven. This time he had more regard to the "mollia tempora fandi," and succeeded very well. He got Mr. Mannini in his interest, and as the shot was getting low in the locker, prevailed upon him and three others to come on board with their chests and baggage, and sent a hasty summons to me and the boy to come ashore with our things, and join the gang at the hide-house. This was unexpected to me; but anything in the way of variety I liked; so we got ready, and were pulled ashore. I stood on the beach while the brig got under weigh, and watched her until she rounded the point, and then went up to the hide-house to take up my quarters for a few months.

[1] The letter i in the Sandwich Island language is sounded like e in the English.

CHAPTER XIX

THE SANDWICH ISLANDERS—HIDE-CURING—WOOD-CUTTING—RATTLE-SNAKES—NEW-COMERS

Here was a change in my life as complete as it had been sudden. In the twinkling of an eye, I was transformed from a sailor into a "beach-comber" and a hide-curer; yet the novelty and the comparative independence of the life were not unpleasant. Our hide-house was a large building, made of rough boards, and intended to hold forty thousand hides. In one corner of it, a small room was parted off, in which four berths were made, where we were to live, with mother earth for our floor. It contained a table, a small locker for pots, spoons, plates, etc., and a small hole cut to let in the light. Here we put our chests, threw our bedding into the berths, and took up our quarters. Over our head was another small room, in which Mr. Russell lived, who had charge of the hide-house; the same man who was for a time an officer of the Pilgrim. There he lived in solitary grandeur; eating and sleeping alone, (and these were his principal occupations,) and communing with his own dignity. The boy was to act as cook; while myself, a giant of a Frenchman named Nicholas, and four Sandwich Islanders, were to cure the hides. Sam, the Frenchman, and myself, lived together in the room, and the four Sandwich Islanders worked and ate with us, but generally slept at the oven. My new messmate, Nicholas, was the most immense man that I had ever seen in my life. He came on the coast in a vessel which was afterwards wrecked, and now let himself out to the different houses to cure hides. He was considerably over six feet, and of a frame so large that he might have been shown for a curiosity. But the most remarkable thing about him was his feet. They were so large that he could not find a pair of shoes in California to fit him, and was obliged to send to Oahu for a pair; and when he got them, he was compelled to wear them down at the heel. He told me once, himself, that he was wrecked in an American brig on the Goodwin Sands, and was sent up to London, to the charge of the American consul, without clothing to his back or shoes to his feet, and was obliged to go about London streets in his stocking feet three or four days, in the month of January, until the consul could have a pair of shoes made for him. His strength was in proportion to his size, and his ignorance to his strength—"strong as an ox, and ignorant as strong." He neither knew how to read nor write. He had been to sea from a boy, and had seen all kinds of service, and been in every kind of vessel: merchantmen, men-of-war, privateers, and slavers; and from what I could gather from his accounts of himself, and from what he once told me, in confidence, after we had become better acquainted, he had even been in worse business than slave-trading. He was once tried for his life in Charleston, South Carolina, and though acquitted, yet he was so frightened that he never would show himself in the United States again; and I could not persuade him that he could never be tried a second time for the same offence. He said he had got safe off from the breakers, and was too good a sailor to risk his timbers again.

Though I knew what his life had been, yet I never had the slightest fear of him. We always got along very well together, and, though so much stronger and larger than I, he showed a respect for my education, and for what he had heard of my situation before coming to sea. "I'll be good friends with you," he used to say, "for by-and-by you'll come out here captain, and then you'll haze me well!" By holding well together, we kept the officer in good order, for he was evidently afraid of Nicholas, and never ordered us, except when employed upon the hides. My other companions, the Sandwich Islanders, deserve particular notice.

A considerable trade has been carried on for several years between California and the Sandwich Islands, and most of the vessels are manned with Islanders; who, as they, for the most part, sign no articles, leave whenever they choose, and let themselves out to cure hides at San Diego, and to supply the places of the men of the American vessels while on the coast. In this way, quite a colony of them had become settled at San Diego, as their headquarters. Some of these had recently gone off in the Ayacucho and Loriotte, and the Pilgrim had taken Mr. Mannini and three others, so that there were not more than twenty left. Of these, four were on pay at the Ayacucho's house, four more working with us, and the rest were living at the oven in a quiet way; for their money was nearly gone, and they must make it last until some other vessel came down to employ them.

During the four months that I lived here, I got well acquainted with all of them, and took the greatest pains to become familiar with their language, habits, and characters. Their language, I could only learn, orally, for they had not any books among them, though many of them had been taught to read and write by the missionaries at home. They spoke a little English, and by a sort of compromise, a mixed language was used on the beach, which could be understood by all. The long name of Sandwich Islanders is dropped, and they are called by the whites, all over the Pacific ocean, "Kanákas," from a word in their own language which they apply to themselves, and to all South Sea Islanders, in distinction from whites, whom they call "Haole." This name, "Kanaka," they answer to, both collectively and individually. Their proper names, in their own language, being difficult to pronounce and remember, they are called by any names which the captains or crews may choose to give them. Some are called after the vessel they are in; others by common names, as Jack, Tom, Bill; and some have fancy names, as Ban-yan, Fore-top, Rope-yarn, Pelican, etc., etc. Of the four who worked at our house one was named "Mr. Bingham," after the missionary at Oahu; another, Hope, after a vessel that he had been in; a third, Tom Davis, the name of his first captain; and the fourth, Pelican, from his fancied resemblance to that bird. Then there was Lagoda-Jack, California-Bill, etc., etc. But by whatever names they might be called, they were the most interesting, intelligent, and kind-hearted people that I ever fell in with. I felt a positive attachment for almost all of them; and many of them I have, to this time, a feeling for, which would lead me to go a great way for the mere pleasure of seeing them, and which will always make me feel a strong interest in the mere name of a Sandwich Islander.

Tom Davis knew how to read, write, and cipher in common arithmetic; had been to the United States, and spoke English quite well. His education was as good as that of three-quarters of the Yankees in California, and his manners and principles a good deal better, and he was so quick of apprehension that he might have been taught navigation, and the elements of many of the sciences, with the most perfect ease. Old "Mr. Bingham" spoke very little English—almost none, and neither knew how to read nor write; but he was the best-hearted old fellow in the world. He must have been over fifty years of age, and had two of his front teeth knocked out, which was done by his parents as a sign of grief at the death of Kamehameha, the great king of the Sandwich Islands. We used to tell him that he ate Captain Cook, and lost his teeth in that way. That was the only thing that ever made him angry. He would always be quite excited at that; and say—"Aole!" (no.) "Me no eat Captain Cook! Me pikinini—small—so high—no more! My father see Captain Cook! Me—no!" None of them liked to have anything said about Captain Cook, for the sailors all believe that he was eaten, and that, they cannot endure to be taunted with.—"New Zealand Kanaka eat white man;—Sandwich Island Kanaka—no. Sandwich Island Kanaka ua like pu na haole—all 'e same a' you!"

Mr. Bingham was a sort of patriarch among them, and was always treated with great respect, though he had not the education and energy which gave Mr. Mannini his power over them. I have spent hours in talking with this old fellow about Kamehameha, the Charlemagne of the Sandwich Islands; his son and successor Riho Riho, who died in England, and was brought to Oahu in the frigate Blonde, Captain Lord Byron, and whose funeral he remembered perfectly; and also about the customs of his country in his boyhood, and the changes which had been made by the missionaries. He never would allow that human beings had been eaten there; and, indeed, it always seemed like an insult to tell so affectionate, intelligent, and civilized a class of men, that such barbarities had been practised in their own country within the recollection of many of them. Certainly, the history of no people on the globe can show anything like so rapid an advance. I would have trusted my life and my fortune in the hands of any one of these people; and certainly had I wished for a favor or act of sacrifice, I would have gone to them all, in turn, before I should have applied to one of my own countrymen on the coast, and should have expected to have seen it done, before my own countrymen had got half through counting the cost. Their costumes, and manner of treating one another, show a simple, primitive generosity, which is truly delightful; and which is often a reproach to our own people. Whatever one has, they all have. Money, food, clothes, they share with one another; even to the last piece of tobacco to put in their pipes. I once heard old Mr. Bingham say, with the highest indignation, to a Yankee trader who was trying to persuade him to keep his money to himself—"No! We no all 'e same a' you!—Suppose one got money, all got money. You;—

suppose one got money—lock him up in chest.—No good!"—"Kanaka all 'e same a' one!" This principle they carry so far, that none of them will eat anything in the sight of others without offering it all round. I have seen one of them break a biscuit, which had been given him, into five parts, at a time when I knew he was on a very short allowance, as there was but little to eat on the beach.

My favorite among all of them, and one who was liked by both officers and men, and by whomever he had anything to do with, was Hope. He was an intelligent, kind-hearted little fellow, and I never saw him angry, though I knew him for more than a year, and have seen him imposed upon by white people, and abused by insolent officers of vessels. He was always civil, and always ready, and never forgot a benefit. I once took care of him when he was ill, getting medicines from the ship's chests, when no captain or officer would do anything for him, and he never forgot it. Every Kanaka has one particular friend, whom he considers himself bound to do everything for, and with whom he has a sort of contract,—an alliance offensive and defensive,—and for whom he will often make the greatest sacrifices. This friend they call aikane; and for such did Hope adopt me. I do not believe I could have wanted anything which he had, that he would not have given me. In return for this, I was always his friend among the Americans, and used to teach him letters and numbers; for he left home before he had learned how to read. He was very curious about Boston (as they call the United States); asking many questions about the houses, the people, etc., and always wished to have the pictures in books explained to him. They were all astonishingly quick in catching at explanations, and many things which I had thought it utterly impossible to make them understand, they often seized in an instant, and asked questions which showed that they knew enough to make them wish to go farther. The pictures of steamboats and railroad cars, in the columns of some newspapers which I had, gave me great difficulty to explain. The grading of the road, the rails, the construction of the carriages, they could easily understand, but the motion produced by steam was a little too refined for them. I attempted to show it to them once by an experiment upon the cook's coppers, but failed; probably as much from my own ignorance as from their want of apprehension; and, I have no doubt, left them with about as clear an idea of the principle as I had myself. This difficulty, of course, existed in the same force with the steamboats and all I could do was to give them some account of the results, in the shape of speed; for, failing in the reason, I had to fall back upon the fact. In my account of the speed I was supported by Tom, who had been to Nantucket, and seen a little steamboat which ran over to New Bedford.

A map of the world, which I once showed them, kept their attention for hours; those who knew how to read pointing out the places and referring to me for the distances. I remember being much amused with a question which Hope asked me. Pointing to the large irregular place which is always left blank round the poles, to denote that it is undiscovered, he looked up and asked.—"Pau?" (Done? ended?)

The system of naming the streets and numbering the houses, they easily understood, and the utility of it. They had a great desire to see America, but were afraid of doubling Cape Horn, for they suffer much in cold weather, and had heard dreadful accounts of the Cape, from those of their number who had been round it.

They smoke a great deal, though not much at a time; using pipes with large bowls, and very short stems, or no stems at all. These, they light, and putting them to their mouths, take a long draught, getting their mouths as full as they can hold, and their cheeks distended, and then let it slowly out through their mouths and nostrils. The pipe is then passed to others, who draw, in the same manner, one pipe-full serving for half a dozen. They never take short, continuous draughts, like Europeans, but one of these "Oahu puffs," as the sailors call them, serves for an hour or two, until some one else lights his pipe, and it is passed round in the same manner. Each Kanaka on the beach had a pipe, flint, steel, tinder, a hand of tobacco, and a jack-knife, which he always carried about with him.

That which strikes a stranger most peculiarly is their style of singing. They run on, in a low, guttural, monotonous sort of chant, their lips and tongues seeming hardly to move, and the sounds modulated solely in the throat. There is very little tune to it, and the words, so far as I could learn, are extempore. They sing about persons and things which are around them, and adopt this method when they do not wish to be understood by any but themselves; and it is very effectual, for with the most careful attention I never could detect a word that I knew. I have often heard Mr. Mannini, who was the most noted improvisatore among them, sing for an hour together, when at work in the midst of Americans and Englishmen; and, by the occasional shouts and laughter of the Kanakas, who were at a distance, it was evident that he was singing about the different men that he was at work with. They have great powers of ridicule, and are excellent mimics; many of them discovering and imitating the peculiarities of our own people, before we had seen them ourselves.

These were the people with whom I was to spend a few months; and who, with the exception of the officer, Nicholas the Frenchman, and the boy, made the whole population of the beach. I ought, perhaps, to except the dogs, for they were an important part of our settlement. Some of the first vessels brought dogs out with them, who, for convenience, were left ashore, and there multiplied, until they came to be a great people. While I was on the beach, the average number was about forty, and probably an equal, or greater number are drowned, or killed in some other way, every year. They are very useful in guarding the beach, the Indians being afraid to come down at night; for it was impossible for any one to get within half a mile of the hide-houses without a general alarm. The father of the colony, old Sachem, so called from the ship in which he was brought out, died while I was there, full of years, and was honorably buried. Hogs, and a few chickens, were the rest of the animal tribe, and formed, like the dogs, a common company, though they were all known and marked, and usually fed at the houses to which they belonged.

I had been but a few hours on the beach, and the Pilgrim was hardly out of sight, when the cry of "Sail ho!" was raised, and a small hermaphrodite brig rounded the point, bore up into the harbor, and came to anchor. It was the Mexican brig Fazio, which we had left at San Pedro, and which had come down to land her tallow, try it all over, and make new bags, and then take it in, and leave the coast. They moored ship, erected their try-works on shore, put up a small tent, in which they all lived, and commenced operations. They made an addition to our society, and we spent many evenings in their tent, where, amid the Babel of English, Spanish, French, Indian, and Kanaka, we found some words that we could understand in common.

The morning after my landing, I began the duties of hide-curing. In order to understand these, it will be necessary to give the whole history of a hide, from the time it is taken from a bullock until it is put on board the vessel to be carried to Boston. When the hide is taken from the bullock, holes are cut round it, near the edge, by which it is staked out to dry. In this manner it dries without shrinking. After they are thus dried in the sun, they are received by the vessels, and brought down to the depot at San Diego. The vessels land them, and leave them in large piles near the houses.

Then begins the hide-curer's duty. The first thing is to put them in soak. This is done by carrying them down at low tide, and making them fast, in small piles, by ropes, and letting the tide come up and cover them. Every day we put in soak twenty-five for each man, which, with us, made an hundred and fifty. There they lie forty-eight hours, when they are taken out, and rolled up, in wheelbarrows, and thrown into the vats. These vats contain brine, made very strong; being sea-water, with great quantities of salt thrown in. This pickles the hides, and in this they lie forty-eight hours; the use of the sea-water, into which they are first put, being merely to soften and clean them. From these vats, they are taken, and lie on a platform twenty-four hours, and then are spread upon the ground, and carefully stretched and staked out, so that they may dry smooth. After they were staked, and while yet wet and soft, we used to go upon them with our knives, and carefully cut off all the bad parts:—the pieces of meat and fat, which would corrupt and infect the whole if stowed away in a vessel for many months, the large flippers, the ears, and all other parts which would prevent close stowage. This was the most difficult part of our duty: as it required much skill to take everything necessary off and not to cut or injure the hide. It was also a long process, as six of us had to clean an hundred and fifty, most of which required a great deal to be done to them, as the Spaniards are very careless in skinning their cattle. Then, too, as we cleaned them while they were staked out, we were obliged to kneel down upon them, which always gives beginners the back-ache. The first day, I was so slow and awkward that I cleaned only eight; at the end of a few days I doubled my number; and in a fortnight or three weeks, could keep up with the others, and clean my proportion—twenty-five.

This cleaning must be got through with before noon; for by that time they get too dry. After the sun has been upon them a few hours, they are carefully gone over with scrapers, to get off all the grease which the sun brings out. This being done, the stakes are pulled up, and the hides carefully doubled, with the hair side out, and left to dry. About the middle of the afternoon they are turned upon the other side, and at sundown piled up and covered over. The next day they are spread out and opened again, and at night, if fully dry, are thrown upon a long, horizontal pole, five at a time, and beat with flails. This takes all the dust from them. Then, being salted, scraped, cleaned, dried, and beaten, they are stowed away in the house. Here ends their history, except that they are taken out again when the vessel is ready to go home, beaten, stowed away on board, carried to Boston, tanned, made into shoes and other articles for which leather is used; and many of them, very probably, in the end, brought back again to California in the shape of shoes, and worn out in pursuit of other bullocks, or in the curing of other hides.

By putting an hundred and fifty in soak every day, we had the same number at each stage of curing, on each day; so that we had, every day, the same work to do upon the same number: an hundred and fifty to put in soak; an hundred and fifty to wash out and put in the vat; the same number to haul from the vat and put on the platform to drain; the same number to spread and stake out and clean; and the same number to beat and stow away in the home. I ought to except Sunday; for, by a prescription which no captain or agent has yet ventured to break in upon, Sunday has been a day of leisure on the beach for years. On Saturday night, the hides, in every stage of progress, are carefully covered up, and not uncovered until Monday morning. On Sundays we had absolutely no work to do, unless it was to kill a bullock, which was sent down for our use about once a week, and sometimes came on Sunday. Another good arrangement was, that we had just so much work to do, and when that was through, the time was our own. Knowing this, we worked hard, and needed no driving. We "turned out" every morning at the first signs of daylight, and allowing a short time, about eight o'clock, for breakfast, generally got through our labor between one and two o'clock, when we dined, and had the rest of the time to ourselves; until just before sundown, when we beat the dry hides and put them in the house, and covered over all the others. By this means we had about three hours to ourselves every afternoon; and at sundown we had our supper, and our work was done for the day. There was no watch to stand, and no topsails to reef. The evenings we generally spent at one another's houses, and I often went up and spent an hour or so at the oven; which was called the "Kanaka Hotel," and the "Oahu Coffee-house." Immediately after dinner we usually took a short siésta to make up for our early rising, and spent the rest of the afternoon according to our own fancies. I generally read, wrote, and made or mended clothes; for necessity, the mother of invention, had taught me these two latter arts. The Kanakas went up to the oven, and spent the time in sleeping, talking, and smoking; and my messmate, Nicholas, who neither knew how to read or write, passed away the time by a long siésta, two or three smokes with his pipe, and a paséo to the other houses. This leisure time is never interfered with, for the captains know that the men earn it by working hard and fast, and that if they interfered with it, the men could easily make their twenty-five hides apiece last through the day. We were pretty independent, too, for the master of the house—"capitan de la casa"—had nothing to say to us, except when we were at work on the hides, and although we could not go up to the town without his permission, this was seldom or never refused.

The great weight of the wet hides, which we were obliged to roll about in wheelbarrows; the continual stooping upon those which were pegged out to be cleaned; and the smell of the vats, into which we were often obliged to get, knee-deep, to press down the hides; all made the work disagreeable and fatiguing;—but we soon got hardened to it, and the comparative independence of our life reconciled us to it; for there was nobody to haze us and find fault; and when we got through, we had only to wash and change our clothes, and our time was our own. There was, however, one exception to the time's being our own; which was, that on two afternoons of every week we were obliged to go off and get wood, for the cook to use in the galley. Wood is very scarce in the vicinity of San Diego; there being no trees of any size, for miles. In the town, the inhabitants burn the small wood which grows in thickets, and for which they send out Indians, in large numbers, every few days. Fortunately, the climate is so fine that they had no need of a fire in their houses, and only use it for cooking. With us the getting of wood was a great trouble; for all that in the vicinity of the houses had been cut down, and we were obliged to go off a mile or two, and to carry it some distance on our backs, as we could not get the hand-cart up the hills and over the uneven places. Two afternoons in the week, generally Monday and Thursday, as soon as we had got through dinner, we started off for the bush, each of us furnished with a hatchet and a long piece of rope, and dragging the hand-cart behind us, and followed by the whole colony of dogs, who were always ready for the bush, and were half mad whenever they saw our preparations. We went with the hand-cart as far as we could conveniently drag it, and leaving it in an open, conspicuous place, separated ourselves; each taking his own course, and looking about for some good place to begin upon. Frequently, we had to go nearly a mile from the hand-cart before we could find any fit place. Having lighted upon a good thicket, the next thing was to clear away the under-brush, and have fair play at the trees. These trees are seldom more than five or six feet high, and the highest that I ever saw in these expeditions could not have been more than twelve; so that, with lopping off the branches and clearing away the underwood, we had a good deal of cutting to do for a very little wood. Having cut enough for a "back-load," the next thing was to make it well fast with the rope, and heaving the bundle upon our backs, and taking the hatchet in hand, to walk off, up hill and down dale, to the hand-cart. Two good back-loads apiece filled the hand-cart; and that was each one's proportion. When each had brought down his second load, we filled the hand-cart, and took our way again slowly back, and unloading, covering the hides for the night, and getting our supper, finished the day's work.

These wooding excursions had always a mixture of something rather pleasant in them. Roaming about in the woods with hatchet in hand, like a backwoodsman, followed by a troop of dogs; starting up of birds, snakes, hares and foxes, and examining the various kinds of trees, flowers, and birds' nests, was at least, a change from the monotonous drag and pull on shipboard. Frequently, too, we had some amusement and adventure. The coati, of which I have before spoken,—a sort of mixture of the fox and wolf breeds,—fierce little animals, with bushy tails and large heads, and a quick, sharp bark, abound here, as in all other parts of California. These, the dogs were very watchful for, and whenever they saw them, started off in full run after them. We had many fine chases; yet, although our dogs ran finely, the rascals generally escaped. They are a match for the dog,—-one to one,—but as the dogs generally went in squads, there was seldom a fair fight. A smaller dog, belonging to us, once attacked a coati, single, and got a good deal worsted, and might perhaps have been killed had we not come to his assistance. We had, however, one dog which gave them a good deal of trouble, and many hard runs. He was a fine, tall fellow, and united strength and agility better than any dog that I have ever seen. He was born at the Islands, his father being an English mastiff, and his mother a greyhound. He had the high head, long legs, narrow body, and springing gait of the latter, and the heavy jaw, thick jowls, and strong fore-quarters of the mastiff. When he was brought to San Diego, an English sailor said that he looked, about the face, precisely like the Duke of Wellington, whom he had once seen at the Tower; and, indeed, there was something about him which resembled the portraits of the Duke. From this time he was christened "Welly," and became the favorite and bully of the beach. He always led the dogs by several yards in the chase, and had killed two coati at different times in single combats. We often had fine sport with these fellows. A quick, sharp bark from a coati, and in an instant every dog was at the height of his speed. A few moments made up for an unfair start, and gave each dog his relative place. Welly, at the head, seemed almost to skim over the bushes; and after him came Fanny, Feliciana, Childers, and the other fleet ones,—the spaniels and terriers; and then behind, followed the heavy corps—bulldogs, etc., for we had every breed. Pursuit by us was in vain, and in about half an hour a few of them would come panting and straggling back.

Beside the coati, the dogs sometimes made prizes of rabbits and hares, which are very plentiful here, and great numbers of which we often shot for our dinners. There was another animal that I was not so much disposed to find amusement from, and that was the rattlesnake. These are very abundant here, especially during the spring of the year. The latter part of the time that I was on shore, I did not meet with so many, but for the first two months we seldom went into "the bush" without one of our number starting some of them. The first that I ever saw, I remember perfectly well. I had left my companions, and was beginning to clear away a fine clump of trees, when just in the midst of the thicket, not more than eight yards from me, one of these fellows set up his hiss. It is a sharp, continuous sound, and resembles very much the letting off of the steam from the small pipe of a steamboat, except that it is on a smaller scale. I knew, by the sound of an axe, that one of my companions was near, and called out to him, to let him know what I had fallen upon. He took it very lightly, and as he seemed inclined to laugh at me for being afraid, I determined to keep my place. I knew that so long as I could hear the rattle, I was safe, for these snakes never make a noise when they are in motion. Accordingly, I kept at my work, and the noise which I made with cutting and breaking the trees kept him in alarm; so that I had the rattle to show me his whereabouts. Once or twice the noise stopped for a short time, which gave me a little uneasiness, and retreating a few steps, I threw something into the bush, at which he would set his rattle agoing; and finding that he had not moved from his first place, I was easy again. In this way I continued at my work until I had cut a full load, never suffering him to be quiet for a moment. Having cut my load, I strapped it together, and got everything ready for starting. I felt that I could now call the others without the imputation of being afraid; and went in search of them. In a few minutes we were all collected, and began an attack upon the bush. The big Frenchman, who was the one that I had called to at first, I found as little inclined to approach the snake as I had been. The dogs, too, seemed afraid of the rattle, and kept up a barking at a safe distance; but the Kanakas showed no fear, and getting long sticks, went into the bush, and keeping a bright look-out, stood within a few feet of him. One or two blows struck near him, and a few stones thrown, started him, and we lost his track, and had the pleasant consciousness that he might be directly under our feet. By throwing stones and chips in different directions, we made him spring his rattle again, and began another attack. This time we drove him into the clear ground, and saw him gliding off, with head and tail erect, when a stone, well aimed, knocked him over the bank, down a declivity of fifteen or twenty feet, and stretched him at his length. Having made sure of him, by a few more stones, we went down, and one of the Kanakas cut off his rattle. These rattles vary in number it is said, according to the age of the snake; though the Indians think they indicate the number of creatures they have killed. We always preserved them as trophies, and at the end of the summer had quite a number. None of our people were ever bitten by them, but one of our dogs died of a bite, and another was supposed to have been bitten, but recovered. We had no remedy for the bite, though it was said that the Indians of the country had, and the Kanakas professed to have an herb which would cure it, but it was fortunately never brought to the test.

Hares and rabbits, as I said before, were abundant, and, during the winter months, the waters are covered with wild ducks and geese. Crows, too, were very numerous, and frequently alighted in great numbers upon our hides, picking at the pieces of dried meat and fat. Bears and wolves are numerous in the upper parts, and in the interior, (and, indeed, a man was killed by a bear within a few miles of San Pedro, while we were there,) but there were none in our immediate neighborhood. The only other animals were horses. Over a dozen of these were owned by different people on the beach, and were allowed to run loose among the hills, with a long lasso attached to them, and pick up feed wherever they could find it. We were sure of seeing them once a day, for there was no water among the hills, and they were obliged to come down to the well which had been dug upon the beach. These horses were bought at, from two, to six and eight dollars apiece, and were held very much as common property. We generally kept one fast to one of the houses every day, so that we could mount him and catch any of the others. Some of them were really fine animals, and gave us many good runs up to the Presidio and over the country.

CHAPTER XX

LEISURE—NEWS FROM HOME—"BURNING THE WATER"

After we had been a few weeks on shore, and had begun to feel broken into the regularity of our life, its monotony was interrupted by the arrival of two vessels from the windward. We were sitting at dinner in our little room, when we heard the cry of "Sail ho!" This, we had learned, did not always signify a vessel, but was raised whenever a woman was seen coming down from the town; or a squaw, or an ox-cart, or anything unusual, hove in sight upon the road; so we took no notice of it. But it soon became so loud and general from all parts of the beach, that we were led to go to the door; and there, sure enough, were two sails coming round the point, and leaning over from the strong north-west wind, which blows down the coast every afternoon. The headmost was a ship, and the other, a brig. Everybody was alive on the beach, and all manner of conjectures were abroad. Some said it was the Pilgrim, with the Boston ship, which we were expecting; but we soon saw that the brig was not the Pilgrim, and the ship with her stump top-gallant masts and rusty sides, could not be a dandy Boston Indiaman. As they drew nearer, we soon discovered the high poop and top-gallant forecastle, and other marks of the Italian ship Rosa, and the brig proved to be the Catalina, which we saw at Santa Barbara, just arrived from Valparaiso. They came to anchor, moored ship, and commenced discharging hides and tallow. The Rosa had purchased the house occupied by the Lagoda, and the Catalina took the other spare one between ours and the Ayacucho's, so that, now, each one was occupied, and the beach, for several days, was all alive. The Catalina had several Kanakas on board, who were immediately besieged by the others, and carried up to the oven, where they had a long pow-wow, and a smoke. Two Frenchmen, who belonged to the Rosa's crew, came in, every evening, to see Nicholas; and from them we learned that the Pilgrim was at San Pedro, and was the only other vessel now on the coast. Several of the Italians slept on shore at their hide-house; and there, and at the tent in which the Fazio's crew lived, we had some very good singing almost every evening. The Italians sang a variety of songs—barcarollas, provincial airs, etc.; in several of which I recognized parts of our favorite operas and sentimental songs. They often joined in a song, taking all the different parts; which produced a fine effect, as many of them had good voices, and all seemed to sing with spirit and feeling. One young man, in particular, had a falsetto as clear as a clarionet.

The greater part of the crews of the vessels came ashore every evening, and we passed the time in going about from one house to another, and listening to all manner of languages. The Spanish was the common ground upon which we all met; for every one knew more or less of that. We had now, out of forty or fifty, representatives from almost every nation under the sun: two Englishmen, three Yankees, two Scotchmen, two Welshmen, one Irishman, three Frenchmen (two of whom were Normans, and the third from Gascony,) one Dutchman, one Austrian, two or three Spaniards, (from old Spain,) half a dozen Spanish-Americans and half-breeds, two native Indians from Chili and the Island of Chiloe, one Negro, one Mulatto, about twenty Italians, from all parts of Italy, as many more Sandwich Islanders, one Otaheitan, and one Kanaka from the Marquesas Islands.

The night before the vessels were ready to sail, all the Europeans united and had an entertainment at the Rosa's hide-house, and we had songs of every nation and tongue. A German gave us "Och! mein lieber Augustin!" the three Frenchmen roared through the Marseilles Hymn; the English and Scotchmen gave us "Rule Britannia," and "Wha'll be King but Charlie?" the Italians and Spaniards screamed through some national affairs, for which I was none the wiser; and we three Yankees made an attempt at the "Star-spangled Banner." After these national tributes had been paid, the Austrian gave us a very pretty little love-song, and the Frenchmen sang a spirited thing called "Sentinelle! O prenez garde a vous!" and then followed the melange which might have been expected. When I left them, the aguardiente and annisou was pretty well in their heads, and they were all singing and talking at once, and their peculiar national oaths were getting as plenty as pronouns.

The next day, the two vessels got under weigh for the windward, and left us in quiet possession of the beach. Our numbers were somewhat enlarged by the opening of the new houses, and the society of the beach a little changed. In charge of the Catalina's house, was an old Scotchman, who, like most of his countrymen, had a pretty good education, and, like many of them, was rather pragmatical, and had a ludicrously solemn conceit. He employed his time in taking care of his pigs, chickens, turkeys, dogs, etc., and in smoking his long pipe. Everything was as neat as a pin in the house, and he was as regular in his hours as a chronometer, but as he kept very much by himself, was not a great addition to our society. He hardly spent a cent all the time he was on the beach, and the others said he was no shipmate. He had been a petty officer on board the British frigate Dublin, Capt. Lord James Townshend, and had great ideas of his own importance. The man in charge of the Rosa's house was an Austrian by birth, but spoke, read, and wrote four languages with ease and correctness. German was his native tongue, but being born near the borders of Italy, and having sailed out of Genoa, the Italian was almost as familiar to him as his own language. He was six years on board of an English man-of-war, where he learned to speak our language with ease, and also to read and write it. He had been several years in Spanish vessels, and had acquired that language so well, that he could read any books in it. He was between forty and fifty years of age, and was a singular mixture of the man-of-war's-man and Puritan. He talked a great deal about propriety and steadiness, and gave good advice to the youngsters and Kanakas, but seldom went up to the town, without coming down "three sheets in the wind." One holyday, he and old Robert (the Scotchman from the Catalina) went up to the town, and got so cozy, talking over old stories and giving one another good advice, that they came down double-backed, on a horse, and both rolled off into the sand as soon as the horse stopped. This put an end to their pretensions, and they never heard the last of it from the rest of the men. On the night of the entertainment at the Rosa's house, I saw old Schmidt, (that was the Austrian's name) standing up by a hogshead, holding on by both hands, and calling out to himself— "Hold on, Schmidt! hold on, my good fellow, or you'll be on your back!" Still, he was an intelligent, good-natured old fellow, and had a chest-full of books, which he willingly lent me to read. In the same house with him was a Frenchman and an Englishman; the latter a regular-built "man-of-war Jack;" a thorough seaman; a hearty, generous fellow; and, at the same time, a drunken, dissolute dog. He made it a point to get drunk once a fortnight, (when he always managed to sleep on the road, and have his money stolen from him,) and to battle the Frenchman once a week. These, with a Chilian, and a half a dozen Kanakas, formed the addition to our company.

In about six weeks from the time when the Pilgrim sailed, we had got all the hides which she left us cured and stowed away; and having cleared up the ground, and emptied the vats, and set everything in order, had nothing more to do until she should come down again, but to supply ourselves with wood. Instead of going twice a week for this purpose, we determined to give one whole week to getting wood, and then we should have enough to last us half through the summer. Accordingly, we started off every morning, after an early breakfast, with our hatchets in hand, and cut wood until the sun was over the point,—which was our only mark of time, as there was not a watch on the beach—and then came back to dinner, and after dinner, started off again with our hand-cart and ropes, and carted and "backed" it down, until sunset. This, we kept up for a week, until we had collected several cords,—enough to last us for six or eight weeks—when we "knocked off" altogether, much to my joy; for, though I liked straying in the woods, and cutting, very well, yet the backing the wood for so great a distance, over an uneven country, was, without exception, the hardest work I had ever done. I usually had to kneel down and contrive to heave the load, which was well strapped together, upon my back, and then rise up and start off with it up the hills and down the vales, sometimes through thickets,—the rough points sticking into the skin, and tearing the clothes, so that, at the end of the week, I had hardly a whole shirt to my back.

We were now through all our work, and had nothing more to do until the Pilgrim should come down again. We had nearly got through our provisions too, as well as our work; for our officer had been very wasteful of them, and the tea, flour, sugar, and molasses, were all gone. We suspected him of sending them up to the town; and he always treated the squaws with molasses, when they came down to the beach. Finding wheat-coffee and dry bread rather poor living, we dubbed together, and I went up to the town on horseback with a great salt-bag behind the saddle, and a few reáls in my pocket, and brought back the bag full of onions, pears, beans, water-melons, and other fruits; for the young woman who tended the garden, finding that I belonged to the American ship, and that we were short of provisions, put in a double portion. With these we lived like fighting-cocks for a week or two, and had, besides, what the sailors call "a blow-out on sleep;" not turning out in the morning until breakfast was ready. I employed several days in overhauling my chest, and mending up all my old clothes, until I had got everything in order—patch upon patch, like a sand-barge's mainsail. Then I took hold of Bowditch's Navigator, which I had always with me. I had been through the greater part of it, and now went carefully through it, from beginning to end working out most of the examples. That done, and there being no signs of the Pilgrim, I made a descent upon old Schmidt, and borrowed and read all the books there were upon the beach. Such a dearth was there of these latter articles, that anything, even a little child's story-book, or the half of a shipping calendar, appeared like a treasure. I actually read a jest-book through, from beginning to end, in one day, as I should a novel, and enjoyed it very much. At last, when I thought that there were no more to be got, I found, at the bottom of old Schmidt's chest, "Mandeville, a Romance, by Godwin, in five volumes." This I had never read, but Godwin's name was enough, and after the wretched trash I had devoured, anything bearing the name of a distinguished intellectual man, was a prize indeed. I bore it off, and for two days I was up early and late, reading with all my might, and actually drinking in delight. It is no extravagance to say that it was like a spring in a desert land.

From the sublime to the ridiculous—so with me, from Mandeville to hide-curing, was but a step; for

Wednesday, July 18th, brought us the brig Pilgrim from the windward. As she came in, we found that she was a good deal altered in her appearance. Her short top-gallant masts were up; her bowlines all unrove (except to the courses); the quarter boom-irons off her lower yards; her jack-cross-trees sent down; several blocks got rid of; running-rigging rove in new places; and numberless other changes of the same character. Then, too, there was a new voice giving orders, and a new face on the quarter-deck,—a short, dark-complexioned man, in a green jacket and a high leather cap. These changes, of course, set the whole beach on the qui-vive, and we were all waiting for the boat to come ashore, that we might have things explained. At length, after the sails were furled and the anchor carried out, the boat pulled ashore, and the news soon flew that the expected ship had arrived at Santa Barbara, and that Captain T—— had taken command of her, and her captain, Faucon, had taken the Pilgrim, and was the green-jacketed man on the quarter-deck. The boat put directly off again, without giving us time to ask any more questions, and we were obliged to wait till night, when we took a little skiff, that lay on the beach, and paddled off. When I stepped aboard, the second mate called me aft, and gave me a large bundle, directed to me, and marked "Ship Alert." This was what I had longed for, yet I refrained from opening it until I went ashore. Diving down into the forecastle, I found the same old crew, and was really glad to see them again. Numerous inquiries passed as to the new ship, the latest news from Boston, etc., etc. S—— had received letters from home, and nothing remarkable had happened. The Alert was agreed on all hands to be a fine ship, and a large one: "Larger than the Rosa"—"Big enough to carry off all the hides in California"—"Rail as high as a man's head"—"A crack ship"—"A regular dandy," etc., etc. Captain T—— took command of her, and she went directly up to Monterey; from thence she was to go to San Francisco, and probably would not be in San Diego under two or three months. Some of the Pilgrim's crew found old ship-mates aboard of her, and spent an hour or two in her forecastle, the evening before she sailed. They said her decks were as white as snow—holystoned every morning, like a man-of-war's; everything on board "shipshape and Bristol fashion;" a fine crew, three mates, a sailmaker and carpenter, and all complete. "They've got a man for mate of that ship, and not a bloody sheep about decks!"—"A mate that knows his duty, and makes everybody do theirs, and won't be imposed upon either by captain or crew." After collecting all the information we could get on this point, we asked something about their new captain. He had hardly been on board long enough for them to know much about him, but he had taken hold strong, as soon as he took command;—sending down the top-gallant masts, and unreeving half the rigging, the very first day.

Having got all the news we could, we pulled ashore; and as soon as we reached the house, I, as might be supposed, proceeded directly to opening my bundle, and found a reasonable supply of duck, flannel shirts, shoes, etc., and, what was still more valuable, a packet of eleven letters. These I sat up nearly all the night to read, and put them carefully away, to be read and re-read again and again at my leisure. Then came a half a dozen newspapers, the last of which gave notice of Thanksgiving, and of the clearance of "ship Alert, Edward H. Faucon, master, for Callao and California, by Bryant, Sturgis & Co." No one has ever been on distant voyages, and after a long absence received a newspaper from home, who cannot understand the delight that they give one. I read every part of them—the houses to let; things lost or stolen; auction sales, and all. Nothing carries you so entirely to a place, and makes you feel so perfectly at home, as a newspaper. The very name of "Boston Daily Advertiser" "sounded hospitably upon the ear."

The Pilgrim discharged her hides, which set us at work again, and in a few days we were in the old routine of dry hides—wet hides—cleaning—beating, etc. Captain Faucon came quietly up to me, as I was at work, with my knife, cutting the meat from a dirty hide, asked me how I liked California, and repeated—"Tityre, tu patulae recubans sub tegmine fagi." Very apropos, thought I, and, at the same time, serves to show that you understand Latin. However, a kind word from a captain is a thing not to be slighted; so I answered him civilly, and made the most of it.

Saturday, July 11th. The Pilgrim set sail for the windward, and left us to go on in our old way. Having laid in such a supply of wood, and the days being now long, and invariably pleasant, we had a good deal of time to ourselves. All the duck I received from home, I soon made up into trowsers and frocks, and displayed, every Sunday, a complete suit of my own make, from head to foot, having formed the remnants of the duck into a cap. Reading, mending, sleeping, with occasional excursions into the bush, with the dogs, in search of coati, hares, and rabbits, or to encounter a rattlesnake, and now and then a visit to the Presidio, filled up our spare time after hide-curing was over for the day. Another amusement, which we sometimes indulged in, was "burning the water" for craw-fish. For this purpose, we procured a pair of grains, with a long staff like a harpoon, and making torches with tarred rope twisted round a long pine stick, took the only boat on the beach, a small skiff, and with a torch-bearer in the bow, a steersman in the stern, and one man on each side with the grains, went off, on dark nights, to burn the water. This is fine sport. Keeping within a few rods of the shore, where the water is not more than three or four feet deep, with a clear sandy bottom, the torches light everything up so that one could almost have seen a pin among the grains of sand. The craw-fish are an easy prey, and we used soon to get a load of them. The other fish were more difficult to catch, yet we frequently speared a number of them, of various kinds and sizes. The Pilgrim brought us down a supply of fish-hooks, which we had never had before, on the beach, and for several days we went down to the Point, and caught a quantity of cod and mackerel. On one of these expeditions, we saw a battle between two Sandwich Islanders and a shark. "Johnny" had been playing about our boat for some time, driving away the fish, and showing his teeth at our bait, when we missed him, and in a few moments heard a great shouting between two Kanakas who were fishing on the rock opposite to us: "E hana hana make i ka ia nui!" "E pii mai Aikane!" etc., etc.; and saw them pulling away on a stout line, and "Johnny Shark" floundering at the other end. The line soon broke; but the Kanakas would not let him off so easily, and sprang directly into the water after him. Now came the tug of war. Before we could get into deep water, one of them seized him by the tail, and ran up with him upon the beach; but Johnny twisted round, turning his head under his body, and, showing his teeth in the vicinity of the Kanaka's hand, made him let go and spring out of the way. The shark now turned tail and made the best of his way, by flapping and floundering, toward deep water; but here again, before he was fairly off, the other Kanaka seized him by the tail, and made a spring towards the beach, his companion at the same time paying away upon him with stones and a large stick. As soon, however, as the shark could turn, he was obliged to let go his hold; but the instant he made toward deep water, they were both behind him, watching their chance to seize him. In this way the battle went on for some time, the shark, in a rage, splashing and twisting about, and the Kanakas, in high excitement, yelling at the top of their voices; but the shark at last got off, carrying away a hook and liner and not a few severe bruises.

CHAPTER XXI

CALIFORNIA AND ITS INHABITANTS

We kept up a constant connection with the Presidio, and by the close of the summer I had added much to my vocabulary, beside having made the acquaintance of nearly everybody in the place, and acquired some knowledge of the character and habits of the people, as well as of the institutions under which they live.

California was first discovered in 1536, by Cortes, and was subsequently visited by numerous other adventurers as well as commissioned voyagers of the Spanish crown. It was found to be inhabited by numerous tribes of Indians, and to be in many parts extremely fertile; to which, of course, was added rumors of gold mines, pearl fishery, etc. No sooner was the importance of the country known, than the Jesuits obtained leave to establish themselves in it, to Christianize and enlighten the Indians. They established missions in various parts of the country toward the close of the seventeenth century, and collected the natives about them, baptizing them into the church, and teaching them the arts of civilized life. To protect the Jesuits in their missions, and at the same time to support the power of the crown over the civilized Indians, two forts were erected and garrisoned, one at San Diego, and the other at Monterey. These were called Presidios, and divided the command of the whole country between them. Presidios have since been established at Santa Barbara and San Francisco; thus dividing the country into four large districts, each with its presidio, and governed by the commandant. The soldiers, for the most part, married civilized Indians; and thus, in the vicinity of each presidio, sprung up, gradually, small towns. In the course of time, vessels began to come into the ports to trade with the missions, and received hides in return; and thus began the great trade of California. Nearly all the cattle in the country belonged to the missions, and they employed their Indians, who became, in fact, their slaves, in tending their vast herds. In the year 1793, when Vancouver visited San Diego, the mission had obtained great wealth and power, and are accused of having depreciated the country with the sovereign, that they might be allowed to retain their possessions. On the expulsion of the Jesuits from the Spanish dominions, the missions passed into the hands of the Franciscans, though without any essential change in their management. Ever since the independence of Mexico, the missions have been going down; until, at last, a law was passed, stripping them of all their possessions, and confining the priests to their spiritual duties; and at the same time declaring all the Indians free and independent Rancheros. The change in the condition of the Indians was, as may be supposed, only nominal: they are virtually slaves, as much as they ever were. But in the missions, the change was complete. The priests have now no power, except in their religious character, and the great possessions of the missions are given over to be preyed upon by the harpies of the civil power, who are sent there in the capacity of administradores, to settle up the concerns; and who usually end, in a few years, by making themselves fortunes, and leaving their stewardships worse than they found them. The dynasty of the priests was much more acceptable to the people of the country, and indeed, to every one concerned with the country, by trade or otherwise, than that of the administradores. The priests were attached perpetually to one mission, and felt the necessity of keeping up its credit. Accordingly, their debts were regularly paid, and the people were, in the main, well treated, and attached to those who had spent their whole lives among them. But the administradores are strangers sent from Mexico, having no interest in the country; not identified in any way with their charge, and, for the most part, men of desperate fortunes—broken down politicians and soldiers—whose only object is to retrieve their condition in as short a time as possible. The change had been made but a few years before our arrival upon the coast, yet, in that short time, the trade was much diminished, credit impaired, and the venerable missions going rapidly to decay. The external arrangements remain the same. There are four presidios, having under their protection the various missions, and pueblos, which are towns formed by the civil power, and containing no mission or presidio. The most northerly presidio is San Francisco; the next Monterey; the next Santa Barbara; including the mission of the same, St. Louis Obispo, and St. Buenaventura, which is the finest mission in the whole country, having very fertile soil and rich vineyards. The last, and most southerly, is San Diego, including the mission of the same, San Juan Campestrano, the Pueblo de los Angelos, the largest town in California, with the neighboring mission of San Gabriel. The priests in spiritual matters are subject to the

Archbishop of Mexico, and in temporal matters to the governor-general, who is the great civil and military head of the country.

The government of the country is an arbitrary democracy; having no common law, and no judiciary. Their only laws are made and unmade at the caprice of the legislature, and are as variable as the legislature itself. They pass through the form of sending representatives to the congress at Mexico, but as it takes several months to go and return, and there is very little communication between the capital and this distant province, a member usually stays there, as permanent member, knowing very well that there will be revolutions at home before he can write and receive an answer; if another member should be sent, he has only to challenge him, and decide the contested election in that way.

Revolutions are matters of constant occurrence in California. They are got up by men who are at the foot of the ladder and in desperate circumstances, just as a new political party is started by such men in our own country. The only object, of course, is the loaves and fishes; and instead of caucusing, paragraphing, libelling, feasting, promising, and lying, as with us, they take muskets and bayonets, and seizing upon the presidio and custom-house, divide the spoils, and declare a new dynasty. As for justice, they know no law but will and fear. A Yankee, who had been naturalized, and become a Catholic, and had married in the country, was sitting in his house at the Pueblo de los Angelos, with his wife and children, when a Spaniard, with whom he had had a difficulty, entered the house, and stabbed him to the heart before them all. The murderer was seized by some Yankees who had settled there, and kept in confinement until a statement of the whole affair could be sent to the governor-general. He refused to do anything about it, and the countrymen of the murdered man, seeing no prospect of justice being administered, made known that if nothing was done, they should try the man themselves. It chanced that, at this time, there was a company of forty trappers and hunters from Kentucky, with their rifles, who had made their head-quarters at the Pueblo; and these, together with the Americans and Englishmen in the place, who were between twenty and thirty in number, took possession of the town, and waiting a reasonable time, proceeded to try the man according to the forms in their own country. A judge and jury were appointed, and he was tried, convicted, sentenced to be shot, and carried out before the town, with his eyes blindfolded. The names of all the men were then put into a hat and each one pledging himself to perform his duty, twelve names were drawn out, and the men took their stations with their rifles, and, firing at the word, laid him dead. He was decently buried, and the place was restored quietly to the proper authorities. A general, with titles enough for an hidalgo, was at San Gabriel, and issued a proclamation as long as the fore-top-bowline, threatening destruction to the rebels, but never stirred from his fort; for forty Kentucky hunters, with their rifles, were a match for a whole regiment of hungry, drawling, lazy half-breeds. This affair happened while we were at San Pedro, (the port of the Pueblo,) and we had all the particulars directly from those who were on the spot. A few months afterwards, another man, whom we had often seen in San Diego, murdered a man and his wife on the high road between the Pueblo and San Louis Rey, and the foreigners not feeling themselves called upon to act in this case, the parties being all natives, nothing was done about it; and I frequently afterwards saw the murderer in San Diego, where he was living with his wife and family.

When a crime has been committed by Indians, justice, or rather vengeance, is not so tardy. One Sunday afternoon, while I was at San Diego, an Indian was sitting on his horse, when another, with whom he had had some difficulty, came up to him, drew a long knife, and plunged it directly into the horse's heart. The Indian sprang from his falling horse, drew out the knife, and plunged it into the other Indian's breast, over his shoulder, and laid him dead. The poor fellow was seized at once, clapped into the calabozo, and kept there until an answer could be received from Monterey. A few weeks afterwards, I saw the poor wretch, sitting on the bare ground, in front of the calabozo, with his feet chained to a stake, and handcuffs about his wrists. I knew there was very little hope for him. Although the deed was done in hot blood, the horse on which he was sitting being his own, and a great favorite, yet he was an Indian, and that was enough. In about a week after I saw him, I heard that he had been shot. These few instances will serve to give one a notion of the distribution of justice in California.

In their domestic relations, these people are no better than in their public. The men are thriftless, proud, and extravagant, and very much given to gaming; and the women have but little education, and a good deal of beauty, and their morality, of course, is none of the best; yet the instances of infidelity are much less frequent than one would at first suppose. In fact, one vice is set over against another; and thus, something like a balance is obtained. The women have but little virtue, but then the jealousy of their husbands is extreme, and their revenge deadly and almost certain. A few inches of cold steel has been the punishment of many an unwary man, who has been guilty, perhaps, of nothing more than indiscretion of manner. The difficulties of the attempt are numerous, and the consequences of discovery fatal. With the unmarried women, too, great watchfulness is used. The main object of the parents is to marry their daughters well, and to this, the slightest slip would be fatal. The sharp eyes of a dueña, and the cold steel of a father or brother, are a protection which the characters of most of them—men and women—render by no means useless; for the very men who would lay down their lives to avenge the dishonor of their own family, would risk the same lives to complete the dishonor of another.

Of the poor Indians, very little care is taken. The priests, indeed, at the missions, are said to keep them very strictly, and some rules are usually made by the alcaldes to punish their misconduct; but it all amounts to but little. Indeed, to show the entire want of any sense of morality or domestic duty among them, I have frequently known an Indian to bring his wife, to whom he was lawfully married in the church, down to the beach, and carry her back again, dividing with her the money which she had got from the sailors. If any of the girls were discovered by the alcalde to be open evil-livers, they were whipped, and kept at work sweeping the square of the presidio, and carrying mud and bricks for the buildings; yet a few reáls would generally buy them off. Intemperance, too, is a common vice among the Indians. The Spaniards, on the contrary, are very abstemious, and I do not remember ever having seen a Spaniard intoxicated.

Such are the people who inhabit a country embracing four or five hundred miles of sea-coast, with several good harbors; with fine forests in the north; the waters filled with fish, and the plains covered with thousands of herds of cattle; blessed with a climate, than which there can be no better in the world; free from all manner of diseases, whether epidemic or endemic; and with a soil in which corn yields from seventy to eighty fold. In the hands of an enterprising people, what a country this might be! we are ready to say. Yet how long would a people remain so, in such a country? The Americans (as those from the United States are called) and Englishmen, who are fast filling up the principal towns, and getting the trade into their hands, are indeed more industrious and effective than the Spaniards; yet their children are brought up Spaniards, in every respect, and if the "California fever" (laziness) spares the first generation, it always attacks the second.

CHAPTER XXII

LIFE ON SHORE—THE ALERT

Saturday, July 18th. This day, sailed the Mexican hermaphrodite brig, Fazio, for San Blas and Mazatlan. This was the brig which was driven ashore at San Pedro in a south-easter, and had been lying at San Diego to repair and take in her cargo. The owner of her had had a good deal of difficulty with the government about the duties, etc., and her sailing had been delayed for several weeks; but everything having been arranged, she got under weigh with a light breeze, and was floating out of the harbor, when two horsemen came dashing down to the beach, at full speed, and tried to find a boat to put off after her; but there being none on the beach, they offered a handful of silver to any Kanaka who would swim off and take a letter on board. One of the Kanakas, a fine, active, well-made young fellow, instantly threw off everything but his duck trowsers, and putting the letter into his hat, swam off, after the vessel. Fortunately, the wind was very light and the vessel was going slowly, so that, although she was nearly a mile off when he started, he gained on her rapidly. He went through the water leaving a wake like a small steamboat. I certainly never saw such swimming before. They saw him coming from the deck, but did not heave-to, suspecting the nature of his errand; yet, the wind continuing light, he swam alongside and got on board, and delivered his letter. The captain read the letter, told the Kanaka there was no answer, and giving him a glass of brandy, left him to jump overboard and find the best of his way to the shore. The Kanaka swam in for the nearest point of land, and, in about an hour, made his appearance at the hide-house. He did not seem at all fatigued, had made three or four dollars, got a glass of brandy, and was in fine spirits. The brig kept on her course, and the government officers, who had come down to forbid her sailing, went back, each with something like a flea in his ear, having depended upon extorting a little more money from the owner.

It was now nearly three months since the Alert arrived at Santa Barbara, and we began to expect her daily. About a half a mile behind the hide-house, was a high hill; and every afternoon, as soon as we had done our work, some one of us walked up to see if there were any sail in sight, coming down before the regular trades, which blow every afternoon. Each day, after the latter part of July, we went up the hill, and came back disappointed. I was anxious for her arrival, for I had been told by letter that the owners in Boston, at the request of my friends, had written to Captain T—— to take me on board the Alert, in case she returned to the United States before the Pilgrim; and I, of course, wished to know whether the order had been received, and what was the destination of the ship. One year more or less might be of small consequence to others, but it was everything to me. It was now just a year since we sailed from Boston, and at the shortest, no vessel could expect to get away under eight or nine months, which would make our absence two years in all. This would be pretty long, but would not be fatal. It would not necessarily be decisive of my future life. But one year more would settle the matter. I should be a sailor for life; and although I had made up my mind to it before I had my letters from home, and was, as I thought, quite satisfied; yet, as soon as an opportunity was held out to me of returning, and the prospect of another kind of life was opened to me, my anxiety to return, and, at least, to have the chance of deciding upon my course for myself, was beyond measure. Beside that, I wished to be "equal to either fortune," and to qualify myself for an officer's berth, and a hide-house was no place to learn seamanship in. I had become experienced in hide-curing, and everything went on smoothly, and I had many opportunities of becoming acquainted with the people, and much leisure for reading and studying navigation; yet practical seamanship could only be got on board ship; therefore, I determined to ask to be taken on board the ship when she arrived. By the first of August, we finished curing all our hides, stored them away, cleaned out our vats, (in which latter work we spent two days, up to our knees in mud and the sediments of six months' hide-curing, in a stench which would drive a donkey from his breakfast,) and got in readiness for the arrival of the ship, and had another leisure interval of three or four weeks; which I spent, as usual, in reading, writing, studying, making and mending my clothes, and getting my wardrobe in complete readiness, in case I should go on board the ship; and in fishing, ranging the woods with the dogs, and in occasional visits to the presidio and mission. A good deal of my time was spent in taking care of a little puppy, which I had selected from thirty-six, that were born within three days of one another, at our house. He was a fine, promising pup, with four white paws, and all the rest of his body of a dark brown.

I built a little kennel for him, and kept him fastened there, away from the other dogs, feeding and disciplining him myself. In a few weeks, I got him in complete subjection, and he grew finely, was very much attached to me, and bid fair to be one of the leading dogs on the beach. I called him Bravo, and the only thing I regretted at the thought of leaving the beach, was parting with him.

Day after day, we went up the hill, but no ship was to be seen, and we began to form all sorts of conjectures as to her whereabouts; and the theme of every evening's conversation at the different houses, and in our afternoon's paséo upon the beach, was the ship—where she could be—had she been to San Francisco?—how many hides she would bring, etc., etc.

Tuesday, August 25th. This morning, the officer in charge of our house went off beyond the point a fishing, in a small canoe, with two Kanakas; and we were sitting quietly in our room at the hide-house, when, just before noon, we heard a complete yell of "Sail ho!" breaking out from all parts of the beach, at once,—from the Kanakas' oven to the Rosa's house. In an instant, every one was out of his house; and there was a fine, tall ship, with royals and skysails set, bending over before the strong afternoon breeze, and coming rapidly round the point. Her yards were braced sharp up; every sail was set, and drew well; the Yankee ensign was flying from her mizen-peak; and having the tide in her favor, she came up like a race-horse. It was nearly six months since a new vessel had entered San Diego, and of course, every one was on the qui-vive. She certainly made a fine appearance. Her light sails were taken in, as she passed the low, sandy tongue of land, and clewing up her head sails, she rounded handsomely to, under her mizen topsail, and let go the anchor at about a cable's length from the shore. In a few minutes, the topsail yards were manned, and all three of the topsails furled at once. From the fore top-gallant yard, the men slid down the stay to furl the jib, and from the mizen top-gallant yard, by the stay, into the maintop, and thence to the yard; and the men on the topsail yards came down the lifts to the yard-arms of the courses. The sails were furled with great care, the bunts triced up by jiggers, and the jibs stowed in cloth. The royal yards were then struck, tackles got upon the yard-arms and the stay, the long-boat hoisted out, a large anchor carried astern, and the ship moored. Then the captain's gig was lowered away from the quarter, and a boat's crew of fine lads, between the ages of fourteen and eighteen, pulled the captain ashore. The gig was a light whale-boat, handsomely painted, and fitted up with cushions, etc., in the stern sheets. We immediately attacked the boat's crew, and got very thick with them in a few minutes. We had much to ask about Boston, their passage out, etc., and they were very curious to know about the life we were leading upon the beach. One of them offered to exchange with me; which was just what I wanted; and we had only to get the permission of the captain.

After dinner, the crew began discharging their hides, and, as we had nothing to do at the hide-houses, we were ordered aboard to help them. I had now my first opportunity of seeing the ship which I hoped was to be my home for the next year. She looked as well on board as she did from without. Her decks were wide and roomy, (there being no poop, or house on deck, which disfigures the after part of most of our vessels,) flush, fore and aft, and as white as snow, which the crew told us was from constant use of holystones. There was no foolish gilding and gingerbread work, to take the eye of landsmen and passengers, but everything was "ship-shape and Bristol fashion." There was no rust, no dirt, no rigging hanging slack, no fag ends of ropes and "Irish pendants" aloft, and the yards were squared "to a t" by lifts and braces.

The mate was a fine, hearty, noisy fellow, with a voice like a lion, and always wide awake. He was "a man, every inch of him," as the sailors said; and though "a bit of a horse," and "a hard customer," yet he was generally liked by the crew. There was also a second and third mate, a carpenter, sailmaker, steward, cook, etc., and twelve, including boys, before the mast. She had, on board, seven thousand hides, which she had collected at the windward, and also horns and tallow. All these we began discharging, from both gangways at once, into the two boats, the second mate having charge of the launch, and the third mate of the pinnace. For several days, we were employed in this way, until all the hides were taken out, when the crew began taking in ballast, and we returned to our old work, hide-curing.

Saturday, Aug. 29th. Arrived, brig Catalina, from the windward.

Sunday, 30th. This was the first Sunday that the crew had been in San Diego, and of course they were all for going up to see the town. The Indians came down early, with horses to let for the day, and all the crew, who could obtain liberty, went off to the Presidio and mission, and did not return until night. I had seen enough of San Diego, and went on board and spent the day with some of the crew, whom I found quietly at work in the forecastle, mending and washing their clothes, and reading and writing. They told me that the ship stopped at Callao in the passage out, and there lay three weeks. She had a passage of little over eighty days from Boston to Callao, which is one of the shortest on record. There, they left the Brandywine frigate, and other smaller American ships of war, and the English frigate Blonde, and a French seventy-four. From Callao they came directly to California, and had visited every port on the coast, including San Francisco. The forecastle in which they lived was large, tolerably well lighted by bulls-eyes, and, being kept perfectly clean, had quite a comfortable appearance; at least, it was far better than the little, black, dirty hole in which I had lived so many months on board the Pilgrim. By the regulations of the ship, the forecastle was cleaned out every morning, and the crew, being very neat, kept it clean by some regulations of their own, such as having a large spitbox always under the steps and between the bits, and obliging every man to hang up his wet clothes, etc. In addition to this, it was holystoned every Saturday morning. In the after part of the ship was a handsome cabin, a dining-room, and a trade-room, fitted out with shelves and furnished with all sorts of goods. Between these and the forecastle was the "between-decks," as high as the gun deck of a frigate; being six feet and a half, under the beams. These between-decks were holystoned regularly, and kept in the most perfect order; the carpenter's bench and tools being in one part, the sailmaker's in another, and boatswain's locker, with the spare rigging, in a third. A part of the crew slept here, in hammocks swung fore and aft from the beams, and triced up every morning. The sides of the between-decks were clapboarded, the knees and stanchions of iron, and the latter made to unship. The crew said she was as tight as a drum, and a fine sea boat, her only fault being, that of most fast ships,—that she was wet, forward. When she was going, as she sometimes would, eight or nine knots on a wind, there would not be a dry spot forward of the gangway. The men told great stories of her sailing, and had great confidence in her as a "lucky ship." She was seven years old, and had always been in the Canton trade, and never had met with an accident of any consequence, and had never made a passage that was not shorter than the average. The third mate, a young man of about eighteen years of age, nephew of one of the owners, had been in the ship from a small boy, and "believed in the ship;" and the chief mate thought more of her than he would of a wife and family.

The ship lay about a week longer in port, when, having discharged her cargo and taken in ballast, she prepared to get under weigh. I now made my application to the captain to go on board. He told me that I could go home in the ship when she sailed (which I knew before); and, finding that I wished to be on board while she was on the coast, said he had no objection, if I could find one of my own age to exchange with me, for the time. This, I easily accomplished, for they were glad to change the scene by a few months on shore, and, moreover, escape the winter and the south-easters; and I went on board the next day, with my chest and hammock, and found myself once more afloat.

CHAPTER XXIII

NEW SHIP AND SHIPMATES—MY WATCHMATE

Tuesday, Sept. 8th. This was my first day's duty on board the ship; and though a sailor's life is a sailor's life wherever it may be, yet I found everything very different here from the customs of the brig Pilgrim. After all hands were called, at day-break, three minutes and a half were allowed for every man to dress and come on deck, and if any were longer than that, they were sure to be overhauled by the mate, who was always on deck, and making himself heard all over the ship. The head-pump was then rigged, and the decks washed down by the second and third mates; the chief mate walking the quarter-deck and keeping a general supervision, but not deigning to touch a bucket or a brush. Inside and out, fore and aft, upper deck and between decks, steerage and forecastle, rail, bulwarks, and water-ways, were washed, scrubbed and scraped with brooms and canvas, and the decks were wet and sanded all over, and then holystoned. The holystone is a large, soft stone, smooth on the bottom, with long ropes attached to each end, by which the crew keep it sliding fore and aft, over the wet, sanded decks. Smaller hand-stones, which the sailors call "prayer-books," are used to scrub in among the crevices and narrow places, where the large holystone will not go. An hour or two, we were kept at this work, when the head-pump was manned, and all the sand washed off the decks and sides. Then came swabs and squilgees; and after the decks were dry, each one went to his particular morning job. There were five boats belonging to the ship,—launch, pinnace, jolly-boat, larboard quarter-boat, and gig,—each of which had a coxswain, who had charge of it, and was answerable for the order and cleanness of it. The rest of the cleaning was divided among the crew; one having the brass and composition work about the capstan; another the bell, which was of brass, and kept as bright as a gilt button; a third, the harness-cask; another, the man-rope stanchions; others, the steps of the forecastle and hatchways, which were hauled up and holystoned. Each of these jobs must be finished before breakfast; and, in the meantime, the rest of the crew filled the scuttle-butt, and the cook scraped his kids (wooden tubs out of which the sailors eat) and polished the hoops, and placed them before the galley, to await inspection. When the decks were dry, the lord paramount made his appearance on the quarter-deck, and took a few turns, when eight bells were struck, and all hands went to breakfast. Half an hour was allowed for breakfast, when all hands were called again; the kids, pots, bread-bags, etc., stowed away; and, this morning, preparations were made for getting under weigh. We paid out on the chain by which we swung; hove in on the other; catted the anchor; and hove short on the first. This work was done in shorter time than was usual on board the brig; for though everything was more than twice as large and heavy, the cat-block being as much as a man could lift, and the chain as large as three of the Pilgrim's, yet there was a plenty of room to move about in, more discipline and system, more men, and more good will. Every one seemed ambitious to do his best: officers and men knew their duty, and all went well. As soon as she was hove short, the mate, on the forecastle, gave the order to loose the sails, and, in an instant, every one sprung into the rigging, up the shrouds, and out on the yards, scrambling by one another,—the first up the best fellow,—cast off the yard-arm gaskets and bunt gaskets, and one man remained on each yard, holding the bunt jigger with a turn round the tye, all ready to let go, while the rest laid down to man the sheets and halyards. The mate then hailed the yards—"All ready forward?"—"All ready the cross-jack yards?" etc., etc., and "Aye, aye, sir!" being returned from each, the word was given to let go; and in the twinkling of an eye, the ship, which had shown nothing but her bare yards, was covered with her loose canvas, from the royal-mast-heads to the decks. Every one then laid down, except one man in each top, to overhaul the rigging, and the topsails were hoisted and sheeted home; all three yards going to the mast-head at once, the larboard watch hoisting the fore, the starboard watch the main, and five light hands, (of whom I was one,) picked from the two watches, the mizen. The yards were then trimmed, the anchor weighed, the cat-block hooked on, the fall stretched out, manned by "all hands and the cook," and the anchor brought to the head with "cheerily men!" in full chorus. The ship being now under weigh, the light sails were set, one after another, and she was under full sail, before she had passed the sandy point. The fore royal, which fell to my lot, (being in the mate's watch,) was more than twice as large as that of the Pilgrim, and, though I could handle the brig's easily, I found my hands full, with this, especially as there were no jacks to the ship; everything being for neatness, and nothing left for Jack to hold on by, but his eyelids.

As soon as we were beyond the point, and all sail out, the order was given, "Go below the watch!" and the crew said that, ever since they had been on the coast, they had had "watch and watch," while going from port to port; and, in fact, everything showed that, though strict discipline was kept, and the utmost was required of every man, in the way of his duty, yet, on the whole, there was very good usage on board. Each one knew that he must be a man, and show himself smart when at his duty, yet every one was satisfied with the usage; and a contented crew, agreeing with one another, and finding no fault, was a contrast indeed with the small, hard-used, dissatisfied, grumbling, desponding crew of the Pilgrim.

It being the turn of our watch to go below, the men went to work, mending their clothes, and doing other little things for themselves; and I, having got my wardrobe in complete order at San Diego, had nothing to do but to read. I accordingly overhauled the chests of the crew, but found nothing that suited me exactly, until one of the men said he had a book which "told all about a great highwayman," at the bottom of his chest, and producing it, I found, to my surprise and joy, that it was nothing else than Bulwer's Paul Clifford. This, I seized immediately, and going to my hammock, lay there, swinging and reading, until the watch was out. The between-decks were clear, the hatchways open, and a cool breeze blowing through them, the ship under easy way, and everything comfortable. I had just got well into the story, when eight bells were struck, and we were all ordered to dinner. After dinner came our watch on deck for four hours, and, at four o'clock, I went below again, turned into my hammock, and read until the dog watch. As no lights were allowed after eight o'clock, there was no reading in the night watch. Having light winds and calms, we were three days on the passage, and each watch below, during the daytime, I spent in the same manner, until I had finished my book. I shall never forget the enjoyment I derived from it. To come across anything with the slightest claims to literary merit, was so unusual, that this was a perfect feast to me. The brilliancy of the book, the succession of capital hits, lively and characteristic sketches, kept me in a constant state of pleasing sensations. It was far too good for a sailor. I could not expect such fine times to last long.

While on deck, the regular work of the ship went on. The sailmaker and carpenter worked between decks, and the crew had their work to do upon the rigging, drawing yarns, making spun-yarn, etc., as usual in merchantmen. The night watches were much more pleasant than on board the Pilgrim. There, there were so few in a watch, that, one being at the wheel, and another on the look-out, there was no one left to talk with; but here, we had seven in a watch, so that we had long yarns, in abundance. After two or three night watches, I became quite well acquainted with all the larboard watch. The sailmaker was the head man of the watch, and was generally considered the most experienced seaman on board. He was a thoroughbred old man-of-war's-man, had been to sea twenty-two years, in all kinds of vessels—men-of-war, privateers, slavers, and merchantmen;—everything except whalers, which a thorough sailor despises, and will always steer clear of, if he can. He had, of course, been in all parts of the world, and was remarkable for drawing a long bow. His yarns frequently stretched through a watch, and kept all hands awake. They were always amusing from their improbability, and, indeed, he never expected to be believed, but spun them merely for amusement; and as he had some humor and a good supply of man-of-war slang and sailor's salt phrases, he always made fun. Next to him in age and experience, and, of course, in standing in the watch, was an Englishman, named Harris, of whom I shall have more to say hereafter. Then, came two or three Americans, who had been the common run of European and South American voyages, and one who had been in a "spouter," and, of course, had all the whaling stories to himself. Last of all, was a broad-backed, thick-headed boy from Cape Cod, who had been in mackerel schooners, and was making his first voyage in a square-rigged vessel. He was born in Hingham, and of course was called "Bucketmaker." The other watch was composed of about the same number. A tall, fine-looking Frenchman, with coal-black whiskers and curly hair, a first-rate seaman, and named John, (one name is enough for a sailor,) was the head man of the watch. Then came two Americans (one of whom had been a dissipated young man of property and family, and was reduced to duck trowsers and monthly wages,) a German, an English lad, named Ben, who belonged on the mizen topsail yard with me, and was a good sailor for his years, and two Boston boys just from the public schools. The carpenter sometimes mustered in the starboard watch, and was an old sea-dog, a Swede by birth, and accounted the best helmsman in the ship. This was our ship's company, beside cook and steward, who were blacks, three mates, and the captain.

The second day out, the wind drew ahead, and we had to beat up the coast; so that, in tacking ship, I could see the regulations of the vessel. Instead of going wherever was most convenient, and running from place to place, wherever work was to be done, each man had his station. A regular tacking and wearing bill was made out. The chief mate commanded on the forecastle, and had charge of the head sails and the forward part of the ship. Two of the best men in the ship—the sailmaker from our watch, and John, the Frenchman, from the other, worked the forecastle. The third mate commanded in the waist, and, with the carpenter and one man, worked the main tack and bowlines; the cook, ex-officio, the fore sheet, and the steward the main. The second mate had charge of the after yards, and let go the lee fore and main braces. I was stationed at the weather cross-jack braces; three other light hands at the lee; one boy at the spanker-sheet and guy; a man and a boy at the main topsail, top-gallant, and royal braces; and all the rest of the crew—men and boys—tallied on to the main brace. Every one here knew his station, must be there when all hands were called to put the ship about, and was answerable for every rope committed to him. Each man's rope must be let go and hauled in at the order, properly made fast, and neatly coiled away when the ship was about. As soon as all hands are at their stations, the captain, who stands on the weather side of the quarter-deck, makes a sign to the man at the wheel to put it down, and calls out "Helm's a lee'!" "Helm's a lee'!" answers the mate on the forecastle, and the head sheets are let go. "Raise tacks and sheets!" says the captain; "tacks and sheets!" is passed forward, and the fore tack and main sheet are let go. The next thing is to haul taut for a swing. The weather cross-jack braces and the lee main braces are each belayed together upon two pins, and ready to be let go; and the opposite braces hauled taut. "Main topsail haul!" shouts the captain; the braces are let go; and if he has taken his time well, the yards swing round like a top; but if he is too late, or too soon, it is like drawing teeth. The after yards are then braced up and belayed, the main sheet hauled aft, the spanker eased over to leeward, and the men from the braces stand by the head yards. "Let go and haul!" says the captain; the second mate lets go the weather fore braces, and the men haul in to leeward. The mate, on the forecastle, looks out for the head yards. "Well, the fore topsail yard!" "Top-gallant yard's well!" "Royal yard too much! Haul into windward! So! well that!" "Well all!" Then the starboard watch board the main tack, and the larboard watch lay forward and board the fore tack and haul down the jib sheet, clapping a tackle upon it, if it blows very fresh. The after yards are then trimmed, the captain generally looking out for them himself. "Well the cross-jack yard!" "Small pull the main top-gallant yard!" "Well that!" "Well the mizen top-gallant yard!" "Cross-jack yards all well!" "Well all aft!" "Haul taut to windward!" Everything being now trimmed and in order, each man coils up the rigging at his own station, and the order is given—"Go below the watch!"

During the last twenty-four hours of the passage, we beat off and on the land, making a tack about once in four hours, so that I had a sufficient opportunity to observe the working of the ship; and certainly, it took no more men to brace about this ship's lower yards, which were more than fifty feet square, than it did those of the Pilgrim, which were not much more than half the size; so much depends upon the manner in which the braces run, and the state of the blocks; and Captain Wilson, of the Ayacucho, who was afterwards a passenger with us, upon a trip to windward, said he had no doubt that our ship worked two men lighter than his brig.

Friday, Sept. 11th. This morning, at four o'clock, went below, San Pedro point being about two leagues ahead, and the ship going on under studding-sails. In about an hour we were waked up by the hauling of the chain about decks, and in a few minutes "All hands ahoy!" was called; and we were all at work, hauling in and making up the studding-sails, overhauling the chain forward, and getting the anchors ready. "The Pilgrim is there at anchor," said some one, as we were running about decks; and taking a moment's look over the rail, I saw my old friend, deeply laden, lying at anchor inside of the kelp. In coming to anchor, as well as in tacking, each one had his station and duty. The light sails were clewed up and furled, the courses hauled up and the jibs down; then came the topsails in the buntlines, and the anchor let go. As soon as she was well at anchor, all hands lay aloft to furl the topsails; and this, I soon found, was a great matter on board this ship; for every sailor knows that a vessel is judged of, a good deal, by the furl of her sails. The third mate, a sailmaker, and the larboard watch went upon the fore topsail yard; the second mate, carpenter, and the starboard watch upon the main; and myself and the English lad, and the two Boston boys, and the young Cape-Cod man, furled the mizen topsail. This sail belonged to us altogether, to reef and to furl, and not a man was allowed to come upon our yard. The mate took us under his special care, frequently making us furl the sail over, three or four times, until we got the bunt up to a perfect cone, and the whole sail without a wrinkle. As soon as each sail was hauled up and the bunt made, the jigger was bent on to the slack of the buntlines, and the bunt triced up, on deck. The mate then took his place between the knightheads to "twig" the fore, on the windlass to twig the main, and at the foot of the mainmast, for the mizen; and if anything was wrong,—too much bunt on one side, clews too taut or too slack, or any sail abaft the yard,—the whole must be dropped again. When all was right, the bunts were triced well up, the yard-arm gaskets passed, so as not to leave a wrinkle forward of the yard—short gaskets with turns close together.

From the moment of letting go the anchor, when the captain ceases his care of things, the chief mate is the great man. With a voice like a young lion, he was hallooing and bawling, in all directions, making everything fly, and, at the same time, doing everything well. He was quite a contrast to the worthy, quiet, unobtrusive mate of the Pilgrim; not so estimable a man, perhaps, but a far better mate of a vessel; and the entire change in Captain T——'s conduct, since he took command of the ship, was owing, no doubt, in a great measure, to this fact. If the chief officer wants force, discipline slackens, everything gets out of joint, the captain interferes continually; that makes a difficulty between them, which encourages the crew, and the whole ends in a three-sided quarrel. But Mr. Brown (the mate of the Alert) wanted no help from anybody; took everything into his own hands; and was more likely to encroach upon the authority of the master, than to need any spurring. Captain T—— gave his directions to the mate in private, and, except in coming to anchor, getting under weigh, tacking, reefing topsails, and other "all-hands-work," seldom appeared in person. This is the proper state of things, and while this lasts, and there is a good understanding aft, everything will go on well.

Having furled all the sails, the royal yards were next to be sent down. The English lad and myself sent down the main, which was larger than the Pilgrim's main top-gallant yard; two more light hands, the fore; and one boy, the mizen. This order, we always kept while on the coast; sending them up and down every time we came in and went out of port. They were all tripped and lowered together, the main on the starboard side, and the fore and mizen, to port. No sooner was she all snug, than tackles were got up on the yards and stays, and the long-boat and pinnace hove out. The swinging booms were then guyed out, and the boats made fast by geswarps, and everything in harbor style. After breakfast, the hatches were taken off, and all got ready to receive hides from the Pilgrim. All day, boats were passing and repassing, until we had taken her hides from her, and left her in ballast trim. These hides made but little show in our hold, though they had loaded the Pilgrim down to the water's edge. This changing of the hides settled the question of the destination of the two vessels, which had been one of some speculation to us. We were to remain in the leeward ports, while the Pilgrim was to sail, the next morning, for San Francisco. After we had knocked off work, and cleared up decks for the night, my friend S—— came on board, and spent an hour with me in our berth between decks. The Pilgrim's crew envied me my place on board the ship, and seemed to think that I had got a little to windward of them; especially in the matter of going home first. S—— was determined to go home on the Alert, by begging or buying; if Captain T—— would not let him come on other terms, he would purchase an exchange with some one of the crew. The prospect of another year after the Alert should sail, was rather "too much of the monkey." About seven o'clock, the mate came down into the steerage, in fine trim for fun, roused the boys out of the berth, turned up the carpenter with his fiddle, sent the steward with lights to put in the between-decks, and set all hands to dancing. The between-decks were high enough to allow of jumping; and being clear, and white, from holystoning, made a fine dancing-hall. Some of the Pilgrim's crew were in the forecastle, and we all turned-to and had a regular sailor's shuffle, till eight bells. The Cape-Cod boy could dance the true fisherman's jig, barefooted, knocking with his heels, and slapping the decks with his bare feet, in time with the music. This was a favorite amusement of the mate's, who always stood at the steerage door, looking on, and if the boys would not dance, he hazed them round with a rope's end, much to the amusement of the men.

The next morning, according to the orders of the agent, the Pilgrim set sail for the windward, to be gone three or four months. She got under weigh with very little fuss, and came so near us as to throw a letter on board, Captain Faucon standing at the tiller himself, and steering her as he would a mackerel smack. When Captain T—— was in command of the Pilgrim, there was as much preparation and ceremony as there would be in getting a seventy-four under weigh. Captain Faucon was a sailor, every inch of him; he knew what a ship was, and was as much at home in one, as a cobbler in his stall. I wanted no better proof of this than the opinion of the ship's crew, for they had been six months under his command, and knew what he was; and if sailors allow their captain to be a good seaman, you may be sure he is one, for that is a thing they are not always ready to say.

After the Pilgrim left us, we lay three weeks at San Pedro, from the 11th of September until the 2nd of October, engaged in the usual port duties of landing cargo, taking off hides, etc., etc. These duties were much easier, and went on much more agreeably, than on board the Pilgrim. "The more, the merrier," is the sailor's maxim; and a boat's crew of a dozen could take off all the hides brought down in a day, without much trouble, by division of labor; and on shore, as well as on board, a good will, and no discontent or grumbling, make everything go well. The officer, too, who usually went with us, the third mate, was a fine young fellow, and made no unnecessary trouble; so that we generally had quite a sociable time, and were glad to be relieved from the restraint of the ship. While here, I often thought of the miserable, gloomy weeks we had spent in this dull place, in the brig; discontent and hard usage on board, and four hands to do all the work on shore. Give me a big ship. There is more room, more hands, better outfit, better regulation, more life, and more company. Another thing was better arranged here: we had a regular gig's crew. A light whale-boat, handsomely painted, and fitted out with stern seats, yoke, tiller-ropes, etc., hung on the starboard quarter, and was used as the gig. The youngest lad in the ship, a Boston boy about thirteen years old, was coxswain of this boat, and had the entire charge of her, to keep her clean, and have her in readiness to go and come at any hour. Four light hands, of about the same size and age, of whom I was one, formed the crew. Each had his oar and seat numbered, and we were obliged to be in our places, have our oars scraped white, our tholepins in, and the fenders over the side. The bow-man had charge of the boat-hook and painter, and the coxswain of the rudder, yoke, and stern-sheets. Our duty was to carry the captain and agent about, and passengers off and on; which last was no trifling duty, as the people on shore have no boats, and every purchaser, from the boy who buys his pair of shoes, to the trader who buys his casks and bales, were to be taken off and on, in our boat. Some days, when people were coming and going fast, we were in the boat, pulling off and on, all day long, with hardly time for our meals; making, as we lay nearly three miles from shore, from forty to fifty miles' rowing in a day. Still, we thought it the best berth in the ship; for when the gig was employed, we had nothing to do with the cargo, except small bundles which the passengers carried with them, and no hides to carry, besides the opportunity of seeing everybody, making acquaintances, hearing the news, etc. Unless the captain or agent were in the boat, we had no officer with us, and often had fine times with the passengers, who were always willing to talk and joke with us. Frequently, too, we were obliged to wait several hours on shore; when we would haul the boat up on the beach, and leaving one to watch her, go up to the nearest house, or spend the time in strolling about the beach, picking up shells, or playing hopscotch, and other games, on the hard sand. The rest of the crew never left the ship, except for bringing heavy goods and taking off hides; and though we were always in the water, the surf hardly leaving us a dry thread from morning till night, yet we were young, and the climate was good, and we thought it much better than the quiet, hum-drum drag and pull on board ship. We made the acquaintance of nearly half of California; for, besides carrying everybody in our boat,—men, women, and children,—all the messages, letters, and light packages went by us, and being known by our dress, we found a ready reception everywhere.

At San Pedro, we had none of this amusement, for, there being but one house in the place, we, of course, had but little company. All the variety that I had, was riding, once a week, to the nearest rancho, to order a bullock down for the ship.

The brig Catalina came in from San Diego, and being bound up to windward, we both got under weigh at the same time, for a trial of speed up to Santa Barbara, a distance of about eighty miles. We hove up and got under sail about eleven o'clock at night, with a light land-breeze, which died away toward morning, leaving us becalmed only a few miles from our anchoring-place. The Catalina, being a small vessel, of less than half our size, put out sweeps and got a boat ahead, and pulled out to sea, during the night, so that she had the sea-breeze earlier and stronger than we did, and we had the mortification of seeing her standing up the coast, with a fine breeze, the sea all ruffled about her, while we were becalmed, in-shore. When the sea-breeze died away, she was nearly out of sight; and, toward the latter part of the afternoon, the regular north-west wind set in fresh, we braced sharp upon it, took a pull at every sheet, tack, and halyard, and stood after her, in fine style, our ship being very good upon a tautened bowline. We had nearly five hours of fine sailing, beating up to windward, by long stretches in and off shore, and evidently gaining upon the Catalina at every tack. When this breeze left us, we were so near as to count the painted ports on her side. Fortunately, the wind died away when we were on our inward tack, and she on her outward, so we were in-shore, and caught the land-breeze first, which came off upon our quarter, about the middle of the first watch. All hands were turned-up, and we set all sail, to the skysails and the royal studding-sails; and with these, we glided quietly through the water, leaving the Catalina, which could not spread so much canvas as we, gradually astern, and, by daylight, were off St. Buenaventura, and our antagonist nearly out of sight. The sea-breeze, however, favored her again, while we were becalmed under the headland, and laboring slowly along, she was abreast of us by noon. Thus we continued, ahead, astern, and abreast of one another, alternately; now, far out at sea, and again, close in under the shore. On the third morning, we came into the great bay of Santa Barbara, two hours behind the brig, and thus lost the bet; though, if the race had been to the point, we should have beaten her by five or six hours. This, however, settled the relative sailing of the vessels, for it was admitted that although she, being small and light, could gain upon us in very light winds, yet whenever there was breeze enough to set us agoing, we walked away from her like hauling in a line; and in beating to windward, which is the best trial of a vessel, we had much the advantage of her.

Sunday, Oct. 4th. This was the day of our arrival; and somehow or other, our captain always managed not only to sail, but to come into port, on a Sunday. The main reason for sailing on the Sabbath is not, as many people suppose, because Sunday is thought a lucky day, but because it is a leisure day. During the six days, the crew are employed upon the cargo and other ship's works, and the Sabbath, being their only day of rest, whatever additional work can be thrown into Sunday, is so much gain to the owners. This is the reason of our coasters, packets, etc, sailing on the Sabbath. They get six good days' work out of the crew, and then throw all the labor of sailing into the Sabbath. Thus it was with us, nearly all the time we were on the coast, and many of our Sabbaths were lost entirely to us. The Catholics on shore have no trading and make no journeys on Sunday, but the American has no national religion, and likes to show his independence of priestcraft by doing as he chooses on the Lord's day.

Santa Barbara looked very much as it did when I left it five months before: the long sand beach, with the heavy rollers, breaking upon it in a continual roar, and the little town, imbedded on the plain, girt by its amphitheatre of mountains. Day after day, the sun shone clear and bright upon the wide bay and the red roofs of the houses; everything being as still as death, the people really hardly seeming to earn their sun-light. Daylight actually seemed thrown away upon them. We had a few visitors, and collected about a hundred hides, and every night, at sundown, the gig was sent ashore, to wait for the captain, who spent his evenings in the town. We always took our monkey-jackets with us, and flint and steel, and made a fire on the beach with the driftwood and the bushes we pulled from the neighboring thickets, and lay down by it, on the sand. Sometimes we would stray up to the town, if the captain was likely to stay late, and pass the time at some of the houses, in which we were almost always well received by the inhabitants. Sometimes earlier and sometimes later, the captain came down; when, after a good drenching in the surf, we went aboard, changed our clothes, and turned in for the night—yet not for all the night, for there was the anchor watch to stand.

This leads me to speak of my watchmate for nine months—and, taking him all in all, the most remarkable man I have ever seen—Tom Harris. An hour, every night, while lying in port, Harris and myself had the deck to ourselves, and walking fore and aft, night after night, for months, I learned his whole character and history, and more about foreign nations, the habits of different people, and especially the secrets of sailors' lives and hardships, and also of practical seamanship, (in which he was abundantly capable of instructing me,) than I could ever have learned elsewhere. But the most remarkable thing about him, was the power of his mind. His memory was perfect; seeming to form a regular chain, reaching from his earliest childhood up to the time I knew him, without one link wanting. His power of calculation, too, was remarkable. I called myself pretty quick at figures, and had been through a course of mathematical studies; but, working by my head, I was unable to keep within sight of this man, who had never been beyond his arithmetic: so rapid was his calculation. He carried in his head not only a log-book of the whole voyage, in which everything was complete and accurate, and from which no one ever thought of appealing, but also an accurate registry of all the cargo; knowing, precisely, where each thing was, and how many hides we took in at every port.

One night, he made a rough calculation of the number of hides that could be stowed in the lower hold, between the fore and main masts, taking the depth of hold and breadth of beam, (for he always knew the dimension of every part of the ship, before he had been a month on board,) and the average area and thickness of a hide; he came surprisingly near the number, as it afterwards turned out. The mate frequently came to him to know the capacity of different parts of the vessel, so he could tell the sailmaker very nearly the amount of canvas he would want for each sail in the ship; for he knew the hoist of every mast, and spread of every sail, on the head and foot, in feet and inches. When we were at sea, he kept a running account, in his head, of the ship's way—the number of knots and the courses; and if the courses did not vary much during the twenty-four hours, by taking the whole progress, and allowing so many eighths southing or northing, to so many easting or westing; he would make up his reckoning just before the captain took the sun at noon, and often came wonderfully near the mark. Calculation of all kinds was his delight. He had, in his chest, several volumes giving accounts of inventions in mechanics, which he read with great pleasure, and made himself master of. I doubt if he ever forgot anything that he read. The only thing in the way of poetry that he ever read was Falconer's Shipwreck, which he was delighted with, and whole pages of which he could repeat. He knew the name of every sailor that had ever been his shipmate, and also, of every vessel, captain, and officer, and the principal dates of each voyage; and a sailor whom he afterwards fell in with, who had been in a ship with Harris nearly twelve years before, was very much surprised at having Harris tell him things about himself which he had entirely forgotten. His facts, whether dates or events, no one thought of disputing; and his opinions, few of the sailors dared to oppose; for, right or wrong, he always had the best of the argument with them. His reasoning powers were remarkable. I have had harder work maintaining an argument with him in a watch, even when I knew myself to be right, and he was only doubting, than I ever had before; not from his obstinacy, but from his acuteness. Give him only a little knowledge of his subject, and, certainly among all the young men of my acquaintance and standing at college, there was not one whom I had not rather meet, than this man. I never answered a question from him, or advanced an opinion to him, without thinking more than once. With an iron memory, he seemed to have your whole past conversation at command, and if you said a thing now which ill agreed with something said months before, he was sure to have you on the hip. In fact, I always felt, when with him, that I was with no common man. I had a positive respect for his powers of mind, and felt often that if half the pains had been spent upon his education which are thrown away, yearly, in our colleges, he would have been a man of great weight in society. Like most self-taught men, he over-estimated the value of an education; and this, I often told him, though I profited by it myself; for he always treated me with respect, and often unnecessarily gave way to me, from an over-estimate of my knowledge. For the intellectual capacities of all the rest of the crew, captain and all, he had the most sovereign contempt. He was a far better sailor, and probably a better navigator, than the captain, and had more brains than all the after part of the ship put together. The sailors said, "Tom's got a head as long as the bowsprit," and if any one got into an argument with him, they would call out—"Ah, Jack! you'd better drop that, as you would a hot potato, for Tom will turn you inside out before you know it."

I recollect his posing me once on the subject of the Corn Laws. I was called to stand my watch, and, coming on deck, found him there before me; and we began, as usual, to walk fore and aft, in the waist. He talked about the Corn Laws; asked me my opinion about them, which I gave him; and my reasons; my small stock of which I set forth to the best advantage, supposing his knowledge on the subject must be less than mine, if, indeed, he had any at all. When I had got through, he took the liberty of differing from me, and, to my surprise, brought arguments and facts connected with the subject which were new to me, to which I was entirely unable to reply. I confessed that I knew almost nothing of the subject, and expressed my surprise at the extent of his information. He said that, a number of years before, while at a boarding-house in Liverpool, he had fallen in with a pamphlet on the subject, and, as it contained calculations, had read it very carefully, and had ever since wished to find some one who could add to his stock of knowledge on the question. Although it was many years since he had seen the book, and it was a subject with which he had no previous acquaintance, yet he had the chain of reasoning, founded upon principles of political economy, perfect in his memory; and his facts, so far as I could judge, were correct; at least, he stated them with great precision. The principles of the steam engine, too, he was very familiar with, having been several months on board of a steamboat, and made himself master of its secrets. He knew every lunar star in both hemispheres, and was a perfect master of his quadrant and sextant. Such was the man, who, at forty, was still a dog before the mast, at twelve dollars a month. The reason of this was to be found in his whole past life, as I had it, at different times, from himself.

He was an Englishman, by birth, a native of Ilfracomb, in Devonshire. His father was skipper of a small coaster, from Bristol, and dying, left him, when quite young, to the care of his mother, by whose exertions he received a common-school education, passing his winters at school and his summers in the coasting trade, until his seventeenth year, when he left home to go upon foreign voyages. Of his mother, he often spoke with the greatest respect, and said that she was a strong-minded woman, and had the best system of education he had ever known; a system which had made respectable men of his three brothers, and failed only in him, from his own indomitable obstinacy. One thing he often mentioned, in which he said his mother differed from all other mothers that he had ever seen disciplining their children; that was, that when he was out of humor and refused to eat, instead of putting his plate away, as most mothers would, and saying that his hunger would bring him to it, in time, she would stand over him and oblige him to eat it—every mouthful of it. It was no fault of hers that he was what I saw him; and so great was his sense of gratitude for her efforts, though unsuccessful, that he determined, at the close of thc voyage, to embark for home with all the wages he should get, to spend with and for his mother, if perchance he should find her alive.

After leaving home, he had spent nearly twenty years, sailing upon all sorts of voyages, generally out of the ports of New York and Boston. Twenty years of vice! Every sin that a sailor knows, he had gone to the bottom of. Several times he had been hauled up in the hospitals, and as often, the great strength of his constitution had brought him out again in health. Several times, too, from his known capacity, he had been promoted to the office of chief mate, and as often, his conduct when in port, especially his drunkenness, which neither fear nor ambition could induce him to abandon, put him back into the forecastle. One night, when giving me an account of his life, and lamenting the years of manhood he had thrown away, he said that there, in the forecastle, at the foot of the steps—a chest of old clothes—was the result of twenty-two years of hard labor and exposure—worked like a horse, and treated like a dog. As he grew older, he began to feel the necessity of some provision for his later years, and came gradually to the conviction that rum had been his worst enemy. One night, in Havana, a young shipmate of his was brought aboard drunk, with a dangerous gash in his head, and his money and new clothes stripped from him. Harris had seen and been in hundreds of such scenes as these, but in his then state of mind, it fixed his determination, and he resolved never to taste another drop of strong drink, of any kind. He signed no pledge, and made no vow, but relied on his own strength of purpose. The first thing with him was a reason, and then a resolution, and the thing was done. The date of his resolution he knew, of course, to the very hour. It was three years before I knew him, and during all that time, nothing stronger than cider or coffee had passed his lips. The sailors never thought of enticing Tom to take a glass, any more than they would of talking to the ship's compass. He was now a temperate man for life, and capable of filling any berth in a ship, and many a high station there is on shore which is held by a meaner man.

He understood the management of a ship upon scientific principles, and could give the reason for hauling every rope; and a long experience, added to careful observation at the time, and a perfect memory, gave him a knowledge of the expedients and resorts in times of hazard, which was remarkable, and for which I became much indebted to him, as he took the greatest pleasure in opening his stores of information to me, in return for what I was able to do for him. Stories of tyranny and hardship which had driven men to piracy;—of the incredible ignorance of masters and mates, and of horrid brutality to the sick, dead, and dying; as well as of the secret knavery and impositions practised upon seamen by connivance of the owners, landlords, and officers; all these he had, and I could not but believe them; for men who had known him for fifteen years had never taken him even in an exaggeration, and, as I have said, his statements were never disputed. I remember, among other things, his speaking of a captain whom I had known by report, who never handed a thing to a sailor, but put it on deck and kicked it to him; and of another, who was of the best connections in Boston, who absolutely murdered a lad from Boston that went out with him before the mast to Sumatra, by keeping him hard at work while ill of the coast fever, and obliging him to sleep in the close steerage. (The same captain has since died of the same fever on the same coast.)

In fact, taking together all that I learned from him of seamanship, of the history of sailors' lives, of practical wisdom, and of human nature under new circumstances,—a great history from which many are shut out,—I would not part with the hours I spent in the watch with that man for any given hours of my life passed in study and social intercourse.

CHAPTER XXIV

SAN DIEGO AGAIN—A DESCENT—HURRIED DEPARTURE—A NEW SHIPMATE

Sunday, Oct. 11th. Set sail this morning for the leeward; passed within sight of San Pedro, and, to our great joy, did not come to anchor, but kept directly on to San Diego, where we arrived and moored ship on.

Thursday, Oct. 15th. Found here the Italian ship La Rosa, from the windward, which reported the brig Pilgrim at San Francisco, all well. Everything was as quiet here as usual. We discharged our hides, horns, and tallow, and were ready to sail again on the following Sunday. I went ashore to my old quarters, and found the gang at the hide-house going on in the even tenor of their way, and spent an hour or two, after dark, at the oven, taking a whiff with my old Kanaka friends, who really seemed glad to see me again, and saluted me as the Aikane of the Kanakas. I was grieved to find that my poor dog Bravo was dead. He had sickened and died suddenly, the very day after I sailed in the Alert.

Sunday was again, as usual, our sailing day, and we got under weigh with a stiff breeze, which reminded us that it was the latter part of the autumn, and time to expect south-easters once more. We beat up against a strong head wind, under reefed top-sails, as far as San Juan, where we came to anchor nearly three miles from the shore, with slip-ropes on our cables, in the old south-easter style of last winter. On the passage up, we had an old sea captain on board, who had married and settled in California, and had not been on salt water for more than fifteen years. He was astonished at the changes and improvements that had been made in ships, and still more at the manner in which we carried sail; for he was really a little frightened; and said that while we had top-gallant sails on, he should have been under reefed topsails. The working of the ship, and her progress to windward, seemed to delight him, for he said she went to windward as though she were kedging.

Tuesday, Oct. 20th. Having got everything ready, we set the agent ashore, who went up to the mission to hasten down the hides for the next morning. This night we had the strictest orders to look out for south-easters; and the long, low clouds seemed rather threatening. But the night passed over without any trouble, and early the next morning, we hove out the long-boat and pinnace, lowered away the quarter-boats, and went ashore to bring off our hides. Here we were again, in this romantic spot; a perpendicular hill, twice the height of the ship's mast-head, with a single circuitous path to the top, and long sand beach at its base, with the swell of the whole Pacific breaking high upon it, and our hides ranged in piles on the overhanging summit. The captain sent me, who was the only one of the crew that had ever been there before, to the top, to count the hides and pitch them down. There I stood again, as six months before, throwing off the hides, and watching them, pitching and scaling, to the bottom, while the men, dwarfed by the distance, were walking to and fro on the beach, carrying the hides, as they picked them up, to the distant boats, upon the tops of their heads. Two or three boat-loads were sent off, until, at last, all were thrown down, and the boats nearly loaded again; when we were delayed by a dozen or twenty hides which had lodged in the recesses of the hill, and which we could not reach by any missiles, as the general line of the side was exactly perpendicular, and these places were caved in, and could not be seen or reached from the top. As hides are worth in Boston twelve and a half cents a pound, and the captain's commission was two per cent, he determined not to give them up; and sent on board for a pair of top-gallant studding-sail halyards, and requested some one of the crew to go to the top, and come down by the halyards. The older sailors said the boys, who were light and active, ought to go, while the boys thought that strength and experience were necessary. Seeing the dilemma, and feeling myself to be near the medium of these requisites, I offered my services, and went up, with one man to tend the rope, and prepared for the descent.

We found a stake fastened strongly into the ground, and apparently capable of holding my weight, to which we made one end of the halyards well fast, and taking the coil, threw it over the brink. The end, we saw, just reached to a landing-place, from which the descent to the beach was easy. Having nothing on but shirt, trowsers, and hat, the common sea-rig of warm weather, I had no stripping to do, and began my descent, by taking hold of the rope in each hand, and slipping down, sometimes with hands and feet round the rope, and sometimes breasting off with one hand and foot against the precipice, and holding on to the rope with the other. In this way I descended until I came to a place which shelved in, and in which the hides were lodged. Keeping hold of the rope with one hand, I scrambled in, and by the other hand and feet succeeded in dislodging all the hides, and continued on my way. Just below this place, the precipice projected again, and going over the projection, I could see nothing below me but the sea and the rocks upon which it broke, and a few gulls flying in mid-air. I got down in safety, pretty well covered with dirt; and for my pains was told, "What a d—d fool you were to risk your life for a half a dozen hides!"

While we were carrying the hides to the boat, I perceived, what I had been too busy to observe before, that heavy black clouds were rolling up from seaward, a strong swell heaving in, and every sign of a south-easter. The captain hurried everything. The hides were pitched into the boats; and, with some difficulty, and by wading nearly up to our armpits, we got the boats through the surf, and began pulling aboard. Our gig's crew towed the pinnace astern of the gig, and the launch was towed by six men in the jolly-boat. The ship was lying three miles off, pitching at her anchor, and the farther we pulled, the heavier grew the swell. Our boat stood nearly up and down several times; the pinnace parted her towline, and we expected every moment to see the launch swamped. We at length got alongside, our boats half full of water; and now came the greatest difficulty of all,—unloading the boats, in a heavy sea, which pitched them about so that it was almost impossible to stand in them; raising them sometimes even with the rail, and again dropping them below the bends. With great difficulty, we got all the hides aboard and stowed under hatches, the yard and stay tackles hooked on, and the launch and pinnace hoisted, checked, and griped. The quarter-boats were then hoisted up, and we began heaving in on the chain. Getting the anchor was no easy work in such a sea, but as we were not coming back to this port, the captain determined not to slip. The ship's head pitched into the sea, and the water rushed through the hawse-holes, and the chain surged so as almost to unship the barrel of the windlass. "Hove short, sir!" said the mate. "Aye, aye! Weather-bit your chain and loose the topsails! Make sail on her, men—with a will!" A few moments served to loose the topsails, which were furled with reefs, to sheet them home, and hoist them up. "Bear a hand!" was the order of the day; and every one saw the necessity of it, for the gale was already upon us. The ship broke out her own anchor, which we catted and fished, after a fashion, and stood off from the lee-shore against a heavy head sea, under reefed topsails, fore-topmast staysail and spanker. The fore course was given to her, which helped her a little; but as she hardly held her own against the sea which was settling her leeward—"Board the main tack!" shouted the captain; when the tack was carried forward and taken to the windlass, and all hands called to the handspikes. The great sail bellied out horizontally as though it would lift up the main stay; the blocks rattled and flew about; but the force of machinery was too much for her. "Heave ho! Heave and pawl! Yo, heave, hearty, ho!" and, in time with the song, by the force of twenty strong arms, the windlass came slowly round, pawl after pawl, and the weather clew of the sail was brought down to the waterways. The starboard watch hauled aft the sheet, and the ship tore through the water like a mad horse, quivering and shaking at every joint, and dashing from its head the foam, which flew off at every blow, yards and yards to leeward. A half hour of such sailing served our turn, when the clews of the sail were hauled up, the sail furled, and the ship, eased of her press, went more quietly on her way. Soon after, the foresail was reefed, and we mizen-top men were sent up to take another reef in the mizen topsail. This was the first time I had taken a weather earing, and I felt not a little proud to sit, astride of the weather yard-arm, pass the earing, and sing out "Haul out to leeward!" From this time until we got to Boston, the mate never suffered any one but our own gang to go upon the mizen topsail yard, either for reefing or furling, and the young English lad and myself generally took the earings between us.

Having cleared the point and got well out to sea, we squared away the yards, made more sail, and stood on, nearly before the wind, for San Pedro. It blew strong, with some rain, nearly all night, but fell calm toward morning, and the gale having gone over, we came-to,—

Thursday, Oct. 22d, at San Pedro, in the old south-easter berth, a league from shore, with a slip-rope on the cable, reefs in the topsails, and rope-yarns for gaskets. Here we lay ten days, with the usual boating, hide-carrying, rolling of cargo up the steep hill, walking barefooted over stones, and getting drenched in salt water.

The third day after our arrival, the Rosa came in from San Juan, where she went the day after the south-easter. Her crew said it was as smooth as a mill-pond, after the gale, and she took off nearly a thousand hides, which had been brought down for us, and which we lost in consequence of the south-easter. This mortified us; not only that an Italian ship should have got to windward of us in the trade, but because every thousand hides went toward completing the forty thousand which we were to collect before we could say good-by to California.

While lying here, we shipped one new hand, an Englishman, of about two or three and twenty, who was quite an acquisition, as he proved to be a good sailor, could sing tolerably, and, what was of more importance to me, had a good education, and a somewhat remarkable history. He called himself George P. Marsh; professed to have been at sea from a small boy, and to have served his time in the smuggling trade between Germany and the coasts of France and England. Thus he accounted for his knowledge of the French language, which he spoke and read as well as he did English; but his cutter education would not account for his English, which was far too good to have been learned in a smuggler; for he wrote an uncommonly handsome hand, spoke with great correctness, and frequently, when in private talk with me, quoted from books, and showed a knowledge of the customs of society, and particularly of the formalities of the various English courts of law, and of Parliament, which surprised me. Still, he would give no other account of himself than that he was educated in a smuggler. A man whom we afterwards fell in with, who had been a shipmate of George's a few years before, said that he heard at the boarding-house from which they shipped, that George had been at college, (probably a naval one, as he knew no Latin or Greek,) where he learned French and mathematics. He was by no means the man by nature that Harris was. Harris had made everything of his mind and character in spite of obstacles; while this man had evidently been born in a different rank, and educated early in life accordingly, but had been a vagabond, and done nothing for himself since. What had been given to him by others, was all that made him to differ from those about him; while Harris had made himself what he was. Neither had George the character, strength of mind, acuteness, or memory of Harris; yet there was about him the remains of a pretty good education, which enabled him to talk perhaps beyond his brains, and a high spirit and sense of honor, which years of a dog's life had not broken. After he had been a little while on board, we learned from him his remarkable history, for the last two years, which we afterwards heard confirmed in such a manner, as put the truth of it beyond a doubt.

He sailed from New York in the year 1833, if I mistake not, before the mast, in the brig Lascar, for Canton. She was sold in the East Indies, and he shipped at Manilla, in a small schooner, bound on a trading voyage among the Ladrone and Pelew Islands. On one of the latter islands, their schooner was wrecked on a reef, and they were attacked by the natives, and, after a desperate resistance, in which all their number except the captain, George, and a boy, were killed or drowned, they surrendered, and were carried bound, in a canoe, to a neighboring island. In about a month after this, an opportunity occurred by which one of their number might get away. I have forgotten the circumstances, but only one could go, and they yielded to the captain, upon his promising to send them aid if he escaped. He was successful in his attempt; got on board an American vessel, went back to Manilla, and thence to America, without making any effort for their rescue, or indeed, as George afterwards discovered, without even mentioning their case to any one in Manilla. The boy that was with George died, and he being alone, and there being no chance for his escape, the natives soon treated him with kindness, and even with attention. They painted him, tattooed his body, (for he would never consent to be marked in the face or hands,) gave him two or three wives; and, in fact, made quite a pet of him. In this way, he lived for thirteen months, in a fine climate, with a plenty to eat, half naked, and nothing to do. He soon, however, became tired, and went round the island, on different pretences, to look out for a sail. One day, he was out fishing in a small canoe with another man, when he saw a large sail to the windward, about a league and a half off, passing abreast of the island and standing westward. With some difficulty, he persuaded the islander to go off with him to the ship, promising to return with a good supply of rum and tobacco. These articles, which the islanders had got a taste of from American traders, were too strong a temptation for the fellow, and he consented. They paddled off in the track of the ship, and lay-to until she came down to them. George stepped on board the ship, nearly naked, painted from head to foot, and in no way distinguishable from his companion until he began to speak. Upon this, the people on board were not a little astonished; and, having learned his story, the captain had him washed and clothed, and sending away the poor astonished native with a knife or two and some tobacco and calico, took George with him on the voyage. This was the ship Cabot, of New York, Captain Low. She was bound to Manilla, from across the Pacific, and George did seaman's duty in her until her arrival in Manilla, when he left her, and shipped in a brig bound to the Sandwich Islands. From Oahu, he came, in the British brig Clementine, to Monterey, as second officer, where, having some difficulty with the captain, he left her, and coming down the coast, joined us at San Pedro. Nearly six months after this, among some papers we received by an arrival from Boston, we found a letter from Captain Low, of the Cabot, published immediately upon his arrival at New York, and giving all the particulars just as we had them from George. The letter was published for the information of the friends of George, and Captain Low added, that he left him at Manilia to go to Oahu, and he had heard nothing of him since.

George had an interesting journal of his adventures in the Pelew Islands, which he had written out at length, in a handsome hand, and in correct English.

CHAPTER XXV

RUMORS OF WAR—A SPOUTER—SLIPPING FOR A SOUTH-EASTER—A GALE

Sunday, November 1st. Sailed this day, (Sunday again,) for Santa Barbara, where we arrived on the 5th. Coming round St. Buenaventura, and nearing the anchorage, we saw two vessels in port, a large full-rigged, and a small hermaphrodite brig. The former, the crew said must be the Pilgrim; but I had been too long in the Pilgrim to be mistaken in her, and I was right in differing from them; for, upon nearer approach, her long, low shear, sharp bows, and raking masts, told quite another story. "Man-of-war brig," said some of them; "Baltimore clipper," said others; the Ayacucho, thought I; and soon the broad folds of the beautiful banner of St. George,—white field with blood-red border and cross,—were displayed from her peak. A few minutes put it beyond a doubt, and we were lying by the side of the Ayacucho, which had sailed from San Diego about nine months before, while we were lying there in the Pilgrim. She had since been to Valparaiso, Callao, and the Sandwich Islands, and had just come upon the coast. Her boat came on board, bringing Captain Wilson; and in half an hour the news was all over the ship that there was a war between the United States and France. Exaggerated accounts reached the forecastle. Battles had been fought, a large French fleet was in the Pacific, etc., etc.; and one of the boat's crew of the Ayacucho said that when they left Callao, a large French frigate and the American frigate Brandywine, which were lying there, were going outside to have a battle, and that the English frigate Blonde was to be umpire, and see fair play. Here was important news for us. Alone, on an unprotected coast, without an American man-of-war within some thousands of miles, and the prospect of a voyage home through the whole length of the Pacific and Atlantic oceans! A French prison seemed a much more probable place of destination than the good port of Boston. However, we were too salt to believe every yarn that comes into the forecastle, and waited to hear the truth of the matter from higher authority. By means of a supercargo's clerk, I got the account of the matter, which was, that the governments had had difficulty about the payment of a debt; that war had been threatened and prepared for, but not actually declared, although it was pretty generally anticipated. This was not quite so bad, yet was no small cause of anxiety. But we cared very little about the matter ourselves. "Happy go lucky" with Jack! We did not believe that a French prison would be much worse than "hide-droghing" on the coast of California; and no one who has not been on a long, dull voyage, shut up in one ship, can conceive of the effect of monotony upon one's thoughts and wishes. The prospect of a change is like a green spot in a desert, and the remotest probability of great events and exciting scenes gives a feeling of delight, and sets life in motion, so as to give a pleasure, which any one not in the same state would be entirely unable to account for. In fact, a more jovial night we had not passed in the forecastle for months. Every one seemed in unaccountably high spirits. An undefined anticipation of radical changes, of new scenes, and great doings, seemed to have possessed every one, and the common drudgery of the vessel appeared contemptible. Here was a new vein opened; a grand theme of conversation, and a topic for all sorts of discussions. National feeling was wrought up. Jokes were cracked upon the only Frenchman in the ship, and comparisons made between "old horse" and "soup meagre," etc., etc.

We remained in uncertainty as to this war for more than two months, when an arrival from the Sandwich Islands brought us the news of an amicable arrangement of the difficulties.

The other vessel which we found in port was the hermaphrodite brig Avon, from the Sandwich Islands. She was fitted up in handsome style; fired a gun and ran her ensign up and down at sunrise and sunset; had a band of four or five pieces of music on board, and appeared rather like a pleasure yacht than a trader; yet, in connection with the Loriotte, Clementine, Bolivar, Convoy, and other small vessels, belonging to sundry Americans at Oahu, she carried on a great trade—legal and illegal—in otter skins, silks, teas, specie, etc.

The second day after our arrival, a full-rigged brig came round the point from the northward, sailed leisurely through the bay, and stood off again for the south-east, in the direction of the large island of Catalina. The next day the Avon got under weigh, and stood in the same direction, bound for San Pedro. This might do for marines and Californians, but we knew the ropes too well. The brig was never again seen on the coast, and the Avon arrived at San Pedro in about a week, with a full cargo of Canton and American goods.

This was one of the means of escaping the heavy duties the Mexicans lay upon all imports. A vessel comes on the coast, enters a moderate cargo at Monterey, which is the only custom-house, and commences trading. In a month or more, having sold a large part of her cargo, she stretches over to Catalina, or other of the large uninhabited islands which lie off the coast, in a trip from port to port, and supplies herself with choice goods from a vessel from Oahu, which has been lying off and on the islands, waiting for her. Two days after the sailing of the Avon, the Loriotte came in from the leeward, and without doubt had also a snatch at the brig's cargo.

Tuesday, Nov. 10th. Going ashore, as usual, in the gig, just before sundown, to bring off the captain, we found, upon taking in the captain and pulling off again, that our ship, which lay the farthest out, had run up her ensign. This meant "Sail ho!" of course, but as we were within the point we could see nothing. "Give way, boys! Give way! Lay out on your oars, and long stroke!" said the captain; and stretching to the whole length of our arms, bending back again, so that our backs touched the thwarts, we sent her through the water like a rocket. A few minutes of such pulling opened the islands, one after another, in range of the point, and gave us a view of the Canal, where was a ship, under top-gallant sails, standing in, with a light breeze, for the anchorage. Putting the boat's head in the direction of the ship, the captain told us to lay out again; and we needed no spurring, for the prospect of boarding a new ship, perhaps from home, hearing the news and having something to tell of when we got back, was excitement enough for us, and we gave way with a will. Captain Nye, of the Loriotte, who had been an old whaleman, was in the stern-sheets, and fell mightily into the spirit of it. "Bend your backs and break your oars!" said he. "Lay me on, Captain Bunker!" "There she flukes!" and other exclamations, peculiar to whalemen. In the meantime, it fell flat calm, and being within a couple of miles of the ship, we expected to board her in a few moments, when a sudden breeze sprung up, dead ahead for the ship, and she braced up and stood off toward the islands, sharp on the larboard tack, making good way through the water. This, of course, brought us up, and we had only to "ease larboard oars; pull round starboard!" and go aboard the Alert, with something very like a flea in the ear. There was a light land-breeze all night, and the ship did not come to anchor until the next morning. As soon as her anchor was down, we went aboard, and found her to be the whaleship, Wilmington and Liverpool Packet, of New Bedford, last from the "off-shore ground," with nineteen hundred barrels of oil. A "spouter" we knew her to be as soon as we saw her, by her cranes and boats, and by her stump top-gallant masts, and a certain slovenly look to the sails, rigging, spars and hull; and when we got on board, we found everything to correspond,—spouter fashion. She had a false deck, which was rough and oily, and cut up in every direction by the chimes of oil casks; her rigging was slack and turning white; no paint on the spars or blocks; clumsy seizings and straps without covers, and homeward-bound splices in every direction. Her crew, too, were not in much better order. Her captain was a slab-sided, shamble-legged Quaker, in a suit of brown, with a broad-brimmed hat, and sneaking about decks, like a sheep, with his head down; and the men looked more like fishermen and farmers than they did like sailors.

Though it was by no means cold weather, (we having on only our red shirts and duck trowsers,) they all had on woollen trowsers—not blue and shipshape—but of all colors—brown, drab, grey, aye, and green, with suspenders over their shoulders, and pockets to put their hands in. This, added to guernsey frocks, striped comforters about the neck, thick cowhide boots, woollen caps, and a strong, oily smell, and a decidedly green look, will complete the description. Eight or ten were on the fore-topsail yard, and as many more in the main, furling the topsails, while eight or ten were hanging about the forecastle, doing nothing. This was a strange sight for a vessel coming to anchor; so we went up to them, to see what was the matter. One of them, a stout, hearty-looking fellow, held out his leg and said he had the scurvy; another had cut his hand; and others had got nearly well, but said that there were plenty aloft to furl the sails, so they were sogering on the forecastle. There was only one "splicer" on board, a fine-looking old tar, who was in the bunt of the fore-topsail. He was probably the only sailor in the ship, before the mast. The mates, of course, and the boat-steerers, and also two or three of the crew, had been to sea before, but only whaling voyages; and the greater part of the crew were raw hands, just from the bush, as green as cabbages, and had not yet got the hay-seed out of their heads. The mizen topsail hung in the bunt-lines until everything was furled forward. Thus a crew of thirty men were half an hour in doing what would have been done in the Alert with eighteen hands to go aloft, in fifteen or twenty minutes.

We found they had been at sea six or eight months, and had no news to tell us; so we left them, and promised to get liberty to come on board in the evening, for some curiosities, etc. Accordingly, as soon as we were knocked off in the evening and had got supper, we obtained leave, took a boat, and went aboard and spent an hour or two. They gave us pieces of whalebone, and the teeth and other parts of curious sea animals, and we exchanged books with them—a practice very common among ships in foreign ports, by which you get rid of the books you have read and re-read, and a supply of new ones in their stead, and Jack is not very nice as to their comparative value.

Thursday, Nov. 12th. This day was quite cool in the early part, and there were black clouds about; but as it was often so in the morning, nothing was apprehended, and all the captains went ashore together, to spend the day. Towards noon, the clouds hung heavily over the mountains, coming half way down the hills that encircle the town of Santa Barbara, and a heavy swell rolled in from the south-east. The mate immediately ordered the gig's crew away, and at the same time, we saw boats pulling ashore from the other vessels. Here was a grand chance for a rowing match, and every one did his best. We passed the boats of the Ayacucho and Loriotte, but could gain nothing upon, and indeed, hardly hold our own with, the long, six-oared boat of the whale-ship. They reached the breakers before us; but here we had the advantage of them, for, not being used to the surf, they were obliged to wait to see us beach our boat, just as, in the same place, nearly a year before, we, in the Pilgrim, were glad to be taught by a boat's crew of Kanakas.

We had hardly got the boats beached, and their heads out, before our old friend, Bill Jackson, the handsome English sailor, who steered the Loriotte's boat, called out that the brig was adrift; and, sure enough, she was dragging her anchors, and drifting down into the bight of the bay. Without waiting for the captain, (for there was no one on board but the mate and steward,) he sprung into the boat, called the Kanakas together, and tried to put off. But the Kanakas, though capital water-dogs, were frightened by their vessel's being adrift, and by the emergency of the case, and seemed to lose their faculties. Twice, their boat filled, and came broadside upon the beach. Jackson swore at them for a parcel of savages, and promised to flog every one of them. This made the matter no better; when we came forward, told the Kanakas to take their seats in the boat, and, going two on each side, walked out with her till it was up to our shoulders, and gave them a shove, when, giving way with their oars, they got her safely into the long, regular swell. In the mean time, boats had put off from our ships and the whaler, and coming all on board the brig together, they let go the other anchor, paid out chain, braced the yards to the wind, and brought the vessel up.

In a few minutes, the captains came hurrying down, on the run; and there was no time to be lost, for the gale promised to be a severe one, and the surf was breaking upon the beach, three deep, higher and higher every instant. The Ayacucho's boat, pulled by four Kanakas, put off first, and as they had no rudder or steering oar, would probably never have got off, had we not waded out with them, as far as the surf would permit. The next that made the attempt was the whale-boat, for we, being the most experienced "beach-combers," needed no help, and staid till the last. Whalemen make the best boats' crews in the world for a long pull, but this landing was new to them, and notwithstanding the examples they had had, they slued round and were hove up—boat, oars, and men—altogether, high and dry upon the sand. The second time, they filled, and had to turn their boat over, and set her off again. We could be of no help to them, for they were so many as to be in one another's way, without the addition of our numbers. The third time, they got off, though not without shipping a sea which drenched them all, and half filled their boat, keeping them baling, until they reached their ship. We now got ready to go off, putting the boat's head out; English Ben and I, who were the largest, standing on each side of the bows, to keep her "head on" to the sea, two more shipping and manning the two after oars, and the captain taking the steering oar. Two or three Spaniards, who stood upon the beach looking at us, wrapped their cloaks about them, shook their heads, and muttered "Caramba!" They had no taste for such doings; in fact, the hydrophobia is a national malady, and shows itself in their persons as well as their actions.

Watching for a "smooth chance," we determined to show the other boats the way it should be done; and, as soon as ours floated, ran out with her, keeping her head on, with all our strength, and the help of the captain's oar, and the two after oarsmen giving way regularly and strongly, until our feet were off the ground, we tumbled into the bows, keeping perfectly still, from fear of hindering the others. For some time it was doubtful how it would go. The boat stood nearly up and down in the water, and the sea, rolling from under her, let her fall upon the water with a force which seemed almost to stave her bottom in. By quietly sliding two oars forward, along the thwarts, without impeding the rowers, we shipped two bow oars, and thus, by the help of four oars and the captain's strong arm, we got safely off, though we shipped several seas, which left us half full of water. We pulled alongside of the Loriotte, put her skipper on board, and found her making preparations for slipping, and then pulled aboard our own ship. Here Mr. Brown, always "on hand," had got everything ready, so that we had only to hook on the gig and hoist it up, when the order was given to loose the sails. While we were on the yards, we saw the Loriotte under weigh, and before our yards were mast-headed, the Ayacucho had spread her wings, and, with yards braced sharp up, was standing athwart our hawse. There is no prettier sight in the world than a full-rigged, clipper-built brig, sailing sharp on the wind. In a moment, our slip-rope was gone, the head-yards filled away, and we were off. Next came the whaler; and in a half an hour from the time when four vessels were lying quietly at anchor, without a rag out, or a sign of motion, the bay was deserted, and four white clouds were standing off to sea. Being sure of clearing the point, we stood off with our yards a little braced in, while the Ayacucho went off with a taut bowline, which brought her to windward of us. During all this day, and the greater part of the night, we had the usual south-easter entertainment, a gale of wind, variegated and finally topped off with a drenching rain of three or four hours. At daybreak, the clouds thinned off and rolled away, and the sun came up clear. The wind, instead of coming out from the northward, as is usual, blew steadily and freshly from the anchoring-ground. This was bad for us, for, being "flying light," with little more than ballast trim, we were in no condition for showing off on a taut bowline, and had depended upon a fair wind, with which, by the help of our light sails and studding-sails, we meant to have been the first at the anchoring-ground; but the Ayacucho was a good league to windward of us, and was standing in, in fine style. The whaler, however, was as far to leeward of us, and the Loriotte was nearly out of sight, among the islands, up the Canal. By hauling every brace and bowline, and clapping watch-tackles upon all the sheets and halyards, we managed to hold our own, and drop the leeward vessels a little in every tack. When we reached the anchoring-ground, the Ayacucho had got her anchor, furled her sails, squared her yards, and was lying as quietly as if nothing had happened for the last twenty-four hours.

We had our usual good luck in getting our anchor without letting go another, and were all snug, with our boats at the boom-ends, in half an hour. In about two hours more, the whaler came in, and made a clumsy piece of work in getting her anchor, being obliged to let go her best bower, and finally, to get out a kedge and a hawser. They were heave-ho-ing, stopping and unstopping, pawling, catting, and fishing, for three hours; and the sails hung from the yards all the afternoon, and were not furled until sundown. The Loriotte came in just after dark, and let go her anchor, making no attempt to pick up the other until the next day.

This affair led to a great dispute as to the sailing of our ship and the Ayacucho. Bets were made between the captains, and the crews took it up in their own way; but as she was bound to leeward and we to windward, and merchant captains cannot deviate, a trial never took place; and perhaps it was well for us that it did not, for the Ayacucho had been eight years in the Pacific, in every part of it—Valparaiso, Sandwich Islands, Canton, California, and all, and was called the fastest merchantman that traded in the Pacific, unless it was the brig John Gilpin, and perhaps the ship Ann McKim of Baltimore.

Saturday, Nov. 14th. This day we got under weigh, with the agent and several Spaniards of note, as passengers, bound up to Monterey. We went ashore in the gig to bring them off with their baggage, and found them waiting on the beach, and a little afraid about going off, as the surf was running very high. This was nuts to us; for we liked to have a Spaniard wet with salt water; and then the agent was very much disliked by the crew, one and all; and we hoped, as there was no officer in the boat, to have a chance to duck them; for we knew that they were such "marines" that they would not know whether it was our fault or not. Accordingly, we kept the boat so far from shore as to oblige them to wet their feet in getting into her; and then waited for a good high comber, and letting the head slue a little round, sent the whole force of the sea into the stern-sheets, drenching them from head to feet. The Spaniards sprang out of the boat, swore, and shook themselves and protested against trying it again; and it was with the greatest difficulty that the agent could prevail upon them to make another attempt. The next time we took care, and went off easily enough, and pulled aboard. The crew came to the side to hoist in their baggage, and we gave them the wink, and they heartily enjoyed the half-drowned looks of the company.

Everything being now ready, and the passengers aboard, we ran up the ensign and broad pennant, (for there was no man-of-war, and we were the largest vessel on the coast,) and the other vessels ran up their ensigns. Having hove short, cast off the gaskets, and made the bunt of each sail fast by the jigger, with a man on each yard; at the word, the whole canvas of the ship was loosed, and with the greatest rapidity possible, everything was sheeted home and hoisted up, the anchor tripped and catheaded, and the ship under headway. We were determined to show the "spouter" how things could be done in a smart ship, with a good crew, though not more than half their number. The royal yards were all crossed at once, and royals and skysails set, and, as we had the wind free, the booms were run out, and every one was aloft, active as cats, laying out on the yards and booms, reeving the studding-sail gear; and sail after sail the captain piled upon her, until she was covered with canvas, her sails looking like a great white cloud resting upon a black speck. Before we doubled the point, we were going at a dashing rate, and leaving the shipping far astern. We had a fine breeze to take us through the Canal, as they call this bay of forty miles long by ten wide. The breeze died away at night, and we were becalmed all day on Sunday, about half way between Santa Barbara and Point Conception. Sunday night we had a light, fair wind, which set us up again; and having a fine sea-breeze on the first part of Monday, we had the prospect of passing, without any trouble, Point Conception,—the Cape Horn of California, where it begins to blow the first of January, and blows all the year round.

Toward the latter part of the afternoon, however, the regular northwest wind, as usual, set in, which brought in our studding-sails, and gave us the chance of beating round the Point, which we were now just abreast of, and which stretched off into the Pacific, high, rocky and barren, forming the central point of the coast for hundreds of miles north and south. A cap-full of wind will be a bag-full here, and before night our royals were furled, and the ship was laboring hard under her top-gallant sails. At eight bells our watch went below, leaving her with as much sail as she could stagger under, the water flying over the forecastle at every plunge. It was evidently blowing harder, but then there was not a cloud in the sky, and the sun had gone down bright.

We had been below but a short time, before we had the usual premonitions of a coming gale: seas washing over the whole forward part of the vessel, and her bows beating against them with a force and sound like the driving of piles. The watch, too, seemed very busy trampling about decks, and singing out at the ropes. A sailor can always tell, by the sound, what sail is coming in, and, in a short time, we heard the top-gallant sails come in, one after another, and then the flying jib. This seemed to ease her a good deal, and we were fast going off to the land of Nod, when—bang, bang, bang—on the scuttle, and "All hands, reef topsails, ahoy!" started us out of our berths; and, it not being very cold weather, we had nothing extra to put on, and were soon on deck. I shall never forget the fineness of the sight. It was a clear, and rather a chilly night; the stars were twinkling with an intense brightness, and as far as the eye could reach, there was not a cloud to be seen. The horizon met the sea in a defined line. A painter could not have painted so clear a sky. There was not a speck upon it. Yet it was blowing great guns from the north-west. When you can see a cloud to windward, you feel that there is a place for the wind to come from; but here it seemed to come from nowhere. No person could have told, from the heavens, by their eyesight alone, that it was not a still summer's night. One reef after another, we took in the topsails, and before we could get them hoisted up, we heard a sound like a short, quick rattling of thunder, and the jib was blown to atoms out of the bolt-rope. We got the topsails set, and the fragments of the jib stowed away, and the fore-topmast staysail set in its place, when the great mainsail gaped open, and the sail ripped from head to foot. "Lay up on that main-yard and furl the sail, before it blows to tatters!" shouted the captain; and in a moment, we were up, gathering the remains of it upon the yard. We got it wrapped, round the yard, and passed gaskets over it as snugly as possible, and were just on deck again, when, with another loud rent, which was heard throughout the ship, the fore-topsail, which had been double-reefed, split in two, athwartships, just below the reefband, from earing to earing. Here again it was down yard, haul out reef-tackles, and lay out upon the yard for reefing. By hauling the reef-tackles chock-a-block, we took the strain from the other earings, and passing the close-reef earing, and knotting the points carefully, we succeeded in setting the sail, close-reefed.

We had but just got the rigging coiled up, and were waiting to hear "go below the watch!" when the main royal worked loose from the gaskets, and blew directly out to leeward, flapping, and shaking the mast like a wand. Here was a job for somebody. The royal must come in or be cut adrift, or the mast would be snapped short off. All the light hands in the starboard watch were sent up, one after another, but they could do nothing with it. At length, John, the tall Frenchman, the head of the starboard watch, (and a better sailor never stepped upon a deck,) sprang aloft, and, by the help of his long arms and legs, succeeded, after a hard struggle,—the sail blowing over the yard-arm to leeward, and the skysail blowing directly over his head—in smothering it, and frapping it with long pieces of sinnet. He came very near being blown or shaken from the yard, several times, but he was a true sailor, every finger a fish-hook. Having made the sail snug, he prepared to send the yard down, which was a long and difficult job; for, frequently, he was obliged to stop and hold on with all his might, for several minutes, the ship pitching so as to make it impossible to do anything else at that height. The yard at length came down safe, and after it, the fore and mizen royal-yards were sent down. All hands were then sent aloft, and for an hour or two we were hard at work, making the booms well fast; unreeving the studding-sail and royal and skysail gear; getting rolling-ropes on the yards; setting up the weather breast-backstays; and making other preparations for a storm. It was a fine night for a gale; just cool and bracing enough for quick work, without being cold, and as bright as day. It was sport to have a gale in such weather as this. Yet it blew like a hurricane. The wind seemed to come with a spite, an edge to it, which threatened to scrape us off the yards. The mere force of the wind was greater than I had ever seen it before; but darkness, cold, and wet are the worst parts of a storm to a sailor.

Having got on deck again, we looked round to see what time of night it was, and whose watch. In a few minutes the man at the wheel struck four bells, and we found that the other watch was out, and our own half out. Accordingly, the starboard watch went below, and left the ship to us for a couple of hours, yet with orders to stand by for a call.

Hardly had they got below, before away went the fore-topmast staysail, blown to ribbons. This was a small sail, which we could manage in the watch, so that we were not obliged to call up the other watch. We laid out upon the bowsprit, where we were under water half the time, and took in the fragments of the sail, and as she must have some head sail on her, prepared to bend another staysail. We got the new one out, into the nettings; seized on the tack, sheets, and halyards, and the hanks; manned the halyards, cut adrift the frapping lines, and hoisted away; but before it was half way up the stay, it was blown all to pieces. When we belayed the halyards, there was nothing left but the bolt-rope. Now large eyes began to show themselves in the foresail, and knowing that it must soon go, the mate ordered us upon the yard to furl it. Being unwilling to call up the watch who had been on deck all night, he roused out the carpenter, sailmaker, cook, steward, and other idlers, and, with their help, we manned the foreyard, and after nearly half an hour's struggle, mastered the sail, and got it well furled round the yard. The force of the wind had never been greater than at this moment. In going up the rigging, it seemed absolutely to pin us down to the shrouds; and on the yard, there was no such thing as turning a face to windward. Yet here was no driving sleet, and darkness, and wet, and cold, as off Cape Horn; and instead of a stiff oil-cloth suit, south-wester caps, and thick boots, we had on hats, round jackets, duck trowsers, light shoes, and everything light and easy. All these things make a great difference to a sailor. When we got on deck, the man at the wheel struck eight bells, (four o'clock in the morning,) and "All starbowlines, ahoy!" brought the other watch up. But there was no going below for us. The gale was now at its height, "blowing like scissors and thumb-screws;" the captain was on deck; the ship, which was light, rolling and pitching as though she would shake the long sticks out of her; and the sail gaping open and splitting, in every direction. The mizen topsail, which was a comparatively new sail, and close-reefed, split, from head to foot, in the bunt; the fore-topsail went, in one rent, from clew to earing, and was blowing to tatters; one of the chain bobstays parted; the spritsail-yard sprung in the slings; the martingale had slued away off to leeward; and, owing to the long dry weather, the lee rigging hung in large bights, at every lurch. One of the main top-gallant shrouds had parted; and, to crown all, the galley had got adrift, and gone over to leeward, and the anchor on the lee bow had worked loose, and was thumping the side. Here was work enough for all hands for half a day. Our gang laid out on the mizen topsail yard, and after more than half an hour's hard work, furled the sail, though it bellied out over our heads, and again, by a slant of the wind, blew in under the yard, with a fearful jerk, and almost threw us off from the foot-ropes.

Double gaskets were passed round the yards, rolling tackles and other gear bowsed taut, and everything made as secure as could be. Coming down, we found the rest of the crew just coming down the fore rigging, having furled the tattered topsail, or, rather, swathed it round the yard, which looked like a broken limb, bandaged. There was no sail now on the ship but the spanker and the close-reefed main topsail, which still held good. But this was too much after sail; and order was given to furl the spanker. The brails were hauled up, and all the light hands in the starboard watch sent out on the gaff to pass the gaskets; but they could do nothing with it. The second mate swore at them for a parcel of "sogers," and sent up a couple of the best men; but they could do no better, and the gaff was lowered down. All hands were now employed in setting up the lee rigging, fishing the spritsail-yard, lashing the galley, and getting tackles upon the martingale, to bowse it to windward. Being in the larboard watch, my duty was forward, to assist in setting up the martingale. Three of us were out on the martingale guys and back-ropes for more than half an hour, carrying out, hooking and unhooking the tackles, several times buried in the seas, until the mate ordered us in, from fear of our being washed off. The anchors were then to be taken up on the rail, which kept all hands on the forecastle for an hour, though every now and then the seas broke over it, washing the rigging off to leeward, filling the lee scuppers breast high, and washing chock aft to the taffrail.

Having got everything secure again, we were promising ourselves some breakfast, for it was now nearly nine o'clock in the forenoon, when the main topsail showed evident signs of giving way. Some sail must be kept on the ship, and the captain ordered the fore and main spencer gaffs to be lowered down, and the two spencers (which were storm sails, bran new, small, and made of the strongest canvas) to be got up and bent; leaving the main topsail to blow away, with a blessing on it, if it would only last until we could set the spencers. These we bent on very carefully, with strong robands and seizings, and making tackles fast to the clews, bowsed them down to the water-ways. By this time the main topsail was among the things that have been, and we went aloft to stow away the remnant of the last sail of all those which were on the ship twenty-four hours before. The spencers were now the only whole sails on the ship, and, being strong and small, and near the deck, presenting but little surface to the wind above the rail, promised to hold out well. Hove-to under these, and eased by having no sail above the tops, the ship rose and fell, and drifted off to leeward like a line-of-battle ship.

It was now eleven o'clock, and the watch was sent below to get breakfast, and at eight bells (noon), as everything was snug, although the gale had not in the least abated, the watch was set, and the other watch and idlers sent below. For three days and three nights, the gale continued with unabated fury, and with singular regularity. There was no lulls, and very little variation in its fierceness. Our ship, being light, rolled so as almost to send the fore yard-arm under water, and drifted off bodily, to leeward. All this time there was not a cloud to be seen in the sky, day or night;—no, not so large as a man's hand. Every morning the sun rose cloudless from the sea, and set again at night, in the sea, in a flood of light. The stars, too, came out of the blue, one after another, night after night, unobscured, and twinkled as clear as on a still frosty night at home, until the day came upon them. All this time, the sea was rolling in immense surges, white with foam, as far as the eye could reach, on every side, for we were now leagues and leagues from shore.

The between-decks being empty, several of us slept there in hammocks, which are the best things in the world to sleep in during a storm; it not being true of them, as it is of another kind of bed, "when the wind blows, the cradle will rock;" for it is the ship that rocks, while they always hang vertically from the beams. During these seventy-two hours we had nothing to do, but to turn in and out, four hours on deck, and four below, eat, sleep, and keep watch. The watches were only varied by taking the helm in turn, and now and then, by one of the sails, which were furled, blowing out of the gaskets, and getting adrift, which sent us up on the yards; and by getting tackles on different parts of the rigging, which were slack. Once, the wheel-rope parted, which might have been fatal to us, had not the chief mate sprung instantly with a relieving tackle to windward, and kept the tiller up, till a new one could be rove. On the morning of the twentieth, at daybreak, the gale had evidently done its worst, and had somewhat abated; so much so, that all hands were called to bend new sails, although it was still blowing as hard as two common gales. One at a time, and with great difficulty and labor, the old sails were unbent and sent down by the bunt-lines, and three new topsails, made for the homeward passage round Cape Horn, and which had never been bent, were got up from the sailroom, and under the care of the sailmaker, were fitted for bending, and sent up by the halyards into the tops, and, with stops and frapping lines, were bent to the yards, close-reefed, sheeted home, and hoisted. These were done one at a time, and with the greatest care and difficulty. Two spare courses were then got up and bent in the same manner and furled, and a storm-jib, with the bonnet off, bent and furled to the boom. It was twelve o'clock before we got through; and five hours of more exhausting labor I never experienced; and no one of that ship's crew, I will venture to say, will ever desire again to unbend and bend five large sails, in the teeth of a tremendous north-wester. Towards night, a few clouds appeared in the horizon, and as the gale moderated, the usual appearance of driving clouds relieved the face of the sky. The fifth day after the commencement of the storm, we shook a reef out of each topsail, and set the reefed foresail, jib and spanker; but it was not until after eight days of reefed topsails that we had a whole sail on the ship; and then it was quite soon enough, for the captain was anxious to make up for leeway, the gale having blown us half the distance to the Sandwich Islands.

Inch by inch, as fast as the gale would permit, we made sail on the ship, for the wind still continued a-head, and we had many days' sailing to get back to the longitude we were in when the storm took us. For eight days more we beat to windward under a stiff top-gallant breeze, when the wind shifted and became variable. A light south-easter, to which we could carry a reefed topmast studding-sail, did wonders for our dead reckoning.

Friday, December 4th, after a passage of twenty days, we arrived at the mouth of the bay of San Francisco.

CHAPTER XXVI

SAN FRANCISCO—MONTEREY

Our place of destination had been Monterey, but as we were to the northward of it when the wind hauled a-head, we made a fair wind for San Francisco. This large bay, which lies in latitude 37° 58', was discovered by Sir Francis Drake, and by him represented to be (as indeed it is) a magnificent bay, containing several good harbors, great depth of water, and surrounded by a fertile and finely wooded country. About thirty miles from the mouth of the bay, and on the south-east side, is a high point, upon which the presidio is built. Behind this, is the harbor in which trading vessels anchor, and near it, the mission of San Francisco, and a newly begun settlement, mostly of Yankee Californians, called Yerba Buena, which promises well. Here, at anchor, and the only vessel, was a brig under Russian colors, from Asitka, in Russian America, which had come down to winter, and to take in a supply of tallow and grain, great quantities of which latter article are raised in the missions at the head of the bay. The second day after our arrival, we went on board the brig, it being Sunday, as a matter of curiosity; and there was enough there to gratify it. Though no larger than the Pilgrim, she had five or six officers, and a crew of between twenty and thirty; and such a stupid and greasy-looking set, I certainly never saw before. Although it was quite comfortable weather, and we had nothing on but straw hats, shirts, and duck trowsers, and were barefooted, they had, every man of them, double-soled boots, coming up to the knees, and well greased; thick woolen trowsers, frocks, waistcoats, pea-jackets, woolen caps, and everything in true Nova Zembla rig; and in the warmest days they made no change. The clothing of one of these men would weigh nearly as much as that of half our crew. They had brutish faces, looked like the antipodes of sailors, and apparently dealt in nothing but grease. They lived upon grease; eat it, drank it, slept in the midst of it, and their clothes were covered with it. To a Russian, grease is the greatest luxury. They looked with greedy eyes upon the tallow-bags as they were taken into the vessel, and, no doubt, would have eaten one up whole, had not the officer kept watch over it. The grease seemed actually coming through their pores, and out in their hair, and on their faces. It seems as if it were this saturation which makes them stand cold and rain so well. If they were to go into a warm climate, they would all die of the scurvy.

The vessel was no better than the crew. Everything was in the oldest and most inconvenient fashion possible; running trusses on the yards, and large hawser cables, coiled all over the decks, and served and parcelled in all directions. The topmasts, top-gallant masts and studding-sail booms were nearly black for want of scraping, and the decks would have turned the stomach of a man-of-war's-man. The galley was down in the forecastle; and there the crew lived, in the midst of the steam and grease of the cooking, in a place as hot as an oven, and as dirty as a pigsty. Five minutes in the forecastle was enough for us, and we were glad to get into the open air. We made some trade with them, buying Indian curiosities, of which they had a great number; such as bead-work, feathers of birds, fur moccasins, etc. I purchased a large robe, made of the skins of some animals, dried and sewed nicely together, and covered all over on the outside with thick downy feathers, taken from the breasts of various birds, and arranged with their different colors, so as to make a brilliant show.

A few days after our arrival, the rainy season set in, and, for three weeks, it rained almost every hour, without cessation. This was bad for our trade, for the collecting of hides is managed differently in this port from what it is in any other on the coast. The mission of San Francisco near the anchorage, has no trade at all, but those of San José, Santa Clara, and others, situated on large creeks or rivers which run into the bay, and distant between fifteen and forty miles from the anchorage, do a greater business in hides than any in California. Large boats, manned by Indians, and capable of carrying nearly a thousand hides apiece, are attached to the missions, and sent down to the vessels with hides, to bring away goods in return. Some of the crews of the vessels are obliged to go and come in the boats, to look out for the hides and goods. These are favorite expeditions with the sailors, in fine weather; but now to be gone three or four days, in open boats, in constant rain, without any shelter, and with cold food, was hard service. Two of our men went up to Santa Clara in one of these boats, and were gone three days, during all which time they had a constant rain, and did not sleep a wink, but passed three long nights, walking fore and aft the boat, in the open air. When they got on board, they were completely exhausted, and took a watch below of twelve hours. All the hides, too, that came down in the boats, were soaked with water, and unfit to put below, so that we were obliged to trice them up to dry, in the intervals of sunshine or wind, upon all parts of the vessel. We got up tricing-lines from the jib-boom-end to each arm of the fore yard, and thence to the main and cross-jack yard-arms. Between the tops, too, and the mast-heads, from the fore to the main swifters, and thence to the mizen rigging, and in all directions athwartships, tricing-lines were run, and strung with hides. The head stays and guys, and the spritsail-yard, were lined, and, having still more, we got out the swinging booms, and strung them and the forward and after guys, with hides. The rail, fore and aft, the windlass, capstan, the sides of the ship, and every vacant place on deck, were covered with wet hides, on the least sign of an interval for drying. Our ship was nothing but a mass of hides, from the cat-harpins to the water's edge, and from the jib-boom-end to the taffrail.

One cold, rainy evening, about eight o'clock, I received orders to get ready to start for San José at four the next morning, in one of these Indian boats, with four days' provisions. I got my oil-cloth clothes, south-wester, and thick boots all ready, and turned into my hammock early, determined to get some sleep in advance, as the boat was to be alongside before daybreak. I slept on till all hands were called in the morning; for, fortunately for me, the Indians, intentionally, or from mistaking their orders, had gone off alone in the night, and were far out of sight. Thus I escaped three or four days of very uncomfortable service.

Four of our men, a few days afterwards, went up in one of the quarter-boats to Santa Clara, to carry the agent, and remained out all night in a drenching rain, in the small boat, where there was not room for them to turn round; the agent having gone up to the mission and left the men to their fate, making no provision for their accommodation, and not even sending them anything to eat. After this, they had to pull thirty miles, and when they got on board, were so stiff that they could not come up the gangway ladder. This filled up the measure of the agent's unpopularity, and never after this could he get anything done by any of the crew; and many a delay and vexation, and many a good ducking in the surf, did he get to pay up old scores, or "square the yards with the bloody quill-driver."

Having collected nearly all the hides that were to be procured, we began our preparations for taking in a supply of wood and water, for both of which, San Francisco is the best place on the coast. A small island, situated about two leagues from the anchorage, called by us "Wood Island," and by the Spaniards "Isle de los Angelos," was covered with trees to the water's edge; and to this, two of our crew, who were Kennebec men, and could handle an axe like a plaything, were sent every morning to cut wood, with two boys to pile it up for them. In about a week, they had cut enough to last us a year, and the third mate, with myself and three others, were sent over in a large, schooner-rigged, open launch, which we had hired of the mission, to take in the wood, and bring it to the ship. We left the ship about noon, but, owing to a strong head wind, and a tide, which here runs four or five knots, did not get into the harbor, formed by two points of the island, where the boats lie, until sundown. No sooner had we come-to, than a strong south-easter, which had been threatening us all day, set in, with heavy rain and a chilly atmosphere. We were in rather a bad situation: an open boat, a heavy rain, and a long night; for in winter, in this latitude, it was dark nearly fifteen hours. Taking a small skiff which we had brought with us, we went ashore, but found no shelter, for everything was open to the rain, and collecting a little wood, which we found by lifting up the leaves and brush, and a few mussels, we put aboard again, and made the best preparations in our power for passing the night. We unbent the mainsail, and formed an awning with it over the after part of the boat, made a bed of wet logs of wood, and, with our jackets on, lay down, about six o'clock, to sleep. Finding the rain running down upon us, and our jackets getting wet through, and the rough, knotty-logs, rather indifferent couches, we turned out; and taking an iron pan which we brought with us, we wiped it out dry, put some stones around it, cut the wet bark from some sticks, and striking a light, made a small fire in the pan. Keeping some sticks near, to dry, and covering the whole over with a roof of boards, we kept up a small fire, by which we cooked our mussels, and ate them, rather for an occupation than from hunger. Still, it was not ten o'clock, and the night was long before us, when one of the party produced an old pack of Spanish cards from his monkey-jacket pocket, which we hailed as a great windfall; and keeping a dim, flickering light by our fagots, we played game after game, till one or two o'clock, when, becoming really tired, we went to our logs again, one sitting up at a time, in turn, to keep watch over the fire. Toward morning, the rain ceased, and the air became sensibly colder, so that we found sleep impossible, and sat up, watching for daybreak. No sooner was it light than we went ashore, and began our preparations for loading our vessel. We were not mistaken in the coldness of the weather, for a white frost was on the ground, a thing we had never seen before in California, and one or two little puddles of fresh water were skimmed over with a thin coat of ice. In this state of the weather and before sunrise, in the grey of the morning, we had to wade off, nearly up to our hips in water, to load the skiff with the wood by armsfull. The third mate remained on board the launch, two more men staid in the skiff, to load and manage it, and all the water-work, as usual, fell upon the two youngest of us; and there we were, with frost on the ground, wading forward and back, from the beach to the boat, with armsfull of wood, barefooted, and our trowsers rolled up. When the skiff went off with her load, we could only keep our feet from freezing by racing up and down the beach on the hard sand, as fast as we could go. We were all day at this work, and towards sundown, having loaded the vessel as deep as she would bear, we hove up our anchor, and made sail, beating out the bay. No sooner had we got into the large bay, than we found a strong tide setting us out to seaward, a thick fog which prevented our seeing the ship, and a breeze too light to set us against the tide; for we were as deep as a sand-barge. By the utmost exertions, we saved ourselves from being carried out to sea, and were glad to reach the leewardmost point of the island, where we came-to, and prepared to pass another night, more uncomfortable than the first, for we were loaded up to the gunwale, and had only a choice among logs and sticks for a resting-place. The next morning, we made sail at slack water, with a fair wind, and got on board by eleven o'clock, when all hands were turned-to, to unload and stow away the wood, which took till night.

Having now taken in all our wood, the next morning a water-party was ordered off with all the casks. From this we escaped, having had a pretty good siege with the wooding. The water-party were gone three days, during which time they narrowly escaped being carried out to sea, and passed one day on an island, where one of them shot a deer, great numbers of which overrun the islands and hills of San Francisco Bay.

While not off, on these wood and water parties, or up the rivers to the missions, we had very easy times on board the ship. We were moored, stem and stern, within a cable's length of the shore, safe from south-easters, and with very little boating to do; and as it rained nearly all the time, awnings were put over the hatchways, and all hands sent down between decks, where we were at work, day after day, picking oakum, until we got enough to caulk the ship all over, and to last the whole voyage. Then we made a whole suit of gaskets for the voyage home, a pair of wheel-ropes from strips of green hide, great quantities of spun-yarn, and everything else that could be made between decks. It being now mid-winter and in high latitude, the nights were very long, so that we were not turned-to until seven in the morning, and were obliged to knock off at five in the evening, when we got supper; which gave us nearly three hours before eight bells, at which time the watch was set.

As we had now been about a year on the coast, it was time to think of the voyage home; and knowing that the last two or three months of our stay would be very busy ones, and that we should never have so good an opportunity to work for ourselves as the present, we all employed our evenings in making clothes for the passage home, and more especially for Cape Horn. As soon as supper was over and the kids cleared away, and each one had taken his smoke, we seated ourselves on our chests round the lamp, which swung from a beam, and each one went to work in his own way, some making hats, others trowsers, others jackets, etc., etc.; and no one was idle. The boys who could not sew well enough to make their own clothes, laid up grass into sinnet for the men, who sewed for them in return. Several of us clubbed together and bought a large piece of twilled cotton, which we made into trowsers and jackets, and giving them several coats of linseed oil, laid them by for Cape Horn. I also sewed and covered a tarpaulin hat, thick and strong enough to sit down upon, and made myself a complete suit of flannel under-clothing, for bad weather. Those who had no south-wester caps, made them, and several of the crew made themselves tarpaulin jackets and trowsers, lined on the inside with flannel. Industry was the order of the day, and every one did something for himself; for we knew that as the season advanced, and we went further south, we should have no evenings to work in.

Friday, December 25th. This day was Christmas; and as it rained all day long, and there were no hides to take in, and nothing especial to do, the captain gave us a holiday, (the first we had had since leaving Boston,) and plum duff for dinner. The Russian brig, following the Old Style, had celebrated their Christmas eleven days before; when they had a grand blow-out and (as our men said) drank, in the forecastle, a barrel of gin, ate up a bag of tallow, and made a soup of the skin.

Sunday, December 27th. We had now finished all our business at this port, and it being Sunday, we unmoored ship and got under weigh, firing a salute to the Russian brig, and another to the Presidio, which were both answered. The commandant of the Presidio, Don Gaudaloupe Villego, a young man, and the most popular, among the Americans and English, of any man in California, was on board when we got under weigh. He spoke English very well, and was suspected of being favorably inclined to foreigners.

We sailed down this magnificent bay with a light wind, the tide, which was running out, carrying us at the rate of four or five knots. It was a fine day; the first of entire sunshine we had had for more than a month. We passed directly under the high cliff on which the Presidio is built, and stood into the middle of the bay, from whence we could see small bays, making up into the interior, on every side; large and beautifully-wooded islands; and the mouths of several small rivers. If California ever becomes a prosperous country, this bay will be the centre of its prosperity. The abundance of wood and water, the extreme fertility of its shores, the excellence of its climate, which is as near to being perfect as any in the world, and its facilities for navigation, affording the best anchoring-grounds in the whole western coast of America, all fit it for a place of great importance; and, indeed, it has attracted much attention, for the settlement of "Yerba Buena," where we lay at anchor, made chiefly by Americans and English, and which bids fair to become the most important trading place on the coast, at this time began to supply traders, Russian ships, and whalers, with their stores of wheat and frijoles.

The tide leaving us, we came to anchor near the mouth of the bay, under a high and beautifully sloping hill, upon which herds of hundreds and hundreds of red deer, and the stag, with his high branching antlers, were bounding about, looking at us for a moment, and then starting off, affrighted at the noises which we made for the purpose of seeing the variety of their beautiful attitudes and motions.

At midnight, the tide having turned, we hove up our anchor and stood out of the bay, with a fine starry heaven above us,—the first we had seen for weeks and weeks. Before the light northerly winds, which blow here with the regularity of trades, we worked slowly along, and made Point Año Nuevo, the northerly point of the Bay of Monterey, on Monday afternoon. We spoke, going in, the brig Diana, of the Sandwich Islands, from the North-west Coast, last from Asitka. She was off the point at the same time with us, but did not get in to the anchoring-ground until an hour or two after us. It was ten o'clock on Tuesday morning when we came to anchor. The town looked just as it did when I saw it last, which was eleven months before, in the brig Pilgrim. The pretty lawn on which it stands, as green as sun and rain could make it; the pine wood on the south; the small river on the north side; the houses, with their white plastered sides and red-tiled roofs, dotted about on the green; the low, white presidio, with its soiled, tri-colored flag flying, and the discordant din of drums and trumpets for the noon parade; all brought up the scene we had witnessed here with so much pleasure nearly a year before, when coming from a long voyage, and our unprepossessing reception at Santa Barbara. It seemed almost like coming to a home.

CHAPTER XXVII

THE SUNDAY WASH-UP—ON SHORE—A SET-TO—A GRANDEE—"SAIL HO!"—A FANDANGO

The only other vessel in port was the Russian government bark, from Asitka, mounting eight guns, (four of which we found to be Quakers,) and having on board the ex-governor, who was going in her to Mazatlan, and thence overland to Vera Cruz. He offered to take letters, and deliver them to the American consul at Vera Cruz, whence they could be easily forwarded to the United States. We accordingly made up a packet of letters, almost every one writing, and dating them "January 1st, 1836." The governor was true to his promise, and they all reached Boston before the middle of March; the shortest communication ever yet made across the country.

The brig Pilgrim had been lying in Monterey through the latter part of November, according to orders, waiting for us. Day after day, Captain Faucon went up to the hill to look out for us, and at last, gave us up, thinking we must have gone down in the gale which we experienced off Point Conception, and which had blown with great fury over the whole coast, driving ashore several vessels in the snuggest ports. An English brig, which had put into San Francisco, lost both her anchors; the Rosa was driven upon a mud bank in San Diego; and the Pilgrim, with great difficulty, rode out the gale in Monterey, with three anchors a-head. She sailed early in December for San Diego and intermedios.

As we were to be here over Sunday, and Monterey was the best place to go ashore on the whole coast, and we had had no liberty-day for nearly three months, every one was for going ashore. On Sunday morning, as soon as the decks were washed, and we had got breakfast, those who had obtained liberty began to clean themselves, as it is called, to go ashore. A bucket of fresh water apiece, a cake of soap, a large coarse towel, and we went to work scrubbing one another, on the forecastle. Having gone through this, the next thing was to get into the head,—one on each side—with a bucket apiece, and duck one another, by drawing up water and heaving over each other, while we were stripped to a pair of trowsers. Then came the rigging-up. The usual outfit of pumps, white stockings, loose white duck trowsers, blue jackets, clean checked shirts, black kerchiefs, hats well varnished, with a fathom of black ribbon over the left eye, a silk handkerchief flying from the outside jacket pocket, and four or five dollars tied up in the back of the neckerchief, and we were "all right." One of the quarter-boats pulled us ashore, and we steamed up to the town. I tried to find the church, in order to see the worship, but was told that there was no service, except a mass early in the morning; so we went about the town, visiting the Americans and English, and the natives whom we had known when we were here before. Toward noon we procured horses, and rode out to the Carmel mission, which is about a league from the town, where we got something in the way of a dinner—beef, eggs, frijoles, tortillas, and some middling wine—from the mayordomo, who, of course, refused to make any charge, as it was the Lord's gift, yet received our present, as a gratuity, with a low bow, a touch of the hat, and "Dios se lo pague!"

After this repast, we had a fine run, scouring the whole country on our fleet horses, and came into town soon after sundown. Here we found our companions who had refused to go to ride with us, thinking that a sailor has no more business with a horse than a fish has with a balloon. They were moored, stem and stern, in a grog-shop, making a great noise, with a crowd of Indians and hungry half-breeds about them, and with a fair prospect of being stripped and dirked, or left to pass the night in the calabozo. With a great deal of trouble, we managed to get them down to the boats, though not without many angry looks and interferences from the Spaniards, who had marked them out for their prey. The Diana's crew,—a set of worthless outcasts, who had been picked up at the islands from the refuse of whale-ships,—were all as drunk as beasts, and had a set-to, on the beach, with their captain, who was in no better state than themselves. They swore they would not go aboard, and went back to the town, were stripped and beaten, and lodged in the calabozo, until the next day, when the captain bought them out. Our forecastle, as usual after a liberty-day, was a scene of tumult all night long, from the drunken ones. They had just got to sleep toward morning, when they were turned up with the rest, and kept at work all day in the water, carrying hides, their heads aching so that they could hardly stand. This is sailor's pleasure.

Nothing worthy of remark happened while we were here, except a little boxing-match on board our own ship, which gave us something to talk about. A broad-backed, big-headed Cape Cod boy, about sixteen years old, had been playing the bully, for the whole voyage, over a slender, delicate-looking boy, from one of the Boston schools, and over whom he had much the advantage, in strength, age, and experience in the ship's duty, for this was the first time the Boston boy had been on salt water. The latter, however, had "picked up his crumbs," was learning his duty, and getting strength and confidence daily; and began to assert his rights against his oppressor. Still, the other was his master, and, by his superior strength, always tackled with him and threw him down. One afternoon, before we were turned-to, these boys got into a violent squabble in the between-decks, when George (the Boston boy) said he would fight Nat, if he could have fair play. The chief mate heard the noise, dove down the hatchway, hauled them both up on deck, and told them to shake hands and have no more trouble for the voyage, or else they should fight till one gave in for beaten. Finding neither willing to make an offer for reconciliation, he called all hands up, (for the captain was ashore, and he could do as he chose aboard,) ranged the crew in the waist, marked a line on the deck, brought the two boys up to it, making them "toe the mark;" then made the bight of a rope fast to a belaying pin, and stretched it across the deck, bringing it just above their waists. "No striking below the rope!" And there they stood, one on each side of it, face to face, and went at it like two game-cocks. The Cape Cod boy, Nat, put in his double-fisters, starting the blood, and bringing the black and blue spots all over the face and arms of the other, whom we expected to see give in every moment: but the more he was hurt, the better he fought. Time after time he was knocked nearly down, but up he came again and faced the mark, as bold as a lion, again to take the heavy blows, which sounded so as to make one's heart turn with pity for him. At length he came up to the mark for the last time, his shirt torn from his body, his face covered with blood and bruises, and his eyes flashing fire, and swore he would stand there until one or the other was killed, and set-to like a young fury. "Hurrah in the bow!" said the men, cheering him on. "Well crowed!" "Never say die, while there's a shot in the locker!" Nat tried to close with him, knowing his advantage, but the mate stopped that, saying there should be fair play, and no fingering. Nat then came up to the mark, but looked white about the mouth, and his blows were not given with half the spirit of his first. He was evidently cowed. He had always been his master, and had nothing to gain, and everything to lose; while the other fought for honor and freedom, under a sense of wrong. It would not do. It was soon over. Nat gave in; not so much beaten, as cowed and mortified; and never afterwards tried to act the bully on board. We took George forward, washed him in the deck-tub, complimented his pluck, and from this time he became somebody on board, having fought himself into notice. Mr. Brown's plan had a good effect, for there was no more quarrelling among the boys for the rest of the voyage.

Wednesday, January 6th. Set sail from Monterey, with a number of Spaniards as passengers, and shaped our course for Santa Barbara. The Diana went out of the bay in company with us, but parted from us off Point Pinos, being bound to the Sandwich Islands. We had a smacking breeze for several hours, and went along at a great rate, until night, when it died away, as usual, and the land-breeze set in, which brought us upon a taut bowline. Among our passengers was a young man who was the best representation of a decayed gentleman I had ever seen. He reminded me much of some of the characters in Gil Blas. He was of the aristocracy of the country, his family being of pure Spanish blood, and once of great importance in Mexico. His father had been governor of the province, and having amassed a large property, settled at San Diego, where he built a large house with a court-yard in front, kept a great retinue of Indians, and set up for the grandee of that part of the country. His son was sent to Mexico, where he received the best education, and went into the first society of the capital. Misfortune, extravagance, and the want of funds, or any manner of getting interest on money, soon eat the estate up, and Don Juan Bandini returned from Mexico accomplished, poor, and proud, and without any office or occupation, to lead the life of most young men of the better families—dissolute and extravagant when the means are at hand; ambitious at heart, and impotent in act; often pinched for bread; keeping up an appearance of style, when their poverty is known to each half-naked Indian boy in the street, and they stand in dread of every small trader and shopkeeper in the place. He had a slight and elegant figure, moved gracefully, danced and waltzed beautifully, spoke the best of Castilian, with a pleasant and refined voice and accent, and had, throughout, the bearing of a man of high birth and figure. Yet here he was, with his passage given him, (as I afterwards learned,) for he had not the means of paying for it, and living upon the charity of our agent. He was polite to every one, spoke to the sailors, and gave four reáls—I dare say the last he had in his pocket—to the steward, who waited upon him. I could not but feel a pity for him, especially when I saw him by the side of his fellow-passenger and townsman, a fat, coarse, vulgar, pretending fellow of a Yankee trader, who had made money in San Diego, and was eating out the very vitals of the Bandinis, fattening upon their extravagance, grinding them in their poverty; having mortgages on their lands, forestalling their cattle, and already making an inroad upon their jewels, which were their last hope.

Don Juan had with him a retainer, who was as much like many of the characters in Gil Blas as his master. He called himself a private secretary, though there was no writing for him to do, and he lived in the steerage with the carpenter and sailmaker. He was certainly a character; could read and write extremely well; spoke good Spanish; had been all over Spanish America, and lived in every possible situation, and served in every conceivable capacity, though generally in that of confidential servant to some man of figure. I cultivated this man's acquaintance, and during the five weeks that he was with us,—for he remained on board until we arrived at San Diego,—I gained a greater knowledge of the state of political parties in Mexico, and the habits and affairs of the different classes of society, than I could have learned from almost any one else. He took great pains in correcting my Spanish, and supplying me with colloquial phrases, and common terms and exclamations in speaking. He lent me a file of late newspapers from the city of Mexico, which were full of triumphal receptions of Santa Ana, who had just returned from Tampico after a victory, and with the preparations for his expedition against the Texans. "Viva Santa Ana!" was the by-word everywhere, and it had even reached California, though there were still many here, among whom was Don Juan Bandini, who were opposed to his government, and intriguing to bring in Bustamente. Santa Ana, they said, was for breaking down the missions; or, as they termed it—"Santa Ana no quiere religion." Yet I had no doubt that the office of administrador of San Diego would reconcile Don Juan to any dynasty, and any state of the church. In these papers, too, I found scraps of American and English news; but which were so unconnected, and I was so ignorant of everything preceding them for eighteen months past, that they only awakened a curiosity which they could not satisfy. One article spoke of Taney as Justicia Mayor de los Estados Unidos, (what had become of Marshall? was he dead, or banished?) and another made known, by news received from Vera Cruz, that "El Vizconde Melbourne" had returned to the office of "primer ministro," in place of Sir Roberto Peel. (Sir Robert Peel had been minister, then? and where were Earl Grey and the Duke of Wellington?) Here were the outlines of a grand parliamentary overturn, the filling up of which I could imagine at my leisure.

The second morning after leaving Monterey, we were off Point Conception. It was a bright, sunny day, and the wind, though strong, was fair; and everything was in striking contrast with our experience in the same place two months before, when we were drifting off from a northwester under a fore and main spencer. "Sail ho!" cried a man who was rigging out a top-gallant studding-sail boom.—"Where away?"—"Weather beam, sir!" and in a few minutes a full-rigged brig was seen standing out from under Point Conception. The studding-sail halyards were let go, and the yards boom-ended, the after yards braced aback, and we waited her coming down. She rounded to, backed her main topsail, and showed her decks full of men, four guns on a side, hammock nettings, and everything man-of-war fashion, except that there was no boatswain's whistle, and no uniforms on the quarter-deck. A short, square-built man, in a rough grey jacket, with a speaking-trumpet in hand, stood in the weather hammock nettings. "Ship ahoy!"—"Hallo!"—"What ship is that, pray?"—"Alert."—"Where are you from, pray?" etc., etc. She proved to be the brig Convoy, from the Sandwich Islands, engaged in otter hunting, among the islands which lie along the coast. Her armament was from her being an illegal trader. The otter are very numerous among these islands, and being of great value, the government require a heavy sum for a license to hunt them, and lay a high duty upon every one shot or carried out of the country. This vessel had no license, and paid no duty, besides being engaged in smuggling goods on board other vessels trading on the coast, and belonging to the same owners in Oahu. Our captain told him to look out for the Mexicans, but he said they had not an armed vessel of his size in the whole Pacific. This was without doubt the same vessel that showed herself off Santa Barbara a few months before. These vessels frequently remain on the coast for years, without making port, except at the islands for wood and water, and an occasional visit to Oahu for a new outfit.

Sunday, January 10th. Arrived at Santa Barbara, and on the following Wednesday, slipped our cable and went to sea, on account of a south-easter. Returned to our anchorage the next day. We were the only vessel in the port. The Pilgrim had passed through the Canal and hove-to off the town, nearly six weeks before, on her passage down from Monterey, and was now at the leeward. She heard here of our safe arrival at San Francisco.

Great preparations were making on shore for the marriage of our agent, who was to marry Donna Anneta De G—— De N—— y C——, youngest daughter of Don Antonio N——, the grandee of the place, and the head of the first family in California. Our steward was ashore three days, making pastry and cake, and some of the best of our stores were sent off with him. On the day appointed for the wedding, we took the captain ashore in the gig, and had orders to come for him at night, with leave to go up to the house and see the fandango. Returning on board, we found preparations making for a salute. Our guns were loaded and run out, men appointed to each, cartridges served out, matches lighted, and all the flags ready to be run up. I took my place at the starboard after gun, and we all waited for the signal from on shore. At ten o'clock the bride went up with her sister to the confessional, dressed in deep black. Nearly an hour intervened, when the great doors of the mission church opened, the bells rang out a loud, discordant peal, the private signal for us was run up by the captain ashore, the bride, dressed in complete white, came out of the church with the bridegroom, followed by a long procession. Just as she stepped from the church door, a small white cloud issued from the bows of our ship, which was full in sight, the loud report echoed among the surrounding hills and over the bay, and instantly the ship was dressed in flags and pennants from stem to stern. Twenty-three guns followed in regular succession, with an interval of fifteen seconds between each when the cloud cleared away, and the ship lay dressed in her colors, all day. At sun-down, another salute of the same number of guns was fired, and all the flags run down. This we thought was pretty well—a gun every fifteen seconds—for a merchantman with only four guns and a dozen or twenty men.

After supper, the gig's crew were called, and we rowed ashore, dressed in our uniform, beached the boat, and went up to the fandango. The bride's father's house was the principal one in the place, with a large court in front, upon which a tent was built, capable of containing several hundred people. As we drew near, we heard the accustomed sound of violins and guitars, and saw a great motion of the people within. Going in, we found nearly all the people of the town—men, women, and children—collected and crowded together, leaving barely room for the dancers; for on these occasions no invitations are given, but every one is expected to come, though there is always a private entertainment within the house for particular friends. The old women sat down in rows, clapping their hands to the music, and applauding the young ones. The music was lively, and among the tunes, we recognized several of our popular airs, which we, without doubt, have taken from the Spanish. In the dancing, I was much disappointed. The women stood upright, with their hands down by their sides, their eyes fixed upon the ground before them, and slided about without any perceptible means of motion; for their feet were invisible, the hem of their dresses forming a perfect circle about them, reaching to the ground. They looked as grave as though they were going through some religious ceremony, their faces as little excited as their limbs; and on the whole, instead of the spirited, fascinating Spanish dances which I had expected, I found the Californian fandango, on the part of the women at least, a lifeless affair. The men did better. They danced with grace and spirit, moving in circles round their nearly stationary partners, and showing their figures to great advantage.

A great deal was said about our friend Don Juan Bandini, and when he did appear, which was toward the close of the evening, he certainly gave us the most graceful dancing that I had ever seen. He was dressed in white pantaloons neatly made, a short jacket of dark silk, gaily figured, white stockings and thin morocco slippers upon his very small feet. His slight and graceful figure was well calculated for dancing, and he moved about with the grace and daintiness of a young fawn. An occasional touch of the toe to the ground, seemed all that was necessary to give him a long interval of motion in the air. At the same time he was not fantastic or flourishing, but appeared to be rather repressing a strong tendency to motion. He was loudly applauded, and danced frequently toward the close of the evening. After the supper, the waltzing began, which was confined to a very few of the "gente de razón," and was considered a high accomplishment, and a mark of aristocracy. Here, too, Don Juan figured greatly, waltzing with the sister of the bride, (Donna Angustia, a handsome woman and a general favorite,) in a variety of beautiful, but, to me, offensive figures, which lasted as much as half an hour, no one else taking the floor. They were repeatedly and loudly applauded, the old men and women jumping out of their seats in admiration, and the young people waving their hats and handkerchiefs. Indeed among people of the character of these Mexicans, the waltz seemed to me to have found its right place. The great amusement of the evening,—which I suppose was owing to its being carnival—was the breaking of eggs filled with cologne, or other essences, upon the heads of the company. One end of the egg is broken and the inside taken out, then it is partly filled with cologne, and the whole sealed up. The women bring a great number of these secretly about them, and the amusement is to break one upon the head of a gentleman when his back is turned. He is bound in gallantry to find out the lady and return the compliment, though it must not be done if the person sees you. A tall, stately Don, with immense grey whiskers, and a look of great importance, was standing before me, when I felt a light hand on my shoulder, and turning round, saw Donna Angustia, (whom we all knew, as she had been up to Monterey, and down again, in the Alert,) with her finger upon her lip, motioning me gently aside. I stepped back a little, when she went up behind the Don, and with one hand knocked off his huge sombrero, and at the same instant, with the other, broke the egg upon his head, and springing behind me, was out of sight in a moment. The Don turned slowly round, the cologne, running down his face, and over his clothes, and a loud laugh breaking out from every quarter. He looked round in vain, for some time, until the direction of so many laughing eyes showed him the fair offender. She was his niece, and a great favorite with him, so old Don Domingo had to join in the laugh. A great many such tricks were played, and many a war of sharp manoeuvering was carried on between couples of the younger people, and at every successful exploit a general laugh was raised.

Another singular custom I was for some time at a loss about. A pretty young girl was dancing, named, after what would appear to us the sacrilegious custom of the country—Espiritu Santo, when a young man went behind her and placed his hat directly upon her head, letting it fall down over her eyes, and sprang back among the crowd. She danced for some time with the hat on, when she threw it off, which called forth a general shout; and the young man was obliged to go out upon the floor and pick it up. Some of the ladies, upon whose heads hats had been placed, threw them off at once, and a few kept them on throughout the dance, and took them off at the end, and held them out in their hands, when the owner stepped out, bowed, and took it from them. I soon began to suspect the meaning of the thing, and was afterward told that it was a compliment, and an offer to become the lady's gallant for the rest of the evening, and to wait upon her home. If the hat was thrown off, the offer was refused, and the gentleman was obliged to pick up his hat amid a general laugh. Much amusement was caused sometimes by gentlemen putting hats on the ladies' heads, without permitting them to see whom it was done by. This obliged them to throw them off, or keep them on at a venture, and when they came to discover the owner, the laugh was often turned upon them. The captain sent for us about ten o'clock, and we went aboard in high spirits, having enjoyed the new scene much, and were of great importance among the crew, from having so much to tell, and from the prospect of going every night until it was over; for these fandangos generally last three days. The next day, two of us were sent up to the town, and took care to come back by way of Capitan Noriego's and take a look into the booth. The musicians were still there, upon their platform, scraping and twanging away, and a few people, apparently of the lower classes, were dancing. The dancing is kept up, at intervals, throughout the day, but the crowd, the spirit, and the élite, come in at night. The next night, which was the last, we went ashore in the same manner, until we got almost tired of the monotonous twang of the instruments, the drawling sounds which the women kept up, as an accompaniment, and the slapping of the hands in time with the music, in place of castanets. We found ourselves as great objects of attention as any persons or anything at the place. Our sailor dresses—and we took great pains to have them neat and shipshape—were much admired, and we were invited, from every quarter, to give them an American sailor's dance; but after the ridiculous figure some of our countrymen cut, in dancing after the Spaniards, we thought it best to leave it to their imaginations. Our agent, with a tight, black, swallow-tailed coat, just imported from Boston, a high stiff cravat, looking as if he had been pinned and skewered, with only his feet and hands left free, took the floor just after Bandini; and we thought they had had enough of Yankee grace.

The last night they kept it up in great style, and were getting into a high-go, when the captain called us off to go aboard, for, it being south-easter season, he was afraid to remain on shore long; and it was well he did not, for that very night, we slipped our cables, as a crowner to our fun ashore, and stood off before a south-easter, which lasted twelve hours, and returned to our anchorage the next day.

CHAPTER XXVIII

AN OLD FRIEND—A VICTIM—CALIFORNIA RANGERS—NEWS FROM HOME—LAST LOOKS

Monday, Feb. 1st. After having been in port twenty-one days, we sailed for San Pedro, where we arrived on the following day, having gone "all fluking," with the weather clew of the mainsail hauled up, the yards braced in a little, and the lower studding-sails just drawing; the wind hardly shifting a point during the passage. Here we found the Ayacucho and the Pilgrim, which last we had not seen since the 11th of September,—nearly five months; and I really felt something like an affection for the old brig which had been my first home, and in which I had spent nearly a year, and got the first rough and tumble of a sea life. She, too, was associated, in my mind with Boston, the wharf from which we sailed, anchorage in the stream, leave-taking, and all such matters, which were now to me like small links connecting me with another world, which I had once been in, and which, please God, I might yet see again. I went on board the first night, after supper; found the old cook in the galley, playing upon the fife which I had given him, as a parting present; had a hearty shake of the hand from him; and dove down into the forecastle, where were my old ship-mates, the same as ever, glad to see me; for they had nearly given us up as lost, especially when they did not find us in Santa Barbara. They had been at San Diego last, had been lying at San Pedro nearly a month, and had received three thousand hides from the pueblo. These were taken from her the next day, which filled us up, and we both got under weigh on the 4th, she bound up to San Francisco again, and we to San Diego, where we arrived on the 6th.

We were always glad to see San Diego; it being the depot, and a snug little place, and seeming quite like home, especially to me, who had spent a summer there. There was no vessel in port, the Rosa having sailed for Valparaiso and Cadiz, and the Catalina for Callao, nearly a month before. We discharged our hides, and in four days were ready to sail again for the windward; and, to our great joy—for the last time! Over thirty thousand hides had been already collected, cured, and stowed away in the house, which, together with what we should collect, and the Pilgrim would bring down from San Francisco, would make out her cargo. The thought that we were actually going up for the last time, and that the next time we went round San Diego point it would be "homeward bound," brought things so near a close, that we felt as though we were just there, though it must still be the greater part of a year before we could see Boston.

I spent one evening, as had been my custom, at the oven with the Sandwich Islanders; but it was far from being the usual noisy, laughing time. It has been said, that the greatest curse to each of the South Sea islands, was the first man who discovered it; and every one who knows anything of the history of our commerce in those parts, knows how much truth there is in this; and that the white men, with their vices, have brought in diseases before unknown to the islanders, and which are now sweeping off the native population of the Sandwich Islands, at the rate of one fortieth of the entire population annually. They seem to be a doomed people. The curse of a people calling themselves Christian, seems to follow them everywhere; and even here, in this obscure place, lay two young islanders, whom I had left strong, active young men, in the vigor of health, wasting away under a disease, which they would never have known but for their intercourse with Christianized Mexico and people from Christian America. One of them was not so ill; and was moving about, smoking his pipe, and talking, and trying to keep up his spirits; but the other, who was my friend, and Aikane—Hope, was the most dreadful object I had ever seen in my life: his eyes sunken and dead, his cheeks fallen in against his teeth, his hands looking like claws; a dreadful cough, which seemed to rack his whole shattered system, a hollow whispering voice, and an entire inability to move himself. There he lay, upon a mat, on the ground, which was the only floor of the oven, with no medicine, no comforts, and no one to care for, or help him, but a few Kanakas, who were willing enough, but could do nothing. The sight of him made me sick, and faint. Poor fellow! During the four months that I lived upon the beach, we were continually together, both in work, and in our excursions in the woods, and upon the water. I really felt a strong affection for him, and preferred him to any of my own countrymen there; and I believe there was nothing which he would not have done for me.

When I came into the oven he looked at me, held out his hand, and said, in a low voice, but with a delightful smile, "Aloha, Aikane! Aloha nui!" I comforted him as well as I could, and promised to ask the captain to help him from the medicine-chest, and told him I had no doubt the captain would do what he could for him, as he had worked in our employ for several years, both on shore and aboard our vessels on the coast. I went aboard and turned into my hammock, but I could not sleep.

Thinking, from my education, that I must have some knowledge of medicine, the Kanakas had insisted upon my examining him carefully; and it was not a sight to be forgotten. One of our crew, an old man-of-war's man, of twenty years' standing, who had seen sin and suffering in every shape, and whom I afterwards took to see Hope, said it was dreadfully worse than anything he had ever seen, or even dreamed of. He was horror-struck, as his countenance showed; yet he had been among the worst cases in our naval hospitals. I could not get the thought of the poor fellow out of my head all night; his horrible suffering, and his apparently inevitable, horrible end.

The next day I told the captain of Hope's state, and asked him if he would be so kind as to go and see him.

"What? a d——d Kanaka?"

"Yes, sir," said I; "but he has worked four years for our vessels, and has been in the employ of our owners, both on shore and aboard."

"Oh! he be d——d!" said the captain, and walked off.

This same man died afterwards of a fever on the deadly coast of Sumatra; and God grant he had better care taken of him in his sufferings, than he ever gave to any one else! Finding nothing was to be got from the captain, I consulted an old shipmate, who had much experience in these matters, and got from him a recipe, which he always kept by him. With this I went to the mate, and told him the case. Mr. Brown had been entrusted with the general care of the medicine-chest, and although a driving fellow, and a taut hand in a watch, he had good feelings, and was always inclined to be kind to the sick. He said that Hope was not strictly one of the crew, but as he was in our employ when taken sick, he should have the medicines; and he got them and gave them to me, with leave to go ashore at night. Nothing could exceed the delight of the Kanakas, when I came bringing the medicines. All their terms of affection and gratitude were spent upon me, and in a sense wasted, (for I could not understand half of them,) yet they made all known by their manner. Poor Hope was so much revived at the bare thought of anything's being done for him, that he was already stronger and better. I knew he must die as he was, and he could but die under the medicines, and any chance was worth running. An oven, exposed to every wind and change of weather, is no place to take calomel; but nothing else would do, and strong remedies must be used, or he was gone. The applications, internal and external, were powerful, and I gave him strict directions to keep warm and sheltered, telling him it was his only chance for life. Twice, after this, I visited him, having only time to run up, while waiting in the boat. He promised to take his medicines regularly until we returned, and insisted upon it that he was doing better.

We got under weigh on the 10th, bound up to San Pedro, and had three days of calm and head winds, making but little progress. On the fourth, we took a stiff south-easter, which obliged us to reef our topsails. While on the yard, we saw a sail on the weather bow, and in about half an hour, passed the Ayacucho, under double-reefed topsails, beating down to San Diego. Arrived at San Pedro on the fourth day, and came-to in the old place, a league from shore, with no other vessel in port, and the prospect of three weeks, or more, of dull life, rolling goods up a slippery hill, carrying hides on our heads over sharp stones, and, perhaps, slipping for a south-easter.

There was but one man in the only house here, and him I shall always remember as a good specimen of a California ranger. He had been a tailor in Philadelphia, and getting intemperate and in debt, he joined a trapping party and went to the Columbia river, and thence down to Monterey, where he spent everything, left his party, and came to the Pueblo de los Angelos, to work at his trade. Here he went dead to leeward among the pulperias, gambling rooms, etc., and came down to San Pedro, to be moral by being out of temptation. He had been in the house several weeks, working hard at his trade, upon orders which he had brought with him, and talked much of his resolution, and opened his heart to us about his past life. After we had been here some time, he started off one morning, in fine spirits, well dressed, to carry the clothes which he had been making to the pueblo, and saying he would bring back his money and some fresh orders the next day. The next day came, and a week passed, and nearly a fortnight, when, one day, going ashore, we saw a tall man, who looked like our friend the tailor, getting out of the back of an Indian's cart, which had just come down from the pueblo. He stood for the house, but we bore up after him; when finding that we were overhauling him, he hove-to and spoke us. Such a sight I never saw before. Barefooted, with an old pair of trowsers tied round his waist by a piece of green hide, a soiled cotton shirt, and a torn Indian hat; "cleaned out," to the last reál, and completely "used up." He confessed the whole matter; acknowledged that he was on his back; and now he had a prospect of a fit of the horrors for a week, and of being worse than useless for months. This is a specimen of the life of half of the Americans and English who are adrift over the whole of California. One of the same stamp was Russell, who was master of the hide-house at San Diego, while I was there, and afterwards turned away for his misconduct. He spent his own money and nearly all the stores among the half-bloods upon the beach, and being turned away, went up to the Presidio, where he lived the life of a desperate "loafer," until some rascally deed sent him off "between two days," with men on horseback, dogs, and Indians in full cry after him, among the hills. One night, he burst into our room at the hide-house, breathless, pale as a ghost, covered with mud, and torn by thorns and briers, nearly naked, and begged for a crust of bread, saying he had neither eaten nor slept for three days. Here was the great Mr. Russell, who a month before was "Don Tomàs," "Capitán de la playa," "Maéstro de la casa," etc., etc., begging food and shelter of Kanakas and sailors. He staid with us till he gave himself up, and was dragged off to the calabozo.

Another, and a more amusing specimen, was one whom we saw at San Francisco. He had been a lad on board the ship California, in one of her first voyages, and ran away and commenced Ranchéro, gambling, stealing horses, etc. He worked along up to San Francisco, and was living on a rancho near there, while we were in port. One morning, when we went ashore in the boat, we found him at the landing-place, dressed in California style,—a wide hat, faded velveteen trowsers, and a blanket cloak thrown over his shoulders—and wishing to go off in the boat, saying he was going to paseár with our captain a little. We had many doubts of the reception he would meet with; but he seemed to think himself company for any one. We took him aboard, landed him at the gangway, and went about our work, keeping an eye upon the quarter-deck, where the captain was walking. The lad went up to him with the most complete assurance, and raising his hat, wished him a good afternoon. Captain T—— turned round, looked at him from head to foot, and saying coolly, "Hallo! who the h—- are you?" kept on his walk. This was a rebuff not to be mistaken, and the joke passed about among the crew by winks and signs, at different parts of the ship. Finding himself disappointed at headquarters, he edged along forward to the mate, who was overseeing some work on the forecastle, and tried to begin a yarn; but it would not do. The mate had seen the reception he had met with aft, and would have no cast-off company. The second mate was aloft, and the third mate and myself were painting the quarter-boat, which hung by the davits, so he betook himself to us; but we looked at one another, and the officer was too busy to say a word. From us, he went to one and another of the crew, but the joke had got before him, and he found everybody busy and silent. Looking over the rail a few moments afterward, we saw him at the galley-door talking to the cook. This was a great comedown, from the highest seat in the synagogue to a seat in the galley with the black cook. At night, too, when supper was called, he stood in the waist for some time, hoping to be asked down with the officers, but they went below, one after another, and left him. His next chance was with the carpenter and sail-maker, and he lounged round the after hatchway until the last had gone down. We had now had fun enough out of him, and taking pity on him, offered him a pot of tea, and a cut at the kid, with the rest, in the forecastle. He was hungry, and it was growing dark, and he began to see that there was no use in playing the caballero any longer, and came down into the forecastle, put into the "grub" in sailor's style, threw off all his airs, and enjoyed the joke as much as any one; for a man must take a joke among sailors. He gave us the whole account of his adventures in the country,—roguery and all—and was very entertaining. He was a smart, unprincipled fellow, was at the bottom of most of the rascally doings of the country, and gave us a great deal of interesting information in the ways of the world we were in.

Saturday, Feb. 13th. Were called up at midnight to slip for a violent north-easter, for this rascally hole of San Pedro is unsafe in every wind but a south-wester, which is seldom known to blow more than once in a half century. We went off with a flowing sheet, and hove-to under the lee of Catalina island, where we lay three days, and then returned to our anchorage.

Tuesday, Feb. 23d. This afternoon, a signal was made from the shore, and we went off in the gig, and found the agent's clerk, who had been up to the pueblo, waiting at the landing-place, with a package under his arm, covered with brown papers and tied carefully with twine. No sooner had we shoved off than he told us there was good news from Santa Barbara. "What's that?" said one of the crew; "has the bloody agent slipped off the hooks? Has the old bundle of bones got him at last?"—"No; better than that. The California has arrived." Letters, papers, news, and, perhaps,—friends, on board! Our hearts were all up in our mouths, and we pulled away like good fellows; for the precious packet could not be opened except by the captain. As we pulled under the stern, the clerk held up the package, and called out to the mate, who was leaning over the taffrail, that the California had arrived.

"Hurrah!" said the mate, so as to be heard fore and aft; "California come, and news from Boston!"

Instantly there was a confusion on board which no one could account for who has not been in the same situation. All discipline seemed for a moment relaxed.

"What's that, Mr. Brown?" said the cook, putting his head out of the galley—"California come?"

"Aye, aye! you angel of darkness, and there's a letter for you from Bullknop 'treet, number two-two-five—green door and brass knocker!"

The packet was sent down into the cabin, and every one waited to hear of the result. As nothing came up, the officers began to feel that they were acting rather a child's part, and turned the crew to again and the same strict discipline was restored, which prohibits speech between man and man, while at work on deck; so that, when the steward came forward with letters for the crew, each man took his letters, carried them below to his chest, and came up again immediately; and not a letter was read until we had cleared up decks for the night.

An overstrained sense of manliness is the characteristic of seafaring men, or, rather, of life on board ship. This often gives an appearance of want of feeling, and even of cruelty. From this, if a man comes within an ace of breaking his neck and escapes, it is made a joke of; and no notice must be taken of a bruise or cut; and any expression of pity, or any show of attention, would look sisterly, and unbecoming a man who has to face the rough and tumble of such a life. From this, too, the sick are neglected at sea, and whatever sailors may be ashore, a sick man finds little sympathy or attention, forward or aft. A man, too, can have nothing peculiar or sacred on board ship; for all the nicer feelings they take pride in disregarding, both in themselves and others. A thin-skinned man could not live an hour on ship-board. One would be torn raw unless he had the hide of an ox. A moment of natural feeling for home and friends, and then the frigid routine of sea-life returned. Jokes were made upon those who showed any interest in the expected news, and everything near and dear was made common stock for rude jokes and unfeeling coarseness, to which no exception could be taken by any one.

Supper, too, must be eaten before the letters were read; and when, at last, they were brought out, they all got round any one who had a letter, and expected to have it read aloud, and have it all in common. If any one went by himself to read, it was—"Fair play, there; and no skulking!" I took mine and went into the sailmaker's berth, where I could read it without interruption. It was dated August, just a year from the time I had sailed from home; and every one was well, and no great change had taken place. Thus, for one year, my mind was set at ease, yet it was already six months from the date of the letter, and what another year would bring to pass, who could tell? Every one away from home thinks that some great thing must have happened, while to those at home there seems to be a continued monotony and lack of incident.

As much as my feelings were taken up by my own intelligence from home, I could not but be amused by a scene in the steerage. The carpenter had been married just before leaving Boston, and during the voyage had talked much about his wife, and had to bear and forbear, as every man, known to be married, must, aboard ship;

yet the certainty of hearing from his wife by the first ship, seemed to keep up his spirits. The California came, the packet was brought on board; no one was in higher spirits than he; but when the letters came forward, there was none for him. The captain looked again, but there was no mistake. Poor "Chips," could eat no supper. He was completely down in the mouth. "Sails" (the sailmaker) tried to comfort him, and told him he was a bloody fool to give up his grub for any woman's daughter, and reminded him that he had told him a dozen times that he'd never see or hear from his wife again.

"Ah!" said "Chips," "you don't know what it is to have a wife, and"—

"Don't I?" said Sails; and then came, for the hundredth time, the story of his coming ashore at New York, from the Constellation frigate, after a cruise of four years round the Horn,—being paid off with over five hundred dollars,—marrying, and taking a couple of rooms in a four-story house,—furnishing the rooms, (with a particular account of the furniture, including a dozen flag-bottomed chairs, which he always dilated upon, whenever the subject of furniture was alluded to,)—going off to sea again, leaving his wife half-pay, like a fool,—coming home and finding her "off, like Bob's horse, with nobody to pay the reckoning;" furniture gone,—flag-bottomed chairs and all;—and with it, his "long togs," the half-pay, his beaver hat, white linen shirts, and everything else. His wife he never saw, or heard of, from that day to this, and never wished to. Then followed a sweeping assertion, not much to the credit of the sex, if true, though he has Pope to back him. "Come, Chips, cheer up like a man, and take some hot grub! Don't be made a fool of by anything in petticoats! As for your wife, you'll never see her again; she was 'up keeleg and off' before you were outside of Cape Cod. You hove your money away like a fool; but every man must learn once, just as I did; so you'd better square the yards with her, and make the best of it."

This was the best consolation "Sails" had to offer, but it did not seem to be just the thing the carpenter wanted; for, during several days, he was very much dejected, and bore with difficulty the jokes of the sailors, and with still more difficulty their attempts at advice and consolation, of most of which the sailmaker's was a good specimen.

Thursday, Feb. 25th. Set sail for Santa Barbara, where we arrived on Sunday, the 28th. We just missed of seeing the California, for she had sailed three days before, bound to Monterey, to enter her cargo and procure her license, and thence to San Francisco, etc. Captain Arthur left files of Boston papers for Captain T——, which, after they had been read and talked over in the cabin, I procured from my friend the third mate. One file was of all the Boston Transcripts for the month of August, 1835, and the rest were about a dozen Daily Advertisers and Couriers, of different dates. After all, there is nothing in a strange land like a newspaper from home. Even a letter, in many respects, is nothing, in comparison with it. It carries you back to the spot, better than anything else. It is almost equal to clairvoyance. The names of the streets, with the things advertised, are almost as good as seeing the signs; and while reading "Boy lost!" one can almost hear the bell and well-known voice of "Old Wilson," crying the boy as "strayed, stolen, or mislaid!" Then there was the Commencement at Cambridge, and the full account of the exercises at the graduating of my own class. A list of all those familiar names, (beginning as usual with Abbot, and ending with W.,) which, as I read them over, one by one, brought up their faces and characters as I had known them in the various scenes of college life. Then I imagined them upon the stage, speaking their orations, dissertations, colloquies, etc., with the gestures and tones of each, and tried to fancy the manner in which each would handle his subject, *****, handsome, showy, and superficial; *****, with his strong head, clear brain, cool self-possession; *****, modest, sensitive, and underrated; *****, the mouth-piece of the debating clubs, noisy, vaporous, and democratic; and so following. Then I could see them receiving their A. Bs. from the dignified, feudal-looking President, with his "auctoritate mihi commissâ," and walking off the stage with their diplomas in their hands; while upon the very same day, their classmate was walking up and down California beach with a hide upon his head.

Every watch below, for a week, I pored over these papers, until I was sure there could be nothing in them that had escaped my attention, and was ashamed to keep them any longer.

Saturday, March 5th. This was an important day in our almanac, for it was on this day that we were first assured that our voyage was really drawing to a close. The captain gave orders to have the ship ready for getting under weigh; and observed that there was a good breeze to take us down to San Pedro. Then we were not going up to windward. Thus much was certain, and was soon known, fore and aft; and when we went in the gig to take him off, he shook hands with the people on the beach, and said that he never expected to see Santa Barbara again. This settled the matter, and sent a thrill of pleasure through the heart of every one in the boat. We pulled off with a will, saying to ourselves (I can speak for myself at least)—"Good-by, Santa Barbara!—This is the last pull here—No more duckings in your breakers, and slipping from your cursed south-easters!" The news was soon known aboard, and put life into everything when we were getting under weigh. Each one was taking his last look at the mission, the town, the breakers on the beach, and swearing that no money would make him ship to see them again; and when all hands tallied on to the cat-fall, the chorus of "Time for us to go!" was raised for the first time, and joined in, with full swing, by everybody. One would have thought we were on our voyage home, so near did it seem to us, though there were yet three months for us on the coast.

We left here the young Englishman, George Marsh, of whom I have before spoken, who was wrecked upon the Pelew Islands. He left us to take the berth of second mate on board the Ayacucho, which was lying in port. He was well qualified for this, and his education would enable him to rise to any situation on board ship. I felt really sorry to part from him. There was something about him which excited my curiosity; for I could not, for a moment, doubt that he was well born, and, in early life, well bred. There was the latent gentleman about him, and the sense of honor, and no little of the pride, of a young man of good family. The situation was offered him only a few hours before we sailed; and though he must give up returning to America, yet I have no doubt that the change from a dog's berth to an officer's, was too agreeable to his feelings to be declined. We pulled him on board the Ayacucho, and when he left the boat he gave each of its crew a piece of money, except myself, and shook hands with me, nodding his head, as much as to say,—"We understand one another," and sprang on board. Had I known, an hour sooner, that he was to leave us, I would have made an effort to get from him the true history of his early life. He knew that I had no faith in the story which he told the crew, and perhaps, in the moment of parting from me, probably forever, he would have given me the true account. Whether I shall ever meet him again, or whether his manuscript narrative of his adventures in the Pelew Islands, which would be creditable to him and interesting to the world, will ever see the light, I cannot tell. His is one of those cases which are more numerous than those suppose, who have never lived anywhere but in their own homes, and never walked but in one line from their cradles to their graves. We must come down from our heights, and leave our straight paths, for the byways and low places of life, if we would learn truths by strong contrasts; and in hovels, in forecastles, and among our own outcasts in foreign lands, see what has been wrought upon our fellow-creatures by accident, hardship, or vice.

Two days brought us to San Pedro, and two days more (to our no small joy) gave us our last view of that place, which was universally called the hell of California, and seemed designed, in every way, for the wear and tear of sailors. Not even the last view could bring out one feeling of regret. No thanks, thought I, as we left the sandy shores in the distance, for the hours I have walked over your stones, barefooted, with hides on my head;—for the burdens I have carried up your steep, muddy hill; for the duckings in your surf; and for the long days and longer nights passed on your desolate hill, watching piles of hides, hearing the sharp bark of your eternal coati, and the dismal hooting of your owls.

As I bade good-by to each successive place, I felt as though one link after another were struck from the chain of my servitude. Having kept close in shore, for the land-breeze, we passed the mission of San Juan Campestráno the same night, and saw distinctly, by the bright moonlight, the hill which I had gone down by a pair of halyards in search of a few paltry hides. "Forsan et haec olim," thought I, and took my last look of that place too. And on the next morning we were under the high point of San Diego. The flood tide took us swiftly in, and we came-to, opposite our hide-house, and prepared to get everything in trim for a long stay. This was our last port. Here we were to discharge everything from the ship, clean her out, smoke her, take in our hides, wood, water, etc., and set sail for Boston. While all this was doing, we were to lie still in one place, and the port was a safe one, and there was no fear of south-easters. Accordingly, having picked out a good berth, in the stream, with a good smooth beach opposite, for a landing-place and within two cables' length of our hide-house, we moored ship, unbent all the sails, sent down the top-gallant yards and all the studding-sail booms, and housed the top-gallant masts. The boats were then hove out, and all the sails, spare spars, the stores, the rigging not rove, and, in fact, everything which was not in daily use, sent ashore, and stowed away in the house. Then went all our hides and horns, and we left hardly anything in the ship but her ballast, and this we made preparation to heave out, the next day. At night, after we had knocked off, and were sitting round in the forecastle, smoking and talking and taking sailor's pleasure, we congratulated ourselves upon being in that situation in which we had wished ourselves every time we had come into San Diego. "If we were only here for the last time," we had often said, "with our top-gallant masts housed and our sails unbent!"—and now we had our wish. Six weeks, or two months, of the hardest work we had yet seen, was before us, and then— "Good-by to California!"

CHAPTER XXIX

LOADING FOR HOME—A SURPRISE—LAST OF AN OLD FRIEND—THE LAST HIDE—A HARD CASE—UP ANCHOR, FOR HOME!—HOMEWARD BOUND

We turned-in early, knowing that we might expect an early call; and sure enough, before the stars had quite faded, "All hands ahoy!" and we were turned-to, heaving out ballast. A regulation of the port forbids any ballast to be thrown overboard; accordingly, our long-boat was lined inside with rough boards and brought alongside the gangway, but where one tub-full went into the boat, twenty went overboard. This is done by every vessel, for the ballast can make but little difference in the channel, and it saves more than a week of labor, which would be spent in loading the boats, rowing them to the point, and unloading them. When any people from the Presidio were on board, the boat was hauled up and ballast thrown in; but when the coast was clear, she was dropped astern again, and the ballast fell overboard. This is one of those petty frauds which every vessel practises in ports of inferior foreign nations, and which are lost sight of, among the countless deeds of greater weight which are hardly less common. Fortunately a sailor, not being a free agent in work aboard ship, is not accountable; yet the fact of being constantly employed, without thought, in such things, begets an indifference to the rights of others.

Friday, and a part of Saturday, we were engaged in this work, until we had thrown out all but what we wanted under our cargo on the passage home; when, as the next day was Sunday, and a good day for smoking ship, we cleared everything out of the cabin and forecastle, made a slow fire of charcoal, birch bark, brimstone, and other matters, on the ballast in the bottom of the hold, calked up the hatches and every open seam, and pasted over the cracks of the windows, and the slides of the scuttles, and companionway. Wherever smoke was seen coming out, we calked and pasted, and, so far as we could, made the ship smoke tight. The captain and officers slept under the awning which was spread over the quarter-deck; and we stowed ourselves away under an old studding-sail, which we drew over one side of the forecastle. The next day, from fear that something might happen, orders were given for no one to leave the ship, and, as the decks were lumbered up with everything, we could not wash them down, so we had nothing to do, all day long. Unfortunately, our books were where we could not get at them, and we were turning about for something to do, when one man recollected a book he had left in the galley. He went after it, and it proved to be Woodstock. This was a great windfall, and as all could not read it at once, I, being the scholar of the company, was appointed reader. I got a knot of six or eight about me, and no one could have had a more attentive audience. Some laughed at the "scholars," and went over the other side of the forecastle, to work, and spin their yarns; but I carried the day, and had the cream of the crew for my hearers. Many of the reflections, and the political parts, I omitted, but all the narrative they were delighted with; especially the descriptions of the Puritans, and the sermons and harangues of the Round-head soldiers. The gallantry of Charles, Dr. Radcliffe's plots, the knavery of "trusty Tompkins,"—in fact, every part seemed to chain their attention. Many things which, while I was reading, I had a misgiving about, thinking them above their capacity, I was surprised to find them enter into completely.

I read nearly all day, until sundown; when, as soon as supper was over, as I had nearly finished, they got a light from the galley; and by skipping what was less interesting, I carried them through to the marriage of Everard, and the restoration of Charles the Second, before eight o'clock.

The next morning, we took the battens from the hatches, and opened the ship. A few stifled rats were found; and what bugs, cockroaches, fleas, and other vermin, there might have been on board, must have unrove their life-lines before the hatches were opened. The ship being now ready, we covered the bottom of the hold over, fore and aft, with dried brush for dunnage, and having levelled everything away, we were ready to take in our cargo. All the hides that had been collected since the California left the coast, (a little more than two years,) amounting to about forty thousand, were cured, dried, and stowed away in the house, waiting for our good ship to take them to Boston.

Now began the operation of taking in our cargo, which kept us hard at work, from the grey of the morning till star-light, for six weeks, with the exception of Sundays, and of just time to swallow our meals. To carry the work on quicker, a division of labor was made. Two men threw the hides down from the piles in the house, two more picked them up and put them on a long horizontal pole, raised a few feet from the ground, where they were beaten, by two more, with flails, somewhat like those used in threshing wheat. When beaten, they were taken from this pole by two more, and placed upon a platform of boards; and ten or a dozen men, with their trowsers rolled up, were constantly going, back and forth, from the platform to the boat, which was kept off where she would just float, with the hides upon their heads. The throwing the hides upon the pole was the most difficult work, and required a sleight of hand which was only to be got by long practice. As I was known for a hide-curer, this post was assigned to me, and I continued at it for six or eight days, tossing, in that time, from eight to ten thousand hides, until my wrists became so lame that I gave in; and was transferred to the gang that was employed in filling the boats, where I remained for the rest of the time. As we were obliged to carry the hides on our heads from fear of their getting wet, we each had a piece of sheepskin sewed into the inside of our hats, with the wool next to our heads, and thus were able to bear the weight, day after day, which would otherwise have soon worn off our hair, and borne hard upon our skulls. Upon the whole, ours was the best berth; for though the water was nipping cold, early in the morning and late at night, and being so continually wet was rather an exposure, yet we got rid of the constant dust and dirt from the beating of the hides, and being all of us young and hearty, did not mind the exposure. The older men of the crew, whom it would have been dangerous to have kept in the water, remained on board with the mate, to stow the hides away, as fast as they were brought off by the boats.

We continued at work in this manner until the lower hold was filled to within four feet of the beams, when all hands were called aboard to commence steeving. As this is a peculiar operation, it will require a minute description.

Before stowing the hides, as I have said, the ballast is levelled off, just above the keelson, and then loose dunnage placed upon it, on which the hides rest. The greatest care is used in stowing, to make the ship hold as many hides as possible. It is no mean art, and a man skilled in it is an important character in California. Many a dispute have I heard raging high between professed "beach-combers," as to whether the hides should be stowed "shingling," or "back-to-back, and flipper-to-flipper;" upon which point there was an entire and bitter division of sentiment among the savans. We adopted each method at different periods of the stowing, and parties ran high in the forecastle, some siding with "old Bill" in favor of the former, and others scouting him, and relying upon "English Bob" of the Ayacucho, who had been eight years in California, and was willing to risk his life and limb for the latter method. At length a compromise was effected, and a middle course, of shifting the ends and backs at every lay, was adopted, which worked well, and which, though they held it inferior to their own, each party granted was better than that of the other.

Having filled the ship up, in this way, to within four feet of her beams, the process of steeving commenced, by which an hundred hides are got into a place where one could not be forced by hand, and which presses the hides to the utmost, sometimes starting the beams of the ship, resembling in its effects the jack-screws which are used in stowing cotton. Each morning we went ashore, and beat and brought off as many hides as we could steeve in the course of the day, and, after breakfast, went down into the hold, where we remained at work until night. The whole length of the hold, from stem to stern, was floored off level, and we began with raising a pile in the after part, hard against the bulkhead of the run, and filling it up to the beams, crowding in as many as we could by hand and pushing in with oars; when a large "book" was made of from twenty-five to fifty hides, doubled at the backs, and put into one another, like the leaves of a book. An opening was then made between two hides in the pile, and the back of the outside hide of the book inserted. Two long, heavy spars, called steeves, made of the strongest wood, and sharpened off like a wedge at one end, were placed with their wedge ends into the inside of the hide which was the centre of the book, and to the other end of each, straps were fitted, into which large tackles were hooked, composed each of two huge purchase blocks, one hooked to the strap on the end of the steeve, and the other into a dog, fastened into one of the beams, as far aft as it could be got. When this was arranged, and the ways greased upon which the book was to slide, the falls of the tackles were stretched forward, and all hands tallied on, and bowsed away until the book was well entered; when these tackles were nippered, straps and toggles clapped upon the falls, and two more luff tackles hooked on, with dogs, in the same manner; and thus, by luff upon luff, the power was multiplied, until into a pile in which one hide more could not be crowded by hand, an hundred or an hundred and fifty were often driven in by this complication of purchases. When the last luff was hooked on, all hands were called to the rope—cook, steward, and all—and ranging ourselves at the falls, one behind the other, sitting down on the hides, with our heads just even with the beams, we set taut upon the tackles, and striking up a song, and all lying back at the chorus, we bowsed the tackles home, and drove the large books chock in out of sight.

The sailor's songs for capstans and falls are of a peculiar kind, having a chorus at the end of each line. The burden is usually sung, by one alone, and, at the chorus, all hands join in,—and the louder the noise, the better. With us, the chorus seemed almost to raise the decks of the ship, and might be heard at a great distance, ashore. A song is as necessary to sailors as the drum and fife to a soldier. They can't pull in time, or pull with a will, without it. Many a time, when a thing goes heavy, with one fellow yo-ho-ing, a lively song, like "Heave, to the girls!" "Nancy oh!" "Jack Cross-tree," etc., has put life and strength into every arm. We often found a great difference in the effect of the different songs in driving in the hides. Two or three songs would be tried, one after the other; with no effect;—not an inch could be got upon the tackles—when a new song, struck up, seemed to hit the humor of the moment, and drove the tackles "two blocks" at once. "Heave round hearty!" "Captain gone ashore!" and the like, might do for common pulls, but in an emergency, when we wanted a heavy, "raise-the-dead" pull, which should start the beams of the ship, there was nothing like "Time for us to go!" "Round the corner," or "Hurrah! hurrah! my hearty bullies!"

This was the most lively part of our work. A little boating and beach work in the morning; then twenty or thirty men down in a close hold, where we were obliged to sit down and slide about, passing hides, and rowsing about the great steeves, tackles, and dogs, singing out at the falls, and seeing the ship filling up every day. The work was as hard as it could well be. There was not a moment's cessation from Monday morning till Saturday night, when we were generally beaten out, and glad to have a full night's rest, a wash and shift of clothes, and a quiet Sunday. During all this time,—which would have startled Dr. Graham—we lived upon almost nothing but fresh beef; fried beefsteaks, three times a day,—morning, noon, and night. At morning and night we had a quart of tea to each man; and an allowance of about a pound of hard bread a day; but our chief article of food was the beef. A mess, consisting of six men, had a large wooden kid piled up with beefsteaks, cut thick, and fried in fat, with the grease poured over them. Round this we sat, attacking it with our jack-knives and teeth, and with the appetite of young lions, and sent back an empty kid to the galley. This was done three times a day. How many pounds each man ate in a day, I will not attempt to compute. A whole bullock (we ate liver and all) lasted us but four days. Such devouring of flesh, I will venture to say, was seldom known before. What one man ate in a day, over a hearty man's allowance, would make a Russian's heart leap into his mouth. Indeed, during all the time we were upon the coast, our principal food was fresh beef, and every man had perfect health; but this was a time of especial devouring; and what we should have done without meat, I cannot tell. Once or twice, when our bullocks failed and we were obliged to make a meal upon dry bread and water, it seemed like feeding upon shavings. Light and dry, feeling unsatisfied, and, at the same time, full, we were glad to see four quarters of a bullock, just killed, swinging from the fore-top. Whatever theories may be started by sedentary men, certainly no men could have gone through more hard work and exposure for sixteen months in more perfect health, and without ailings and failings, than our ship's crew, let them have lived upon Hygeia's own baking and dressing.

Friday, April 15th. Arrived, brig Pilgrim, from the windward. It was a sad sight for her crew to see us getting ready to go off the coast, while they, who had been longer on the coast than the Alert, were condemned to another year's hard service. I spent an evening on board, and found them making the best of the matter, and determined to rough it out as they might; but my friend S—— was determined to go home in the ship, if money or interest could bring it to pass. After considerable negotiating and working, he succeeded in persuading my English friend, Tom Harris,—my companion in the anchor watch—for thirty dollars, some clothes, and an intimation from Captain Faucon that he should want a second mate before the voyage was up, to take his place in the brig as soon as she was ready to go up to windward.

The first opportunity I could get to speak to Captain Faucon, I asked him to step up to the oven and look at Hope, whom he knew well, having had him on board his vessel. He went to see him, but said that he had so little medicine, and expected to be so long on the coast, that he could do nothing for him, but that Captain Arthur would take care of him when he came down in the California, which would be in a week or more. I had been to see Hope the first night after we got into San Diego this last time, and had frequently since spent the early part of a night in the oven. I hardly expected, when I left him to go to windward, to find him alive upon my return. He was certainly as low as he could well be when I left him, and what would be the effect of the medicines that I gave him, I hardly then dared to conjecture. Yet I knew that he must die without them. I was not a little rejoiced, therefore, and relieved, upon our return, to see him decidedly better. The medicines were strong, and took hold and gave a check to the disorder which was destroying him; and, more than that, they had begun the work of exterminating it. I shall never forget the gratitude that he expressed. All the Kanakas attributed his escape solely to my knowledge, and would not be persuaded that I had not all the secrets of the physical system open to me and under my control. My medicines, however, were gone, and no more could be got from the ship, so that his life was left to hang upon the arrival of the California.

Sunday, April 24th. We had now been nearly seven weeks in San Diego, and had taken in the greater part of our cargo, and were looking out, every day, for the arrival of the California, which had our agent on board; when, this afternoon, some Kanakas, who had been over the hill for rabbits and to fight rattlesnakes, came running down the path, singing out, "Kail ho!" with all their might. Mr. H., our third mate, was ashore, and asking them particularly about the size of the sail, etc., and learning that it was "Moku—Nui Moku," hailed our ship, and said that the California was on the other side of the point. Instantly, all hands were turned up, the bow guns run out and loaded, the ensign and broad pennant set, the yards squared by lifts and braces, and everything got ready to make a good appearance. The instant she showed her nose round the point, we began our salute. She came in under top-gallant sails, clewed up and furled her sails in good order, and came-to, within good swinging distance of us. It being Sunday, and nothing to do, all hands were on the forecastle, criticising the new-comer. She was a good, substantial ship, not quite so long as the Alert, and wall-sided and kettle-bottomed, after the latest fashion of south-shore cotton and sugar wagons; strong, too, and tight, and a good average sailor, but with no pretensions to beauty, and nothing in the style of a "crack ship." Upon the whole, we were perfectly satisfied that the Alert might hold up her head with a ship twice as smart as she.

At night, some of us got a boat and went on board, and found a large, roomy forecastle, (for she was squarer forward than the Alert,) and a crew of a dozen or fifteen men and boys, sitting around on their chests, smoking and talking, and ready to give a welcome to any of our ship's company. It was just seven months since they left Boston, which seemed but yesterday to us. Accordingly, we had much to ask, for though we had seen the newspapers that she brought, yet these were the very men who had been in Boston and seen everything with their own eyes. One of the green-hands was a Boston boy, from one of the public schools, and, of course, knew many things which we wished to ask about, and on inquiring the names of our two Boston boys, found that they had been schoolmates of his. Our men had hundreds of questions to ask about Ann street, the boarding-houses, the ships in port, the rate of wages, and other matters.

Among her crew were two English man-of-war's-men, so that, of course, we soon had music. They sang in the true sailor's style, and the rest of the crew, which was a remarkably musical one, joined in the choruses. They had many of the latest sailor songs, which had not yet got about among our merchantmen, and which they were very choice of. They began soon after we came on board, and kept it up until after two bells, when the second mate came forward and called "the Alerts away!" Battle-songs, drinking-songs, boat-songs, love-songs, and everything else, they seemed to have a complete assortment of, and I was glad to find that "All in the Downs," "Poor Tom Bowline," "The Bay of Biscay," "List, ye Landsmen!" and all those classical songs of the sea, still held their places. In addition to these, they had picked up at the theatres and other places a few songs of a little more genteel cast, which they were very proud of; and I shall never forget hearing an old salt, who had broken his voice by hard drinking on shore, and bellowing from the mast-head in a hundred northwesters, with all manner of ungovernable trills and quavers in the high notes, breaking into a rough falsetto—and in the low ones, growling along like the dying away of the boatswain's "all hands ahoy!" down the hatch-way, singing, "Oh, no, we never mention him."

"Perhaps, like me, he struggles with
Each feeling of regret;
But if he's loved as I have loved,
He never can forget!"

The last line, being the conclusion, he roared out at the top of his voice, breaking each word up into half a dozen syllables. This was very popular, and Jack was called upon every night to give them his "sentimental song." No one called for it more loudly than I, for the complete absurdity of the execution, and the sailors' perfect satisfaction in it, were ludicrous beyond measure.

The next day, the California commenced unloading her cargo; and her boats' crews, in coming and going, sang their boat-songs, keeping time with their oars. This they did all day long for several days, until their hides were all discharged, when a gang of them were sent on board the Alert, to help us steeve our hides. This was a windfall for us, for they had a set of new songs for the capstan and fall, and ours had got nearly worn out by six weeks' constant use. I have no doubt that this timely reinforcement of songs hastened our work several days.

Our cargo was now nearly all taken in; and my old friend, the Pilgrim, having completed her discharge, unmoored, to set sail the next morning on another long trip to windward. I was just thinking of her hard lot, and congratulating myself upon my escape from her, when I received a summons into the cabin. I went aft, and there found, seated round the cabin table, my own captain, Captain Faucon of the Pilgrim, and Mr. R——, the agent. Captain T—— turned to me and asked abruptly—

"D——, do you want to go home in the ship?"

"Certainly, sir," said I; "I expect to go home in the ship."

"Then," said he, "you must get some one to go in your place on board the Pilgrim."

I was so completely "taken aback" by this sudden intimation, that for a moment I could make no reply. I knew that it would be hopeless to attempt to prevail upon any of the ship's crew to take twelve months more upon the California in the brig. I knew, too, that Captain T—— had received orders to bring me home in the Alert, and he had told me, when I was at the hide-house, that I was to go home in her; and even if this had not been so, it was cruel to give me no notice of the step they were going to take, until a few hours before the brig would sail. As soon as I had got my wits about me, I put on a bold front, and told him plainly that I had a letter in my chest informing me that he had been written to, by the owners in Boston, to bring me home in the ship, and moreover, that he had told me that I was to go in the ship.

To have this told him, and to be opposed in such a manner, was more than my lord paramount had been used to.

He turned fiercely upon me, and tried to look me down, and face me out of my statement; but finding that that wouldn't do, and that I was entering upon my defence in such a way as would show to the other two that he was in the wrong,—he changed his ground, and pointed to the shipping papers of the Pilgrim, from which my name had never been erased, and said that there was my name,—that I belonged to her,—that he had an absolute discretionary power,—and, in short, that I must be on board the Pilgrim by the next morning with my chest and hammock, or have some one ready to go in my place, and that he would not hear another word from me. No court or star chamber could proceed more summarily with a poor devil, than this trio was about to do with me; condemning me to a punishment worse than a Botany Bay exile, and to a fate which would alter the whole current of my future life; for two years more in California would have made me a sailor for the rest of my days. I felt all this, and saw the necessity of being determined. I repeated what I had said, and insisted upon my right to return in the ship.

I "raised my arm, and tauld my crack,
Before them a'."

But it would have all availed me nothing, had I been "some poor body," before this absolute, domineering tribunal. But they saw that I would not go, unless "vi et armis," and they knew that I had friends and interest enough at home to make them suffer for any injustice they might do me. It was probably this that turned the matter; for the captain changed his tone entirely, and asked me if, in case any one went in my place, I would give him the same sum that S—— gave Harris to exchange with him. I told him that if any one was sent on board the brig, I should pity him, and be willing to help him to that, or almost any amount; but would not speak of it as an exchange.

"Very well," said he. "Go forward about your business, and send English Ben here to me!"

I went forward with a light heart, but feeling as angry, and as much contempt as I could well contain between my teeth. English Ben was sent aft, and in a few moments came forward, looking as though he had received his sentence to be hung. The captain had told him to get his things ready to go on board the brig the next morning; and that I would give him thirty dollars and a suit of clothes. The hands had "knocked off" for dinner, and were standing about the forecastle, when Ben came forward and told his story. I could see plainly that it made a great excitement, and that, unless I explained the matter to them, the feeling would be turned against me. Ben was a poor English boy, a stranger in Boston, and without friends or money; and being an active, willing lad, and a good sailor for his years, was a general favorite. "Oh, yes!" said the crew, "the captain has let you off, because you are a gentleman's son, and have got friends, and know the owners; and taken Ben, because he is poor, and has got nobody to say a word for him!" I knew that this was too true to be answered, but I excused myself from any blame, and told them that I had a right to go home, at all events. This pacified them a little, but Jack had got a notion that a poor lad was to be imposed upon, and did not distinguish very clearly; and though I knew that I was in no fault, and, in fact, had barely escaped the grossest injustice, yet I felt that my berth was getting to be a disagreeable one. The notion that I was not "one of them," which, by a participation in all their labor and hardships, and having no favor shown me, had been laid asleep, was beginning to revive. But far stronger than any feeling for myself, was the pity I felt for the poor lad. He had depended upon going home in the ship; and from Boston, was going immediately to Liverpool, to see his friends. Beside this, having begun the voyage with very few clothes, he had taken up the greater part of his wages in the slop-chest, and it was every day a losing concern to him; and, like all the rest of the crew, he had a hearty hatred of California, and the prospect of eighteen months or two years more of hide-droghing seemed completely to break down his spirit. I had determined not to go myself, happen what would, and I knew that the captain would not dare to attempt to force me. I knew, too, that the two captains had agreed together to get some one, and that unless I could prevail upon somebody to go voluntarily, there would be no help for Ben. From this consideration, though I had said that I would have nothing to do with an exchange, I did my best to get some one to go voluntarily. I offered to give an order upon the owners in Boston for six months' wages, and also all the clothes, books, and other matters, which I should not want upon the voyage home. When this offer was published in the ship, and the case of poor Ben was set forth in strong colors, several, who would not have dreamed of going themselves, were busy in talking it up to others, who, they thought, might be tempted to accept it; and, at length, one fellow, a harum-scarum lad, whom we called Harry Bluff, and who did not care what country or ship he was in, if he had clothes enough and money enough—partly from pity for Ben, and partly from the thought he should have "cruising money" for the rest of his stay,—came forward, and offered to go and "sling his hammock in the bloody hooker." Lest his purpose should cool, I signed an order for the sum upon the owners in Boston, gave him all the clothes I could spare, and sent him aft to the captain, to let him know what had been done. The skipper accepted the exchange, and was, doubtless, glad to have it pass off so easily. At the same time he cashed the order, which was endorsed to him,[1] and the next morning, the lad went aboard the brig, apparently in good spirits, having shaken hands with each of us and wished us a pleasant passage home, jingling the money in his pockets, and calling out, "Never say die, while there's a shot in the locker." The same boat carried off Harris, my old watchmate, who had previously made an exchange with my friend S——.

I was sorry to part with Harris. Nearly two hundred hours (as we had calculated it) had we walked the ship's deck together, at anchor watch, when all hands were below, and talked over and over every subject which came within the ken of either of us. He gave me a strong gripe with his hand; and I told him, if he came to Boston again, not to fail to find me out, and let me see an old watchmate. The same boat brought on board S——, my friend, who had begun the voyage with me from Boston, and, like me, was going back to his family and to the society which we had been born and brought up in. We congratulated one another upon finding what we had long talked over and wished for, thus brought about; and none on board the ship were more glad than ourselves to see the old brig standing round the point, under full sail. As she passed abreast of us, we all collected in the waist, and gave her three loud, hearty cheers, waving our hats in the air. Her crew sprang into the rigging and chains, answered us with three as loud, to which we, after the nautical custom, gave one in return. I took my last look of their familiar faces as they got over the rail, and saw the old black cook put his head out of the galley, and wave his cap over his head. The crew flew aloft to loose the top-gallant sails and royals; the two captains waved their hands to one another; and, in ten minutes, we saw the last inch of her white canvas, as she rounded the point.

Relieved as I was to see her well off, (and I felt like one who had just sprung from an iron trap which was closing upon him) I had yet a feeling of regret at taking the last look at the old craft in which I had spent a year, and the first year, of my sailor's life—which had been my first home in the new world into which I had entered—and with which I had associated so many things,—my first leaving home, my first crossing the equator, Cape Horn, Juan Fernandez, death at sea, and other things, serious and common. Yet, with all this, and the feeling I had for my old shipmates, condemned to another term of California life, the thought that we were done with it, and that one week more would see us on our way to Boston, was a cure for everything.

Friday, May 6th, completed the taking of our cargo, and was a memorable day in our calendar. The time when we were to take in our last hide, we had looked forward to, for sixteen months, as the first bright spot. When the last hide was stowed away, and the hatches calked down, the tarpaulins battened on to them, the long-boat hoisted in and secured, and the decks swept down for the night,—the chief mate sprang upon the top of the long-boat, called all hands into the waist, and giving us a signal by swinging his cap over his head,—we gave three long, loud cheers, which came from the bottom of our hearts, and made the hills and valleys ring again. In a moment, we heard three, in answer, from the

California's crew, who had seen us taking in our long-boat, and—"the cry they heard—its meaning knew."

The last week, we had been occupied in taking in a supply of wood and water for the passage home, and bringing on board the spare spars, sails, etc. I was sent off with a party of Indians to fill the water-casks, at a spring, about three miles from the shipping, and near the town, and was absent three days, living at the town, and spending the daytime in filling the casks and transporting them on ox-carts to the landing-place, whence they were taken on board by the crew with boats. This being all done with, we gave one day to bending our sails; and at night, every sail, from the courses to the skysails, was bent, and every studding-sail ready for setting.

Before our sailing, an unsuccessful attempt was made by one of the crew of the California to effect an exchange with one of our number. It was a lad, between fifteen and sixteen years of age, who went by the name of the "reefer," having been a midshipman in an East India Company's ship. His singular character and story had excited our interest ever since the ship came into the port. He was a delicate, slender little fellow, with a beautiful pearly complexion, regular features, forehead as white as marble, black haired, curling beautifully, rounded, tapering, delicate fingers, small feet, soft voice, gentle manners, and, in fact, every sign of having been well born and bred. At the same time there was something in his expression which showed a slight deficiency of intellect. How great the deficiency was, or what it resulted from; whether he was born so; whether it was the result of disease or accident; or whether, as some said, it was brought on by his distress of mind, during the voyage, I cannot say. From his own account of himself, and from many circumstances which were known in connection with his story, he must have been the son of a man of wealth. His mother was an Italian woman. He was probably a natural son, for in scarcely any other way could the incidents of his early life be accounted for. He said that his parents did not live together, and he seemed to have been ill treated by his father. Though he had been delicately brought up, and indulged in every way, (and he had then with him trinkets which had been given him at home,) yet his education had been sadly neglected; and when only twelve years old, he was sent as midshipman in the Company's service. His own story was, that he afterwards ran away from home, upon a difficulty which he had with his father, and went to Liverpool, whence he sailed in the ship Rialto, Captain Holmes, for Boston. Captain Holmes endeavored to get him a passage back, but there being no vessel to sail for some time, the boy left him, and went to board at a common sailor's boarding-house, in Ann street, where he supported himself for a few weeks by selling some of his valuables. At length, according to his own account, being desirous of returning home, he went to a shipping-office, where the shipping articles of the California were open. Upon asking where the ship was going, he was told by the shipping-master that she was bound to California. Not knowing where that was, he told him that he wanted to go to Europe, and asked if California was in Europe. The shipping-master answered him in a way which the boy did not understand, and advised him to ship. The boy signed the articles, received his advance, laid out a little of it in clothes, and spent the rest, and was ready to go on board, when, upon the morning of sailing, he heard that the ship was bound upon the North-west Coast, on a two or three years' voyage, and was not going to Europe. Frightened at this prospect, he slipped away when the crew was going aboard, wandered up into another part of the town, and spent all the forenoon in straying about the common, and the neighboring streets.

Having no money, and all his clothes and other things being in the chest, on board, and being a stranger, he became tired and hungry, and ventured down toward the shipping, to see if the vessel had sailed. He was just turning the corner of a street, when the shipping-master, who had been in search of him, popped upon him, seized him, and carried him on board. He cried and struggled, and said he did not wish to go in the ship, but the topsails were at the mast-head, the fasts just ready to be cast off, and everything in the hurry and confusion of departure, so that he was hardly noticed; and the few who did inquire about the matter were told that it was merely a boy who had spent his advance and tried to run away. Had the owners of the vessel known anything of the matter, they would have interfered at once; but they either knew nothing of it, or heard, like the rest, that it was only an unruly boy who was sick of his bargain. As soon as the boy found himself actually at sea, and upon a voyage of two or three years in length, his spirits failed him; he refused to work, and became so miserable, that Captain Arthur took him into the cabin, where he assisted the steward, and occasionally pulled and hauled about decks. He was in this capacity when we saw him; and though it was much better for him than the life in the forecastle, and the hard work, watching, and exposure, which his delicate frame could not have borne, yet, to be joined with a black fellow in waiting upon a man whom he probably looked upon as but little, in point of education and manners, above one of his father's servants, was almost too much for his spirit to bear. Had he entered upon his situation of his own free will, he could have endured it; but to have been deceived, and, in addition to that, forced into it, was intolerable. He made every effort to go home in our ship, but his captain refused to part with him except in the way of exchange, and that he could not effect. If this account of the whole matter, which we had from the boy, and which was confirmed by all the crew, be correct, I cannot understand why Captain Arthur should have refused to let him go, especially being a captain who had the name, not only with that crew, but with all whom he had ever commanded, of an unusually kind-hearted man.

The truth is, the unlimited power which merchant captains have, upon long voyages on strange coasts, takes away a sense of responsibility, and too often, even in men otherwise well-disposed, substitutes a disregard for the rights and feelings of others. The lad was sent on shore to join the gang at the hide-house; from whence, I was afterwards rejoiced to hear, he effected his escape, and went down to Callao in a small Spanish schooner; and from Callao, he probably returned to England.

Soon after the arrival of the California, I spoke to Captain Arthur about Hope; and as he had known him on the voyage before, and was very fond of him, he immediately went to see him, gave him proper medicines, and, under such care, he began rapidly to recover. The Saturday night before our sailing, I spent an hour in the oven, and took leave of my Kanaka friends; and, really, this was the only thing connected with leaving California which was in any way unpleasant. I felt an interest and affection for many of these simple, true-hearted men, such as I never felt before but for a near relation. Hope shook me by the hand, said he should soon be well again, and ready to work for me when I came upon the coast, next voyage, as officer of the ship; and told me not to forget, when I became captain, how to be kind to the sick. Old "Mr. Bingham" and "King Mannini" went down to the boat with me, shook me heartily by the hand, wished us a good voyage, and went back to the oven, chanting one of their deep monotonous songs, the burden of which I gathered to be about us and our voyage.

Sunday, May 8th. This promised to be our last day in California.

Our forty thousand hides, thirty thousand horns, besides several barrels of otter and beaver skins, were all stowed below, and the hatches calked down. All our spare spars were taken on board and lashed; our water-casks secured; and our live stock, consisting of four bullocks, a dozen sheep, a dozen or more pigs, and three or four dozen of poultry, were all stowed away in their different quarters: the bullocks in the long-boat, the sheep in a pen on the fore-hatch, and the pigs in a sty under the bows of the long-boat, and the poultry in their proper coop; and the jolly-boat was full of hay for the sheep and bullocks. Our unusually large cargo, together with the stores for a five months' voyage, brought the ship channels down into the water. In addition to this, she had been steeved so thoroughly, and was so bound by the compression of her cargo, forced into her by so powerful machinery, that she was like a man in a straight-jacket, and would be but a dull sailer, until she had worked herself loose.

The California had finished discharging her cargo, and was to get under weigh at the same time with us. Having washed down decks and got our breakfast, the two vessels lay side by side, in complete readiness for sea, our ensigns hanging from the peaks, and our tall spars reflected from the glassy surface of the river, which, since sunrise, had been unbroken by a ripple. At length, a few whiffs came across the water, and, by eleven o'clock, the regular north-west wind set steadily in. There was no need of calling all hands, for we had all been hanging about the forecastle the whole forenoon, and were ready for a start upon the first sign of a breeze.

All eyes were aft upon the captain, who was walking the deck, with, every now and then, a look to windward. He made a sign to the mate, who came forward, took his station, deliberately between the knight-heads, cast a glance aloft, and called out, "All hands, lay aloft and loose the sails!" We were half in the rigging before the order came, and never since we left Boston were the gaskets off the yards, and the rigging overhauled, in a shorter time. "All ready forward, sir!"—"All ready the main!"—"Cross-jack yards all ready, sir!"—"Lay down, all hands but one on each yard!" The yard-arm and bunt gaskets were cast off; and each sail hung by the jigger, with one man standing by the tie to let it go. At the same moment that we sprang aloft, a dozen hands sprang into the rigging of the California, and in an instant were all over her yards; and her sails, too, were ready to be dropped at the word. In the mean time our bow gun had been loaded and run out, and its discharge was to be the signal for dropping sails. A cloud of smoke came out of our bows; the echoes of the gun rattled our farewell among the hills of California; and the two ships were covered, from head to foot, with their white canvas. For a few minutes, all was uproar and apparent confusion: men flying about like monkeys in the rigging; ropes and blocks flying; orders given and answered, and the confused noises of men singing out at the ropes. The top-sails came to the mast-heads with "Cheerily, men!" and, in a few minutes, every sail was set; for the wind was light. The head sails were backed, the windlass came round "slip-slap" to the cry of the sailors;—"Hove short, sir," said the mate;—"Up with him!"—"Aye, aye, sir."—A few hearty and long heaves, and the anchor showed its head. "Hook cat!"—The fall was stretched along the decks; all hands laid hold;—"Hurrah, for the last time," said the mate; and the anchor came to the cat-head to the tune of "Time for us to go," with a loud chorus. Everything was done quick, as though it were for the last time. The head yards were filled away, and our ship began to move through the water on her homeward-bound course.

The California had got under weigh at the same moment; and we sailed down the narrow bay abreast and were just off the mouth, and finding ourselves gradually shooting ahead of her, were on the point of giving her three parting cheers, when, suddenly, we found ourselves stopped short, and the California ranging fast ahead of us. A bar stretches across the mouth of the harbor, with water enough to float common vessels, but, being low in the water, and having kept well to leeward, as we were bound to the southward, we had stuck fast, while the California, being light, had floated over.

We kept all sail on, in the hope of forcing over, but failing in this, we hove aback, and lay waiting for the tide, which was on the flood, to take us back into the channel. This was somewhat of a damper to us, and the captain looked not a little mortified and vexed. "This is the same place where the Rosa got ashore," observed the redheaded second mate, most mal-a-propos. A malediction on the

Rosa, and him too, was all the answer he got, and he slunk off to leeward. In a few minutes, the force of the wind and the rising of the tide backed us into the stream, and we were on our way to our old anchoring-place, the tide setting swiftly up, and the ship barely manageable, in the light breeze. We came-to, in our old berth, opposite the hide-house, whose inmates were not a little surprised to see us return. We felt as though we were tied to California; and some of the crew swore that they never should get clear of the bloody coast.

In about half an hour, which was near high water, the order was given to man the windlass, and again the anchor was catted; but not a word was said about the last time. The California had come back on finding that we had returned, and was hove-to, waiting for us, off the point. This time we passed the bar safely, and were soon up with the California, who filled away, and kept us company.

She seemed desirous of a trial of speed, and our captain accepted the challenge, although we were loaded down to the bolts of our chain plates, as deep as a sand-barge, and bound so taut with our cargo that we were no more fit for a race than a man in fetters;—while our antagonist was in her best trim. Being clear of the point, the breeze became stiff, and the royal masts bent under our sails, but we would not take them in until we saw three boys spring aloft into the rigging of the California; when they were all furled at once, but with orders to stay aloft at the top-gallant mastheads, and loose them again at the word. It was my duty to furl the fore royal; and while standing by to loose it again, I had a fine view of the scene. From where I stood, the two vessels seemed nothing but spars and sails, while their narrow decks, far below, slanting over by the force of the wind aloft, appeared hardly capable of supporting the great fabrics raised upon them. The California was to windward of us, and had every advantage; yet, while the breeze was stiff, we held our own. As soon as it began to slacken, she ranged a little ahead, and the order was given to loose the royals. In an instant the gaskets were off and the bunt dropped. "Sheet home the fore royal!—Weather sheet's home!"—"Hoist away, sir!" is bawled from aloft. "Overhaul your clew-lines!" shouts the mate. "Aye, aye, sir, all clear!"—"taut leech! belay! Well the lee brace; haul taut to windward"—and the royals are set. These brought us up again; but the wind continuing light, the California set hers, and it was soon evident that she was walking away from us. Our captain then hailed, and said that he should keep off to his course; adding—"She isn't the Alert now. If I had her in your trim, she would have been out of sight by this time." This was good-naturedly answered from the California, and she braced sharp up, and stood close upon the wind up the coast; while we squared away our yards, and stood before the wind to the south-south-west. The California's crew manned her weather rigging, waved their hats in the air, and gave up three hearty cheers, which we answered as heartily, and the customary single cheer came back to us from over the water. She stood on her way, doomed to eighteen months' or two years' hard service upon that hated coast, while we were making our way to our home, to which every hour and every mile was bringing us nearer.

As soon as we parted company with the California, all hands were sent aloft to set the studding-sails. Booms were rigged out, tacks and halyards rove, sail after sail packed upon her, until every available inch of canvas was spread, that we might not lose a breath of the fair wind. We could now see how much she was cramped and deadened by her cargo; for with a good breeze on her quarter, and every stitch of canvas spread, we could not get more than six knots out of her. She had no more life in her than if she were water-logged. The log was hove several times; but she was doing her best. We had hardly patience with her, but the older sailors said—"Stand by! you'll see her work herself loose in a week or two, and then she'll walk up to Cape Horn like a race-horse."

When all sail had been set, and the decks cleared up, the California was a speck in the horizon, and the coast lay like a low cloud along the north-east. At sunset they were both out of sight, and we were once more upon the ocean where sky and water meet.

[1] When the crew were paid off in Boston, the owners answered the order, but generously refused to deduct the amount from the pay-roll, saying that the exchange was made under compulsion. They also allowed S—— his exchange money.

CHAPTER XXX

BEGINNING THE LONG RETURN VOYAGE—A SCARE

At eight o'clock all hands were called aft, and the watches set for the voyage. Some changes were made; but I was glad to find myself still in the larboard watch. Our crew was somewhat diminished; for a man and a boy had gone in the Pilgrim; another was second mate of the Ayacucho; and a third, the oldest man of the crew, had broken down under the hard work and constant exposure on the coast, and, having had a stroke of the palsy, was left behind at the hide-house under the charge of Captain Arthur. The poor fellow wished very much to come home in the ship; and he ought to have been brought home in her. But a live dog is better than a dead lion, and a sick sailor belongs to nobody's mess; so he was sent ashore with the rest of the lumber, which was only in the way. By these diminutions, we were short-handed for a voyage round Cape Horn in the dead of winter. Besides S—— and myself, there were only five in the forecastle; who, together with four boys in the steerage, the sailmaker, carpenter, etc., composed the whole crew. In addition to this, we were only three or four days out, when the sailmaker, who was the oldest and best seaman on board, was taken with the palsy, and was useless for the rest of the voyage. The constant wading in the water, in all weathers, to take off hides, together with the other labors, is too much for old men, and for any who have not good constitutions. Beside these two men of ours, the second officer of the California and the carpenter of the Pilgrim broke down under the work, and the latter died at Santa Barbara. The young man, too, who came out with us from Boston in the Pilgrim, had to be taken from his berth before the mast and made clerk, on account of a fit of rheumatism which attacked him soon after he came upon the coast. By the loss of the sailmaker, our watch was reduced to five, of whom two were boys, who never steered but in fine weather, so that the other two and myself had to stand at the wheel four hours apiece out of every twenty-four; and the other watch had only four helmsmen. "Never mind—we're homeward bound!" was the answer to everything; and we should not have minded this, were it not for the thought that we should be off Cape Horn in the very dead of winter. It was now the first part of May; and two months would bring us off the cape in July, which is the worst month in the year there; when the sun rises at nine and sets at three, giving eighteen hours night, and there is snow and rain, gales and high seas, in abundance.

The prospect of meeting this in a ship half manned, and loaded so deep that every heavy sea must wash her fore and aft, was by no means pleasant. The Alert, in her passage out, doubled the Cape in the month of February, which is midsummer; and we came round in the Pilgrim in the latter part of October, which we thought was bad enough. There was only one of our crew who had been off there in the winter, and that was in a whaleship, much lighter and higher than our ship; yet he said they had man-killing weather for twenty days without intermission, and their decks were swept twice, and they were all glad enough to see the last of it. The Brandywine frigate, also, in her passage round, had sixty days off the Cape, and lost several boats by the heavy sea. All this was for our comfort; yet pass it we must; and all hands agreed to make the best of it.

During our watches below we overhauled our clothes, and made and mended everything for bad weather. Each of us had made for himself a suit of oil-cloth or tarpaulin, and these we got out, and gave thorough coatings of oil or tar, and hung upon the stays to dry.

Our stout boots, too, we covered over with a thick mixture of melted grease and tar, and hung out to dry. Thus we took advantage of the warm sun and fine weather of the Pacific to prepare for its other face. In the forenoon watches below, our forecastle looked like the workshop of what a sailor is,—a Jack at all trades. Thick stockings and drawers were darned and patched; mittens dragged from the bottom of the chest and mended; comforters made for the neck and ears; old flannel shirts cut up to line monkey jackets; south-westers lined with flannel, and a pot of paint smuggled forward to give them a coat on the outside; and everything turned to hand; so that, although two years had left us but a scanty wardrobe, yet the economy and invention which necessity teaches a sailor, soon put each of us in pretty good trim for bad weather, even before we had seen the last of the fine. Even the cobbler's art was not out of place. Several old shoes were very decently repaired, and with waxed ends, an awl, and the top of an old boot, I made me quite a respectable sheath for my knife.

There was one difficulty, however, which nothing that we could do would remedy; and that was the leaking of the forecastle, which made it very uncomfortable in bad weather, and rendered half of the berths tenantless. The tightest ships, in a long voyage, from the constant strain which is upon the bowsprit, will leak, more or less, round the heel of the bowsprit, and the bitts, which come down into the forecastle; but, in addition to this, we had an unaccountable leak on the starboard bow, near the cat-head, which drove us from the forward berths on that side, and, indeed, when she was on the starboard tack, from all the forward berths. One of the after berths, too, leaked in very bad weather; so that in a ship which was in other respects as tight as a bottle, and brought her cargo to Boston perfectly dry, we had, after every effort made to prevent it, in the way of caulking and leading, a forecastle with only three dry berths for seven of us. However, as there is never but one watch below at a time, by 'turning in and out,' we did pretty well. And there being, in our watch, but three of us who lived forward, we generally had a dry berth apiece in bad weather.[1]

All this, however, was but anticipation. We were still in fine weather in the North Pacific, running down the north-east trades, which we took on the second day after leaving San Diego.

Sunday, May 15th, one week out, we were in latitude 14° 56' N., long. 116° 14' W., having gone, by reckoning, over thirteen hundred miles in seven days. In fact, ever since leaving San Diego, we had had a fair wind, and as much as we wanted of it. For seven days, our lower and topmast studding-sails were set all the time, and our royals and top-gallant studding-sails, whenever she could stagger under them. Indeed, the captain had shown, from the moment we got to sea, that he was to have no boy's play, but that the ship had got to carry all she could, and that he was going to make up, by "cracking on" to her, what she wanted in lightness. In this way, we frequently made three degrees of latitude, besides something in longitude, in the course of twenty-four hours.—Our days were spent in the usual ship's work. The rigging which had become slack from being long in port was to be set up; breast backstays got up; studding-sail booms rigged upon the main yard;

and the royal studding-sails got ready for the light trades; ring-tail set; and new rigging fitted and sails got ready for Cape Horn. For, with a ship's gear, as well as a sailor's wardrobe, fine weather must be improved to get ready for the bad to come. Our forenoon watch below, as I have said, was given to our own work, and our night watches were spent in the usual manner:—a trick at the wheel, a look-out on the forecastle, a nap on a coil of rigging under the lee of the rail; a yarn round the windlass-end; or, as was generally my way, a solitary walk fore and aft, in the weather waist, between the windlass-end and the main tack. Every wave that she threw aside brought us nearer home, and every day's observation at noon showed a progress which, if it continued, would in less than five months, take us into Boston Bay. This is the pleasure of life at sea,—fine weather, day after day, without interruption,—fair wind, and a plenty of it,—and homeward bound. Every one was in good humor; things went right; and all was done with a will. At the dog watch, all hands came on deck, and stood round the weather side of the forecastle, or sat upon the windlass, and sung sea songs, and those ballads of pirates and highwaymen, which sailors delight in. Home, too, and what we should do when we got there, and when and how we should arrive, was no infrequent topic. Every night, after the kids and pots were put away, and we had lighted our pipes and cigars at the galley, and gathered about the windlass, the first question was,—

"Well, Tom, what was the latitude to-day?"

"Why fourteen, north, and she has been going seven knots ever since."

"Well, this will bring us up to the line in five days."

"Yes, but these trades won't last twenty-four hours longer," says an old salt, pointing with the sharp of his hand to leeward,—"I know that by the look of the clouds."

Then came all manner of calculations and conjectures as to the continuance of the wind, the weather under the line, the south-east trades, etc., and rough guesses as to the time the ship would be up with the Horn; and some, more venturous, gave her so many days to Boston light, and offered to bet that she would not exceed it.

"You'd better wait till you get round Cape Horn," says an old croaker.

"Yes," says another, "you may see Boston, but you've got to 'smell hell' before that good day."

Rumors also of what had been said in the cabin, as usual, found their way forward. The steward had heard the captain say something about the straits of Magellan, and the man at the wheel fancied he had heard him tell the "passenger" that, if he found the wind ahead and the weather very bad off the Cape, he should stick her off for New Holland, and come home round the Cape of Good Hope.

This passenger—the first and only one we had had, except to go from port to port, on the coast, was no one else than a gentleman whom I had known in my better days; and the last person I should have expected to have seen on the coast of California—Professor N——, of Cambridge. I had left him quietly seated in the chair of Botany and Ornithology, in Harvard University; and the next I saw of him, was strolling about San Diego beach, in a sailor's pea-jacket, with a wide straw hat, and barefooted, with his trowsers roiled up to his knees, picking up stones and shells. He had travelled overland to the North-west Coast, and come down in a small vessel to Monterey. There he learned that there was a ship at the leeward, about to sail for Boston; and, taking passage in the Pilgrim, which was then at Monterey, he came slowly down, visiting the intermediate ports, and examining the trees, plants, earths, birds, etc., and joined us at San Diego shortly before we sailed. The second mate of the Pilgrim told me that they had an old gentleman on board who knew me, and came from the college that I had been in.

He could not recollect his name, but said he was a "sort of an oldish man," with white hair, and spent all his time in the bush, and along the beach, picking up flowers and shells, and such truck, and had a dozen boxes and barrels, full of them. I thought over everybody who would be likely to be there, but could fix upon no one; when, the next day, just as we were about to shove off from the beach, he came down to the boat, in the rig I have described, with his shoes in his hand, and his pockets full of specimens. I knew him at once, though I should not have been more surprised to have seen the Old South steeple shoot up from the hide-house. He probably had no less difficulty in recognizing me. As we left home about the same time, we had nothing to tell one another; and, owing to our different situations on board, I saw but little of him on the passage home. Sometimes, when I was at the wheel of a calm night, and the steering required no attention, and the officer of the watch was forward, he would come aft and hold a short yarn with me; but this was against the rules of the ship, as is, in fact, all intercourse between passengers and the crew. I was often amused to see the sailors puzzled to know what to make of him, and to hear their conjectures about him and his business. They were as much puzzled as our old sailmaker was with the captain's instruments in the cabin.

He said there were three:—the chro-nometer, the chre-nometer, and the the-nometer. (Chronometer, barometer, and thermometer.) The Pilgrim's crew christened Mr. N. "Old Curious," from his zeal for curiosities, and some of them said that he was crazy, and that his friends let him go about and amuse himself in this way. Why else a rich man (sailors call every man rich who does not work with his hands, and wears a long coat and cravat) should leave a Christian country, and come to such a place as California, to pick up shells and stones, they could not understand. One of them, however, an old salt, who had seen something more of the world ashore, set all to rights, as he thought,—"Oh, 'vast there!—You don't know anything about them craft. I've seen them colleges, and know the ropes. They keep all such things for cur'osities, and study 'em, and have men a' purpose to go and get 'em. This old chap knows what he's about. He a'n't the child you take him for. He'll carry all these things to the college, and if they are better than any that they have had before, he'll be head of the college. Then, by-and-by, somebody else will go after some more, and if they beat him, he'll have to go again, or else give up his berth. That's the way they do it. This old covey knows the ropes. He has worked a traverse over 'em, and come 'way out here, where nobody's ever been afore, and where they'll never think of coming." This explanation satisfied Jack; and as it raised Mr. N.'s credit for capacity, and was near enough to the truth for common purposes, I did not disturb it.

With the exception of Mr. N., we had no one on board but the regular ship's company, and the live stock. Upon this, we had made a considerable inroad. We killed one of the bullocks every four days, so that they did not last us up to the line. We, or, rather, they, then began upon the sheep and the poultry, for these never come into Jack's mess.[2] The pigs were left for the latter part of the voyage, for they are sailors, and can stand all weathers. We had an old sow on board, the mother of a numerous progeny, who had been twice round the Cape of Good Hope, and once round Cape Horn. The last time going round, was very nearly her death. We heard her squealing and moaning one dark night, after it had been snowing and hailing for several hours, and getting into the sty, we found her nearly frozen to death. We got some straw, an old sail, and other things, and wrapped her up in a corner of the sty, where she staid until we got into fine weather again.

Wednesday, May 18th. Lat. 9° 54' N., long. 113° 17' W. The north-east trades had now left us, and we had the usual variable winds, which prevail near the line, together with some rain. So long as we were in these latitudes, we had but little rest in our watch on deck at night, for, as the winds were light and variable, and we could not lose a breath, we were all the watch bracing the yards, and taking in and making sail, and "humbugging" with our flying kites. A little puff of wind on the larboard quarter, and then—"larboard fore braces!" and studding-booms were rigged out, studding-sails set alow and aloft, the yards trimmed, and jibs and spanker in; when it would come as calm as a duck-pond, and the man at the wheel stand with the palm of his hand up, feeling for the wind. "Keep her off a little!" "All aback forward, sir!" cries a man from the forecastle. Down go the braces again; in come the studding-sails, all in a mess, which half an hour won't set right; yards braced sharp up; and she's on the starboard tack, close hauled.

The studding-sails must now be cleared away, and set up in the tops, and on the booms. By the time this is done, and you are looking out for a soft plank for a nap,—"Lay aft here, and square in the head yards!" and the studding-sails are all set again on the starboard side. So it goes until it is eight bells,—call the watch,—heave the log,—relieve the wheel, and go below the larboard watch.

Sunday, May 22d. Lat. 5° 14' N., long. 166° 45' W. We were now a fortnight out, and within five degrees of the line, to which two days of good breeze would take us; but we had, for the most part, what sailors call "an Irishman's hurricane,—right up and down."

This day it rained nearly all day, and being Sunday, and nothing to do, we stopped up the scuppers and filled the decks with rain water, and bringing all our clothes on deck, had a grand wash, fore and aft. When this was through, we stripped to our drawers, and taking pieces of soap and strips of canvas for towels, we turned-to and soaped, washed, and scrubbed one another down, to get off, as we said, the California dust; for the common wash in salt water, which is all Jack can get, being on an allowance of fresh, had little efficacy, and was more for taste than utility. The captain was below all the afternoon, and we had something nearer to a Saturnalia than anything we had yet seen; for the mate came into the scuppers, with a couple of boys to scrub him, and got into a battle with them in heaving water. By unplugging the holes, we let the soap-suds off the decks, and in a short time had a new supply of rain water, in which we had a grand rinsing. It was surprising to see how much soap and fresh water did for the complexions of many of us; how much of what we supposed to be tan and sea-blacking, we got rid of. The next day, the sun rising clear, the ship was covered, fore and aft, with clothes of all sorts, hanging out to dry.

As we approached the line, the wind became more easterly, and the weather clearer, and in twenty days from San Diego,—

Saturday, May 28th, at about three P. M., with a fine breeze from the east-south-east, we crossed the equator. In twenty-four hours after crossing the line, which was very unusual, we took the regular south-east trades. These winds come a little from the eastward of south-east, and, with us, they blew directly from the east-south-east, which was fortunate for us, for our course was south-by-west, and we could thus go one point free. The yards were braced so that every sail drew, from the spanker to the flying-jib; and the upper yards being squared in a little, the fore and main top-gallant studding-sails were set, and just drew handsomely. For twelve days this breeze blew steadily, not varying a point, and just so fresh that we could carry our royals; and, during the whole time, we hardly started a brace. Such progress did we make, that at the end of seven days from the time we took the breeze, on

Sunday, June 5th, we were in lat. 19° 29' S., and long. 118° 01' W., having made twelve hundred miles in seven days, very nearly upon a taut bowline. Our good ship was getting to be herself again, had increased her rate of sailing more than one-third since leaving San Diego. The crew ceased complaining of her, and the officers hove the log every two hours with evident satisfaction. This was glorious sailing. A steady breeze; the light trade-wind clouds over our heads; the incomparable temperature of the Pacific,—neither hot nor cold; a clear sun every day, and clear moon and stars each night; and new constellations rising in the south, and the familiar ones sinking in the north, as we went on our course,—"stemming nightly toward the pole." Already we had sunk the north star and the Great Bear in the northern horizon, and all hands looked out sharp to the southward for the Magellan Clouds, which, each succeeding night, we expected to make. "The next time we see the north star," said one, "we shall be standing to the northward, the other side of the Horn." This was true enough, and no doubt it would be a welcome sight; for sailors say that in coming home from round Cape Horn, and the Cape of Good Hope, the north star is the first land you make.

These trades were the same that, in the passage out in the Pilgrim, lasted nearly all the way from Juan Fernandez to the line; blowing steadily on our starboard quarter for three weeks, without our starting a brace, or even brailing down the skysails. Though we had now the same wind, and were in the same latitude with the Pilgrim on her passage out, yet we were nearly twelve hundred miles to the westward of her course; for the captain, depending upon the strong south-west winds which prevail in high southern latitudes during the winter months, took the full advantage of the trades, and stood well to the westward, so far that we passed within about two hundred miles of Ducie's Island.

It was this weather and sailing that brought to my mind a little incident that occurred on board the Pilgrim, while we were in the same latitude. We were going along at a great rate, dead before the wind, with studding-sails out on both sides, alow and aloft, on a dark night, just after midnight, and everything was as still as the grave, except the washing of the water by the vessel's side; for, being before the wind, with a smooth sea, the little brig, covered with canvas, was doing great business, with very little noise. The other watch was below, and all our watch, except myself and the man at the wheel, were asleep under the lee of the boat. The second mate, who came out before the mast, and was always very thick with me, had been holding a yarn with me, and just gone aft to his place on the quarter-deck, and I had resumed my usual walk to and from the windlass-end, when, suddenly, we heard a loud scream coming from ahead, apparently directly from under the bows. The darkness, and complete stillness of the night, and the solitude of the ocean, gave to the sound a dreadful and almost supernatural effect. I stood perfectly still, and my heart beat quick.

The sound woke up the rest of the watch, who stood looking at one another. "What, in the name of God, is that?" said the second mate, coming slowly forward. The first thought I had was, that it might be a boat, with the crew of some wrecked vessel, or perhaps the boat of some whaleship, out over night, and we had run them down in the darkness. Another scream, but less loud than the first. This started us, and we ran forward, and looked over the bows, and over the sides, to leeward, but nothing was to be seen or heard. What was to be done. Call the captain, and heave the ship aback? Just at this moment, in crossing the forecastle, one of the men saw a light below, and looking down the scuttle, saw the watch all out of their berths, and afoul of one poor fellow, dragging him out of his berth, and shaking him, to wake him out of a nightmare.

They had been waked out of their sleep, and as much alarmed at the scream as we were, and were hesitating whether to come on deck, when the second sound, coming directly from one of the berths, revealed the cause of the alarm. The fellow got a good shaking for the trouble he had given. We made a joke of the matter and we could well laugh, for our minds were not a little relieved by its ridiculous termination.

We were now close upon the southern tropical line, and, with so fine a breeze, were daily leaving the sun behind us, and drawing nearer to Cape Horn, for which it behoved us to make every preparation. Our rigging was all examined and overhauled, and mended, or replaced with new, where it was necessary: new and strong bobstays fitted in the place of the chain ones, which were worn out; the spritsail yard and martingale guys and back-ropes set well taut; bran new fore and main braces rove; top-gallant sheets, and wheel-ropes, made of green hide, laid up in the form of rope, were stretched and fitted; and new top-sail clewlines, etc., rove; new fore-topmast back-stays fitted; and other preparations made, in good season, that the ropes might have time to stretch and become limber before we got into cold weather.

Sunday, June 12th. Lat. 26° 04' S., 116° 31' W. We had now lost the regular trades, and had the winds variable, principally from the westward, and kept on, in a southerly course, sailing very nearly upon a meridian, and at the end of the week,

Sunday, June 19th, were in lat. 34° 15' S., and long. 116° 38' W.

[1] On removing the cat-head, after the ship arrived at Boston, it was found that there were two holes under it which had been bored for the purpose of driving tree-nails, and which, accidentally, had not been plugged up when the cat-head was placed over them. This was sufficient to account for the leak, and for our not having been able to discover and stop it.

[2] The customs as to the allowance of "grub" are very nearly the same in all American merchantmen. Whenever a pig is killed, the sailors have one mess from it. The rest goes to the cabin. The smaller live stock, poultry, etc., they never taste.

And, indeed, they do not complain of this, for it would take a great deal to supply them with a good meal, and without the accompaniments, (which could hardly be furnished to them,) it would not be much better than salt beef. But even as to the salt beef, they are scarcely dealt fairly with; for whenever a barrel is opened, before any of the beef is put into the harness-cask, the steward comes up, and picks it all over, and takes out the best pieces, (those that have any fat in them) for the cabin.

This was done in both the vessels I was in, and the men said that it was usual in other vessels. Indeed, it is made no secret, but some of the crew are usually called to help in assorting and putting away the pieces. By this arrangement the hard, dry pieces, which the sailors call "old horse," come to their share.

There is a singular piece of rhyme, traditional among sailors, which they say over such pieces of beef. I do not know that it ever appeared in print before. When seated round the kid, if a particularly bad piece is found, one of them takes it up, and addressing it, repeats these lines: "Old horse! old horse! what brought you here?"

—"From Sacarap to Portland pier
I've carted stone this many a year:
Till, killed by blows and sore abuse,
They salted me down for sailors' use.

The sailors they do me despise:
They turn me over and damn my eyes;
Cut off my meat, and pick my bones,
And pitch the rest to Davy Jones."

There is a story current among seamen, that a beef-dealer was convicted, at Boston, of having sold old horse for ship's stores, instead of beef, and had been sentenced to be confined in jail, until he should eat the whole of it; and that he is now lying in Boston jail. I have heard this story often, on board other vessels beside those of our own nation. It is very generally believed, and is always highly commended, as a fair instance of retaliatory justice.

CHAPTER XXXI

BAD PROSPECTS—FIRST TOUCH OF CAPE HORN—ICEBERGS—TEMPERANCE SHIPS—LYING-UP—ICE—DIFFICULTY ON BOARD—CHANGE OF COURSE—STRAITS OF MAGELLAN

There now began to be a decided change in the appearance of things. The days became shorter and shorter; the sun running lower in its course each day, and giving less and less heat; and the nights so cold as to prevent our sleeping on deck; the Magellan Clouds in sight, of a clear night; the skies looking cold and angry; and, at times, a long, heavy, ugly sea, setting in from the southwards told us what we were coming to. Still, however, we had a fine, strong breeze, and kept on our way, under as much sail as our ship would bear. Toward the middle of the week, the wind hauled to the southward, which brought us upon a taut bowline, made the ship meet, nearly head on, the heavy swell which rolled from that direction; and there was something not at all encouraging in the manner in which she met it. Being so deep and heavy, she wanted the buoyancy which should have carried her over the seas, and she dropped heavily into them, the water washing over the decks; and every now and then, when an unusually large sea met her fairly upon the bows, she struck it with a sound as dead and heavy as that with which a sledge-hammer falls upon the pile, and took the whole of it in upon the forecastle, and rising, carried it aft in the scuppers, washing the rigging off the pins, and carrying along with it everything which was loose on deck. She had been acting in this way all of our forenoon watch below; as we could tell by the washing of the water over our heads, and the heavy breaking of the seas against her bows, (with a sound as though she were striking against a rock,) only the thickness of the plank from our heads, as we lay in our berths, which are directly against the bows. At eight bells, the watch was called, and we came on deck, one hand going aft to take the wheel, and another going to the galley to get the grub for dinner. I stood on the forecastle, looking at the seas, which were rolling high, as far as the eye could reach, their tops white with foam, and the body of them of a deep indigo blue, reflecting the bright rays of the sun. Our ship rose slowly over a few of the largest of them, until one immense fellow came rolling on, threatening to cover her, and which I was sailor enough to know, by "the feeling of her" under my feet, she would not rise over. I sprang upon the knight-heads, and seizing hold of the fore-stay with my hands, drew myself upon it. My feet were just off the stanchion, when she struck fairly into the middle of the sea, and it washed her fore and aft, burying her in the water. As soon as she rose out of it, I looked aft, and everything forward of the main-mast, except the long-boat, which was griped and double-lashed down to the ring-bolts, was swept off clear. The galley, the pig-sty, the hen-coop, and a large sheep-pen which had been built upon the forehatch, were all gone, in the twinkling of an eye—leaving the deck as clean as a chin new-reaped—and not a stick left, to show where they had stood. In the scuppers lay the galley, bottom up, and a few boards floating about, the wreck of the sheep-pen,—and half a dozen miserable sheep floating among them, wet through, and not a little frightened at the sudden change that had come upon them. As soon as the sea had washed by, all hands sprung out of the forecastle to see what had become of the ship and in a few moments the cook and old Bill crawled out from under the galley, where they had been lying in the water, nearly smothered, with the galley over them. Fortunately, it rested against the bulwarks, or it would have broken some of their bones. When the water ran off, we picked the sheep up, and put them in the long-boat, got the galley back in its place, and set things a little to rights; but, had not our ship had uncommonly high bulwarks and rail, everything must have been washed overboard, not excepting Old Bill and the cook.

Bill had been standing at the galley-door, with the kid of beef in his hand for the forecastle mess, when, away he went, kid, beef, and all. He held on to the kid till the last, like a good fellow, but the beef was gone, and when the water had run off, we saw it lying high and dry, like a rock at low tide—nothing could hurt that. We took the loss of our beef very easily, consoling ourselves with the recollection that the cabin had more to lose than we; and chuckled not a little at seeing the remains of the chicken-pie and pan-cakes floating in the scuppers. "This will never do!" was what some said, and every one felt. Here we were, not yet within a thousand miles of the latitude of Cape Horn, and our decks swept by a sea not one half so high as we must expect to find there. Some blamed the captain for loading his ship so deep, when he knew what he must expect; while others said that the wind was always southwest, off the Cape, in the winter; and that, running before it, we should not mind the seas so much. When we got down into the forecastle, Old Bill, who was somewhat of a croaker,—having met with a great many accidents at sea—said that if that was the way she was going to act, we might as well make our wills, and balance the books at once, and put on a clean shirt. "'Vast there, you bloody old owl! You're always hanging out blue lights! You're frightened by the ducking you got in the scuppers, and can't take a joke! What's the use in being always on the look-out for Davy Jones?" "Stand by!" says another, "and we'll get an afternoon watch below, by this scrape;" but in this they were disappointed, for at two bells, all hands were called and set to work, getting lashings upon everything on deck; and the captain talked of sending down the long top-gallant masts; but, as the sea went down toward night, and the wind hauled abeam, we left them standing, and set the studding-sails.

The next day, all hands were turned-to upon unbending the old sails, and getting up the new ones; for a ship, unlike people on shore, puts on her best suit in bad weather. The old sails were sent down, and three new topsails, and new fore and main courses, jib, and fore-topmast staysail, which were made on the coast, and never had been used, were bent, with a complete set of new earings, robands and reef-points; and reef-tackles were rove to the courses, and spilling-lines to the top-sails. These, with new braces and clew-lines, fore and aft, gave us a good suit of running rigging.

The wind continued westerly, and the weather and sea less rough since the day on which we shipped the heavy sea, and we were making great progress under studding-sails, with our light sails all set, keeping a little to the eastward of south; for the captain, depending upon westerly winds off the Cape, had kept so far to the westward, that though we were within about five hundred miles of the latitude of Cape Horn, we were nearly seventeen hundred miles to the westward of it. Through the rest of the week, we continued on with a fair wind, gradually, as we got more to the southward, keeping a more easterly course, and bringing the wind on our larboard quarter, until—

Sunday, June 26th, when, having a fine, clear day, the captain got a lunar observation, as well as his meridian altitude, which made us in lat. 47° 50' S., long. 113° 49' W.; Cape Horn bearing, according to my calculation, E. S. E. 1/2 E., and distant eighteen hundred miles.

Monday, June 27th. During the first part of this day, the wind continued fair, and, as we were going before it, it did not feel very cold, so that we kept at work on deck, in our common clothes and round jackets. Our watch had an afternoon watch below, for the first time since leaving San Diego, and having inquired of the third mate what the latitude was at noon, and made our usual guesses as to the time she would need, to be up with the Horn, we turned-in, for a nap. We were sleeping away "at the rates of knots," when three knocks on the scuttle, and "All hands ahoy!" started us from our berths. What could be the matter? It did not appear to be blowing hard, and looking up through the scuttle, we could see that it was a clear day, overhead; yet the watch were taking in sail.

We thought there must be a sail in sight, and that we were about to heave-to and speak her; and were just congratulating ourselves upon it—for we had seen neither sail nor land since we had left port—when we heard the mate's voice on deck, (he turned-in "all standing," and was always on deck the moment he was called,) singing out to the men who were taking in the studding-sails, and asking where his watch were. We did not wait for a second call, but tumbled up the ladder; and there, on the starboard bow, was a bank of mist, covering sea and sky, and driving directly for us. I had seen the same before, in my passage round in the Pilgrim, and knew what it meant, and that there was no time to be lost. We had nothing on but thin clothes, yet there was not a moment to spare, and at it we went.

The boys of the other watch were in the tops, taking in the top-gallant studding-sails, and the lower and topmast studding-sails were coming down by the run. It was nothing but "haul down and clew up," until we got all the studding-sails in, and the royals, flying-jib, and mizen top-gallant sail furled, and the ship kept off a little, to take the squall. The fore and main top-gallant sails were still on her, for the "old man" did not mean to be frightened in broad daylight, and was determined to carry sail till the last minute.

We all stood waiting for its coming, when the first blast showed us that it was not be trifled with. Rain, sleet, snow, and wind, enough to take our breath from us, and make the toughest turn his back to windward! The ship lay nearly over on her beam-ends; the spars and rigging snapped and cracked; and her top-gallant masts bent like whip-sticks. "Clew up the fore and main top-gallant sails!" shouted the captain, and all hands sprang to the clewlines. The decks were standing nearly at an angle of forty-five degrees, and the ship going like a mad steed through the water, the whole forward part of her in a smother of foam. The halyards were let go and the yard clewed down, and the sheets started, and in a few minutes the sails smothered and kept in by clewlines and buntlines.—"Furl 'em, sir?" asked the mate.—"Let go the topsail halyards, fore and aft!" shouted the captain, in answer, at the top of his voice. Down came the topsail yards, the reef-tackles were manned and hauled out, and we climbed up to windward, and sprang into the weather rigging. The violence of the wind, and the hail and sleet, driving nearly horizontally across the ocean, seemed actually to pin us down to the rigging. It was hard work making head against them. One after another, we got out upon the yards. And here we had work to do; for our new sails, which had hardly been bent long enough to get the starch out of them, were as stiff as boards, and the new earings and reef-points, stiffened with the sleet, knotted like pieces of iron wire. Having only our round jackets and straw hats on, we were soon wet through, and it was every moment growing colder. Our hands were soon stiffened and numbed, which, added to the stiffness of everything else, kept us a good while on the yard. After we had got the sail hauled upon the yard, we had to wait a long time for the weather earing to be passed; but there was no fault to be found, for French John was at the earing, and a better sailor never laid out on a yard; so we leaned over the yard, and beat our hands upon the sail to keep them from freezing. At length the word came—"Haul out to leeward,"—and we seized the reef-points and hauled the band taut for the lee earing. "taut band—Knot away," and we got the first reef fast, and were just going to lay down, when—"Two reefs—two reefs!" shouted the mate, and we had a second reef to take, in the same way. When this was fast, we laid down on deck, manned the halyards to leeward, nearly up to our knees in water, set the topsail, and then laid aloft on the main topsail yard, and reefed that sail in the same manner; for, as I have before stated, we were a good deal reduced in numbers, and, to make it worse, the carpenter, only two days before, cut his leg with an axe, so that he could not go aloft. This weakened us so that we could not well manage more than one topsail at a time, in such weather as this, and, of course, our labor was doubled. From the main topsail yard, we went upon the main yard, and took a reef in the mainsail. No sooner had we got on deck, than—"Lay aloft there, mizen-top-men, and close-reef the mizen topsail!" This called me; and being nearest to the rigging, I got first aloft, and out to the weather earing. English Ben was on the yard just after me, and took the lee earing, and the rest of our gang were soon on the yard, and began to fist the sail, when the mate considerately sent up the cook and steward, to help us. I could now account for the long time it took to pass the other earings, for, to do my best, with a strong hand to help me at the dog's ear, I could not get it passed until I heard them beginning to complain in the bunt. One reef after another we took in, until the sail was close-reefed, when we went down and hoisted away at the halyards. In the mean time, the jib had been furled and the staysail set, and the ship, under her reduced sail, had got more upright and was under management; but the two top-gallant sails were still hanging in the buntlines, and slatting and jerking as though they would take the masts out of her. We gave a look aloft, and knew that our work was not done yet; and, sure enough, no sooner did the mate see that we were on deck, than—"Lay aloft there, four of you, and furl the top-gallant sails!" This called me again, and two of us went aloft, up the fore rigging, and two more up the main, upon the top-gallant yards.

The shrouds were now iced over, the sleet having formed a crust or cake round all the standing rigging, and on the weather side of the masts and yards. When we got upon the yard, my hands were so numb that I could not have cast off the knot of the gasket to have saved my life. We both lay over the yard for a few seconds, beating our hands upon the sail, until we started the blood into our fingers' ends, and at the next moment our hands were in a burning heat. My companion on the yard was a lad, who came out in the ship a weak, puny boy, from one of the Boston schools,—

"no larger than a spritsail sheet knot," nor "heavier than a paper of lamp-black," and "not strong enough to haul a shad off a gridiron," but who was now "as long as a spare topmast, strong enough to knock down an ox, and hearty enough to eat him." We fisted the sail together, and after six or eight minutes of hard hauling and pulling and beating down the sail, which was as stiff as sheet iron, we managed to get it furled; and snugly furled it must be, for we knew the mate well enough to be certain that if it got adrift again, we should be called up from our watch below, at any hour of the night, to furl it.

I had been on the look-out for a moment to jump below and clap on a thick jacket and south-wester; but when we got on deck we found that eight bells had been struck, and the other watch gone below, so that there were two hours of dog watch for us, and a plenty of work to do. It had now set in for a steady gale from the south-west; but we were not yet far enough to the southward to make a fair wind of it, for we must give Terra del Fuego a wide berth. The decks were covered with snow, and there was a constant driving of sleet. In fact, Cape Horn had set in with good earnest. In the midst of all this, and before it became dark, we had all the studding-sails to make up and stow away, and then to lay aloft and rig in all the booms, fore and aft, and coil away the tacks, sheets, and halyards. This was pretty tough work for four or five hands, in the face of a gale which almost took us off the yards, and with ropes so stiff with ice that it was almost impossible to bend them. I was nearly half an hour out on the end of the fore yard, trying to coil away and stop down the topmast studding-sail tack and lower halyards. It was after dark when we got through, and we were not a little pleased to hear four bells struck, which sent us below for two hours, and gave us each a pot of hot tea with our cold beef and bread, and, what was better yet, a suit of thick, dry clothing, fitted for the weather, in place of our thin clothes, which were wet through and now frozen stiff.

This sudden turn, for which we were so little prepared, was as unacceptable to me as to any of the rest; for I had been troubled for several days with a slight tooth-ache, and this cold weather, and wetting and freezing, were not the best things in the world for it.

I soon found that it was getting strong hold, and running over all parts of my face; and before the watch was out I went aft to the mate, who had charge of the medicine-chest, to get something for it.

But the chest showed like the end of a long voyage, for there was nothing that would answer but a few drops of laudanum, which must be saved for any emergency; so I had only to bear the pain as well as I could.

When we went on deck at eight bells, it had stopped snowing, and there were a few stars out, but the clouds were still black, and it was blowing a steady gale. Just before midnight, I went aloft and sent down the mizen royal yard, and had the good luck to do it to the satisfaction of the mate, who said it was done "out of hand and ship-shape." The next four hours below were but little relief to me, for I lay awake in my berth, the whole time, from the pain in my face, and heard every bell strike, and, at four o'clock, turned out with the watch, feeling little spirit for the hard duties of the day.

Bad weather and hard work at sea can be borne up against very well, if one only has spirit and health; but there is nothing brings a man down, at such a time, like bodily pain and want of sleep.

There was, however, too much to do to allow time to think; for the gale of yesterday, and the heavy seas we met with a few days before, while we had yet ten degrees more southing to make, had convinced the captain that we had something before us which was not to be trifled with, and orders were given to send down the long top-gallant masts. The top-gallant and royal yards were accordingly struck, the flying jib-boom rigged in, and the top-gallant masts sent down on deck, and all lashed together by the side of the long-boat.

The rigging was then sent down and coiled away below, and everything was made snug aloft. There was not a sailor in the ship who was not rejoiced to see these sticks come down; for, so long as the yards were aloft, on the least sign of a lull, the top-gallant sails were loosed, and then we had to furl them again in a snow-squall, and shin up and down single ropes caked with ice, and send royal yards down in the teeth of a gale coming right from the south pole. It was an interesting sight, too, to see our noble ship, dismantled of all her top-hamper of long tapering masts and yards, and boom pointed with spear-head, which ornamented her in port; and all that canvas, which a few days before had covered her like a cloud, from the truck to the water's edge, spreading far out beyond her hull on either side, now gone; and she, stripped, like a wrestler for the fight. It corresponded, too, with the desolate character of her situation;—alone, as she was, battling with storms, wind, and ice, at this extremity of the globe, and in almost constant night.

Friday, July 1st. We were now nearly up to the latitude of Cape Horn, and having over forty degrees of easting to make, we squared away the yards before a strong westerly gale, shook a reef out of the fore-topsail, and stood on our way, east-by-south, with the prospect of being up with the Cape in a week or ten days. As for myself, I had had no sleep for forty-eight hours; and the want of rest, together with constant wet and cold, had increased the swelling, so that my face was nearly as large as two, and I found it impossible to get my mouth open wide enough to eat. In this state, the steward applied to the captain for some rice to boil for me, but he only got a—"No! d— you! Tell him to eat salt junk and hard bread, like the rest of them." For this, of course, I was much obliged to him, and in truth it was just what I expected. However, I did not starve, for the mate, who was a man as well as a sailor, and had always been a good friend to me, smuggled a pan of rice into the galley, and told the cook to boil it for me, and not let the "old man" see it. Had it been fine weather, or in port, I should have gone below and lain by until my face got well; but in such weather as this, and short-handed as we were, it was not for me to desert my post; so I kept on deck, and stood my watch and did my duty as well as I could.

Saturday, July 2nd. This day the sun rose fair, but it ran too low in the heavens to give any heat, or thaw out our sails and rigging; yet the sight of it was pleasant; and we had a steady "reef topsail breeze" from the westward. The atmosphere, which had previously been clear and cold, for the last few hours grew damp, and had a disagreeable, wet chilliness in it; and the man who came from the wheel said he heard the captain tell "the passenger" that the thermometer had fallen several degrees since morning, which he could not account for in any other way than by supposing that there must be ice near us; though such a thing had never been heard of in this latitude, at this season of the year. At twelve o'clock we went below, and had just got through dinner, when the cook put his head down the scuttle and told us to come on deck and see the finest sight that we had ever seen. "Where away, cook?" asked the first man who was up. "On the larboard bow." And there lay, floating in the ocean, several miles off, an immense, irregular mass, its top and points covered with snow, and its center of a deep indigo color.

This was an iceberg, and of the largest size, as one of our men said who had been in the Northern ocean. As far as the eye could reach, the sea in every direction was of a deep blue color, the waves running high and fresh, and sparkling in the light, and in the midst lay this immense mountain-island, its cavities and valleys thrown into deep shade, and its points and pinnacles glittering in the sun.

All hands were soon on deck, looking at it, and admiring in various ways its beauty and grandeur. But no description can give any idea of the strangeness, splendor, and, really, the sublimity, of the sight.

Its great size;—for it must have been from two to three miles in circumference, and several hundred feet in height;—its slow motion, as its base rose and sank in the water, and its high points nodded against the clouds; the dashing of the waves upon it, which, breaking high with foam, lined its base with a white crust; and the thundering sound of the cracking of the mass, and the breaking and tumbling down of huge pieces; together with its nearness and approach, which added a slight element of fear,—all combined to give to it the character of true sublimity. The main body of the mass was, as I have said, of an indigo color, its base crusted with frozen foam; and as it grew thin and transparent toward the edges and top, its color shaded off from a deep blue to the whiteness of snow.

It seemed to be drifting slowly toward the north, so that we kept away and avoided it. It was in sight all the afternoon; and when we got to leeward of it, the wind died away, so that we lay-to quite near it for a greater part of the night. Unfortunately, there was no moon, but it was a clear night, and we could plainly mark the long, regular heaving of the stupendous mass, as its edges moved slowly against the stars. Several times in our watch loud cracks were heard, which sounded as though they must have run through the whole length of the iceberg, and several pieces fell down with a thundering crash, plunging heavily into the sea. Toward morning, a strong breeze sprang up, and we filled away, and left it astern, and at daylight it was out of sight. The next day, which was

Sunday, July 3d, the breeze continued strong, the air exceedingly chilly, and the thermometer low. In the course of the day we saw several icebergs, of different sizes, but none so near as the one which we saw the day before. Some of them, as well as we could judge, at the distance at which we were, must have been as large as that, if not larger. At noon we were in latitude 55° 12' south, and supposed longitude 89° 5' west. Toward night the wind hauled to the southward, and headed us off our course a little, and blew a tremendous gale; but this we did not mind, as there was no rain nor snow, and we were already under close sail.

Monday, July 4th. This was "independence day" in Boston. What firing of guns, and ringing of bells, and rejoicings of all sorts, in every part of our country! The ladies (who have not gone down to Nahant, for a breath of cool air, and sight of the ocean) walking the streets with parasols over their heads, and the dandies in their white pantaloons and silk stockings! What quantities of ice-cream have been eaten, and what quantities of ice brought into the city from a distance, and sold out by the lump and the pound! The smallest of the islands which we saw today would have made the fortune of poor Jack, if he had had it in Boston; and I dare say he would have had no objection to being there with it. This, to be sure, was no place to keep the fourth of July. To keep ourselves warm, and the ship out of the ice, was as much as we could do. Yet no one forgot the day; and many were the wishes, and conjectures, and comparisons, both serious and ludicrous, which were made among all hands. The sun shone bright as long as it was up, only that a scud of black clouds was ever and anon driving across it. At noon we were in lat. 54° 27' S., and long. 85° 5' W., having made a good deal of easting, but having lost in our latitude by the heading of the wind. Between daylight and dark—that is, between nine o'clock and three—we saw thirty-four ice islands, of various sizes; some no bigger than the hull of our vessel, and others apparently nearly as large as the one that we first saw; though, as we went on, the islands became smaller and more numerous; and, at sundown of this day, a man at the mast-head saw large fields of floating ice called "field-ice" at the south-east.

This kind of ice is much more dangerous than the large islands, for those can be seen at a distance, and kept away from; but the field-ice, floating in great quantities, and covering the ocean for miles and miles, in pieces of every size—large, flat, and broken cakes, with here and there an island rising twenty and thirty feet, and as large as the ship's hull;—this, it is very difficult to sheer clear of. A constant look-out was necessary; for any of these pieces, coming with the heave of the sea, were large enough to have knocked a hole in the ship, and that would have been the end of us; for no boat (even if we could have got one out) could have lived in such a sea; and no man could have lived in a boat in such weather. To make our condition still worse, the wind came out due east, just after sundown, and it blew a gale dead ahead, with hail and sleet, and a thick fog, so that we could not see half the length of the ship. Our chief reliance, the prevailing westerly gales, was thus cut off; and here we were, nearly seven hundred miles to the westward of the Cape, with a gale dead from the eastward, and the weather so thick that we could not see the ice with which we were surrounded, until it was directly under our bows.

At four, P. M. (it was then quite dark) all hands were called, and sent aloft in a violent squall of hail and rain, to take in sail. We had now all got on our "Cape Horn rig"—thick boots, south-westers coming down over our neck and ears, thick trowsers and jackets, and some with oil-cloth suits over all. Mittens, too, we wore on deck, but it would not do to go aloft with them on, for it was impossible to work with them, and, being wet and stiff, they might let a man slip overboard, for all the hold he could get upon a rope; so, we were obliged to work with bare hands, which, as well as our faces, were often cut with the hail-stones, which fell thick and large. Our ship was now all cased with ice,—hull, spars, and standing rigging;—and the running rigging so stiff that we could hardly bend it so as to belay it, or, still worse, take a knot with it; and the sails nearly as stiff as sheet iron. One at a time, (for it was a long piece of work and required many hands,) we furled the courses, mizen topsail, and fore-topmast staysail, and close-reefed the fore and main topsails, and hove the ship to under the fore, with the main hauled up by the clewlines and buntlines, and ready to be sheeted home, if we found it necessary to make sail to get to windward of an ice island. A regular look-out was then set, and kept by each watch in turn, until the morning. It was a tedious and anxious night. It blew hard the whole time, and there was an almost constant driving of either rain, hail, or snow. In addition to this, it was "as thick as muck," and the ice was all about us. The captain was on deck nearly the whole night, and kept the cook in the galley, with a roaring fire, to make coffee for him, which he took every few hours, and once or twice gave a little to his officers; but not a drop of anything was there for the crew. The captain, who sleeps all the daytime, and comes and goes at night as he chooses, can have his brandy and water in the cabin, and his hot coffee at the galley; while Jack, who has to stand through everything, and work in wet and cold, can have nothing to wet his lips or warm his stomach.

This was a "temperance ship," and, like too many such ships, the temperance was all in the forecastle. The sailor, who only takes his one glass as it is dealt out to him, is in danger of being drunk; while the captain, who has all under his hand, and can drink as much as he chooses, and upon whose self-possession and cool judgment the lives of all depend, may be trusted with any amount, to drink at his will. Sailors will never be convinced that rum is a dangerous thing, by taking it away from them, and giving it to the officers; nor that, that temperance is their friend, which takes from them what they have always had, and gives them nothing in the place of it. By seeing it allowed to their officers, they will not be convinced that it is taken from them for their good; and by receiving nothing in its place, they will not believe that it is done in kindness. On the contrary, many of them look upon the change as a new instrument of tyranny. Not that they prefer rum. I never knew a sailor, in my life, who would not prefer a pot of hot coffee or chocolate, in a cold night, to all the rum afloat. They all say that rum only warms them for a time; yet, if they can get nothing better, they will miss what they have lost. The momentary warmth and glow from drinking it; the break and change which is made in a long, dreary watch by the mere calling all hands aft and serving of it out; and the simply having some event to look forward to, and to talk about; give it an importance and a use which no one can appreciate who has not stood his watch before the mast. On my passage round Cape Horn before, the vessel that I was in was not under temperance articles, and grog was served out every middle and morning watch, and after every reefing of topsails; and though

I had never drank rum before, and never intend to again, I took my allowance then at the capstan, as the rest did, merely for the momentary warmth it gave the system, and the change in our feelings and aspect of our duties on the watch. At the same time, as I have stated, there was not a man on board who would not have pitched the rum to the dogs, (I have heard them say so, a dozen times) for a pot of coffee or chocolate; or even for our common beverage—"water bewitched, and tea begrudged," as it was.*[1]*

The temperance reform is the best thing that ever was undertaken for the sailor; but when the grog is taken from him, he ought to have something in its place. As it is now, in most vessels, it is a mere saving to the owners; and this accounts for the sudden increase of temperance ships, which surprised even the best friends of the cause. If every merchant, when he struck grog from the list of the expenses of his ship, had been obliged to substitute as much coffee, or chocolate, as would give each man a pot-full when he came off the topsail yard, on a stormy night;—I fear Jack might have gone to ruin on the old road.[2] But this is not doubling Cape Horn. Eight hours of the night, our watch was on deck, and during the whole of that time we kept a bright look-out: one man on each bow, another in the bunt of the fore yard, the third mate on the scuttle, one on each quarter, and a man always standing by the wheel. The chief mate was everywhere, and commanded the ship when the captain was below.

When a large piece of ice was seen in our way, or drifting near us, the word was passed along, and the ship's head turned one way and another; and sometimes the yards squared or braced up. There was little else to do than to look out; and we had the sharpest eyes in the ship on the forecastle. The only variety was the monotonous voice of the look-out forward—"Another island!"—"Ice ahead!"—"Ice on the lee bow!"—"Hard up the helm!"—"Keep her off a little!"—"Stead-y!"

In the meantime, the wet and cold had brought my face into such a state that I could neither eat nor sleep; and though I stood it out all night, yet, when it became light, I was in such a state, that all hands told me I must go below, and lie-by for a day or two, or I should be laid up for a long time, and perhaps have the lock-jaw.

When the watch was changed I went into the steerage, and took off my hat and comforter, and showed my face to the mate, who told me to go below at once, and stay in my berth until the swelling went down, and gave the cook orders to make a poultice for me, and said he would speak to the captain.

I went below and turned-in, covering myself over with blankets and jackets, and lay in my berth nearly twenty-four hours, half asleep and half awake, stupid, from the dull pain. I heard the watch called, and the men going up and down, and sometimes a noise on deck, and a cry of "ice," but I gave little attention to anything. At the end of twenty-four hours the pain went down, and I had a long sleep, which brought me back to my proper state; yet my face was so swollen and tender, that I was obliged to keep to my berth for two or three days longer. During the two days I had been below, the weather was much the same that it had been, head winds, and snow and rain; or, if the wind came fair, too foggy, and the ice too thick, to run. At the end of the third day the ice was very thick; a complete fog-bank covered the ship. It blew a tremendous gale from the eastward, with sleet and snow, and there was every promise of a dangerous and fatiguing night. At dark, the captain called all hands aft, and told them that not a man was to leave the deck that night; that the ship was in the greatest danger; any cake of ice might knock a hole in her, or she might run on an island and go to pieces. No one could tell whether she would be a ship the next morning. The look-outs were then set, and every man was put in his station. When I heard what was the state of things, I began to put on my clothes to stand it out with the rest of them, when the mate came below, and looking at my face, ordered me back to my berth, saying that if we went down, we should all go down together, but if I went on deck I might lay myself up for life. This was the first word I had heard from aft; for the captain had done nothing, nor inquired how I was, since I went below.

In obedience to the mate's orders, I went back to my berth; but a more miserable night I never wish to spend. I never felt the curse of sickness so keenly in my life. If I could only have been on deck with the rest, where something was to be done, and seen, and heard; where there were fellow-beings for companions in duty and danger—but to be cooped up alone in a black hole, in equal danger, but without the power to do, was the hardest trial. Several times, in the course of the night, I got up, determined to go on deck; but the silence which showed that there was nothing doing, and the knowledge that I might make myself seriously ill, for nothing, kept me back. It was not easy to sleep, lying, as I did, with my head directly against the bows, which might be dashed in by an island of ice, brought down by the very next sea that struck her. This was the only time I had been ill since I left Boston, and it was the worst time it could have happened. I felt almost willing to bear the plagues of Egypt for the rest of the voyage, if I could but be well and strong for that one night. Yet it was a dreadful night for those on deck.

A watch of eighteen hours, with wet, and cold, and constant anxiety, nearly wore them out; and when they came below at nine o'clock for breakfast, they almost dropped asleep on their chests, and some of them were so stiff that they could with difficulty sit down. Not a drop of anything had been given them during the whole time, (though the captain, as on the night that I was on deck, had his coffee every four hours,) except that the mate stole a potful of coffee for two men to drink behind the galley, while he kept a look-out for the captain. Every man had his station, and was not allowed to leave it; and nothing happened to break the monotony of the night, except once setting the main topsails to run clear of a large island to leeward, which they were drifting fast upon. Some of the boys got so sleepy and stupefied, that they actually fell asleep at their posts; and the young third mate, whose station was the exposed one of standing on the fore scuttle, was so stiff, when he was relieved, that he could not bend his knees to get down. By a constant look-out, and a quick shifting of the helm, as the islands and pieces came in sight, the ship went clear of everything but a few small pieces, though daylight showed the ocean covered for miles. At daybreak it fell a dead calm, and with the sun, the fog cleared a little, and a breeze sprung up from the westward, which soon grew into a gale. We had now a fair wind, daylight, and comparatively clear weather; yet, to the surprise of every one, the ship continued hove-to. Why does not he run? What is the captain about? was asked by every one; and from questions, it soon grew into complaints and murmurings. When the daylight was so short, it was too bad to lose it, and a fair wind, too, which every one had been praying for. As hour followed hour, and the captain showed no sign of making sail, the crew became impatient, and there was a good deal of talking and consultation together, on the forecastle. They had been beaten out with the exposure and hardship, and impatient to get out of it, and this unaccountable delay was more than they could bear in quietness, in their excited and restless state. Some said that the captain was frightened,—completely cowed, by the dangers and difficulties that surrounded us, and was afraid to make sail; while others said that in his anxiety and suspense he had made a free use of brandy and opium, and was unfit for his duty. The carpenter, who was an intelligent man, and a thorough seaman, and had great influence with the crew, came down into the forecastle, and tried to induce the crew to go aft and ask the captain why he did not run, or request him, in the name of all hands, to make sail. This appeared to be a very reasonable request, and the crew agreed that if he did not make sail before noon, they would go aft. Noon came, and no sail was made. A consultation was held again, and it was proposed to take the ship from the captain and give the command of her to the mate, who had been heard to say that, if he could have his way, the ship would have been half the distance to the Cape before night,—ice or no ice. And so irritated and impatient had the crew become, that even this proposition, which was open mutiny, punishable with state prison, was entertained, and the carpenter went to his berth, leaving it tacitly understood that something serious would be done, if things remained as they were many hours longer. When the carpenter left, we talked it all over, and I gave my advice strongly against it. Another of the men, too, who had known something of the kind attempted in another ship by a crew who were dissatisfied with their captain, and which was followed with serious consequences, was opposed to it. S——, who soon came down, joined us, and we determined to have nothing to do with it. By these means, they were soon induced to give it up, for the present, though they said they would not lie where they were much longer without knowing the reason.

The affair remained in this state until four o'clock, when an order came forward for all hands to come aft upon the quarter-deck. In about ten minutes they came forward again, and the whole affair had been blown. The carpenter, very prematurely, and without any authority from the crew, had sounded the mate as to whether he would take command of the ship, and intimated an intention to displace the captain; and the mate, as in duty bound, had told the whole to the captain, who immediately sent for all hands aft. Instead of violent measures, or, at least, an outbreak of quarter-deck bravado, threats, and abuse, which they had every reason to expect, a sense of common danger and common suffering seemed to have tamed his spirit, and begotten something like a humane fellow-feeling; for he received the crew in a manner quiet, and even almost kind. He told them what he had heard, and said that he did not believe that they would try to do any such thing as was intimated; that they had always been good men,—obedient, and knew their duty, and he had no fault to find with them; and asked them what they had to complain of—said that no one could say that he was slow to carry sail, (which was true enough;) and that, as soon as he thought it was safe and proper, he should make sail. He added a few words about their duty in their present situation, and sent them forward, saying that he should take no further notice of the matter; but, at the same time, told the carpenter to recollect whose power he was in, and that if he heard another word from him he would have cause to remember him to the day of his death.

This language of the captain had a very good effect upon the crew, and they returned quietly to their duty.

For two days more the wind blew from the southward and eastward; or in the short intervals when it was fair, the ice was too thick to run; yet the weather was not so dreadfully bad, and the crew had watch and watch. I still remained in my berth, fast recovering, yet still not well enough to go safely on deck. And I should have been perfectly useless; for, from having eaten nothing for nearly a week, except a little rice, which I forced into my mouth the last day or two, I was as weak as an infant. To be sick in a forecastle is miserable indeed. It is the worst part of a dog's life; especially in bad weather. The forecastle, shut up tight to keep out the water and cold air;—the watch either on deck, or asleep in their berths;—no one to speak to;—the pale light of the single lamp, swinging to and fro from the beam, so dim that one can scarcely see, much less read by it;—the water dropping from the beams and carlines, and running down the sides; and the forecastle so wet, and dark, and cheerless, and so lumbered up with chests and wet clothes, that sitting up is worse than lying in the berth! These are some of the evils. Fortunately, I needed no help from any one, and no medicine; and if I had needed help, I don't know where I should have found it. Sailors are willing enough; but it is true, as is often said—No one ships for nurse on board a vessel. Our merchant ships are always under-manned, and if one man is lost by sickness, they cannot spare another to take care of him. A sailor is always presumed to be well, and if he's sick, he's a poor dog. One has to stand his wheel, and another his lookout, and the sooner he gets on deck again, the better.

Accordingly, as soon as I could possibly go back to my duty, I put on my thick clothes and boots and south-wester, and made my appearance on deck. Though I had been but a few days below, yet everything looked strangely enough. The ship was cased in ice,—decks, sides, masts, yards, and rigging. Two close-reefed top-sails were all the sail she had on, and every sail and rope was frozen so stiff in its place, that it seemed as though it would be impossible to start anything. Reduced, too, to her top-masts, she had altogether a most forlorn and crippled appearance. The sun had come up brightly; the snow was swept off the decks, and ashes thrown upon them, so that we could walk, for they had been as slippery as glass.

It was, of course, too cold to carry on any ship's work, and we had only to walk the deck and keep ourselves warm. The wind was still ahead, and the whole ocean, to the eastward, covered with islands and field-ice. At four bells the order was given to square away the yards; and the man who came from the helm said that the captain had kept her off to N. N. E. What could this mean? Some said that he was going to put into Valparaiso, and winter, and others that he was going to run out of the ice and cross the Pacific, and go home round the Cape of Good Hope. Soon, however, it leaked out, and we found that we were running for the straits of Magellan. The news soon spread through the ship, and all tongues were at work, talking about it. No one on board had been through the straits, but I had in my chest an account of the passage of the ship A. J. Donelson, of New York, through those straits, a few years before.

The account was given by the captain, and the representation was as favorable as possible. It was soon read by every one on board, and various opinions pronounced. The determination of our captain had at least this good effect; it gave every one something to think and talk about, made a break in our life, and diverted our minds from the monotonous dreariness of the prospect before us.

Having made a fair wind of it, we were going off at a good rate, and leaving the thickest of the ice behind us. This, at least, was something.

Having been long enough below to get my hands well warmed and softened, the first handling of the ropes was rather tough; but a few days hardened them, and as soon as I got my mouth open wide enough to take in a piece of salt beef and hard bread, I was all right again.

Sunday, July 10th. Lat. 54° 10', long. 79° 07'. This was our position at noon. The sun was out bright; the ice was all left behind, and things had quite a cheering appearance. We brought our wet pea-jackets and trowsers on deck, and hung them up in the rigging, that the breeze and the few hours of sun might dry them a little; and, by the permission of the cook, the galley was nearly filled with stockings and mittens, hung round to be dried. Boots, too, were brought up; and having got a little tar and slush from below, we gave them a thick coat. After dinner, all hands were turned-to, to get the anchors over the bows, bend on the chains, etc. The fish-tackle was got up, fish-davit rigged out, and after two or three hours of hard and cold work, both the anchors were ready for instant use, a couple of kedges got up, a hawser coiled away upon the fore-hatch, and the deep-sea-lead-line overhauled and got ready. Our spirits returned with having something to do; and when the tackle was manned to bowse the anchor home, notwithstanding the desolation of the scene, we struck up "Cheerily ho!" in full chorus. This pleased the mate, who rubbed his hands and cried out—"That's right, my boys; never say die! That sounds like the old crew!" and the captain came up, on hearing the song, and said to the passenger, within hearing of the man at the wheel,—"That sounds like a lively crew. They'll have their song so long as there're enough left for a chorus!"

This preparation of the cable and anchors was for the passage of the straits; for, being very crooked, and with a variety of currents, it is necessary to come frequently to anchor. This was not, by any means, a pleasant prospect, for, of all the work that a sailor is called upon to do in cold weather, there is none so bad as working the ground-tackle. The heavy chain cables to be hauled and pulled about the decks with bare hands; wet hawsers, slip-ropes, and buoy-ropes to be hauled aboard, dripping in water, which is running up your sleeves, and freezing; clearing hawse under the bows; getting under weigh and coming-to, at all hours of the night and day, and a constant look-out for rocks and sands and turns of tides;—these are some of the disagreeables of such a navigation to a common sailor. Fair or foul, he wants to have nothing to do with the ground-tackle between port and port. One of our hands, too, had unluckily fallen upon a half of an old newspaper which contained an account of the passage, through the straits, of a Boston brig, called, I think, the Peruvian, in which she lost every cable and anchor she had, got aground twice, and arrived at Valparaiso in distress. This was set off against the account of the A. J. Donelson, and led us to look forward with less confidence to the passage, especially as no one on board had ever been through, and the captain had no very perfect charts. However, we were spared any further experience on the point; for the next day, when we must have been near the Cape of Pillars, which is the south-west point of the mouth of the straits, a gale set in from the eastward, with a heavy fog, so that we could not see half of the ship's length ahead. This, of course, put an end to the project, for the present; for a thick fog and a gale blowing dead ahead are not the most favorable circumstances for the passage of difficult and dangerous straits. This weather, too, seemed likely to last for some time, and we could not think of beating about the mouth of the straits for a week or two, waiting for a favorable opportunity; so we braced up on the larboard tack, put the ship's head due south, and struck her off for Cape Horn again.

[1] The proportions of the ingredients of the tea that was made for us (and ours, as I have before stated, was a favorable specimen of American merchantmen) were, a pint of tea, and a pint and a half of molasses, to about three gallons of water.

These are all boiled down together in the "coppers," and before serving it out, the mess is stirred up with a stick, so as to give each man his fair share of sweetening and tea-leaves. The tea for the cabin is, of course, made in the usual way, in a tea-pot, and drank with sugar.

[2] I do not wish these remarks, so far as they relate to the saving of expense in the outfit, to be applied to the owners of our ship, for she was supplied with an abundance of stores, of the best kind that are given to seamen;, though the dispensing of them is necessarily left to the captain, Indeed, so high was the reputation of "the employ" among men and

officers, for the character and outfit of their vessels, and for their liberality in conducting their voyages, that when it was known that they had a ship fitting out for a long voyage, and that hands were to be shipped at a certain time,—a half hour before the time, as one of the crew told me, numbers of sailors were steering down the wharf, hopping over the barrels, like flocks of sheep.

CHAPTER XXXII

ICE AGAIN—A BEAUTIFUL AFTERNOON—CAPE HORN—"LAND HO!"—HEADING FOR HOME

In our first attempt to double the Cape, when we came up to the latitude of it, we were nearly seventeen hundred miles to the westward, but, in running for the straits of Magellan, we stood so far to the eastward, that we made our second attempt at a distance of not more than four or five hundred miles; and we had great hopes, by this means, to run clear of the ice; thinking that the easterly gales, which had prevailed for a long time, would have driven it to the westward. With the wind about two points free, the yards braced in a little, and two close-reefed topsails and a reefed foresail on the ship, we made great way toward the southward and, almost every watch, when we came on deck, the air seemed to grow colder, and the sea to run higher. Still, we saw no ice, and had great hopes of going clear of it altogether, when, one afternoon, about three o'clock, while we were taking a siesta during our watch below, "All hands!" was called in a loud and fearful voice. "Tumble up here, men!—tumble up!—don't stop for your clothes—before we're upon it!" We sprang out of our berths and hurried upon deck.

The loud, sharp voice of the captain was heard giving orders, as though for life or death, and we ran aft to the braces, not waiting to look ahead, for not a moment was to be lost. The helm was hard up, the after yards shaking, and the ship in the act of wearing.

Slowly, with stiff ropes and iced rigging, we swung the yards round, everything coming hard, and with a creaking and rending sound, like pulling up a plank which had been frozen into the ice. The ship wore round fairly, the yards were steadied, and we stood off on the other tack, leaving behind us, directly under our larboard quarter, a large ice island, peering out of the mist, and reaching high above our tops, while astern; and on either side of the island, large tracts of field-ice were dimly seen, heaving and rolling in the sea. We were now safe, and standing to the northward; but, in a few minutes more, had it not been for the sharp look-out of the watch, we should have been fairly upon the ice, and left our ship's old bones adrift in the Southern ocean. After standing to the northward a few hours, we wore ship, and the wind having hauled, we stood to the southward and eastward. All night long, a bright lookout was kept from every part of the deck; and whenever ice was seen on the one bow or the other, the helm was shifted and the yards braced, and by quick working of the ship she was kept clear. The accustomed cry of "Ice ahead!"—"Ice on the lee bow!"—"Another island!" in the same tones, and with the same orders following them, seemed to bring us directly back to our old position of the week before.

During our watch on deck, which was from twelve to four, the wind came out ahead, with a pelting storm of hail and sleet, and we lay hove-to, under a close-reefed main topsail, the whole watch. During the next watch it fell calm, with a drenching rain, until daybreak, when the wind came out to the westward, and the weather cleared up, and showed us the whole ocean, in the course which we should have steered, had it not been for the head wind and calm, completely blocked up with ice. Here then our progress was stopped, and we wore ship, and once more stood to the northward and eastward; not for the straits of Magellan, but to make another attempt to double the Cape, still farther to the eastward; for the captain was determined to get round if perseverance could do it; and the third time, he said, never failed.

With a fair wind we soon ran clear of the field-ice, and by noon had only the stray islands floating far and near upon the ocean.

The sun was out bright, the sea of a deep blue, fringed with the white foam of the waves which ran high before a strong south-wester; our solitary ship tore on through the water, as though glad to be out of her confinement; and the ice islands lay scattered upon the ocean here and there, of various sizes and shapes, reflecting the bright rays of the sun, and drifting slowly northward before the gale. It was a contrast to much that we had lately seen, and a spectacle not only of beauty, but of life; for it required but little fancy to imagine these islands to be animate masses which had broken loose from the "thrilling regions of thick-ribbed ice," and were working their way, by wind and current, some alone, and some in fleets, to milder climes. No pencil has ever yet given anything like the true effect of an iceberg. In a picture, they are huge, uncouth masses, stuck in the sea, while their chief beauty and grandeur,—their slow, stately motion; the whirling of the snow about their summits, and the fearful groaning and cracking of their parts,—the picture cannot give. This is the large iceberg; while the small and distant islands, floating on the smooth sea, in the light of a clear day, look like little floating fairy isles of sapphire.

From a north-east course we gradually hauled to the eastward, and after sailing about two hundred miles, which brought us as near to the western coast of Terra del Fuego as was safe, and having lost sight of the ice altogether,—for the third time we put the ship's head to the southward, to try the passage of the Cape. The weather continued clear and cold, with a strong gale from the westward, and we were fast getting up with the latitude of the Cape, with a prospect of soon being round. One fine afternoon, a man who had gone into the fore-top to shift the rolling tackles, sung out, at the top of his voice, and with evident glee,—"Sail ho!" Neither land nor sail had we seen since leaving San Diego; and any one who has traversed the length of a whole ocean alone, can imagine what an excitement such an announcement produced on board. "Sail ho!" shouted the cook, jumping out of his galley; "Sail ho!" shouted a man, throwing back the slide of the scuttle, to the watch below, who were soon out of their berths and on deck; and "Sail ho!" shouted the captain down the companion-way to the passenger in the cabin. Besides the pleasure of seeing a ship and human beings in so desolate a place, it was important for us to speak a vessel, to learn whether there was ice to the eastward, and to ascertain the longitude; for we had no chronometer, and had been drifting about so long that we had nearly lost our reckoning, and opportunities for lunar observations are not frequent or sure in such a place as Cape Horn. For these various reasons, the excitement in our little community was running high, and conjectures were made, and everything thought of for which the captain would hail, when the man aloft sung out—"Another sail, large on the weather bow!"

This was a little odd, but so much the better, and did not shake our faith in their being sails. At length the man in the top hailed, and said he believed it was land, after all. "Land in your eye!" said the mate, who was looking through a telescope; "they are ice islands, if I can see a hole through a ladder;" and a few moments showed the mate to be right and all our expectations fled; and instead of what we most wished to see, we had what we most dreaded, and what we hoped we had seen the last of. We soon, however, left these astern, having passed within about two miles of them; and at sundown the horizon was clear in all directions.

Having a fine wind, we were soon up with and passed the latitude of the Cape, and having stood far enough to the southward to give it a wide berth, we began to stand to the eastward, with a good prospect of being round and steering to the northward on the other side, in a very few days.

But ill luck seemed to have lighted upon us. Not four hours had we been standing on in this course, before it fell dead calm; and in half an hour it clouded up; a few straggling blasts, with spits of snow and sleet, came from the eastward; and in an hour more, we lay hove-to under a close-reefed main topsail, drifting bodily off to leeward before the fiercest storm that we had yet felt, blowing dead ahead, from the eastward. It seemed as though the genius of the place had been roused at finding that we had nearly slipped through his fingers, and had come down upon us with tenfold fury. The sailors said that every blast, as it shook the shrouds, and whistled through the rigging, said to the old ship, "No, you don't!"—"No, you don't!"

For eight days we lay drifting about in this manner. Sometimes,—generally towards noon,—it fell calm; once or twice a round copper ball showed itself for a few moments in the place where the sun ought to have been; and a puff or two came from the westward, giving some hope that a fair wind had come at last. During the first two days, we made sail for these puffs, shaking the reefs out of the topsails and boarding the tacks of the courses; but finding that it only made work for us when the gale set in again, it was soon given up, and we lay-to under our close-reefs.

We had less snow and hail than when we were farther to the westward, but we had an abundance of what is worse to a sailor in cold weather—drenching rain. Snow is blinding, and very bad when coming upon a coast, but, for genuine discomfort, give me rain with freezing weather. A snow-storm is exciting, and it does not wet through the clothes (which is important to a sailor); but a constant rain there is no escaping from. It wets to the skin, and makes all protection vain. We had long ago run through all our dry clothes, and as sailors have no other way of drying them than by the sun, we had nothing to do but to put on those which were the least wet.

At the end of each watch, when we came below, we took off our clothes and wrung them out; two taking hold of a pair of trowsers,—one at each end,—and jackets in the same way. Stockings, mittens, and all, were wrung out also and then hung up to drain and chafe dry against the bulk-heads. Then, feeling of all our clothes, we picked out those which were the least wet, and put them on, so as to be ready for a call, and turned-in, covered ourselves up with blankets, and slept until three knocks on the scuttle and the dismal sound of "All starbowlines ahoy! Eight bells, there below! Do you hear the news?" drawled out from on deck, and the sulky answer of "Aye, aye!" from below, sent us up again.

On deck, all was as dark as a pocket, and either a dead calm, with the rain pouring steadily down, or, more generally, a violent gale dead ahead, with rain pelting horizontally, and occasional variations of hail and sleet;—decks afloat with water swashing from side to side, and constantly wet feet; for boots could not be wrung out like drawers, and no composition could stand the constant soaking. In fact, wet and cold feet are inevitable in such weather, and are not the least of those little items which go to make up the grand total of the discomforts of a winter passage round the Cape. Few words were spoken between the watches as they shifted, the wheel was relieved, the mate took his place on the quarter-deck, the look-outs in the bows; and each man had his narrow space to walk fore and aft in, or, rather, to swing himself forward and back in, from one belaying pin to another,—for the decks were too slippery with ice and water to allow of much walking. To make a walk, which is absolutely necessary to pass away the time, one of us hit upon the expedient of sanding the deck; and afterwards, whenever the rain was not so violent as to wash it off, the weatherside of the quarter-deck and a part of the waist and forecastle were sprinkled with the sand which we had on board for holystoning; and thus we made a good promenade, where we walked fore and aft, two and two, hour after hour, in our long, dull, and comfortless watches. The bells seemed to be an hour or two apart, instead of half an hour, and an age to elapse before the welcome sound of eight bells. The sole object was to make the time pass on. Any change was sought for, which would break the monotony of the time; and even the two hours' trick at the wheel, which came round to each of us, in turn, once in every other watch, was looked upon as a relief. Even the never-failing resource of long yarns, which eke out many a watch, seemed to have failed us now; for we had been so long together that we had heard each other's stories told over and over again, till we had them by heart; each one knew the whole history of each of the others, and we were fairly and literally talked out. Singing and joking, we were in no humor for, and, in fact, any sound of mirth or laughter would have struck strangely upon our ears, and would not have been tolerated, any more than whistling, or a wind instrument. The last resort, that of speculating upon the future, seemed now to fail us, for our discouraging situation, and the danger we were really in, (as we expected every day to find ourselves drifted back among the ice) "clapped a stopper" upon all that. From saying—"when we get home"—we began insensibly to alter it to—"if we get home"—and at last the subject was dropped by a tacit consent.

In this state of things, a new light was struck out, and a new field opened, by a change in the watch. One of our watch was laid up for two or three days by a bad hand, (for in cold weather the least cut or bruise ripens into a sore,) and his place was supplied by the carpenter. This was a windfall, and there was quite a contest, who should have the carpenter to walk with him. As "Chips" was a man of some little education, and he and I had had a good deal of intercourse with each other, he fell in with me in my walk. He was a Fin, but spoke English very well, and gave me long accounts of his country;—the customs, the trade, the towns, what little he knew of the government, (I found he was no friend of Russia), his voyages, his first arrival in America, his marriage and courtship;—he had married a countrywoman of his, a dress-maker, whom he met with in Boston. I had very little to tell him of my quiet, sedentary life at home; and, in spite of our best efforts, which had protracted these yarns through five or six watches, we fairly talked one another out, and I turned him over to another man in the watch, and put myself upon my own resources.

I commenced a deliberate system of time-killing, which united some profit with a cheering up of the heavy hours. As soon as I came on deck, and took my place and regular walk, I began with repeating over to myself a string of matters which I had in my memory, in regular order. First, the multiplication table and the tables of weights and measures; then the states of the union, with their capitals; the counties of England, with their shire towns; the kings of England in their order; and a large part of the peerage, which I committed from an almanac that we had on board; and then the Kanaka numerals. This carried me through my facts, and, being repeated deliberately, with long intervals, often eked out the two first bells. Then came the ten commandments; the thirty-ninth chapter of Job, and a few other passages from Scripture. The next in the order, that I never varied from, came Cowper's Castaway, which was a great favorite with me; the solemn measure and gloomy character of which, as well as the incident that it was founded upon, made it well suited to a lonely watch at sea. Then his lines to Mary, his address to the jackdaw, and a short extract from Table Talk; (I abounded in Cowper, for I happened to have a volume of his poems in my chest;) "Ille et nefasto" from Horace, and Goethe's Erl King. After I had got through these, I allowed myself a more general range among everything that I could remember, both in prose and verse. In this way, with an occasional break by relieving the wheel, heaving the log, and going to the scuttle-butt for a drink of water, the longest watch was passed away; and I was so regular in my silent recitations, that if there was no interruption by ship's duty, I could tell very nearly the number of bells by my progress.

Our watches below were no more varied than the watch on deck.

All washing, sewing, and reading was given up; and we did nothing but eat, sleep, and stand our watch, leading what might be called a Cape Horn life. The forecastle was too uncomfortable to sit up in; and whenever we were below, we were in our berths. To prevent the rain, and the sea-water which broke over the bows, from washing down, we were obliged to keep the scuttle closed, so that the forecastle was nearly air-tight. In this little, wet, leaky hole, we were all quartered, in an atmosphere so bad that our lamp, which swung in the middle from the beams, sometimes actually burned blue, with a large circle of foul air about it. Still I was never in better health than after three weeks of this life. I gained a great deal of flesh, and we all ate like horses. At every watch, when we came below, before turning-in, the bread barge and beef kid were overhauled. Each man drank his quart of hot tea night and morning; and glad enough we were to get it, for no nectar and ambrosia were sweeter to the lazy immortals, than was a pot of hot tea, a hard biscuit, and a slice of cold salt beef, to us after a watch on deck. To be sure, we were mere animals and had this life lasted a year instead of a month we should have been little better than the ropes in the ship. Not a razor, nor a brush, nor a drop of water, except the rain and the spray, had come near us all the time; for we were on an allowance of fresh water; and who would strip and wash himself in salt water on deck, in the snow and ice, with the thermometer at zero?

After about eight days of constant easterly gales, the wind hauled occasionally a little to the southward, and blew hard, which, as we were well to the southward, allowed us to brace in a little and stand on, under all the sail we could carry. These turns lasted but a short while, and sooner or later it set again from the old quarter; yet each time we made something, and were gradually edging along to the eastward. One night, after one of these shifts of the wind, and when all hands had been up a great part of the time, our watch was left on deck, with the mainsail hanging in the buntlines, ready to be set if necessary. It came on to blow worse and worse, with hail and snow beating like so many furies upon the ship, it being as dark and thick as night could make it. The mainsail was blowing and slatting with a noise like thunder, when the captain came on deck, and ordered it to be furled. The mate was about to call all hands, when the captain stopped him, and said that the men would be beaten out if they were called up so often; that as our watch must stay on deck, it might as well be doing that as anything else.

Accordingly, we went upon the yard; and never shall I forget that piece of work. Our watch had been so reduced by sickness, and by some having been left in California, that, with one man at the wheel, we had only the third mate and three beside myself, to go aloft; so that at most, we could only attempt to furl one yard-arm at a time. We manned the weather yard-arm, and set to work to make a furl of it. Our lower masts being short, and our yards very square, the sail had a head of nearly fifty feet, and a short leach, made still shorter by the deep reef which was in it, which brought the clew away out on the quarters of the yard, and made a bunt nearly as square as the mizen royal-yard. Beside this difficulty, the yard over which we lay was cased with ice, the gaskets and rope of the foot and leach of the sail as stiff and hard as a piece of suction-hose, and the sail itself about as pliable as though it had been made of sheets of sheathing copper. It blew a perfect hurricane, with alternate blasts of snow, hail, and rain. We had to fist the sail with bare hands. No one could trust himself to mittens, for if he slipped, he was a gone man. All the boats were hoisted in on deck, and there was nothing to be lowered for him. We had need of every finger God had given us. Several times we got the sail upon the yard, but it blew away again before we could secure it. It required men to lie over the yard to pass each turn of the gaskets, and when they were passed, it was almost impossible to knot them so that they would hold. Frequently we were obliged to leave off altogether and take to beating our hands upon the sail, to keep them from freezing.

After some time,—which seemed forever,—we got the weather side stowed after a fashion, and went over to leeward for another trial.

This was still worse, for the body of the sail had been blown over to leeward, and as the yard was a-cock-bill by the lying over of the vessel, we had to light it all up to windward. When the yard-arms were furled, the bunt was all adrift again, which made more work for us. We got all secure at last, but we had been nearly an hour and a half upon the yard, and it seemed an age. It just struck five bells when we went up, and eight were struck soon after we came down. This may seem slow work, but considering the state of everything, and that we had only five men to a sail with just half as many square yards of canvas in it as the mainsail of the Independence, sixty-gun ship, which musters seven hundred men at her quarters, it is not wonderful that we were no quicker about it. We were glad enough to get on deck, and still more, to go below. The oldest sailor in the watch said, as he went down,—"I shall never forget that main yard;—it beats all my going a fishing. Fun is fun, but furling one yard-arm of a course, at a time, off Cape Horn, is no better than man-killing."

During the greater part of the next two days, the wind was pretty steady from the southward. We had evidently made great progress, and had good hope of being soon up with the Cape, if we were not there already. We could put but little confidence in our reckoning, as there had been no opportunities for an observation, and we had drifted too much to allow of our dead reckoning being anywhere near the mark. If it would clear off enough to give a chance for an observation, or if we could make land, we should know where we were; and upon these, and the chances of falling in with a sail from the eastward, we depended almost entirely.

Friday, July 22d. This day we had a steady gale from the southward, and stood on under close sail, with the yards eased a little by the weather braces, the clouds lifting a little, and showing signs of breaking away. In the afternoon, I was below with Mr. H——, the third mate, and two others, filling the bread locker in the steerage from the casks, when a bright gleam of sunshine broke out and shone down the companion-way and through the skylight, lighting up everything below, and sending a warm glow through the heart of every one. It was a sight we had not seen for weeks,—an omen, a god-send. Even the roughest and hardest face acknowledged its influence. Just at that moment we heard a loud shout from all parts of the deck, and the mate called out down the companion-way to the captain, who was sitting in the cabin. What he said, we could not distinguish, but the captain kicked over his chair, and was on deck at one jump. We could not tell what it was; and, anxious as we were to know, the discipline of the ship would not allow of our leaving our places. Yet, as we were not called, we knew there was no danger. We hurried to get through with our job, when, seeing the steward's black face peering out of the pantry, Mr. H—— hailed him, to know what was the matter. "Lan' o, to be sure, sir! No you hear 'em sing out, 'Lan' o?' De cap'em say 'im Cape Horn!"

This gave us a new start, and we were soon through our work, and on deck; and there lay the land, fair upon the larboard beam, and slowly edging away upon the quarter. All hands were busy looking at it—the captain and mates from the quarter-deck, the cook from his galley, and the sailors from the forecastle; and even Mr. N., the passenger, who had kept in his shell for nearly a month, and hardly been seen by anybody, and who we had almost forgotten was on board, came out like a butterfly, and was hopping round as bright as a bird.

The land was the island of Staten Land, and, just to the eastward of Cape Horn; and a more desolate-looking spot I never wish to set eyes upon;—bare, broken, and girt with rocks and ice, with here and there, between the rocks and broken hillocks, a little stunted vegetation of shrubs. It was a place well suited to stand at the junction of the two oceans, beyond the reach of human cultivation, and encounter the blasts and snows of a perpetual winter. Yet, dismal as it was, it was a pleasant sight to us; not only as being the first land we had seen, but because it told us that we had passed the Cape,—were in the Atlantic,—and that, with twenty-four hours of this breeze, might bid defiance to the Southern Ocean. It told us, too, our latitude and longitude better than any observation; and the captain now knew where we were, as well as if we were off the end of Long wharf.

In the general joy, Mr. N. said he should like to go ashore upon the island and examine a spot which probably no human being had ever set foot upon; but the captain intimated that he would see the island—specimens and all,—in—another place, before he would get out a boat or delay the ship one moment for him.

We left the land gradually astern; and at sundown had the Atlantic Ocean clear before us.

CHAPTER XXXIII

CRACKING ON—PROGRESS HOMEWARD—A PLEASANT SUNDAY—A FINE SIGHT—BY-PLAY

It is usual, in voyages round the Cape from the Pacific, to keep to the eastward of the Falkland Islands; but as it had now set in a strong, steady, and clear south-wester, with every prospect of its lasting, and we had had enough of high latitudes, the captain determined to stand immediately to the northward, running inside the Falkland Islands. Accordingly, when the wheel was relieved at eight o'clock, the order was given to keep her due north, and all hands were turned up to square away the yards and make sail. In a moment, the news ran through the ship that the captain was keeping her off, with her nose straight for Boston, and Cape Horn over her taffrail. It was a moment of enthusiasm. Every one was on the alert, and even the two sick men turned out to lend a hand at the halyards. The wind was now due south-west, and blowing a gale to which a vessel close hauled could have shown no more than a single close-reefed sail; but as we were going before it, we could carry on.

Accordingly, hands were sent aloft, and a reef shaken out of the top-sails, and the reefed foresail set. When we came to masthead the topsail yards, with all hands at the halyards, we struck up "Cheerily, men," with a chorus which might have been heard half-way to Staten Land. Under her increased sail, the ship drove on through the water. Yet she could bear it well; and the captain sang out from the quarter-deck—"Another reef out of that fore-topsail, and give it to her!" Two hands sprang aloft; the frozen reef-points and earings were cast adrift, the halyards manned, and the sail gave out her increased canvas to the gale. All hands were kept on deck to watch the effect of the change. It was as much as she could well carry, and with a heavy sea astern, it took two men at the wheel to steer her. She flung the foam from her bows; the spray breaking aft as far as the gangway. She was going at a prodigious rate.

Still, everything held. Preventer braces were reeved and hauled taut; tackles got upon the backstays; and each thing done to keep all snug and strong. The captain walked the deck at a rapid stride, looked aloft at the sails, and then to windward; the mate stood in the gangway, rubbing his hands, and talking aloud to the ship—"Hurrah, old bucket! the Boston girls have got hold of the tow-rope!" and the like; and we were on the forecastle, looking to see how the spars stood it, and guessing the rate at which she was going,—when the captain called out—"Mr. Brown, get up the topmast studding-sail! What she can't carry she may drag!" The mate looked a moment; but he would let no one be before him in daring.

He sprang forward—"Hurrah, men! rig out the topmast studding-sail boom! Lay aloft, and I'll send the rigging up to you!"—We sprang aloft into the top; lowered a girt-line down, by which we hauled up the rigging; rove the tacks and halyards; ran out the boom and lashed it fast, and sent down the lower halyards, as a preventer. It was a clear starlight night, cold and blowing; but everybody worked with a will. Some, indeed, looked as though they thought the "old man" was mad, but no one said a word. We had had a new topmast studding-sail made with a reef in it,—a thing hardly ever heard of, and which the sailors had ridiculed a good deal, saying that when it was time to reef a studding-sail, it was time to take it in. But we found a use for it now; for, there being a reef in the topsail, the studding-sail could not be set without one in it also. To be sure, a studding-sail with reefed topsails was rather a new thing; yet there was some reason in it, for if we carried that away, we should lose only a sail and a boom; but a whole topsail might have carried away the mast and all.

While we were aloft, the sail had been got out, bent to the yard, reefed, and ready for hoisting. Waiting for a good opportunity, the halyards were manned and the yard hoisted fairly up to the block; but when the mate came to shake the catspaw out of the downhaul, and we began to boom-end the sail, it shook the ship to her centre. The boom buckled up and bent like a whip-stick, and we looked every moment to see something go; but, being of the short, tough upland spruce, it bent like whalebone, and nothing could break it. The carpenter said it was the best stick he had ever seen. The strength of all hands soon brought the tack to the boom-end, and the sheet was trimmed down, and the preventer and the weather brace hauled taut to take off the strain. Every rope-yarn seemed stretched to the utmost, and every thread of canvas; and with this sail added to her, the ship sprang through the water like a thing possessed. The sail being nearly all forward, it lifted her out of the water, and she seemed actually to jump from sea to sea. From the time her keel was laid, she had never been so driven; and had it been life or death with every one of us, she could not have borne another stitch of canvas.

Finding that she would bear the sail, the hands were sent below, and our watch remained on deck. Two men at the wheel had as much as they could do to keep her within three points of her course, for she steered as wild as a young colt. The mate walked the deck, looking at the sails, and then over the side to see the foam fly by her, slapping his hands upon his thighs and talking to the ship—"Hurrah, you jade, you've got the scent!—you know where you're going!" And when she leaped over the seas, and almost out of the water, and trembled to her very keel, the spars and masts snapping and creaking,—"There she goes!—There she goes,—handsomely!—as long as she cracks she holds!"—while we stood with the rigging laid down fair for letting go, and ready to take in sail and clear away, if anything went. At four bells we hove the log, and she was going eleven knots fairly; and had it not been for the sea from aft which sent the ship home, and threw her continually off her course, the log would have shown her to have been going much faster. I went to the wheel with a young fellow from the Kennebec, who was a good helmsman; and for two hours we had our hands full. A few minutes showed us that our monkey-jackets must come off; and, cold as it was, we stood in our shirt-sleeves, in a perspiration; and were glad enough to have it eight bells, and the wheel relieved. We turned-in and slept as well as we could, though the sea made a constant roar under her bows, and washed over the forecastle like a small cataract.

At four o'clock, we were called again. The same sail was still on the vessel, and the gale, if there was any change, had increased a little. No attempt was made to take the studding-sail in; and, indeed, it was too late now. If we had started anything toward taking it in, either tack or halyards, it would have blown to pieces, and carried something away with it. The only way now was to let everything stand, and if the gale went down, well and good; if not, something must go—the weakest stick or rope first—and then we could get it in. For more than an hour she was driven on at such a rate that she seemed actually to crowd the sea into a heap before her; and the water poured over the spritsail yard as it would over a dam. Toward daybreak the gale abated a little, and she was just beginning to go more easily along, relieved of the pressure, when Mr. Brown, determined to give her no respite, and depending upon the wind's subsiding as the sun rose, told us to get along the lower studding-sail. This was an immense sail, and held wind enough to last a Dutchman a week,—hove-to. It was soon ready, the boom topped up, preventer guys rove, and the idlers called up to man the halyards; yet such was still the force of the gale, that we were nearly an hour setting the sail; carried away the outhaul in doing it, and came very near snapping off the swinging boom. No sooner was it set than the ship tore on again like one that was mad, and began to steer as wild as a hawk. The men at the wheel were puffing and blowing at their work, and the helm was going hard up and hard down, constantly. Add to this, the gale did not lessen as the day came on, but the sun rose in clouds. A sudden lurch threw the man from the weather wheel across the deck and against the side. The mate sprang to the wheel, and the man, regaining his feet, seized the spokes, and they hove the wheel up just in time to save her from broaching to; though nearly half the studding-sail went under water; and as she came to, the boom stood up at an angle of forty five degrees. She had evidently more on her than she could bear; yet it was in vain to try to take it in—the clewline was not strong enough; and they were thinking of cutting away, when another wide yaw and a come-to, snapped the guys, and the swinging boom came in, with a crash, against the lower rigging. The outhaul block gave way, and the topmast studding-sail boom bent in a manner which I never before supposed a stick could bend. I had my eye on it when the guys parted, and it made one spring and buckled up so as to form nearly a half circle, and sprang out again to its shape.

The clewline gave way at the first pull; the cleat to which the halyards were belayed was wrenched off, and the sail blew round the spritsail yards and head guys, which gave us a bad job to get it in.

A half hour served to clear all away, and she was suffered to drive on with her topmast studding-sail set, it being as much as she could stagger under.

During all this day and the next night, we went on under the same sail, the gale blowing with undiminished force; two men at the wheel all the time; watch and watch, and nothing to do but to steer and look out for the ship, and be blown along;—until the noon of the next day—

Sunday, July 24th, when we were in latitude 50° 27' S., longitude 62° 13' W., having made four degrees of latitude in the last twenty-four hours. Being now to northward of the Falkland Islands, the ship was kept off, north-east, for the equator; and with her head for the equator, and Cape Horn over her taffrail, she went gloriously on; every heave of the sea leaving the Cape astern, and every hour bringing us nearer to home, and to warm weather. Many a time, when blocked up in the ice, with everything dismal and discouraging about us, had we said,—if we were only fairly round, and standing north on the other side, we should ask for no more:—and now we had it all, with a clear sea, and as much wind as a sailor could pray for. If the best part of the voyage is the last part, surely we had all now that we could wish. Every one was in the highest spirits, and the ship seemed as glad as any of us at getting out of her confinement. At each change of the watch, those coming on deck asked those going below—"How does she go along?" and got for answer, the rate, and the customary addition—"Aye! and the Boston girls have had hold of the tow-rope all the watch, and can't haul half the slack in!" Each day the sun rose higher in the horizon, and the nights grew shorter; and at coming on deck each morning, there was a sensible change in the temperature. The ice, too, began to melt from off the rigging and spars, and, except a little which remained in the tops and round the hounds of the lower masts, was soon gone. As we left the gale behind us, the reefs were shaken out of the topsails, and sail made as fast as she could bear it; and every time all hands were sent to the halyards, a song was called for, and we hoisted away with a will.

Sail after sail was added, as we drew into fine weather; and in one week after leaving Cape Horn, the long topgallant masts were got up, topgallant and royal yards crossed, and the ship restored to her fair proportions.

The Southern Cross we saw no more after the first night; the Magellan Clouds settled lower and lower in the horizon; and so great was our change of latitude each succeeding night, that we sank some constellation in the south, and raised another in the northern horizon.

Sunday, July 31st. At noon we were in lat. 36° 41' S., long. 38° 08' W.; having traversed the distance of two thousand miles, allowing for changes of course, in nine days. A thousand miles in four days and a half!—This is equal to steam.

Soon after eight o'clock, the appearance of the ship gave evidence that this was the first Sunday we had yet had in fine weather. As the sun came up clear, with the promise of a fair, warm day, and, as usual on Sunday, there was no work going on, all hands turned-to upon clearing out the forecastle. The wet and soiled clothes which had accumulated there during the past month, were brought up on deck; the chests moved; brooms, buckets of water, swabs, scrubbing-brushes, and scrapers carried down, and applied, until the forecastle floor was as white as chalk, and everything neat and in order. The bedding from the berths was then spread on deck, and dried, and aired; the deck-tub filled with water; and a grand washing begun of all the clothes which were brought up. Shirts, frocks, drawers, trowsers, jackets, stockings, of every shape and color, wet and dirty—many of them mouldy from having been lying a long time wet in a foul corner—these were all washed and scrubbed out, and finally towed overboard for half an hour; and then made fast in the rigging to dry. Wet boots and shoes were spread out to dry in sunny places on deck; and the whole ship looked like a back yard on a washing day. After we had done with our clothes, we began upon our own persons. A little fresh water, which we had saved from our allowance, was put in buckets, and with soap and towels, we had what sailors call a fresh-water wash. The same bucket, to be sure, had to go through several hands, and was spoken for by one after another, but as we rinsed off in salt water, pure from the ocean, and the fresh was used only to start the accumulated grime and blackness of five weeks, it was held of little consequence.

We soaped down and scrubbed one another with towels and pieces of canvas, stripping to it; and then, getting into the head, threw buckets of water upon each other. After this, came shaving, and combing, and brushing; and when, having spent the first part of the day in this way, we sat down on the forecastle, in the afternoon, with clean duck trowsers, and shirts on, washed, shaved, and combed, and looking a dozen shades lighter for it, reading, sewing, and talking at our ease, with a clear sky and warm sun over our heads, a steady breeze over the larboard quarter, studding-sails out alow and aloft, and all the flying kites aboard;—we felt that we had got back into the pleasantest part of a sailor's life. At sundown the clothes were all taken down from the rigging—clean and dry—and stowed neatly away in our chests; and our southwesters, thick boots, guernsey frocks, and other accompaniments of bad weather, put out of the way, we hoped, for the rest of the voyage, as we expected to come upon the coast early in the autumn.

Notwithstanding all that has been said about the beauty of a ship under full sail, there are very few who have ever seen a ship, literally, under all her sail. A ship coming in or going out of port, with her ordinary sails, and perhaps two of three studding-sails, is commonly said to be under full sail; but a ship never has all her sail upon her, except when she has a light, steady breeze, very nearly, but not quite, dead aft, and so regular that it can be trusted, and is likely to last for some time. Then, with all her sails, light and heavy, and studding-sails, on each side, alow and aloft, she is the most glorious moving object in the world. Such a sight, very few, even some who have been at sea a great deal, have ever beheld; for from the deck of your own vessel you cannot see her, as you would a separate object.

One night, while we were in these tropics, I went out to the end of the flying-jib-boom, upon some duty, and, having finished it, turned round, and lay over the boom for a long time, admiring the beauty of the sight before me. Being so far out from the deck, I could look at the ship, as at a separate vessel;—and there rose up from the water, supported only by the small black hull, a pyramid of canvas, spreading out far beyond the hull, and towering up almost, as it seemed in the indistinct night air, to the clouds. The sea was as still as an inland lake; the light trade-wind was gently and steadily breathing from astern; the dark blue sky was studded with the tropical stars; there was no sound but the rippling of the water under the stem; and the sails were spread out, wide and high;—the two lower studding-sails stretching, on each side, far beyond the deck; the topmast studding-sails, like wings to the topsails; the top-gallant studding-sails spreading fearlessly out above them; still higher, the two royal studding-sails, looking like two kites flying from the same string; and, highest of all, the little skysail, the apex of the pyramid, seeming actually to touch the stars, and to be out of reach of human hand. So quiet, too, was the sea, and so steady the breeze, that if these sails had been sculptured marble, they could not have been more motionless. Not a ripple upon the surface of the canvas; not even a quivering of the extreme edges of the sail—so perfectly were they distended by the breeze. I was so lost in the sight, that I forgot the presence of the man who came out with me, until he said, (for he, too, rough old man-of-war's-man as he was, had been gazing at the show,) half to himself, still looking at the marble sails—"How quietly they do their work!"

The fine weather brought work with it; as the ship was to be put in order for coming into port. This may give a landsman some notion of what is done on board ship.—All the first part of a passage is spent in getting a ship ready for sea, and the last part in getting her ready for port. She is, as sailors say, like a lady's watch, always out of repair. The new, strong sails, which we had up off Cape Horn, were to be sent down, and the old set, which were still serviceable in fine weather, to be bent in their place; all the rigging to be set up, fore and aft; the masts stayed; the standing rigging to be tarred down; lower and topmast rigging rattled down, fore and aft; the ship scraped, inside and out, and painted; decks varnished; new and neat knots, seizings and coverings to be fitted; and every part put in order, to look well to the owner's eye, on coming into Boston. This, of course, was a long matter; and all hands were kept on deck at work for the whole of each day, during the rest of the voyage. Sailors call this hard usage; but the ship must be in crack order, and "we're homeward bound" was the answer to everything.

We went on for several days, employed in this way, nothing remarkable occurring; and, at the latter part of the week, fell in with the south-east trades, blowing about east-south-east, which brought them nearly two points abaft our beam. These blew strong and steady, so that we hardly started a rope, until we were beyond their latitude. The first day of "all hands," one of those little incidents occurred, which are nothing in themselves, but are great matters in the eyes of a ship's company, as they serve to break the monotony of a voyage, and afford conversation to the crew for days afterwards. These small matters, too, are often interesting, as they show the customs and state of feeling on shipboard.

In merchant vessels, the captain gives his orders as to the ship's work, to the mate, in a general way, and leaves the execution of them, with the particular ordering, to him. This has become so fixed a custom, that it is like a law, and is never infringed upon by a wise master, unless his mate is no seaman; in which case, the captain must often oversee things for himself. This, however, could not be said of our chief mate; and he was very jealous of any encroachment upon the borders of his authority.

On Monday morning, the captain told him to stay the fore-topmast plumb. He accordingly came forward, turned all hands to, with tackles on the stays and back-stays, coming up with the seizings, hauling here, belaying there, and full of business, standing between the knightheads to sight the mast,—when the captain came forward, and also began to give orders. This made confusion, and the mate, finding that he was all aback, left his place and went aft, saying to the captain—

"If you come forward, sir, I'll go aft. One is enough on the forecastle."

This produced a reply, and another fierce answer; and the words flew, fists were doubled up, and things looked threateningly.

"I'm master of this ship."

"Yes, sir, and I'm mate of her, and know my place! My place is forward, and yours is aft!"

"My place is where I choose! I command the whole ship; and you are mate only so long as I choose!"

"Say the word, Capt. T., and I'm done! I can do a man's work aboard! I didn't come through the cabin windows! If I'm not mate, I can be man," etc., etc.

This was all fun for us, who stood by, winking at each other, and enjoying the contest between the higher powers. The captain took the mate aft; and they had a long talk, which ended in the mate's returning to his duty. The captain had broken through a custom, which is a part of the common-law of a ship, and without reason; for he knew that his mate was a sailor, and needed no help from him; and the mate was excusable for being angry. Yet he was wrong, and the captain right. Whatever the captain does is right, ipso facto, and any opposition to it is wrong, on board ship; and every officer and man knows this when he signs the ship's articles.

It is a part of the contract. Yet there has grown up in merchant vessels a series of customs, which have become a well understood system, and have almost the force of prescriptive law. To be sure, all power is in the captain, and the officers hold their authority only during his will; and the men are liable to be called upon for any service; yet, by breaking in upon these usages, many difficulties have occurred on board ship, and even come into courts of justice, which are perfectly unintelligible to any one not acquainted with the universal nature and force of these customs. Many a provocation has been offered, and a system of petty oppression pursued towards men, the force and meaning of which would appear as nothing to strangers, and doubtless do appear so to many "'long-shore" juries and judges.

The next little diversion, was a battle on the forecastle one afternoon, between the mate and the steward. They had been on bad terms the whole voyage; and had threatened a rupture several times. This afternoon, the mate asked him for a tumbler of water, and he refused to get it for him, saying that he waited upon nobody but the captain: and here he had the custom on his side. But in answering, he left off "the handle to the mate's name." This enraged the mate, who called him a "black soger;" and at it they went, clenching, striking, and rolling over and over; while we stood by, looking on, and enjoying the fun. The darky tried to butt him, but the mate got him down, and held him, the steward singing out, "Let me go, Mr. Brown, or there'll be blood spilt!" In the midst of this, the captain came on deck, separated them, took the steward aft, and gave him half a dozen with a rope's end.

The steward tried to justify himself; but he had been heard to talk of spilling blood, and that was enough to earn him his flogging; and the captain did not choose to inquire any further.

CHAPTER XXXIV

NARROW ESCAPES—THE EQUATOR—TROPICAL SQUALLS—A THUNDER STORM

The same day, I met with one of those narrow escapes, which are so often happening in a sailor's life. I had been aloft nearly all the afternoon, at work, standing for as much as an hour on the fore top-gallant yard, which was hoisted up, and hung only by the tie; when, having got through my work, I balled up my yarns, took my serving-board in my hand, laid hold deliberately of the top-gallant rigging, took one foot from the yard, and was just lifting the other, when the tie parted, and down the yard fell. I was safe, by my hold upon the rigging, but it made my heart beat quick. Had the tie parted one instant sooner, or had I stood an instant longer on the yard, I should inevitably have been thrown violently from the height of ninety or a hundred feet, overboard; or, what is worse, upon the deck. However, "a miss is as good as a mile;" a saying which sailors very often have occasion to use. An escape is always a joke on board ship. A man would be ridiculed who should make a serious matter of it. A sailor knows too well that his life hangs upon a thread, to wish to be always reminded of it; so, if a man has an escape, he keeps it to himself, or makes a joke of it. I have often known a man's life to be saved by an instant of time, or by the merest chance,—the swinging of a rope,—and no notice taken of it. One of our boys, when off Cape Horn, reefing topsails of a dark night, and when there were no boats to be lowered away, and where, if a man fell overboard he must be left behind,—lost his hold of the reef-point, slipped from the foot-rope, and would have been in the water in a moment, when the man who was next to him on the yard caught him by the collar of his jacket, and hauled him up upon the yard, with—"Hold on, another time, you young monkey, and be d——d to you!"—and that was all that was heard about it.

Sunday, August 7th. Lat. 25° 59' S., long. 27° 0' W. Spoke the English bark Mary-Catherine, from Bahia, bound to Calcutta. This was the first sail we had fallen in with, and the first time we had seen a human form or heard the human voice, except of our own number, for nearly a hundred days. The very yo-ho-ing of the sailors at the ropes sounded sociably upon the ear. She was an old, damaged-looking craft, with a high poop and top-gallant forecastle, and sawed off square, stem and stern, like a true English "tea-wagon," and with a run like a sugar-box. She had studding-sails out alow and aloft, with a light but steady breeze, and her captain said he could not get more than four knots out of her and thought he should have a long passage. We were going six on an easy bowline.

The next day, about three P. M., passed a large corvette-built ship, close upon the wind, with royals and skysails set fore and aft, under English colors. She was standing south-by-east, probably bound round Cape Horn. She had men in her tops, and black mast-heads; heavily sparred, with sails cut to a t, and other marks of a man-of-war. She sailed well, and presented a fine appearance; the proud, aristocratic-looking banner of St. George, the cross in a blood-red field, waving from the mizen. We probably were as fine a sight, with our studding-sails spread far out beyond the ship on either side, and rising in a pyramid to royal studding-sails and sky-sails, burying the hull in canvas, and looking like what the whale-men on the Banks, under their stump top-gallant masts, call "a Cape Horn-er under a cloud of sail."

Friday, August 12th. At daylight made the island of Trinidad, situated in lat. 20° 28' S., long. 29° 08' W. At twelve M., it bore N. W. 1/2 N., distant twenty-seven miles. It was a beautiful day, the sea hardly ruffled by the light trades, and the island looking like a small blue mound rising from a field of glass.

Such a fair and peaceful-looking spot is said to have been, for a long time, the resort of a band of pirates, who ravaged the tropical seas.

Thursday, August 18th. At three P. M., made the island of Fernando Naronha, lying in lat. 3° 55' S., long. 32° 35' W.; and between twelve o'clock Friday night and one o'clock Saturday morning, crossed the equator, for the fourth time since leaving Boston, in long. 35° W.; having been twenty-seven days from Staten Land—a distance, by the courses we had made, of more than four thousand miles.

We were now to the northward of the line, and every day added to our latitude. The Magellan Clouds, the last sign of South latitude, were sunk in the horizon, and the north star, the Great Bear, and the familiar signs of northern latitudes, were rising in the heavens.

Next to seeing land, there is no sight which makes one realize more that he is drawing near home, than to see the same heavens, under which he was born, shining at night over his head. The weather was extremely hot, with the usual tropical alternations of a scorching sun and squalls of rain; yet not a word was said in complaint of the heat, for we all remembered that only three or four weeks before we would have given nearly our all to have been where we now were. We had plenty of water, too, which we caught by spreading an awning, with shot thrown in to make hollows. These rain squalls came up in the manner usual between the tropics.—A clear sky; burning, vertical sun; work going lazily on, and men about decks with nothing but duck trowsers, checked shirts, and straw hats; the ship moving as lazily through the water; the man at the helm resting against the wheel, with his hat drawn over his eyes; the captain below, taking an afternoon nap; the passenger leaning over the taffrail, watching a dolphin following slowly in our wake; the sailmaker mending an old topsail on the lee side of the quarter-deck; the carpenter working at his bench, in the waist; the boys making sinnet; the spun-yarn winch whizzing round and round, and the men walking slowly fore and aft with their yarns.—A cloud rises to windward, looking a little black; the sky-sails are brailed down; the captain puts his head out of the companion-way, looks at the cloud, comes up, and begins to walk the deck.—The cloud spreads and comes on;—the tub of yarns, the sail, and other matters, are thrown below, and the sky-light and booby-hatch put on, and the slide drawn over the forecastle.—"Stand by the royal halyards;"—the man at the wheel keeps a good weather helm, so as not to be taken aback. The squall strikes her. If it is light, the royal yards are clewed down, and the ship keeps on her way; but if the squall takes strong hold, the royals are clewed up, fore and aft; light hands lay aloft and furl them; top-gallant yards clewed down, flying-jib hauled down, and the ship kept off before it,—the man at the helm laying out his strength to heave the wheel up to windward. At the same time a drenching rain, which soaks one through in an instant. Yet no one puts on a jacket or cap; for if it is only warm, a sailor does not mind a ducking; and the sun will soon be out again. As soon as the force of the squall has passed, though to a common eye the ship would seem to be in the midst of it,—"Keep her up to her course, again!"—"Keep her up, sir," (answer);—"Hoist away the top-gallant yards!"—"Run up the flying jib!"—"Lay aloft, you boys, and loose the royals!"—and all sail is on her again before she is fairly out of the squall; and she is going on in her course. The sun comes out once more, hotter than ever, dries up the decks and the sailors' clothes; the hatches are taken off; the sail got up and spread on the quarter-deck; spun-yarn winch set a whirling again; rigging coiled up; captain goes below; and every sign of an interruption is removed.

These scenes, with occasional dead calms, lasting for hours, and sometimes for days, are fair specimens of the Atlantic tropics. The nights were fine; and as we had all hands all day, the watch were allowed to sleep on deck at night, except the man at the wheel, and one look-out on the forecastle. This was not so much expressly allowed, as winked at. We could do it if we did not ask leave. If the look-out was caught napping, the whole watch was kept awake.

We made the most of this permission, and stowed ourselves away upon the rigging, under the weather rail, on the spars, under the windlass, and in all the snug corners; and frequently slept out the watch, unless we had a wheel or a look-out. And we were glad enough to get this rest; for under the "all hands" system, out of every other thirty-six hours, we had only four below; and even an hour's sleep was a gain not to be neglected. One would have thought so, to have seen our watch, some nights, sleeping through a heavy rain. And often have we come on deck, and finding a dead calm and a light, steady rain, and determined not to lose our sleep, have laid a coil of rigging down so as to keep us out of the water which was washing about decks, and stowed ourselves away upon it, covering a jacket over us, and slept as soundly as a Dutchman between two feather beds.

For a week or ten days after crossing the line, we had the usual variety of calms, squalls, head winds, and fair winds;—at one time braced sharp upon the wind, with a taut bowline, and in an hour after, slipping quietly along, with a light breeze over the taffrail, and studding-sails out on both sides;—until we fell in with the north-east trade-winds; which we did on the afternoon of

Sunday, August 28th, in lat. 12° N. The trade-wind clouds had been in sight for a day or two previously, and we expected to take them every hour. The light southerly breeze, which had been blowing languidly during the first part of the day, died away toward noon, and in its place came puffs from the north-east, which caused us to take our studding-sails in and brace up; and in a couple of hours more, we were bowling gloriously along, dashing the spray far ahead and to leeward, with the cool, steady north-east trades, freshening up the sea, and giving us as much as we could carry our royals to. These winds blew strong and steady, keeping us generally upon a bowline, as our course was about north-north-west; and sometimes, as they veered a little to the eastward, giving us a chance at a main top-gallant studding-sail; and sending us well to the northward, until—

Sunday, Sept. 4th, when they left us, in lat. 22° N., long. 51° W., directly under the tropic of Cancer.

For several days we lay "humbugging about" in the Horse latitudes, with all sorts of winds and weather, and occasionally, as we were in the latitude of the West Indies—a thunder storm. It was hurricane month, too, and we were just in the track of the tremendous hurricane of 1830, which swept the North Atlantic, destroying almost everything before it. The first night after the tradewinds left us, while we were in the latitude of the island of Cuba, we had a specimen of a true tropical thunder storm. A light breeze had been blowing directly from aft during the first part of the night which gradually died away, and before midnight it was dead calm, and a heavy black cloud had shrouded the whole sky. When our watch came on deck at twelve o'clock, it was as black as Erebus; the studding-sails were all taken in, and the royals furled; not a breath was stirring; the sails hung heavy and motionless from the yards; and the perfect stillness, and the darkness, which was almost palpable, were truly appalling. Not a word was spoken, but every one stood as though waiting for something to happen. In a few minutes the mate came forward; and in a low tone, which was almost a whisper, told us to haul down the jib. The fore and mizen top-gallant sails were taken in, in the same silent manner; and we lay motionless upon the water, with an uneasy expectation, which, from the long suspense, became actually painful. We could hear the captain walking the deck, but it was too dark to see anything more than one's hand before the face. Soon the mate came forward again, and gave an order, in a low tone, to clew up the main top-gallant sail; and so infectious was the awe and silence, that the clewlines and buntlines were hauled up without any of the customary singing out at the ropes. An English lad and myself went up to furl it; and we had just got the bunt up, when the mate called out to us, something, we did not hear what,—but supposing it to be an order to bear-a-hand, we hurried, and made all fast, and came down, feeling our way among the rigging. When we got down we found all hands looking aloft, and there, directly over where we had been standing, upon the main top-gallant-mast-head, was a ball of light, which the sailors name a corposant (corpus sancti), and which the mate had called out to us to look at. They were all watching it carefully, for sailors have a notion that if the corposant rises in the rigging, it is a sign of fair weather, but if it comes lower down, there will be a storm. Unfortunately, as an omen, it came down, and showed itself on the top-gallant yard-arm. We were off the yard in good season, for it is held a fatal sign to have the pale light of the corposant thrown upon one's face. As it was, the English lad did not feel comfortably at having had it so near him, and directly over his head. In a few minutes it disappeared, and showed itself again on the fore top-gallant yard; and after playing about for some time, disappeared again; when the man on the forecastle pointed to it upon the flying-jib-boom-end. But our attention was drawn from watching this, by the falling of some drops of rain and by a perceptible increase of the darkness, which seemed suddenly to add a new shade of blackness to the night. In a few minutes, low, grumbling thunder was heard, and some random flashes of lightning came from the south-west. Every sail was taken in but the topsails, still, no squall appeared to be coming. A few puffs lifted the topsails, but they fell again to the mast, and all was as still as ever. A moment more, and a terrific flash and peal broke simultaneously upon us, and a cloud appeared to open directly over our heads and let down the water in one body, like a falling ocean. We stood motionless, and almost stupefied; yet nothing had been struck. Peal after peal rattled over our heads, with a sound which seemed actually to stop the breath in the body, and the "speedy gleams" kept the whole ocean in a glare of light. The violent fall of rain lasted but a few minutes, and was succeeded by occasional drops and showers; but the lightning continued incessant for several hours, breaking the midnight darkness with irregular and blinding flashes. During all which time there was not a breath stirring, and we lay motionless, like a mark to be shot at, probably the only object on the surface of the ocean for miles and miles. We stood hour after hour, until our watch was out, and we were relieved, at four o'clock. During all this time, hardly a word was spoken; no bells were struck, and the wheel was silently relieved. The rain fell at intervals in heavy showers, and we stood drenched through and blinded by the flashes, which broke the Egyptian darkness with a brightness which seemed almost malignant; while the thunder rolled in peals, the concussion of which appeared to shake the very ocean. A ship is not often injured by lightning, for the electricity is separated by the great number of points she presents, and the quantity of iron which she has scattered in various parts. The electric fluid ran over our anchors, top-sail sheets and ties; yet no harm was done to us. We went below at four o'clock, leaving things in the same state. It is not easy to sleep, when the very next flash may tear the ship in two, or set her on fire; or where the deathlike calm may be broken by the blast of a hurricane, taking the masts out of the ship. But a man is no sailor if he cannot sleep when he turns-in, and turn out when he's called. And when, at seven bells, the customary "All the larboard watch, ahoy?" brought us on deck, it was a fine, clear, sunny morning, the ship going leisurely along, with a good breeze and all sail set.

CHAPTER XXXV

A DOUBLE-REEF-TOP-SAIL BREEZE—SCURVY—A FRIEND IN NEED—PREPARING FOR PORT—THE GULF STREAM

From the latitude of the West Indies, until we got inside the Bermudas, where we took the westerly and south-westerly winds, which blow steadily off the coast of the United States early in the autumn, we had every variety of weather, and two or three moderate gales, or, as sailors call them, double-reef-topsail breezes, which came on in the usual manner, and of which one is a specimen of all.—A fine afternoon; all hands at work, some in the rigging, and others on deck; a stiff breeze, and ship close upon the wind, and skysails brailed down.—Latter part of the afternoon, breeze increases, ship lies over to it, and clouds look windy. Spray begins to fly over the forecastle, and wets the yarns the boys are knotting;—ball them up and put them below.—Mate knocks off work and clears up decks earlier than usual, and orders a man who has been employed aloft to send the royal halyards over to windward, as he comes down. Breast backstays hauled taut, and tackle got upon the martingale back-rope.—One of the boys furls the mizen royal.—Cook thinks there is going to be "nasty work," and has supper ready early.—Mate gives orders to get supper by the watch, instead of all hands, as usual.—While eating supper, hear the watch on deck taking in the royals.—Coming on deck, find it is blowing harder, and an ugly head sea is running.—Instead of having all hands on the forecastle in the dog watch, smoking, singing, and telling yarns, one watch goes below and turns-in, saying that it's going to be an ugly night, and two hours' sleep is not to be lost.

Clouds look black and wild; wind rising, and ship working hard against a heavy sea, which breaks over the forecastle, and washes aft through the scuppers. Still, no more sail is taken in, for the captain is a driver, and, like all drivers, very partial to his top-gallant sails. A top-gallant sail, too, makes the difference between a breeze and a gale. When a top-gallant sail is on a ship, it is only a breeze, though I have seen ours set over a reefed topsail, when half the bowsprit was under water, and it was up to a man's knees in the scuppers. At eight bells, nothing is said about reefing the topsails, and the watch go below, with orders to "stand by for a call." We turn-in, growling at the "old man" for not reefing the topsails when the watch was changed, but putting it off so as to call all hands, and break up a whole watch below. Turn-in "all standing," and keep ourselves awake, saying there is no use in going asleep to be waked up again.—Wind whistles on deck, and ship works hard, groaning and creaking, and pitching into a heavy head sea, which strikes against the bows, with a noise like knocking upon a rock.—The dim lamp in the forecastle swings to and fro, and things "fetch away" and go over to leeward.—"Doesn't that booby of a second mate ever mean to take in his top-gallant sails?—He'll have the sticks out of her soon," says old Bill, who was always growling, and, like most old sailors, did not like to see a ship abused.—By-and-by an order is given—"Aye, aye, sir!" from the forecastle;—rigging is heaved down on deck;—the noise of a sail is heard fluttering aloft, and the short, quick cry which sailors make when hauling upon clewlines.—"Here comes his fore-top-gallant sail in!"—We are wide awake, and know all that's going on as well as if we were on deck.—A well-known voice is heard from the mast-head singing out the officer of the watch to haul taut the weather brace.—"Hallo! There's S—— aloft to furl the sail!"—Next thing, rigging is heaved down directly over our heads, and a long-drawn cry and a rattling of hanks announce that the flying-jib has come in.—The second mate holds on to the main top-gallant sail until a heavy sea is shipped, and washes over the forecastle as though the whole ocean had come aboard; when a noise further aft shows that that sail, too, is taking in. After this, the ship is more easy for a time; two bells are struck, and we try to get a little sleep. By-and-by, bang, bang, bang, on the scuttle—"All ha-a-ands, a ho-o-y!"—We spring out of our berths, clap on a monkey-jacket and southwester, and tumble up the ladder.—Mate up before us, and on the forecastle, singing out like a roaring bull; the captain singing out on the quarter-deck, and the second mate yelling, like a hyena, in the waist. The ship is lying over half upon her beam-ends; lee scuppers under water, and forecastle all in a smother of foam.—Rigging all let go, and washing about decks; topsail yards down upon the caps, and sails flapping and beating against the masts; and starboard watch hauling out the reef-tackles of the main topsail. Our watch haul out the fore, and lay aloft and put two reefs into it, and reef the foresail, and race with the starboard watch, to see which will mast-head its topsail first. All hands tally-on to the main tack, and while some are furling the jib, and hoisting the staysail, we mizen-topmen double-reef the mizen topsail and hoist it up. All being made fast—"Go below, the watch!" and we turn-in to sleep out the rest of the time, which is perhaps an hour and a half. During all the middle, and for the first part of the morning watch, it blows as hard as ever, but toward daybreak it moderates considerably, and we shake a reef out of each topsail, and set the top-gallant sails over them and when the watch come up, at seven bells, for breakfast, shake the other reefs out, turn all hands to upon the halyards, get the watch-tackle upon the top-gallant sheets and halyards, set the flying-jib, and crack on to her again.

Our captain had been married only a few weeks before he left Boston; and, after an absence of over two years, it may be supposed he was not slow in carrying sail. The mate, too, was not to be beaten by anybody; and the second mate, though he was afraid to press sail, was afraid as death of the captain, and being between two fears, sometimes carried on longer than any of them. We snapped off three flying-jib booms in twenty-four hours, as fast as they could be fitted and rigged out; sprung the spritsail yard; and made nothing of studding-sail booms. Beside the natural desire to get home, we had another reason for urging the ship on. The scurvy had begun to show itself on board. One man had it so badly as to be disabled and off duty, and the English lad, Ben, was in a dreadful state, and was daily growing worse. His legs swelled and pained him so that he could not walk; his flesh lost its elasticity, so that if it was pressed in, it would not return to its shape; and his gums swelled until he could not open his mouth. His breath, too, became very offensive; he lost all strength and spirit; could eat nothing; grew worse every day; and, in fact, unless something was done for him, would be a dead man in a week, at the rate at which he was sinking. The medicines were all, or nearly all, gone; and if we had had a chest-full, they would have been of no use; for nothing but fresh provisions and terra firma has any effect upon the scurvy. This disease is not so common now as formerly; and is attributed generally to salt provisions, want of cleanliness, the free use of grease and fat (which is the reason of its prevalence among whalemen,) and, last of all, to laziness. It never could have been from the latter cause on board our ship;

nor from the second, for we were a very cleanly crew, kept our forecastle in neat order, and were more particular about washing and changing clothes than many better-dressed people on shore. It was probably from having none but salt provisions, and possibly from our having run very rapidly into hot weather, after having been so long in the extremest cold.

Depending upon the westerly winds, which prevail off the coast in the autumn, the captain stood well to the westward, to run inside of the Bermudas, and in the hope of falling in with some vessel bound to the West Indies or the Southern States. The scurvy had spread no farther among the crew, but there was danger that it might; and these cases were bad ones.

Sunday, Sept. 11th. Lat. 30° 04' N., long. 63° 23' W.; the Bermudas bearing north-north-west, distant one hundred and fifty miles. The next morning, about ten o'clock, "Sail ho!" was cried on deck; and all hands turned up to see the stranger. As she drew nearer, she proved to be an ordinary-looking hermaphrodite brig, standing south-south-east; and probably bound out, from the Northern States, to the West Indies; and was just the thing we wished to see. She hove-to for us, seeing that we wished to speak her; and we ran down to her; boom-ended our studding-sails; backed our main topsail, and hailed her—"Brig, ahoy!"—"Hallo!"—"Where are you from, pray?"—"From New York, bound to Curaçoa."—"Have you any fresh provisions to spare?"—"Aye, aye! plenty of them!" We lowered away the quarter-boat, instantly; and the captain and four hands sprang in, and were soon dancing over the water, and alongside the brig. In about half an hour, they returned with half a boat-load of potatoes and onions, and each vessel filled away, and kept on her course. She proved to be the brig Solon, of Plymouth, from the Connecticut river, and last from New York, bound to the Spanish Main, with a cargo of fresh provisions, mules, tin bake-pans, and other notions. The onions were genuine and fresh; and the mate of the brig told the men in the boat, as he passed the bunches over the side, that the girls had strung them on purpose for us the day he sailed. We had supposed, on board, that a new president had been chosen, the last winter, and, just as we filled away, the captain hailed and asked who was president of the United States. They answered, Andrew Jackson; but thinking that the old General could not have been elected for a third time, we hailed again, and they answered—Jack Downing; and left us to correct the mistake at our leisure.

It was just dinner-time when we filled away; and the steward, taking a few bunches of onions for the cabin, gave the rest to us, with a bottle of vinegar. We carried them forward, stowed them away in the forecastle, refusing to have them cooked, and ate them raw, with our beef and bread. And a glorious treat they were. The freshness and crispness of the raw onion, with the earthy taste, give it a great relish to one who has been a long time on salt provisions.

We were perfectly ravenous after them. It was like a scent of blood to a hound. We ate them at every meal, by the dozen; and filled our pockets with them, to eat in our watch on deck; and the bunches, rising in the form of a cone, from the largest at the bottom, to the smallest, no larger than a strawberry, at the top, soon disappeared.

The chief use, however, of the fresh provisions, was for the men with the scurvy. One of them was able to eat, and he soon brought himself to, by gnawing upon raw potatoes; but the other, by this time, was hardly able to open his mouth; and the cook took the potatoes raw, pounded them in a mortar, and gave him the juice to drink. This he swallowed, by the tea-spoonful at a time, and rinsed it about his gums and throat. The strong earthy taste and smell of this extract of the raw potato at first produced a shuddering through his whole frame, and after drinking it, an acute pain, which ran through all parts of his body; but knowing, by this, that it was taking strong hold, he persevered, drinking a spoonful every hour or so, and holding it a long time in his mouth; until, by the effect of this drink, and of his own restored hope, (for he had nearly given up, in despair) he became so well as to be able to move about, and open his mouth enough to eat the raw potatoes and onions pounded into a soft pulp. This course soon restored his appetite and strength; and in ten days after we spoke the Solon, so rapid was his recovery, that, from lying helpless and almost hopeless in his berth, he was at the mast-head, furling a royal.

With a fine south-west wind, we passed inside of the Bermudas; and notwithstanding the old couplet, which was quoted again and again by those who thought we should have one more touch of a storm before our voyage was up,—

"If the Bermudas let you pass,
You must beware of Hatteras—"

we were to the northward of Hatteras, with good weather, and beginning to count, not the days, but the hours, to the time when we should be at anchor in Boston harbor.

Our ship was in fine order, all hands having been hard at work upon her from daylight to dark, every day but Sunday, from the time we got into warm weather on this side the Cape.

It is a common notion with landsmen that a ship is in her finest condition when she leaves port to enter upon her voyage; and that she comes home, after a long absence,

"With over-weathered ribs and ragged sails;
Lean, rent and beggared by the strumpet wind."

But so far from that, unless a ship meets with some accident, or comes upon the coast in the dead of winter, when work cannot be done upon the rigging, she is in her finest order at the end of the voyage. When she sails from port, her rigging is generally slack; the masts need staying; the decks and sides are black and dirty from taking in cargo; riggers' seizings and overhand knots in place of nice seamanlike work; and everything, to a sailor's eye, adrift.

But on the passage home, the fine weather between the tropics is spent in putting the ship into the neatest order. No merchant vessel looks better than an Indiaman, or a Cape Horn-er, after a long voyage; and many captains and mates will stake their reputation for seamanship upon the appearance of their ship when she hauls into the dock. All our standing rigging, fore and aft, was set up and tarred; the masts stayed; the lower and top-mast rigging rattled down, (or up, as the fashion now is;) and so careful were our officers to keep the rattlins taut and straight, that we were obliged to go aloft upon the ropes and shearpoles with which the rigging was swifted in; and these were used as jury rattlins until we got close upon the coast. After this, the ship was scraped, inside and out, decks, masts, booms and all; a stage being rigged outside, upon which we scraped her down to the water-line; pounding the rust off the chains, bolts and fastenings. Then, taking two days of calm under the line, we painted her on the outside, giving her open ports in her streak, and finishing off the nice work upon the stern, where sat Neptune in his car, holding his trident, drawn by sea-horses; and re-touched the gilding and coloring of the cornucopia which ornamented her billet-head. The inside was then painted, from the skysail truck to the waterways—the yards black; mast-heads and tops, white; monkey-rail, black, white, and yellow; bulwarks, green; plank-shear, white; waterways, lead color, etc., etc. The anchors and ring-bolts, and other iron work, were blackened with coal-tar; and the steward kept at work, polishing the brass of the wheel, bell, capstan, etc. The cabin, too, was scraped, varnished, and painted; and the forecastle scraped and scrubbed; there being no need of paint and varnish for Jack's quarters. The decks were then scraped and varnished, and everything useless thrown overboard; among which the empty tar barrels were set on fire and thrown overboard, on a dark night, and left blazing astern, lighting up the ocean for miles. Add to all this labor, the neat work upon the rigging;—the knots, flemish-eyes, splices, seizings, coverings, pointings, and graftings, which show a ship in crack order. The last preparation, and which looked still more like coming into port, was getting the anchors over the bows, bending the cables, rowsing the hawsers up from between decks, and overhauling the deep-sea-lead-line.

Thursday, September 15th. This morning the temperature and peculiar appearance of the water, the quantities of gulf-weed floating about, and a bank of clouds lying directly before us, showed that we were on the border of the Gulf Stream. This remarkable current, running north-east, nearly across the ocean, is almost constantly shrouded in clouds, and is the region of storms and heavy seas. Vessels often run from a clear sky and light wind, with all sail, at once into a heavy sea and cloudy sky, with double-reefed topsails. A sailor told me that on a passage from Gibraltar to Boston, his vessel neared the Gulf Stream with a light breeze, clear sky, and studding-sails out, alow and aloft; while, before it, was a long line of heavy, black clouds, lying like a bank upon the water, and a vessel coming out of it, under double-reefed topsails, and with royal yards sent down. As they drew near, they began to take in sail after sail, until they were reduced to the same condition; and, after twelve or fourteen hours of rolling and pitching in a heavy sea, before a smart gale, they ran out of the bank on the other side, and were in fine weather again, and under their royals and skysails. As we drew into it, the sky became cloudy, the sea high, and everything had the appearance of the going off, or the coming on, of a storm. It was blowing no more than a stiff breeze; yet the wind, being north-east, which is directly against the course of the current, made an ugly, chopping sea, which heaved and pitched the vessel about, so that we were obliged to send down the royal yards, and to take in our light sails. At noon, the thermometer, which had been repeatedly lowered into the water, showed the temperature to be seventy; which was considerably above that of the air,—as is always the case in the centre of the Stream. A lad who had been at work at the royal mast-head, came down upon the deck, and took a turn round the long-boat; and looking very pale, said he was so sick that he could stay aloft no longer, but was ashamed to acknowledge it to the officer. He went up again, but soon gave out and came down, and leaned over the rail, "as sick as a lady passenger."

He had been to sea several years, and had, he said, never been sick before. He was made so by the irregular, pitching motion of the vessel, increased by the height to which he had been above the hull, which is like the fulcrum of the lever. An old sailor, who was at work on the top-gallant yard, said he felt disagreeably all the time, and was glad, when his job was done, to get down into the top, or upon the deck. Another hand was sent to the royal mast-head, who staid nearly an hour, but gave up. The work must be done, and the mate sent me. I did very well for some time, but began at length to feel very unpleasantly, though I had never been sick since the first two days from Boston, and had been in all sorts of weather and situations. Still, I kept my place, and did not come down, until I had got through my work, which was more than two hours. The ship certainly never acted so badly before. She was pitched and jerked about in all manner of ways; the sails seeming to have no steadying power over her. The tapering points of the masts made various curves and angles against the sky overhead, and sometimes, in one sweep of an instant, described an arc of more than forty-five degrees, bringing up with a sudden jerk which made it necessary to hold on with both hands, and then sweeping off, in another long, irregular curve. I was not positively sick, and came down with a look of indifference, yet was not unwilling to get upon the comparative terra firma of the deck. A few hours more carried us through, and when we saw the sun go down, upon our larboard beam, in the direction of the continent of North America, we had left the bank of dark, stormy clouds astern, in the twilight.

CHAPTER XXXVI

SOUNDINGS—SIGHTS FROM HOME—BOSTON HARBOR—LEAVING THE SHIP

Friday, Sept. 16th. Lat. 38° N., long. 69° 00' W. A fine south-west wind; every hour carrying us nearer in toward land. All hands on deck at the dog watch, and nothing talked about, but our getting in; where we should make the land; whether we should arrive before Sunday; going to church; how Boston would look; friends; wages paid;—and the like. Every one was in the best of spirits; and, the voyage being nearly at an end, the strictness of discipline was relaxed; for it was not necessary to order in a cross tone, what every one was ready to do with a will.

The little differences and quarrels which a long voyage breeds on board a ship, were forgotten, and every one was friendly; and two men, who had been on the eve of a battle half the voyage, were laying out a plan together for a cruise on shore. When the mate came forward, he talked to the men, and said we should be on George's Bank before to-morrow noon; and joked with the boys, promising to go and see them, and to take them down to Marblehead in a coach.

Saturday, 17th. The wind was light all day, which kept us back somewhat; but a fine breeze springing up at nightfall, we were running fast in toward the land. At six o'clock we expected to have the ship hove-to for soundings, as a thick fog, coming up showed we were near them; but no order was given, and we kept on our way. Eight o'clock came, and the watch went below, and, for the whole of the first hour, the ship was tearing on, with studding-sails out, alow and aloft, and the night as dark as a pocket. At two bells the captain came on deck, and said a word to the mate, when the studding sails were hauled into the tops, or boom-ended, the after yards backed, the deep-sea-lead carried forward, and everything got ready for sounding. A man on the spritsail yard with the lead, another on the cathead with a handful of the line coiled up, another in the fore chains, another in the waist, and another in the main chains, each with a quantity of the line coiled away in his hand. "All ready there, forward?"—"Aye, aye, sir!"—"He-e-e-ave!"—"Watch! ho! watch!" sings out the man on the spritsail yard, and the heavy lead drops into the water. "Watch! ho! watch!" bawls the man on the cat-head, as the last fake of the coil drops from his hand, and "Watch! ho! watch!" is shouted by each one as the line falls from his hold; until it comes to the mate, who tends the lead, and has the line in coils on the quarter-deck. Eighty fathoms, and no bottom! A depth as great as the height of St. Peter's! The line is snatched in a block upon the swifter, and three or four men haul it in and coil it away. The after yards are braced full, the studding-sails hauled out again, and in a few minutes more the ship had her whole way upon her. At four bells, backed again, hove the lead, and—soundings! at sixty fathoms! Hurrah for Yankee land! Hand over hand, we hauled the lead in, and the captain, taking it to the light, found black mud on the bottom.

Studding-sails taken in; after yards filled, and ship kept on under easy sail all night; the wind dying away.

The soundings on the American coast are so regular that a navigator knows as well where he has made land, by the soundings, as he would by seeing the land. Black mud is the soundings of Block Island. As you go toward Nantucket, it changes to a dark sand; then, sand and white shells; and on George's Banks, white sand; and so on. Being off Block Island, our course was due east, to Nantucket Shoals, and the South Channel; but the wind died away and left us becalmed in a thick fog, in which we lay the whole of Sunday. At noon of

Sunday, 18th, Block Island bore, by calculation, N. W. 1/4 W. fifteen miles; but the fog was so thick all day that we could see nothing.

Having got through the ship's duty, and washed and shaved, we went below, and had a fine time overhauling our chests, laying aside the clothes we meant to go ashore in and throwing overboard all that were worn out and good for nothing. Away went the woollen caps in which we had carried hides upon our heads, for sixteen months, on the coast of California; the duck frocks, for tarring down rigging; and the worn-out and darned mittens and patched woollen trowsers which had stood the tug of Cape Horn.

We hove them overboard with a good will; for there is nothing like being quit of the very last appendages and remnants of our evil fortune. We got our chests all ready for going ashore, ate the last "duff" we expected to have on board the ship Alert; and talked as confidently about matters on shore as though our anchor were on the bottom.

"Who'll go to church with me a week from to-day?"

"I will," says Jack; who said aye to everything.

"Go away, salt water!" says Tom. "As soon as I get both legs ashore, I'm going to shoe my heels, and button my ears behind me, and start off into the bush, a straight course, and not stop till I'm out of the sight of salt water!"

"Oh! belay that! Spin that yarn where nobody knows your filling! If you get once moored, stem and stern, in old B——'s grog-shop, with a coal fire ahead and the bar under your lee, you won't see daylight for three weeks!"

"No!" says Tom, "I'm going to knock off grog, and go and board at the Home, and see if they won't ship me for a deacon!"

"And I," says Bill, "am going to buy a quadrant and ship for navigator of a Hingham packet!"

These and the like jokes served to pass the time while we were lying waiting for a breeze to clear up the fog and send us on our way.

Toward night a moderate breeze sprang up; the fog however continuing as thick as before; and we kept on to the eastward. About the middle of the first watch, a man on the forecastle sang out, in a tone which showed that there was not a moment to be lost,—"Hard up the helm!" and a great ship loomed up out of the fog, coming directly down upon us. She luffed at the same moment, and we just passed one another; our spanker boom grazing over her quarter. The officer of the deck had only time to hail, and she answered, as she went into the fog again, something about Bristol—probably, a whaleman from Bristol, Rhode Island, bound out. The fog continued through the night, with a very light breeze, before which we ran to the eastward, literally feeling our way along. The lead was heaved every two hours, and the gradual change from black mud to sand, showed that we were approaching Nantucket South Shoals. On Monday morning, the increased depth and deep blue color of the water, and the mixture of shells and white sand which we brought up, upon sounding, showed that we were in the channel, and nearing George's; accordingly, the ship's head was put directly to the northward, and we stood on, with perfect confidence in the soundings, though we had not taken an observation for two days, nor seen land; and the difference of an eighth of a mile out of the way might put us ashore. Throughout the day a provokingly light wind prevailed, and at eight o'clock, a small fishing schooner, which we passed, told us we were nearly abreast of Chatham lights.

Just before midnight, a light land-breeze sprang up, which carried us well along; and at four o'clock, thinking ourselves to the northward of Race Point, we hauled upon the wind and stood into the bay, west-north-west, for Boston light, and commenced firing guns for a pilot. Our watch went below at four o'clock, but could not sleep, for the watch on deck were banging away at the guns every few minutes. And, indeed, we cared very little about it, for we were in Boston Bay; and if fortune favored us, we could all "sleep in" the next night, with nobody to call the watch every four hours.

We turned out, of our own will, at daybreak, to get a sight of land.

In the grey of the morning, one or two small fishing smacks peered out of the mist; and when the broad day broke upon us, there lay the low sand-hills of Cape Cod, over our larboard quarter, and before us, the wide waters of Massachusetts Bay, with here and there a sail gliding over its smooth surface. As we drew in toward the mouth of the harbor, as toward a focus, the vessels began to multiply until the bay seemed actually alive with sails gliding about in every direction; some on the wind, and others before it, as they were bound to or from the emporium of trade and centre of the bay. It was a stirring sight for us, who had been months on the ocean without seeing anything but two solitary sails; and over two years without seeing more than the three or four traders on an almost desolate coast. There were the little coasters, bound to and from the various towns along the south shore, down in the bight of the bay, and to the eastward; here and there a square-rigged vessel standing out to seaward; and, far in the distance, beyond Cape Ann, was the smoke of a steamer, stretching along in a narrow, black cloud upon the water. Every sight was full of beauty and interest. We were coming back to our homes; and the signs of civilization, and prosperity, and happiness, from which we had been so long banished, were multiplying about us. The high land of Cape Ann and the rocks and shore of Cohasset were full in sight, the lighthouses, standing like sentries in white before the harbors, and even the smoke from the chimney on the plains of Hingham was seen rising slowly in the morning air. One of our boys was the son of a bucket-maker; and his face lighted up as he saw the tops of the well-known hills which surround his native place. About ten o'clock a little boat came bobbing over the water, and put a pilot on board, and sheered off in pursuit of other vessels bound in.

Being now within the scope of the telegraph stations, our signals were run up at the fore, and in half an hour afterwards, the owner on 'change, or in his counting-room, knew that his ship was below; and the landlords, runners, and sharks in Ann street learned that there was a rich prize for them down in the bay: a ship from round the Horn, with a crew to be paid off with two years' wages.

The wind continuing very light, all hands were sent aloft to strip off the chafing gear; and battens, parcellings, roundings, hoops, mats, and leathers, came flying from aloft, and left the rigging neat and clean, stripped of all its sea bandaging. The last touch was put to the vessel by painting the skysail poles; and I was sent up to the fore, with a bucket of white paint and a brush, and touched her off, from the truck to the eyes of the royal rigging. At noon, we lay becalmed off the lower light-house; and it being about slack water, we made little progress. A firing was heard in the direction of Hingham, and the pilot said there was a review there.

The Hingham boy got wind of this, and said if the ship had been twelve hours sooner, he should have been down among the soldiers, and in the booths, and having a grand time. As it was, we had little prospect of getting in before night. About two o'clock a breeze sprang up ahead, from the westward, and we began beating up against it. A full-rigged brig was beating in at the same time, and we passed one another, in our tacks, sometimes one and sometimes the other, working to windward, as the wind and tide favored or opposed. It was my trick at the wheel from two till four; and I stood my last helm, making between nine hundred and a thousand hours which I had spent at the helms of our two vessels. The tide beginning to set against us, we made slow work; and the afternoon was nearly spent, before we got abreast of the inner light. In the meantime, several vessels were coming down, outward bound; among which, a fine, large ship, with yards squared, fair wind and fair tide, passed us like a race-horse, the men running out upon her yards to rig out the studding-sail booms. Toward sundown the wind came off in flaws, sometimes blowing very stiff, so that the pilot took in the royals, and then it died away; when, in order to get us in before the tide became too strong, the royals were set again. As this kept us running up and down the rigging all the time, one hand was sent aloft at each mast-head, to stand-by to loose and furl the sails, at the moment of the order. I took my place at the fore, and loosed and furled the royal five times between Rainsford Island and the Castle. At one tack we ran so near to Rainsford Island, that, looking down from the royal yard, the island, with its hospital buildings, nice gravelled walks, and green plats, seemed to lie directly under our yard-arms. So close is the channel to some of these islands, that we ran the end of our flying-jib-boom over one of the out-works of the fortifications on George's Island; and had an opportunity of seeing the advantages of that point as a fortified place; for, in working up the channel, we presented a fair stem and stern, for raking, from the batteries, three or four times. One gun might have knocked us to pieces.

We had all set our hearts upon getting up to town before night and going ashore, but the tide beginning to run strong against us, and the wind, what there was of it, being ahead, we made but little by weather-bowing the tide, and the pilot gave orders to cock-bill the anchor and overhaul the chain. Making two long stretches, which brought us into the roads, under the lee of the castle, he clewed up the topsails, and let go the anchor; and for the first time since leaving San Diego,—one hundred and thirty-five days—our anchor was upon bottom. In half an hour more, we were lying snugly, with all sails furled, safe in Boston harbor; our long voyage ended; the well-known scene about us; the dome of the State House fading in the western sky; the lights of the city starting into sight, as the darkness came on; and at nine o'clock the clangor of the bells, ringing their accustomed peals; among which the Boston boys tried to distinguish the well-known tone of the Old South.

We had just done furling the sails, when a beautiful little pleasure-boat luffed up into the wind, under our quarter, and the junior partner of the firm to which our ship belonged, jumped on board. I saw him from the mizen topsail yard, and knew him well.

He shook the captain by the hand, and went down into the cabin, and in a few moments came up and inquired of the mate for me.

The last time I had seen him, I was in the uniform of an undergraduate of Harvard College, and now, to his astonishment, there came down from aloft a "rough alley" looking fellow, with duck trowsers and red shirt, long hair, and face burnt as black as an Indian's. He shook me by the hand, congratulated me upon my return and my appearance of health and strength, and said my friends were all well. I thanked him for telling me what I should not have dared to ask; and if—

"the first bringer of unwelcome news
Hath but a losing office; and his tongue
Sounds ever after like a sullen bell—"

certainly I shall ever remember this man and his words with pleasure.

The captain went up to town in the boat with Mr. H——, and left us to pass another night on board ship, and to come up with the morning's tide under command of the pilot.

So much did we feel ourselves to be already at home, in anticipation, that our plain supper of hard bread and salt beef was barely touched; and many on board, to whom this was the first voyage, could scarcely sleep. As for myself, by one of those anomalous changes of feeling of which we are all the subjects, I found that I was in a state of indifference, for which I could by no means account. A year before, while carrying hides on the coast, the assurance that in a twelvemonth we should see Boston, made me half wild; but now that I was actually there, and in sight of home, the emotions which I had so long anticipated feeling, I did not find, and in their place was a state of very nearly entire apathy. Something of the same experience was related to me by a sailor whose first voyage was one of five years upon the North-west Coast. He had left home, a lad, and after several years of very hard and trying experience, found himself homeward bound; and such was the excitement of his feelings that, during the whole passage, he could talk and think of nothing else but his arrival, and how and when he should jump from the vessel and take his way directly home. Yet when the vessel was made fast to the wharf and the crew dismissed, he seemed suddenly to lose all feeling about the matter. He told me that he went below and changed his dress; took some water from the scuttle-butt and washed himself leisurely; overhauled his chest, and put his clothes all in order; took his pipe from its place, filled it, and sitting down upon his chest, smoked it slowly for the last time. Here he looked round upon the forecastle in which he had spent so many years, and being alone and his shipmates scattered, he began to feel actually unhappy. Home became almost a dream; and it was not until his brother (who had heard of the ship's arrival) came down into the forecastle and told him of things at home, and who were waiting there to see him, that he could realize where he was, and feel interest enough to put him in motion toward that place for which he had longed, and of which he had dreamed, for years. There is probably so much of excitement in prolonged expectation, that the quiet realizing of it produces a momentary stagnation of feeling as well as of effort. It was a good deal so with me. The activity of preparation, the rapid progress of the ship, the first making land, the coming up the harbor, and old scenes breaking upon the view, produced a mental as well as bodily activity, from which the change to a perfect stillness, when both expectation and the necessity of labor failed, left a calmness, almost of indifference, from which I must be roused by some new excitement. And the next morning, when all hands were called, and we were busily at work, clearing the decks, and getting everything in readiness for going up to the wharves,—loading the guns for a salute, loosing the sails, and manning the windlass—mind and body seemed to wake together.

About ten o'clock, a sea-breeze sprang up, and the pilot gave orders to get the ship under weigh. All hands manned the windlass, and the long-drawn "Yo, heave, ho!" which we had last heard dying away among the desolate hills of San Diego, soon brought the anchor to the bows; and, with a fair wind and tide, a bright sunny morning, royals and sky-sails set, ensign, streamer, signals, and pennant, flying, and with our guns firing, we came swiftly and handsomely up to the city. Off the end of the wharf, we rounded-to and let go our anchor; and no sooner was it on the bottom, than the decks were filled with people: custom-house officers; Topliff's agent, to inquire for news; others, inquiring for friends on board, or left upon the coast; dealers in grease, besieging the galley to make a bargain with the cook for his slush;

"loafers" in general; and last and chief, boarding-house runners, to secure their men.

Nothing can exceed the obliging disposition of these runners, and the interest they take in a sailor returned from a long voyage with a plenty of money. Two or three of them, at different times, took me by the hand; remembered me perfectly; were quite sure I had boarded with them before I sailed; were delighted to see me back; gave me their cards; had a hand-cart waiting on the wharf, on purpose to take my things up: would lend me a hand to get my chest ashore; bring a bottle of grog on board if we did not haul in immediately,—and the like. In fact, we could hardly get clear of them, to go aloft and furl the sails. Sail after sail, for the hundredth time, in fair weather and in foul, we furled now for the last time together, and came down and took the warp ashore, manned the capstan, and with a chorus which waked up half the North End, and rang among the buildings in the dock, we hauled her in to the wharf. Here, too, the landlords and runners were active and ready, taking a bar to the capstan, lending a hand at the ropes, laughing and talking and telling the news. The city bells were just ringing one when the last turn was made fast, and the crew dismissed; and in five minutes more, not a soul was left on board the good ship Alert, but the old ship-keeper, who had come down from the counting-house to take charge of her.

CONCLUDING CHAPTER

I trust that they who have followed me to the end of my narrative, will not refuse to carry their attention a little farther, to the concluding remarks which I here present to them.

This chapter is written after the lapse of a considerable time since the end of my voyage, and after a return to my former pursuits; and in it I design to offer those views of what may be done for seamen, and of what is already doing, which I have deduced from my experiences, and from the attention which I have since gladly given to the subject.

The romantic interest which many take in the sea, and in those who live upon it, may be of use in exciting their attention to this subject, though I cannot but feel sure that all who have followed me in my narrative must be convinced that the sailor has no romance in his every-day life to sustain him, but that it is very much the same plain, matter-of-fact drudgery and hardship, which would be experienced on shore. If I have not produced this conviction, I have failed in persuading others of what my own experience has most fully impressed upon myself.

There is a witchery in the sea, its songs and stories, and in the mere sight of a ship, and the sailor's dress, especially to a young mind, which has done more to man navies, and fill merchantmen, than all the press-gangs of Europe. I have known a young man with such a passion for the sea, that the very creaking of a block stirred up his imagination so that he could hardly keep his feet on dry ground; and many are the boys, in every seaport, who are drawn away, as by an almost irresistible attraction, from their work and schools, and hang about the decks and yards of vessels, with a fondness which, it is plain, will have its way. No sooner, however, has the young sailor begun his new life in earnest, than all this fine drapery falls off, and he learns that it is but work and hardship, after all. This is the true light in which a sailor's life is to be viewed; and if in our books, and anniversary speeches, we would leave out much that is said about "blue water," "blue jackets," "open hearts," "seeing God's hand on the deep," and so forth, and take this up like any other practical subject, I am quite sure we should do full as much for those we wish to benefit. The question is, what can be done for sailors, as they are,—men to be fed, and clothed, and lodged, for whom laws must be made and executed, and who are to be instructed in useful knowledge, and, above all, to be brought under religious influence and restraint? It is upon these topics that I wish to make a few observations.

In the first place, I have no fancies about equality on board ship, It is a thing out of the question, and certainly, in the present state of mankind, not to be desired. I never knew a sailor who found fault with the orders and ranks of the service; and if I expected to pass the rest of my life before the mast, I would not wish to have the power of the captain diminished an iota. It is absolutely necessary that there should be one head and one voice, to control everything, and be responsible for everything. There are emergencies which require the instant exercise of extreme power. These emergencies do not allow of consultation; and they who would be the captain's constituted advisers might be the very men over whom he would be called upon to exert his authority. It has been found necessary to vest in every government, even the most democratic, some extraordinary, and, at first sight, alarming powers; trusting in public opinion, and subsequent accountability to modify the exercise of them. These are provided to meet exigencies, which all hope may never occur, but which yet by possibility may occur, and if they should, and there were no power to meet them instantly, there would be an end put to the government at once. So it is with the authority of the shipmaster. It will not answer to say that he shall never do this and that thing, because it does not seem always necessary and advisable that it should be done. He has great cares and responsibilities; is answerable for everything; and is subject to emergencies which perhaps no other man exercising authority among civilized people is subject to. Let him, then, have powers commensurate with his utmost possible need; only let him be held strictly responsible for the exercise of them. Any other course would be injustice, as well as bad policy.

In the treatment of those under his authority, the captain is amenable to the common law, like any other person. He is liable at common law for murder, assault and battery, and other offences; and in addition to this, there is a special statute of the United States which makes a captain or other officer liable to imprisonment for a term not exceeding five years, and to a fine not exceeding a thousand dollars, for inflicting any cruel punishment upon, withholding food from, or in any other way maltreating a seaman. This is the state of the law on the subject; while the relation in which the parties stand, and the peculiar necessities, excuses, and provocations arising from that relation, are merely circumstances to be considered in each case. As to the restraints upon the master's exercise of power, the laws themselves seem, on the whole, to be sufficient. I do not see that we are in need, at present, of more legislation on the subject. The difficulty lies rather in the administration of the laws; and this is certainly a matter that deserves great consideration, and one of no little embarrassment.

In the first place, the courts have said that public policy requires the power of the master and officers should be sustained. Many lives and a great amount of property are constantly in their hands, for which they are strictly responsible. To preserve these, and to deal justly by the captain, and not lay upon him a really fearful responsibility, and then tie up his hands, it is essential that discipline should be supported. In the second place, there is always great allowance to be made for false swearing and exaggeration by seamen, and for combinations among them against their officers; and it is to be remembered that the latter have often no one to testify on their side. These are weighty and true statements, and should not be lost sight of by the friends of seamen. On the other hand, sailors make many complaints, some of which are well founded.

On the subject of testimony, seamen labor under a difficulty full as great as that of the captain. It is a well-known fact, that they are usually much better treated when there are passengers on board.

The presence of passengers is a restraint upon the captain, not only from his regard to their feelings and to the estimation in which they may hold him, but because he knows they will be influential witnesses against him if he is brought to trial. Though officers may sometimes be inclined to show themselves off before passengers, by freaks of office and authority, yet cruelty they would hardly dare to be guilty of. It is on long and distant voyages, where there is no restraint upon the captain, and none but the crew to testify against him, that sailors need most the protection of the law. On such voyages as these, there are many cases of outrageous cruelty on record, enough to make one heartsick, and almost disgusted with the sight of man; and many, many more, which have never come to light, and never will be known, until the sea shall give up its dead. Many of these have led to mutiny and piracy,—stripe for stripe, and blood for blood. If on voyages of this description the testimony of seamen is not to be received in favor of one another, or too great a deduction is made on account of their being seamen, their case is without remedy; and the captain, knowing this, will be strengthened in that disposition to tyrannize which the possession of absolute power, without the restraints of friends and public opinion, is too apt to engender.

It is to be considered, also, that the sailor comes into court under very different circumstances from the master. He is thrown among landlords, and sharks of all descriptions; is often led to drink freely; and comes upon the stand unaided, and under a certain cloud of suspicion as to his character and veracity. The captain, on the other hand, is backed by the owners and insurers, and has an air of greater respectability; though, after all, he may have but a little better education than the sailor, and sometimes, (especially among those engaged in certain voyages that I could mention) a very hackneyed conscience.

These are the considerations most commonly brought up on the subject of seamen's evidence; and I think it cannot but be obvious to every one that here, positive legislation would be of no manner of use. There can be no rule of law regulating the weight to be given to seamen's evidence. It must rest in the mind of the judge and jury; and no enactment or positive rule of court could vary the result a hair, in any one case. The effect of a sailor's testimony in deciding a case must depend altogether upon the reputation of the class to which he belongs, and upon the impression he himself produces in court by his deportment, and by those infallible marks of character which always tell upon a jury.

In fine, after all the well-meant and specious projects that have been brought forward, we seem driven back to the belief, that the best means of securing a fair administration of the laws made for the protection of seamen, and certainly the only means which can create any important change for the better, is the gradual one of raising the intellectual and religious character of the sailor, so that as an individual and as one of a class, he may, in the first instance, command the respect of his officers, and if any difficulty should happen, may upon the stand carry that weight which an intelligent and respectable man of the lower class almost always does with a jury. I know there are many men who, when a few cases of great hardship occur, and it is evident that there is an evil somewhere, think that some arrangement must be made, some law passed, or some society got up, to set all right at once. On this subject there can be no call for any such movement; on the contrary, I fully believe that any public and strong action would do harm, and that we must be satisfied to labor in the less easy and less exciting task of gradual improvement, and abide the issue of things working slowly together for good.

Equally injudicious would be any interference with the economy of the ship. The lodging, food, hours of sleep, etc., are all matters which, though capable of many changes for the better, must yet be left to regulate themselves. And I am confident that there will be, and that there is now a gradual improvement in all such particulars. The forecastles of most of our ships are small, black, and wet holes, which few landsmen would believe held a crew of ten or twelve men on a voyage of months or years; and often, indeed in most cases, the provisions are not good enough to make a meal anything more than a necessary part of a day's duty;[1] and on the score of sleep, I fully believe that the lives of merchant seamen are shortened by the want of it. I do not refer to those occasions when it is necessarily broken in upon; but, for months, during fine weather, in many merchantmen, all hands are kept, throughout the day, and, then, there are eight hours on deck for one watch each night. Thus it is usually the case that at the end of a voyage, where there has been the finest weather, and no disaster, the crew have a wearied and worn-out appearance. They never sleep longer than four hours at a time, and are seldom called without being really in need of more rest. There is no one thing that a sailor thinks more of as a luxury of life on shore, than a whole night's sleep. Still, all these things must be left to be gradually modified by circumstances.

Whenever hard cases occur, they should be made known, and masters and owners should be held answerable, and will, no doubt, in time, be influenced in their arrangements and discipline by the increased consideration in which sailors are held by the public.

It is perfectly proper that the men should live in a different part of the vessel from the officers; and if the forecastle is made large and comfortable, there is no reason why the crew should not live there as well as in any other part. In fact, sailors prefer the forecastle. It is their accustomed place, and in it they are out of the sight and hearing of their officers.

As to their food and sleep, there are laws, with heavy penalties, requiring a certain amount of stores to be on board, and safely stowed; and, for depriving the crew unnecessarily of food or sleep, the captain is liable at common law, as well as under the statute before referred to. Farther than this, it would not be safe to go.

The captain must be the judge when it is necessary to keep his crew from their sleep; and sometimes a retrenching, not of the necessaries, but of some of the little niceties of their meals, as, for instance, duff on Sunday, may be a mode of punishment, though I think generally an injudicious one.

I could not do justice to this subject without noticing one part of the discipline of a ship, which has been very much discussed of late, and has brought out strong expressions of indignation from many,—I mean the infliction of corporal punishment. Those who have followed me in my narrative will remember that I was witness to an act of great cruelty inflicted upon my own shipmates; and indeed I can sincerely say that the simple mention of the word flogging, brings up in me feelings which I can hardly control. Yet, when the proposition is made to abolish it entirely and at once; to prohibit the captain from ever, under any circumstances, inflicting corporal punishment; I am obliged to pause, and, I must say, to doubt exceedingly the expediency of making any positive enactment which shall have that effect. If the design of those who are writing on this subject is merely to draw public attention to it, and to discourage the practice of flogging, and bring it into disrepute, it is well; and, indeed, whatever may be the end they have in view, the mere agitation of the question will have that effect, and, so far, must do good. Yet I should not wish to take the command of a ship to-morrow, running my chance of a crew, as most masters must, and know, and have my crew know, that I could not, under any circumstances, inflict even moderate chastisement. I should trust that I might never have to resort to it; and, indeed, I scarcely know what risk I would not run, and to what inconvenience I would not subject myself, rather than do so. Yet not to have the power of holding it up in terrorem, and indeed of protecting myself, and all under my charge, by it, if some extreme case should arise, would be a situation I should not wish to be placed in myself, or to take the responsibility of placing another in.

Indeed, the difficulties into which masters and officers are liable to be thrown, are not sufficiently considered by many whose sympathies are easily excited by stories, frequent enough, and true enough of outrageous abuse of this power. It is to be remembered that more than three-fourths of the seamen in our merchant vessels are foreigners. They are from all parts of the world. A great many from the north of Europe, beside Frenchmen, Spaniards, Portuguese, Italians, men from all parts of the Mediterranean, together with Lascars, Negroes, and, perhaps worst of all, the off-casts of British men-of-war, and men from our own country who have gone to sea because they could not be permitted to live on land.

As things now are, many masters are obliged to sail without knowing anything of their crews, until they get out at sea. There may be pirates or mutineers among them; and one bad man will often infect all the rest; and it is almost certain that some of them will be ignorant foreigners, hardly understanding a word of our language, accustomed all their lives to no influence but force, and perhaps nearly as familiar with the use of the knife as with that of the marline-spike. No prudent master, however peaceably inclined, would go to sea without his pistols and handcuffs. Even with such a crew as I have supposed, kindness and moderation would be the best policy, and the duty of every conscientious man; and the administering of corporal punishment might be dangerous, and of doubtful use. But the question is not, what a captain ought generally to do, but whether it shall be put out of the power of every captain, under any circumstances, to make use of, even moderate, chastisement. As the law now stands, a parent may correct moderately his child, and the master his apprentice; and the case of the shipmaster has been placed upon the same principle. The statutes, and the common law as expounded in the decisions of courts, and in the books of commentators, are express and unanimous to this point, that the captain may inflict moderate corporal chastisement, for a reasonable cause. If the punishment is excessive, or the cause not sufficient to justify it, he is answerable; and the jury are to determine, by their verdict in each case, whether, under all the circumstances, the punishment was moderate, and for a justifiable cause.

This seems to me to be as good a position as the whole subject can be left in. I mean to say, that no positive enactment, going beyond this, is needed, or would be a benefit either to masters or men, in the present state of things. This again would seem to be a case which should be left to the gradual working of its own cure. As seamen improve, punishment will become less necessary; and as the character of officers is raised, they will be less ready to inflict it; and, still more, the infliction of it upon intelligent and respectable men, will be an enormity which will not be tolerated by public opinion, and by juries, who are the pulse of the body politic. No one can have a greater abhorrence of the infliction of such punishment than I have, and a stronger conviction that severity is bad policy with a crew; yet I would ask every reasonable man whether he had not better trust to the practice becoming unnecessary and disreputable; to the measure of moderate chastisement and a justifiable cause being better understood, and thus, the act becoming dangerous, and in course of time to be regarded as an unheard-of barbarity—than to take the responsibility of prohibiting it, at once, in all cases, and in what ever degree, by positive enactment?

There is, however, one point connected with the administration of justice to seamen, to which I wish seriously to call the attention of those interested in their behalf, and, if possible, also of some of those concerned in that administration. This is, the practice which prevails of making strong appeals to the jury in mitigation of damages, or to the judge, after a verdict has been rendered against a captain or officer, for a lenient sentence, on the grounds of their previous good character, and of their being poor, and having friends and families depending upon them for support. These appeals have been allowed a weight which is almost incredible, and which, I think, works a greater hardship upon seamen than any one other thing in the laws, or the execution of them. Notwithstanding every advantage the captain has over the seaman in point of evidence, friends, money, and able counsel, it becomes apparent that he must fail in his defence. An appeal is then made to the jury, if it is a civil action, or to the judge for a mitigated sentence, if it is a criminal prosecution, on the two grounds I have mentioned. The same form is usually gone through in every case. In the first place, as to the previous good character of the party. Witnesses are brought from the town in which he resides, to testify to his good character, and to his unexceptionable conduct when on shore. They say that he is a good father, or husband, or son, or neighbor, and that they never saw in him any signs of a cruel or tyrannical disposition. I have even known evidence admitted to show the character he bore when a boy at school. The owners of the vessel, and other merchants, and perhaps the president of the insurance company, are then introduced; and they testify to his correct deportment, express their confidence in his honesty, and say that they have never seen anything in his conduct to justify a suspicion of his being capable of cruelty or tyranny. This evidence is then put together, and great stress is laid upon the extreme respectability of those who give it. They are the companions and neighbors of the captain, it is said,—men who know him in his business and domestic relations, and who knew him in his early youth. They are also men of the highest standing in the community, and who, as the captain's employers, must be supposed to know his character. This testimony is then contrasted with that of some half dozen obscure sailors, who, the counsel will not forget to add, are exasperated against the captain because he has found it necessary to punish them moderately, and who have combined against him, and if they have not fabricated a story entirely, have at least so exaggerated it, that little confidence can be placed in it.

The next thing to be done is to show to the court and jury that the captain is a poor man, and has a wife and family, or other friends, depending upon him for support; that if he is fined, it will only be taking bread from the mouths of the innocent and helpless, and laying a burden upon them which their whole lives will not be able to work off; and that if he is imprisoned, the confinement, to be sure, he will have to bear, but the distress consequent upon the cutting him off from his labor and means of earning his wages, will fall upon a poor wife and helpless children, or upon an infirm parent. These two topics, well put, and urged home earnestly, seldom fail of their effect.

In deprecation of this mode of proceeding, and in behalf of men who I believe are every day wronged by it, I would urge a few considerations which seem to me to be conclusive.

First, as to the evidence of the good character the captain sustains on shore. It is to be remembered that masters of vessels have usually been brought up in a forecastle; and upon all men, and especially upon those taken from lower situations, the conferring of absolute power is too apt to work a great change. There are many captains whom I know to be cruel and tyrannical men at sea, who yet, among their friends, and in their families, have never lost the reputation they bore in childhood. In fact, the sea-captain is seldom at home, and when he is, his stay is short, and during the continuance of it he is surrounded by friends who treat him with kindness and consideration, and he has everything to please, and at the same time to restrain him. He would be a brute indeed, if, after an absence of months or years, during his short stay, so short that the novelty and excitement of it has hardly time to wear off, and the attentions he receives as a visitor and stranger hardly time to slacken,—if, under such circumstances, a townsman or neighbor would be justified in testifying against his correct and peaceable deportment. With the owners of the vessel, also, to which he is attached, and among merchants and insurers generally, he is a very different man from what he may be at sea, when his own master, and the master of everybody and everything about him. He knows that upon such men, and their good opinion of him, he depends for his bread. So far from their testimony being of any value in determining what his conduct would be at sea, one would expect that the master who would abuse and impose upon a man under his power, would be the most compliant and deferential to his employers at home.

As to the appeal made in the captain's behalf on the ground of his being poor and having persons depending upon his labor for support, the main and fatal objection to it is, that it will cover every case of the kind, and exempt nearly the whole body of masters and officers from the punishment the law has provided for them. There are very few, if any masters or other officers of merchantmen in our country, who are not poor men, and having either parents, wives, children, or other relatives, depending mainly or wholly upon their exertions for support in life. Few others follow the sea for subsistence. Now if this appeal is to have weight with courts in diminishing the penalty the law would otherwise inflict, is not the whole class under a privilege which will, in a degree, protect it in wrong-doing? It is not a thing that happens now and then. It is the invariable appeal, the last resort, of counsel, when everything else has failed. I have known cases of the most flagrant nature, where after every effort has been made for the captain, and yet a verdict rendered against him, and all other hope failed, this appeal has been urged, and with such success that the punishment has been reduced to something little more than nominal, the court not seeming to consider that it might be made in almost every such case that could come before them. It is a little singular, too, that it seems to be confined to cases of shipmasters and officers. No one ever heard of a sentence, for an offence committed on shore, being reduced by the court on the ground of the prisoner's poverty, and the relation in which he may stand to third persons. On the contrary, it had been thought that the certainty that disgrace and suffering will be brought upon others as well as himself, is one of the chief restraints upon the criminally disposed. Besides, this course works a peculiar hardship in the case of the sailor. For if poverty is the point in question, the sailor is the poorer of the two; and if there is a man on earth who depends upon whole limbs and an unbroken spirit for support, it is the sailor. He, too, has friends to whom his hard earnings may be a relief, and whose hearts will bleed at any cruelty or indignity practised upon him. Yet I never knew this side of the case to be once adverted to in these arguments addressed to the leniency of the court, which are now so much in vogue; and certainly they are never allowed a moment's consideration when a sailor is on trial for revolt, or for an injury done to an officer. Notwithstanding the many difficulties which lie in a seaman's way in a court of justice, presuming that they will be modified in time, there would be little to complain of, were it not for these two appeals.

It is no cause of complaint that the testimony of seamen against their officers is viewed with suspicion, and that great allowance is made for combinations and exaggeration. On the contrary, it is the judge's duty to charge the jury on these points strongly. But there is reason for objection, when, after a strict cross-examination of witnesses, after the arguments of counsel, and the judge's charge, a verdict is found against the master, that the court should allow the practice of hearing appeals to its lenity, supported solely by evidence of the captain's good conduct when on shore, (especially where the case is one in which no evidence but that of sailors could have been brought against the accused), and then, on this ground, and on the invariable claims of the wife and family, be induced to cut down essentially the penalty imposed by a statute made expressly for masters and officers of merchantmen, and for no one else.

There are many particulars connected with the manning of vessels, the provisions given to crews, and the treatment of them while at sea, upon which there might be a good deal said; but as I have, for the most part, remarked upon them as they came up in the course of my narrative, I will offer nothing further now, except on the single point of the manner of shipping men. This, it is well known, is usually left entirely to the shipping-masters, and is a cause of a great deal of difficulty, which might be remedied by the captain, or owner, if he has any knowledge of seamen, attending to it personally. One of the members of the firm to which our ship belonged, Mr. S——, had been himself a master of a vessel, and generally selected the crew from a number sent down to him from the shipping-office. In this way he almost always had healthy, serviceable, and respectable men; for any one who has seen much of sailors can tell pretty well at first sight, by a man's dress, countenance, and deportment, what he would be on board ship. This same gentleman was also in the habit of seeing the crew together, and speaking to them previously to their sailing. On the day before our ship sailed, while the crew were getting their chests and clothes on board, he went down into the forecastle and spoke to them about the voyage, the clothing they would need, the provision he had made for them, and saw that they had a lamp and a few other conveniences. If owners or masters would more generally take the same pains, they would often save their crews a good deal of inconvenience, beside creating a sense of satisfaction and gratitude, which makes a voyage begin under good auspices, and goes far toward keeping up a better state of feeling throughout its continuance.

It only remains for me now to speak of the associated public efforts which have been making of late years for the good of seamen: a far more agreeable task than that of finding fault, even where fault there is. The exertions of the general association, called the American Seamen's Friend Society, and of the other smaller societies throughout the Union, have been a true blessing to the seaman; and bid fair, in course of time, to change the whole nature of the circumstances in which he is placed, and give him a new name, as well as a new character. These associations have taken hold in the right way, and aimed both at making the sailor's life more comfortable and creditable, and at giving him spiritual instruction. Connected with these efforts, the spread of temperance among seamen, by means of societies, called, in their own nautical language, Windward-Anchor Societies, and the distribution of books; the establishment of Sailors' Homes, where they can be comfortably and cheaply boarded, live quietly and decently, and be in the way of religious services, reading and conversation; also the institution of Savings Banks for Seamen; the distribution of tracts and Bibles;—are all means which are silently doing a great work for this class of men. These societies make the religious instruction of seamen their prominent object. If this is gained, there is no fear but that all other things necessary will be added unto them. A sailor never becomes interested in religion, without immediately learning to read, if he did not know how before; and regular habits, forehandedness (if I may use the word) in worldly affairs, and hours reclaimed from indolence and vice, which follow in the wake of the converted man, make it sure that he will instruct himself in the knowledge necessary and suitable to his calling. The religious change is the great object. If this is secured, there is no fear but that knowledge of things of the world will come in fast enough. With the sailor, as with all other men in fact, the cultivation of the intellect, and the spread of what is commonly called useful knowledge, while religious instruction is neglected, is little else than changing an ignorant sinner into an intelligent and powerful one. That sailor upon whom, of all others, the preaching of the Cross is least likely to have effect, is the one whose understanding has been cultivated, while his heart has been left to its own devices. I fully believe that those efforts which have their end in the intellectual cultivation of the sailor; in giving him scientific knowledge; putting it in his power to read everything, without securing, first of all, a right heart which shall guide him in judgment; in giving him political information, and interesting him in newspapers;—an end in the furtherance of which he is exhibited at ladies' fairs and public meetings, and complimented for his gallantry and generosity,—are all doing a harm which the labors of many faithful men cannot undo.

The establishment of Bethels in most of our own seaports, and in many foreign ports frequented by our vessels, where the gospel is regularly preached and the opening of "Sailors' Homes," which I have before mentioned, where there are usually religious services and other good influences, are doing a vast deal in this cause. But it is to be remembered that the sailor's home is on the deep. Nearly all his life must be spent on board ship; and to secure a religious influence there, should be the great object. The distribution of Bibles and tracts into cabins and forecastles, will do much toward this. There is nothing which will gain a sailor's attention sooner, and interest him more deeply, than a tract, especially one which contains a story. It is difficult to engage their attention in mere essays and arguments, but the simplest and shortest story, in which home is spoken of, kind friends, a praying mother or sister, a sudden death, and the like, often touches the heart of the roughest and most abandoned. The Bible is to the sailor a sacred book. It may lie in the bottom of his chest, voyage after voyage; but he never treats it with positive disrespect. I never knew but one sailor who doubted its being the inspired word of God; and he was one who had received an uncommonly good education, except that he had been brought up without any early religious influence. The most abandoned man of our crew, one Sunday morning, asked one of the boys to lend him his Bible. The boy said he would, but was afraid he would make sport of it. "No!" said the man, "I don't make sport of God Almighty." This is a feeling general among sailors, and is a good foundation for religious influence.

A still greater gain is made whenever, by means of a captain who is interested in the eternal welfare of those under his command, there can be secured the performance of regular religious exercises, and the exertion, on the side of religion, of that mighty influence which a captain possesses for good, or for evil. There are occurrences at sea which he may turn to great account,—a sudden death, the apprehension of danger, or the escape from it, and the like; and all the calls for gratitude and faith. Besides, this state of thing alters the whole current of feeling between the crew and their commander. His authority assumes more of the parental character; and kinder feelings exist. Godwin, though an infidel, in one of his novels, describing the relation in which a tutor stood to his pupil, says that the conviction the tutor was under, that he and his ward were both alike awaiting a state of eternal happiness or misery, and that they must appear together before the same judgment-seat, operated so upon his naturally morose disposition, as to produce a feeling of kindness and tenderness toward his ward, which nothing else could have caused. Such must be the effect upon the relation of master and common seaman.

There are now many vessels sailing under such auspices, in which great good is done. Yet I never happened to fall in with one of them. I did not hear a prayer made, a chapter read in public, nor see anything approaching to a religious service, for two years and a quarter. There were, in the course of the voyage, many incidents which made, for the time, serious impressions upon our minds, and which might have been turned to our good; but there being no one to use the opportunity, and no services, the regular return of which might have kept something of the feeling alive in us, the advantage of them was lost, to some, perhaps, forever.

The good which a single religious captain may do can hardly be calculated. In the first place, as I have said, a kinder state of feeling exists on board the ship. There is no profanity allowed; and the men are not called by any opprobrious names, which is a great thing with sailors. The Sabbath is observed. This gives the men a day of rest, even if they pass it in no other way. Such a captain, too, will not allow a sailor on board his ship to remain unable to read his Bible and the books given to him; and will usually instruct those who need it, in writing, arithmetic, and navigation; since he has a good deal of time on his hands, which he can easily employ in such a manner. He will also have regular religious services; and, in fact, by the power of his example, and, where it can judiciously be done, by the exercise of his authority, will give a character to the ship and all on board. In foreign ports, a ship is known by her captain; for, there being no general rules in the merchant service, each master may adopt a plan of his own. It is to be remembered, too, that there are, in most ships, boys of a tender age, whose characters for life are forming, as well as old men, whose lives must be drawing toward a close. The greater part of sailors die at sea; and when they find their end approaching, if it does not, as is often the case, come without warning, they cannot, as on shore, send for a clergyman, or some religious friend, to speak to them of that hope in a Saviour, which they have neglected, if not despised, through life; but if the little hull does not contain such an one within its compass, they must be left without human aid in their great extremity. When such commanders and such ships, as I have just described, shall become more numerous, the hope of the friends of seamen will be greatly strengthened; and it is encouraging to remember that the efforts among common sailors will soon raise up such a class; for those of them who are brought under these influences will inevitably be the ones to succeed to the places of trust and authority. If there is on earth an instance where a little leaven may leaven the whole lump, it is that of the religious shipmaster.

It is to the progress of this work among seamen that we must look with the greatest confidence for the remedying of those numerous minor evils and abuses that we so often hear of. It will raise the character of sailors, both as individuals and as a class. It will give weight to their testimony in courts of justice, secure better usage to them on board ship, and add comforts to their lives on shore and at sea. There are some laws that can be passed to remove temptation from their way and to help them in their progress; and some changes in the jurisdiction of the lower courts, to prevent delays, may, and probably will, be made. But, generally speaking, more especially in things which concern the discipline of ships, we had better labor in this great work, and view with caution the proposal of new laws and arbitrary regulations, remembering that most of those concerned in the making of them must necessarily be little qualified to judge of their operation.

Without any formal dedication of my narrative to that body of men, of whose common life it is intended to be a picture, I have yet borne them constantly in mind during its preparation. I cannot but trust that those of them, into whose hands it may chance to fall, will find in it that which shall render any professions of sympathy and good wishes on my part unnecessary. And I will take the liberty, on parting with my reader, who has gone down with us to the ocean, and "laid his hand upon its mane," to commend to his kind wishes, and to the benefit of his efforts, that class of men with whom, for a time, my lot was cast. I wish the rather to do this, since I feel that whatever attention this book may gain, and whatever favor it may find, I shall owe almost entirely to that interest in the sea, and those who follow it, which is so easily excited in us all.

[1] I am not sure that I have stated, in the course of my narrative, the manner in which sailors eat, on board ship. There are neither tables, knives, forks, nor plates, in a forecastle; but the kid (a wooden tub, with iron hoops) is placed on the floor and the crew sit round it, and each man cuts for himself with the common jack-knife or sheath-knife, that he carries about him. They drink their tea out of tin pots, holding little less than a quart each.

These particulars are not looked upon as hardships, and, indeed, may be considered matters of choice. Sailors, in our merchantmen, furnish their own eating utensils, as they do many of the instruments which they use in the ship's work, such as knives, palms and needles, marline-spikes, rubbers, etc. And considering their mode of life in other respects, the little time they would have for laying and clearing away a table with its apparatus, and the room it would take up in a forecastle, as well as the simple character of their meals, consisting generally of only one piece of meat,—it is certainly a convenient method, and, as the kid and pans are usually kept perfectly clean, a neat and simple one. I had supposed these things to be generally known, until I heard, a few months ago, a lawyer of repute, who has had a good deal to do with marine cases, ask a sailor upon the stand whether the crew had "got up from table" when a certain thing happened.

TWENTY-FOUR YEARS AFTER

It was in the winter of 1835-6 that the ship Alert, in the prosecution of her voyage for hides on the remote and almost unknown coast of California, floated into the vast solitude of the Bay of San Francisco. All around was the stillness of nature. One vessel, a Russian, lay at anchor there, but during our whole stay not a sail came or went. Our trade was with remote Missions, which sent hides to us in launches manned by their Indians. Our anchorage was between a small island, called Yerba Buena, and a gravel beach in a little bight or cove of the same name, formed by two small projecting points. Beyond, to the westward of the landing-place, were dreary sand-hills, with little grass to be seen, and few trees, and beyond them higher hills, steep and barren, their sides gullied by the rains. Some five or six miles beyond the landing-place, to the right, was a ruinous Presidio, and some three or four miles to the left was the Mission of Dolores, as ruinous as the Presidio, almost deserted, with but few Indians attached to it, and but little property in cattle. Over a region far beyond our sight there were no other human habitations, except that an enterprising Yankee, years in advance of his time, had put up, on the rising ground above the landing, a shanty of rough boards, where he carried on a very small retail trade between the hide ships and the Indians. Vast banks of fog, invading us from the North Pacific, drove in through the entrance, and covered the whole bay; and when they disappeared, we saw a few well-wooded islands, the sand-hills on the west, the grassy and wooded slopes on the east, and the vast stretch of the bay to the southward, where we were told lay the Missions of Santa Clara and San José, and still longer stretches to the northward and northeastward, where we understood smaller bays spread out, and large rivers poured in their tributes of waters. There were no settlements on these bays or rivers, and the few ranchos and Missions were remote and widely separated. Not only the neighborhood of our anchorage, but the entire region of the great bay, was a solitude. On the whole coast of California there was not a lighthouse, a beacon, or a buoy, and the charts were made up from old and disconnected surveys by British, Russian, and Mexican voyagers. Birds of prey and passage swooped and dived about us, wild beasts ranged through the oak groves, and as we slowly floated out of the harbor with the tide, herds of deer came to the water's edge, on the northerly side of the entrance, to gaze at the strange spectacle.

On the evening of Saturday, the 13th of August, 1859, the superb steamship Golden Gate, gay with crowds of passengers, and lighting the sea for miles around with the glare of her signal lights of red, green, and white, and brilliant with lighted saloons and staterooms, bound up from the Isthmus of Panama, neared the entrance to San Francisco, the great centre of a world-wide commerce. Miles out at sea, on the desolate rocks of the Farallones, gleamed the powerful rays of one of the most costly and effective light-houses in the world. As we drew in through the Golden Gate, another light-house met our eyes, and in the clear moonlight of the unbroken California summer we saw, on the right, a large fortification protecting the narrow entrance, and just before us the little island of Alcatraz confronted us,—one entire fortress. We bore round the point toward the old anchoring-ground of the hide ships, and there, covering the sand-hills and the valleys, stretching from the water's edge to the base of the great hills, and from the old Presidio to the Mission, flickering all over with the lamps of its streets and houses, lay a city of one hundred thousand inhabitants. Clocks tolled the hour of midnight from its steeples, but the city was alive from the salute of our guns, spreading the news that the fortnightly steamer had come, bringing mails and passengers from the Atlantic world. Clipper ships of the largest size lay at anchor in the stream, or were girt to the wharves; and capacious high-pressure steamers, as large and showy as those of the Hudson or Mississippi, bodies of dazzling light, awaited the delivery of our mails to take their courses up the Bay, stopping at Benicia and the United States Naval Station, and then up the great tributaries—the Sacramento, San Joaquin, and Feather Rivers—to the far inland cities of Sacramento, Stockton, and Marysville.

The dock into which we drew, and the streets about it, were densely crowded with express wagons and hand-carts to take luggage, coaches and cabs for passengers, and with men,—some looking out for friends among our hundreds of passengers,—

agents of the press, and a greater multitude eager for newspapers and verbal intelligence from the great Atlantic and European world. Through this crowd I made my way, along the well-built and well-lighted streets, as alive as by day, where boys in high-keyed voices were already crying the latest New York papers; and between one and two o'clock in the morning found myself comfortably abed in a commodious room, in the Oriental Hotel, which stood, as well as I could learn, on the filled-up cove, and not far from the spot where we used to beach our boats from the Alert.

Sunday, August 14th. When I awoke in the morning, and looked from my windows over the city of San Francisco, with its storehouses, towers, and steeples; its court-houses, theatres, and hospitals; its daily journals; its well-filled learned professions; its fortresses and light-houses; its wharves and harbor, with their thousand-ton clipper ships, more in number than London or Liverpool sheltered that day, itself one of the capitals of the American Republic, and the sole emporium of a new world, the awakened Pacific; when I looked across the bay to the eastward, and beheld a beautiful town on the fertile, wooded shores of the Contra Costa, and steamers, large and small, the ferryboats to the Contra Costa, and capacious freighters and passenger-carriers to all parts of the great bay and its tributaries, with lines of their smoke in the horizon,—when I saw all these things, and reflected on what I once was and saw here, and what now surrounded me, I could scarcely keep my hold on reality at all, or the genuineness of anything, and seemed to myself like one who had moved in "worlds not realized."

I could not complain that I had not a choice of places of worship. The Roman Catholics have an archbishop, a cathedral, and five or six smaller churches, French, German, Spanish, and English; and the Episcopalians, a bishop, a cathedral, and three other churches; the Methodists and Presbyterians have three or four each, and there are Congregationalists, Baptists, a Unitarian, and other societies. On my way to church, I met two classmates of mine at Harvard standing in a door-way, one a lawyer and the other a teacher, and made appointments for a future meeting. A little farther on I came upon another Harvard man, a fine scholar and wit, and full of cleverness and good-humor, who invited me to go to breakfast with him at the French house—he was a bachelor, and a late riser on Sundays. I asked him to show me the way to

Bishop Kip's church. He hesitated, looked a little confused, and admitted that he was not as well up in certain classes of knowledge as in others, but, by a desperate guess, pointed out a wooden building at the foot of the street, which any one might have seen could not be right, and which turned out to be an African Baptist meeting-house. But my friend had many capital points of character, and I owed much of the pleasure of my visit to his attentions.

The congregation at the Bishop's church was precisely like one you would meet in New York, Philadelphia, or Boston. To be sure, the identity of the service makes one feel at once at home, but the people were alike, nearly all of the English race, though from all parts of the Union. The latest French bonnets were at the head of the chief pews, and business men at the foot. The music was without character, but there was an instructive sermon, and the church was full.

I found that there were no services at any of the Protestant churches in the afternoon. They have two services on Sunday; at 11 A. M., and after dark. The afternoon is spent at home, or in friendly visiting, or teaching of Sunday Schools, or other humane and social duties.

This is as much the practice with what at home are called the strictest denominations as with any others. Indeed, I found individuals, as well as public bodies, affected in a marked degree by a change of oceans and by California life. One Sunday afternoon I was surprised at receiving the card of a man whom I had last known, some fifteen years ago, as a strict and formal deacon of a Congregational Society in New England. He was a deacon still, in San Francisco, a leader in all pious works, devoted to his denomination and to total abstinence,—the same internally, but externally—what a change! Gone was the downcast eye, the bated breath, the solemn, non-natural voice, the watchful gait, stepping as if he felt responsible for the balance of the moral universe! He walked with a stride, an uplifted open countenance, his face covered with beard, whiskers, and mustache, his voice strong and natural;—and, in short, he had put off the New England deacon and become a human being. In a visit of an hour I learned much from him about the religious societies, the moral reforms, the "Dashaways,"—total abstinence societies, which had taken strong hold on the young and wilder parts of society,—and then of the Vigilance Committee, of which he was a member, and of more secular points of interest.

In one of the parlors of the hotel, I saw a man of about sixty years of age, with his feet bandaged and resting in a chair, whom somebody addressed by the name of Lies.[1] Lies! thought I, that must be the man who came across the country from Kentucky to Monterey while we lay there in the Pilgrim in 1835, and made a passage in the Alert, when he used to shoot with his rifle bottles hung from the top-gallant studding-sail-boom-ends. He married the beautiful Doña Rosalía Vallejo, sister of Don Guadalupe. There were the old high features and sandy hair. I put my chair beside him, and began conversation, as any one may do in California. Yes, he was the Mr. Lies; and when I gave my name he professed at once to remember me, and spoke of my book. I found that almost—I might perhaps say quite—every American in California had read it; for when California "broke out," as the phrase is, in 1848, and so large a portion of the Anglo-Saxon race flocked to it, there was no book upon California but mine. Many who were on the coast at the time the book refers to, and afterwards read it, and remembered the Pilgrim and Alert, thought they also remembered me. But perhaps more did remember me than I was inclined at first to believe, for the novelty of a collegian coming out before the mast had drawn more attention to me than I was aware of at the time.

Late in the afternoon, as there were vespers at the Roman Catholic churches, I went to that of Notre Dame des Victoires. The congregation was French, and a sermon in French was preached by an Abbé; the music was excellent, all things airy and tasteful, and making one feel as if in one of the chapels in Paris. The Cathedral of St. Mary, which I afterwards visited, where the Irish attend, was a contrast indeed, and more like one of our stifling Irish Catholic churches in Boston or New York, with intelligence in so small a proportion to the number of faces. During the three Sundays I was in San Francisco, I visited three of the Episcopal churches, and the Congregational, a Chinese Mission Chapel, and on the Sabbath (Saturday) a Jewish synagogue. The Jews are a wealthy and powerful class here. The Chinese, too, are numerous, and do a great part of the manual labor and small shop-keeping, and have some wealthy mercantile houses.

It is noticeable that European Continental fashions prevail generally in this city,—French cooking, lunch at noon, and dinner at the end of the day, with café noir after meals, and to a great extent the European Sunday,—to all which emigrants from the United States and Great Britain seem to adapt themselves. Some dinners which were given to me at French restaurants were, it seemed to me,—a poor judge of such matters, to be sure,—as sumptuous and as good, in dishes and wines, as I have found in Paris. But I had a relish-maker which my friends at table did not suspect—the remembrance of the forecastle dinners I ate here twenty-four years before.

August 17th. The customs of California are free; and any person who knows about my book speaks to me. The newspapers have announced the arrival of the veteran pioneer of all. I hardly walk out without meeting or making acquaintances. I have already been invited to deliver the anniversary oration before the Pioneer Society, to celebrate the settlement of San Francisco. Any man is qualified for election into the society who came to California before 1853. What moderns they are! I tell them of the time when Richardson's shanty of 1835—not his adobe house of 1836—was the only human habitation between the Mission and the Presidio, and when the vast bay, with all its tributaries and recesses, was a solitude,—and yet I am but little past forty years of age. They point out the place where Richardson's adobe house stood, and tell me that the first court and first town council were convened in it, the first Protestant worship performed in it, and in it the first capital trial by the Vigilance Committee held. I am taken down to the wharves, by antiquaries of a ten or twelve years' range, to identify the two points, now known as Clark's and Rincon, which formed the little cove of Yerba Buena, where we used to beach our boats,—now filled up and built upon. The island we called "Wood Island," where we spent the cold days and nights of December, in our launch, getting wood for our year's supply, is clean shorn of trees; and the bare rocks of Alcatraz Island, an entire fortress. I have looked at the city from the water and islands from the city, but I can see nothing that recalls the times gone by, except the venerable Mission, the ruinous Presidio, the high hills in the rear of the town, and the great stretches of the bay in all directions.

To-day I took a California horse of the old style,—the run, the loping gait,—and visited the Presidio. The walls stand as they did, with some changes made to accommodate a small garrison of United States troops. It has a noble situation, and I saw from it a clipper ship of the very largest class, coming through the Gate, under her fore-and-aft sails. Thence I rode to the Fort, now nearly finished, on the southern shore of the Gate, and made an inspection of it. It is very expensive and of the latest style. One of the engineers here is Custis Lee, who has just left West Point at the head of his class,—a son of Colonel Robert E. Lee, who distinguished himself in the Mexican War.

Another morning I ride to the Mission Dolores. It has a strangely solitary aspect, enhanced by its surroundings of the most uncongenial, rapidly growing modernisms; the hoar of ages surrounded by the brightest, slightest, and rapidest of modern growths. Its old belfries still clanged with the discordant bells, and Mass was saying within, for it is used as a place of worship for the extreme south part of the city.

In one of my walks about the wharves, I found a pile of dry hides lying by the side of a vessel. Here was something to feelingly persuade me what I had been, to recall a past scarce credible to myself. I stood lost in reflection. What were these hides—what were they not?—to us, to me, a boy, twenty-four years ago? These were our constant labor, our chief object, our almost habitual thought. They brought us out here, they kept us here, and it was only by getting them that we could escape from the coast and return to home and civilized life. If it had not been that I might be seen, I should have seized one, slung it over my head, walked off with it, and thrown it by the old toss—I do not believe yet a lost art—to the ground. How they called up to my mind the months of curing at San Diego, the year and more of beach and surf work, and the steering of the ship for home! I was in a dream of San Diego, San Pedro—with its hills so steep for taking up goods, and its stones so hard to our bare feet—and the cliffs of San Juan! All this, too, is no more! The entire hide-business is of the past, and to the present inhabitants of California a dim tradition. The gold discoveries drew off all men from the gathering or cure of hides, the inflowing population made an end of the great droves of cattle; and now not a vessel pursues the—I was about to say dear—the dreary once hated business of gathering hides upon the coast, and the beach of San Diego is abandoned and its hide-houses have disappeared. Meeting a respectable-looking citizen on the wharf, I inquired of him how the hide-trade was carried on. "O," said he, "there is very little of it, and that is all here. The few that are brought in are placed under sheds in winter, or left out on the wharf in summer, and are loaded from the wharves into the vessels alongside. They form parts of cargoes of other materials." I really felt too much, at the instant, to express to him the cause of my interest in the subject, and only added, "Then the old business of trading up and down the coast and curing hides for cargoes is all over?" "O yes, sir," said he, "those old times of the Pilgrim and Alert and California, that we read about, are gone by."

Saturday, August 20th. The steamer Senator makes regular trips up and down the coast, between San Francisco and San Diego, calling at intermediate ports. This is my opportunity to revisit the old scenes. She sails to-day, and I am off, steaming among the great clippers anchored in the harbor, and gliding rapidly round the point, past Alcatraz Island, the light-house, and through the fortified Golden Gate, and bending to the southward,—all done in two or three hours, which, in the Alert, under canvas, with head tides, variable winds, and sweeping currents to deal with, took us full two days.

Among the passengers I noticed an elderly gentleman, thin, with sandy hair and face that seemed familiar. He took off his glove and showed one shrivelled hand. It must be he! I went to him and said, "Captain Wilson, I believe." Yes, that was his name. "I knew you, sir, when you commanded the Ayacucho on this coast, in old hide-droghing times, in 1835-6." He was quickened by this, and at once inquiries were made on each side, and we were in full talk about the Pilgrim and Alert, Ayacucho and Loriotte, the California and Lagoda. I found he had been very much flattered by the praise I had bestowed in my book on his seamanship, especially in bringing the Pilgrim to her berth in San Diego harbor, after she had drifted successively into the Lagoda and Loriotte, and was coming into him. I had made a pet of his brig, the Ayacucho, which pleased him almost as much as my remembrance of his bride and their wedding, which I saw at Santa Barbara in 1836. Doña Ramona was now the mother of a large family, and Wilson assured me that if I would visit him at his rancho, near San Luis Obispo, I should find her still a handsome woman, and very glad to see me. How we walked the deck together, hour after hour, talking over the old times,—the ships, the captains, the crews, the traders on shore, the ladies, the Missions, the south-easters! indeed, where could we stop? He had sold the Ayacucho in Chili for a vessel of war, and had given up the sea, and had been for years a ranchero. (I learned from others that he had become one of the most wealthy and respectable farmers in the State, and that his rancho was well worth visiting.) Thompson, he said, hadn't the sailor in him; and he never could laugh enough at his fiasco in San Diego, and his reception by Bradshaw. Faucon was a sailor and a navigator. He did not know what had become of George Marsh (ante, pp. 199-202, 252), except that he left him in Callao; nor could he tell me anything of handsome Bill Jackson (ante, p. 86), nor of Captain Nye of the Loriotte. I told him all I then knew of the ships, the masters, and the officers. I found he had kept some run of my history, and needed little information. Old Señor Noriego of Santa Barbara, he told me, was dead, and Don Carlos and Don Santiago, but I should find their children there, now in middle life. Doña Augustia, he said, I had made famous by my praises of her beauty and dancing, and I should have from her a royal reception. She had been a widow, and remarried since, and had a daughter as handsome as herself. The descendants of Noriego had taken the ancestral name of De la Guerra, as they were nobles of Old Spain by birth; and the boy Pablo, who used to make passages in the Alert, was now Don Pablo de la Guerra, a Senator in the State Legislature for Santa Barbara County.

The points in the country, too, he noticed, as he passed them,—Santa Cruz, San Luis Obispo, Point Año Nuevo, the opening to Monterey, which to my disappointment we did not visit. No; Monterey, the prettiest town on the coast, and its capital and seat of customs, had got no advantage from the great changes, was out of the way of commerce and of the travel to the mines and great rivers, and was not worth stopping at. Point Conception we passed in the night, a cheery light gleaming over the waters from its tar light-house, standing on its outermost peak. Point Conception! That word was enough to recall all our experiences and dreads of gales, swept decks, topmast carried away, and the hardships of a coast service in the winter. But Captain Wilson tells me that the climate has altered; that the southeasters are no longer the bane of the coast they once were, and that vessels now anchor inside the kelp at Santa Barbara and San Pedro all the year round. I should have thought this owing to his spending his winters on a rancho instead of the deck of the Ayacucho, had not the same thing been told me by others.

Passing round Point Conception, and steering easterly, we opened the islands that form, with the main-land, the canal of Santa Barbara. There they are, Santa Cruz and Santa Rosa; and there is the beautiful point, Santa Buenaventura; and there lies Santa Barbara on its plain, with its amphitheatre of high hills and distant mountains. There is the old white Mission with its belfries, and there the town, with its one-story adobe houses, with here and there a two-story wooden house of later build; yet little is it altered,—the same repose in the golden sunlight and glorious climate, sheltered by its hills; and then, more remindful than anything else, there roars and tumbles upon the beach the same grand surf of the great Pacific as on the beautiful day when the Pilgrim, after her five months' voyage, dropped her weary anchors here; the same bright blue ocean, and the surf making just the same monotonous, melancholy roar, and the same dreamy town, and gleaming white Mission, as when we beached our boats for the first time, riding over the breakers with shouting Kanakas, the three small hide-traders lying at anchor in the offing. But now we are the only vessel, and that an unromantic, sail-less, spar-less, engine-driven hulk!

I landed in the surf, in the old style, but it was not high enough to excite us, the only change being that I was somehow unaccountably a passenger, and did not have to jump overboard and steady the boat, and run her up by the gunwales.

Santa Barbara has gained but little. I should not know, from anything I saw, that she was now a seaport of the United States, a part of the enterprising Yankee nation, and not still a lifeless Mexican town. At the same old house, where Señor Noriego lived, on the piazza in front of the court-yard, where was the gay scene of the marriage of our agent, Mr. Robinson, to Doña Anita, where Don Juan Bandini and Doña Augustia danced, Don Pablo de la Guerra received me in a courtly fashion. I passed the day with the family, and in walking about the place; and ate the old dinner with its accompaniments of frijoles, native olives and grapes, and native wines. In due time I paid my respects to Doña Augustia, and notwithstanding what Wilson told me, I could hardly believe that after twenty-four years there would still be so much of the enchanting woman about her.

She thanked me for the kind and, as she called them, greatly exaggerated compliments I had paid her; and her daughter told me that all travellers who came to Santa Barbara called to see her mother, and that she herself never expected to live long enough to be a belle.

Mr. Alfred Robinson, our agent in 1835-6, was here, with a part of his family. I did not know how he would receive me, remembering what I had printed to the world about him at a time when I took little thought that the world was going to read it; but there was no sign of offence, only cordiality which gave him, as between us, rather the advantage in status.

The people of this region are giving attention to sheep-raising, wine-making, and the raising of olives, just enough to keep the town from going backwards.

But evening is drawing on, and our boat sails to-night. So, refusing a horse or carriage, I walk down, not unwilling to be a little early, that I may pace up and down the beach, looking off to the islands and the points, and watching the roaring, tumbling billows. How softening is the effect of time! It touches us through the affections. I almost feel as if I were lamenting the passing away of something loved and dear,—the boats, the Kanakas, the hides, my old shipmates. Death, change, distance, lend them a character which makes them quite another thing from the vulgar, wearisome toil of uninteresting, forced manual labour.

The breeze freshened as we stood out to sea, and the wild waves rolled over the red sun, on the broad horizon of the Pacific; but it is summer, and in summer there can be no bad weather in California. Every day is pleasant. Nature forbids a drop of rain to fall by day or night, or a wind to excite itself beyond a fresh summer breeze.

The next morning we found ourselves at anchor in the Bay of San Pedro. Here was this hated, this thoroughly detested spot. Although we lay near, I could scarce recognize the hill up which we rolled and dragged and pushed and carried our heavy loads, and down which we pitched the hides, to carry them barefooted over the rocks to the floating long-boat. It was no longer the landing-place. One had been made at the head of the creek, and boats discharged and took off cargoes from a mole or wharf, in a quiet place, safe from southeasters. A tug ran to take off passengers from the steamer to the wharf,—for the trade of Los Angeles is sufficient to support such a vessel. I got the captain to land me privately, in a small boat, at the old place by the hill. I dismissed the boat, and, alone, found my way to the high ground. I say found my way, for neglect and weather had left but few traces of the steep road the hide-vessels had built to the top. The cliff off which we used to throw the hides, and where I spent nights watching them, was more easily found. The population was doubled, that is to say, there were two houses, instead of one, on the hill. I stood on the brow and looked out toward the offing, the Santa Catalina Island, and, nearer, the melancholy Dead Man's Island, with its painful tradition, and recalled the gloomy days that followed the flogging, and fancied the Pilgrim at anchor in the offing. But the tug is going toward our steamer, and I must awake and be off. I walked along the shore to the new landing-place, where were two or three store-houses and other buildings, forming a small depot; and a stage-coach, I found, went daily between this place and the Pueblo. I got a seat on the top of the coach, to which were tackled six little less than wild California horses. Each horse had a man at his head, and when the driver had got his reins in hand he gave the word, all the horses were let go at once, and away they went on a spring, tearing over the ground, the driver only keeping them from going the wrong way, for they had a wide, level pampa to run over the whole thirty miles to the Pueblo. This plain is almost treeless, with no grass, at least none now in the drought of mid-summer, and is filled with squirrel-holes, and alive with squirrels. As we changed horses twice, we did not slacken our speed until we turned into the streets of the Pueblo.

The Pueblo de los Angeles I found a large and flourishing town of about twenty thousand inhabitants, with brick sidewalks, and blocks of stone or brick houses. The three principal traders when we were here for hides in the Pilgrim and Alert are still among the chief traders of the place,—Stearns, Temple, and Warner, the two former being reputed very rich. I dined with Mr. Stearns, now a very old man, and met there Don Juan Bandini, to whom I had given a good deal of notice in my book. From him, as indeed from every one in this town, I met with the kindest attentions. The wife of Don Juan, who was a beautiful young girl when we were on the coast, Doña Refugio, daughter of Don Santiago Argüello, the commandante of San Diego, was with him, and still handsome. This is one of several instances I have noticed of the preserving quality of the California climate. Here, too, was Henry Mellus, who came out with me before the mast in the Pilgrim, and left the brig to be agent's clerk on shore. He had experienced varying fortunes here, and was now married to a Mexican lady, and had a family. I dined with him, and in the afternoon he drove me round to see the vineyards, the chief objects in this region. The vintage of last year was estimated at half a million of gallons. Every year new square miles of ground are laid down to vineyards, and the Pueblo promises to be the centre of one of the largest wine-producing regions in the world. Grapes are a drug here, and I found a great abundance of figs, olives, peaches, pears, and melons. The climate is well suited to these fruits, but is too hot and dry for successful wheat crops.

Towards evening, we started off in the stage coach, with again our relays of six mad horses, and reached the creek before dark, though it was late at night before we got on board the steamer, which was slowly moving her wheels, under way for San Diego.

As we skirted along the coast, Wilson and I recognized, or thought we did, in the clear moonlight, the rude white Mission of San Juan Capistrano, and its cliff, from which I had swung down by a pair of halyards to save a few hides,—a boy who could not be prudential, and who caught at every chance for adventure.

As we made the high point off San Diego, Point Loma, we were greeted by the cheering presence of a light-house. As we swept round it in the early morning, there, before us, lay the little harbor of San Diego, its low spit of sand, where the water runs so deep; the opposite flats, where the Alert grounded in starting for home; the low hills, without trees, and almost without brush; the quiet little beach;—but the chief objects, the hide houses, my eye looked for in vain. They were gone, all, and left no mark behind.

I wished to be alone, so I let the other passengers go up to the town, and was quietly pulled ashore in a boat, and left to myself. The recollections and the emotions all were sad, and only sad.

Fugit, interea fugit irreparabile tempus.

The past was real. The present, all about me, was unreal, unnatural, repellant. I saw the big ships lying in the stream, the Alert, the California, the Rosa, with her Italians; then the handsome Ayacucho, my favorite; the poor, dear old Pilgrim, the home of hardship and hopelessness; the boats passing to and fro; the cries of the sailors at the capstan or falls; the peopled beach; the large hide-houses with their gangs of men; and the Kanakas interspersed everywhere. All, all were gone! not a vestige to mark where one hide-house stood. The oven, too, was gone. I searched for its site, and found, where I thought it should be, a few broken bricks and bits of mortar. I alone was left of all, and how strangely was I here! What changes to me! Where were they all? Why should I care for them,—poor Kanakas and sailors, the refuse of civilization, the outlaws and beach-combers of the Pacific! Time and death seemed to transfigure them. Doubtless nearly all were dead; but how had they died, and where? In hospitals, in fever-climes, in dens of vice, or falling from the mast, or dropping exhausted from the wreck,—

"When for a moment, like a drop of rain,
He sinks into thy depths with bubbling groan,
Without a grave, unknelled, uncoffined, and unknown."

The light-hearted boys are now hardened middle-aged men, if the seas, rocks, fevers, and the deadlier enemies that beset a sailor's life on shore have spared them; and the then strong men have bowed themselves, and the earth or sea has covered them.

Even the animals are gone,—the colony of dogs, the broods of poultry, the useful horses; but the coyotes bark still in the woods, for they belong not to man, and are not touched by his changes.

I walked slowly up the hill, finding my way among the few bushes, for the path was long grown over, and sat down where we used to rest in carrying our burdens of wood, and to look out for vessels that might, though so seldom, be coming down from the windward.

To rally myself by calling to mind my own better fortune and nobler lot, and cherished surroundings at home, was impossible. Borne down by depression, the day being yet at its noon, and the sun over the old point—it is four miles to the town, the Presidio,—I have walked it often, and can do it once more,—I passed the familiar objects, and it seemed to me that I remembered them better than those of any other place I had ever been in;—the opening to the little cave; the low hills where we cut wood and killed rattlesnakes, and where our dogs chased the coyotes; and the black ground where so many of the ship's crew and beach-combers used to bring up on their return at the end of a liberty day, and spend the night sub Jove.

The little town of San Diego has undergone no change whatever that I can see. It certainly has not grown. It is still, like Santa Barbara, a Mexican town. The four principal houses of the gente de razon—of the Bandinis, Estudillos, Argüellos, and Picos—are the chief houses now; but all the gentlemen—and their families, too, I believe—are gone. The big vulgar shop-keeper and trader, Fitch, is long since dead; Tom Wrightington, who kept the rival pulpería, fell from his horse when drunk, and was found nearly eaten up by coyotes; and I can scarce find a person whom I remember. I went into a familiar one-story adobe house, with its piazza and earthen floor, inhabited by a respectable lower-class family by the name of Muchado, and inquired if any of the family remained, when a bright-eyed middle-aged woman recognized me, for she had heard I was on board the steamer, and told me she had married a shipmate of mine, Jack Stewart, who went out as second mate the next voyage, but left the ship and married and settled here. She said he wished very much to see me. In a few minutes he came in, and his sincere pleasure in meeting me was extremely grateful. We talked over old times as long as I could afford to. I was glad to hear that he was sober and doing well. Doña Tomasa Pico I found and talked with. She was the only person of the old upper class that remained on the spot, if I rightly recollect. I found an American family here, with whom I dined,—Doyle and his wife, nice young people, Doyle agent for the great line of coaches to run to the frontier of the old States.

I must complete my acts of pious remembrance, so I take a horse and make a run out to the old Mission, where Ben Stimson and I went the first liberty day we had after we left Boston (ante, p. 115). All has gone to decay. The buildings are unused and ruinous, and the large gardens show now only wild cactuses, willows, and a few olive-trees. A fast run brings me back in time to take leave of the few I knew and who knew me, and to reach the steamer before she sails. A last look—yes, last for life—to the beach, the hills, the low point, the distant town, as we round Point Loma and the first beams of the light-house strike out towards the setting sun.

Wednesday, August 24th. At anchor at San Pedro by daylight. But instead of being roused out of the forecastle to row the long-boat ashore and bring off a load of hides before breakfast, we were served with breakfast in the cabin, and again took our drive with the wild horses to the Pueblo and spent the day; seeing nearly the same persons as before, and again getting back by dark. We steamed again for Santa Barbara, where we only lay an hour, and passed through its canal and round Point Conception, stopping at San Luis Obispo to land my friend, as I may truly call him after this long passage together, Captain Wilson, whose most earnest invitation to stop here and visit him at his rancho I was obliged to decline.

Friday evening, 26th August, we entered the Golden Gate, passed the light-houses and forts, and clipper ships at anchor, and came to our dock, with this great city, on its high hills and rising surfaces, brilliant before us, and full of eager life.

Making San Francisco my head-quarters, I paid visits to various parts of the State,—down the Bay to Santa Clara, with its live oaks and sycamores, and its Jesuit College for boys; and San José, where is the best girls' school in the State, kept by the Sisters of Notre Dame,—a town now famous for a year's session of "The legislature of a thousand drinks,"—and thence to the rich Almaden quicksilver mines, returning on the Contra Costa side through the rich agricultural country, with its ranchos and the vast grants of the Castro and Soto families, where farming and fruit-raising are done on so large a scale. Another excursion was up the San Joaquin to Stockton, a town of some ten thousand inhabitants, a hundred miles from San Francisco, and crossing the Tuolumne and Stanislaus and Merced, by the little Spanish town of Hornitos, and Snelling's Tavern, at the ford of the Merced, where so many fatal fights are had. Thence I went to Mariposa County, and Colonel Fremont's mines, and made an interesting visit to "the Colonel," as he is called all over the country, and Mrs. Fremont, a heroine equal to either fortune, the salons of Paris and the drawing-rooms of New York and Washington, or the roughest life of the remote and wild mining regions of Mariposa,—with their fine family of spirited, clever children. After a rest there, we went on to Clark's Camp and the Big Trees, where I measured one tree ninety-seven feet in circumference without its bark, and the bark is usually eighteen inches thick; and rode through another which lay on the ground, a shell, with all the insides out—rode through it mounted, and sitting at full height in the saddle; then to the wonderful Yo Semite Valley,—itself a stupendous miracle of nature, with its Dome, its Capitan, its walls of three thousand feet of perpendicular height,—but a valley of streams, of waterfalls from the torrent to the mere shimmer of a bridal veil, only enough to reflect a rainbow, with their plunges of twenty-five hundred feet, or their smaller falls of eight hundred, with nothing at the base but thick mists, which form and trickle, and then run and at last plunge into the blue Merced that flows through the centre of the valley. Back by the Coulterville trail, the peaks of Sierra Nevada in sight, across the North Fork of the Merced, by Gentry's Gulch, over hills and through cañons, to Fremont's again, and thence to Stockton and San Francisco—all this at the end of August, when there has been no rain for four months, and the air is dear and very hot, and the ground perfectly dry; windmills, to raise water for artificial irrigation of small patches, seen all over the landscape, while we travel through square miles of hot dust, where they tell us, and truly that in winter and early spring we should be up to our knees in flowers; a country, too, where surface gold-digging is so common and unnoticed that the large, six-horse stage-coach, in which I travelled from Stockton to Hornitos, turned off in the high road for a Chinaman, who, with his pan and washer, was working up a hole which an American had abandoned, but where the minute and patient industry of the Chinaman averaged a few dollars a day.

These visits were so full of interest, with grandeurs and humors of all sorts, that I am strongly tempted to describe them. But I remember that I am not to write a journal of a visit over the new California, but to sketch briefly the contrasts with the old spots of 1835-6, and I forbear.

How strange and eventful has been the brief history of this marvellous city, San Francisco! In 1835 there was one board shanty. In 1836, one adobe house on the same spot. In 1847, a population of four hundred and fifty persons, who organized a town government. Then came the auri sacra fames, the flocking together of many of the worst spirits of Christendom; a sudden birth of a city of canvas and boards, entirely destroyed by fire five times in eighteen months, with a loss of sixteen millions of dollars, and as often rebuilt, until it became a solid city of brick and stone, of nearly one hundred thousand inhabitants, with all the accompaniments of wealth and culture, and now (in 1859) the most quiet and well-governed city of its size in the United States. But it has been through its season of Heaven-defying crime, violence, and blood, from which it was rescued and handed back to soberness, morality, and good government, by that peculiar invention of Anglo-Saxon Republican America, the solemn, awe-inspiring Vigilance Committee of the most grave and responsible citizens, the last resort of the thinking and the good, taken to only when vice, fraud, and ruffianism have intrenched themselves behind the forms of law, suffrage, and ballot, and there is no hope but in organized force, whose action must be instant and thorough, or its state will be worse than before. A history of the passage of this city through those ordeals, and through its almost incredible financial extremes, should be written by a pen which not only accuracy shall govern, but imagination shall inspire.

I cannot pause for the civility of referring to the many kind attentions I received, and the society of educated men and women from all parts of the Union I met with; where New England, the Carolinas, Virginia, and the new West sat side by side with English, French, and German civilization.

My stay in California was interrupted by an absence of nearly four months, when I sailed for the Sandwich Islands in the noble Boston clipper ship Mastiff, which was burned at sea to the water's edge; we escaping in boats, and carried by a friendly British bark into Honolulu, whence, after a deeply interesting visit of three months in that most fascinating group of islands, with its natural and its moral wonders, I returned to San Francisco in an American whaler, and found myself again in my quarters on the morning of Sunday, December 11th, 1859.

My first visit after my return was to Sacramento, a city of about forty thousand inhabitants, more than a hundred miles inland from San Francisco, on the Sacramento, where was the capital of the State, and where were fleets of river steamers, and a large inland commerce. Here I saw the inauguration of a Governor, Mr. Latham, a young man from Massachusetts, much my junior; and met a member of the State Senate, a man who, as a carpenter, repaired my father's house at home some ten years before; and two more Senators from southern California, relics of another age,—Don Andres Pico, from San Diego; and Don Pablo de la Guerra, whom I have mentioned as meeting at Santa Barbara. I had a good deal of conversation with these gentlemen, who stood alone in an assembly of Americans, who had conquered their country, spared pillars of the past. Don Andres had fought us at San Pazqual and Sepulveda's rancho, in 1846, and as he fought bravely, not a common thing among the Mexicans, and, indeed, repulsed Kearney, is always treated with respect. He had the satisfaction, dear to the proud Spanish heart, of making a speech before a Senate of Americans, in favor of the retention in office of an officer of our army who was wounded at San Pazqual and whom some wretched caucus was going to displace to carry out a political job. Don Andres's magnanimity and indignation carried the day.

My last visit in this part of the country was to a new and rich farming region, the Napa Valley, the United States Navy Yard at Mare Island, the river gold workings, and the Geysers, and old Mr. John Yount's rancho. On board the steamer, found Mr. Edward Stanley, formerly member of Congress from North Carolina, who became my companion for the greater part of my trip. I also met—a revival on the spot of an acquaintance of twenty years ago—Don Guadalupe Vallejo; I may say acquaintance, for although I was then before the mast, he knew my story, and, as he spoke English well, used to hold many conversations with me, when in the boat or on shore. He received me with true earnestness, and would not hear of my passing his estate without visiting him. He reminded me of a remark I made to him once, when pulling him ashore in the boat, when he was commandante at the Presidio. I learned that the two Vallejos, Guadalupe and Salvador, owned, at an early time, nearly all Napa and Sonoma, having princely estates. But they have not much left. They were nearly ruined by their bargain with the State, that they would put up the public buildings if the Capital should be placed at Vallejo, then a town of some promise. They spent $100,000, the Capital was moved there, and in two years removed to San José on another contract. The town fell to pieces, and the houses, chiefly wooden, were taken down and removed. I accepted the old gentleman's invitation so far as to stop at Vallejo to breakfast.

The United States Navy Yard, at Mare Island, near Vallejo, is large and well placed, with deep fresh water. The old Independence, and the sloop Decatur, and two steamers were there, and they were experimenting on building a despatch boat, the Saginaw, of California timber.

I have no excuse for attempting to describe my visit through the fertile and beautiful Napa Valley, nor even, what exceeded that in interest, my visit to old John Yount at his rancho, where I heard from his own lips some of his most interesting stories of hunting and trapping and Indian fighting, during an adventurous life of forty years of such work, between our back settlements in Missouri and Arkansas, and the mountains of California, trapping in Colorado and Gila,—and his celebrated dream, thrice repeated, which led him to organize a party to go out over the mountains, that did actually rescue from death by starvation the wretched remnants of the Donner party.

I must not pause for the dreary country of the Geysers, the screaming escapes of steam, the sulphur, the boiling caldrons of black and yellow and green, and the region of Gehenna, through which runs a quiet stream of pure water; nor for the park scenery, and captivating ranchos of the Napa Valley, where farming is done on so grand a scale—where I have seen a man plough a furrow by little red flags on sticks, to keep his range by, until nearly out of sight, and where, the wits tell us, he returns the next day on the back furrow; a region where, at Christmas time, I have seen old strawberries still on the vines, by the side of vines in full blossom for the next crop, and grapes in the same stages, and open windows, and yet a grateful wood fire on the hearth in early morning; nor for the titanic operations of hydraulic surface mining, where large mountain streams are diverted from their ancient beds, and made to do the work, beyond the reach of all other agents, of washing out valleys and carrying away hills, and changing the whole surface of the country, to expose the stores of gold hidden for centuries in the darkness of their earthly depths.

January 10th, 1860. I am again in San Francisco, and my revisit to California is closed. I have touched too lightly and rapidly for much impression upon the reader on my last visit into the interior; but, as I have said, in a mere continuation to a narrative of a sea-faring life on the coast, I am only to carry the reader with me on a visit to those scenes in which the public has long manifested so gratifying an interest. But it seemed to me that slight notices of these entirely new parts of the country would not be out of place, for they serve to put in strong contrast with the solitudes of 1835-6 the developed interior, with its mines, and agricultural wealth, and rapidly filling population, and its large cities, so far from the coast, with their education, religion, arts, and trade.

On the morning of the 11th January, 1860, I passed, for the eighth time, through the Golden Gate, on my way across the delightful Pacific to the Oriental world, with its civilization three thousand years older than that I was leaving behind. As the shores of California faded in the distance, and the summits of the Coast Range sank under the blue horizon, I bade farewell—yes, I do not doubt, forever—to those scenes which, however changed or unchanged, must always possess an ineffable interest for me.

It is time my fellow-travellers and I should part company. But I have been requested by a great many persons to give some account of the subsequent history of the vessels and their crews, with which I had made them acquainted. I attempt the following sketches in deference to these suggestions, and not, I trust, with any undue estimate of the general interest my narrative may have created.

Something less than a year after my return in the Alert, and when, my eyes having recovered, I was again in college life, I found one morning in the newspapers, among the arrivals of the day before, "The brig Pilgrim, Faucon, from San Diego, California." In a few hours I was down in Ann Street, and on my way to Hackstadt's boarding-house, where I knew Tom Harris and others would lodge. Entering the front room, I heard my name called from amid a group of blue-jackets, and several sunburned, tar-colored men came forward to speak to me. They were, at first, a little embarrassed by the dress and style in which they had never seen me, and one of them was calling me Mr. Dana; but I soon stopped that, and we were shipmates once more. First, there was Tom Harris, in a characteristic occupation. I had made him promise to come and see me when we parted in San Diego; he had got a directory of Boston, found the street and number of my father's house, and, by a study of the plan of the city, had laid out his course, and was committing it to memory. He said he could go straight to the house without asking a question. And so he could, for I took the book from him, and he gave his course, naming each street and turn to right or left, directly to the door.

Tom had been second mate of the Pilgrim, and had laid up no mean sum of money. True to his resolution, he was going to England to find his mother, and he entered into the comparative advantages of taking his money home in gold or in bills,—a matter of some moment, as this was in the disastrous financial year of 1837. He seemed to have his ideas well arranged, but I took him to a leading banker, whose advice he followed; and, declining my invitation to go up and show himself to my friends, he was off for New York that afternoon, to sail the next day for Liverpool. The last I ever saw of Tom Harris was as he passed down Tremont Street on the sidewalk, a man dragging a hand-cart in the street by his side, on which were his voyage-worn chest, his mattress, and a box of nautical instruments.

Sam seemed to have got funny again, and he and John the Swede learned that Captain Thompson had several months before sailed in command of a ship for the coast of Sumatra, and that their chance of proceedings against him at law was hopeless. Sam was afterwards lost in a brig off the coast of Brazil, when all hands went down. Of John and the rest of the men I have never heard. The Marblehead boy, Sam, turned out badly; and, although he had influential friends, never allowed them to improve his condition. The old carpenter, the Fin, of whom the cook stood in such awe (ante p. 41), had fallen sick and died in Santa Barbara, and was buried ashore. Jim Hall, from the Kennebec, who sailed with us before the mast, and was made second mate in Foster's place, came home chief mate of the Pilgrim. I have often seen him since. His lot has been prosperous, as he well deserved it should be. He has commanded the largest ships, and when I last saw him, was going to the Pacific coast of South America, to take charge of a line of mail steamers. Poor, luckless Foster I have twice seen. He came into my rooms in Boston, after I had become a barrister and my narrative had been published, and told me he was chief mate of a big ship; that he had heard I had said some things unfavorable of him in my book; that he had just bought it, and was going to read it that night, and if I had said anything unfair of him, he would punish me if he found me in State Street. I surveyed him from head to foot, and said to him, "Foster, you were not a formidable man when I last knew you, and I don't believe you are now." Either he was of my opinion, or thought I had spoken of him well enough, for the next (and last) time I met him he was civil and pleasant.

I believe I omitted to state that Mr. Andrew B. Amerzene, the chief mate of the Pilgrim, an estimable, kind, and trustworthy man, had a difficulty with Captain Faucon, who thought him slack, was turned off duty, and sent home with us in the Alert. Captain Thompson, instead of giving him the place of a mate off duty, put him into the narrow between-decks, where a space, not over four feet high, had been left out among the hides, and there compelled him to live the whole wearisome voyage, through trades and tropics, and round Cape Horn, with nothing to do,—not allowed to converse or walk with the officers, and obliged to get his grub himself from the galley, in the tin pot and kid of a common sailor. I used to talk with him as much as I had opportunity to, but his lot was wretched, and in every way wounding to his feelings. After our arrival, Captain Thompson was obliged to make him compensation for this treatment. It happens that I have never heard of him since.

Henry Mellus, who had been in a counting-house in Boston, and left the forecastle, on the coast, to be agent's clerk, and whom I met, a married man, at Los Angeles in 1859, died at that place a few years ago, not having been successful in commercial life. Ben Stimson left the sea for the fresh water and prairies, and settled in Detroit as a merchant, and when I visited that city, in 1863, I was rejoiced to find him a prosperous and respected man, and the same generous-hearted shipmate as ever.

This ends the catalogue of the Pilgrim's original crew, except her first master, Captain Thompson. He was not employed by the same firm again, and got up a voyage to the coast of Sumatra for pepper. A cousin and classmate of mine, Mr. Channing, went as supercargo, not having consulted me as to the captain. First, Captain Thompson got into difficulties with another American vessel on the coast, which charged him with having taken some advantage of her in getting pepper; and then with the natives, who accused him of having obtained too much pepper for his weights. The natives seized him, one afternoon, as he landed in his boat, and demanded of him to sign an order on the supercargo for the Spanish dollars that they said were due them, on pain of being imprisoned on shore. He never failed in pluck, and now ordered his boat aboard, leaving him ashore, the officer to tell the supercargo to obey no direction except under his hand. For several successive days and nights, his ship, the Alciope, lay in the burning sun, with rain-squalls and thunder-clouds coming over the high mountains, waiting for a word from him. Toward evening of the fourth or fifth day he was seen on the beach, hailing for the boat. The natives, finding they could not force more money from him, were afraid to hold him longer, and had let him go. He sprang into the boat, urged her off with the utmost eagerness, leaped on board the ship like a tiger, his eyes flashing and his face full of blood, ordered the anchor aweigh, and the topsails set, the four guns, two on a side, loaded with all sorts of devilish stuff, and wore her round, and, keeping as close into the bamboo village as he could, gave them both broadsides, slam-bang into the midst of the houses and people, and stood out to sea! As his excitement passed off, headache, languor, fever, set in,—the deadly coast-fever, contracted from the water and night-dews on shore and his maddened temper. He ordered the ship to Penang, and never saw the deck again. He died on the passage, and was buried at sea. Mr. Channing, who took care of him in his sickness and delirium, caught the fever from him, but, as we gratefully remember, did not die until the ship made port, and he was under the kindly roof of a hospitable family in Penang. The chief mate, also, took the fever, and the second mate and crew deserted; and although the chief mate recovered and took the ship to Europe and home, the voyage was a melancholy disaster. In a tour I made round the world in 1859-1860, of which my revisit to California was the beginning, I went to Penang. In that fairy-like scene of sea and sky and shore, as beautiful as material earth can be, with its fruits and flowers of a perpetual summer,—somewhere in which still lurks the deadly fever,—I found the tomb of my kinsman, classmate, and friend. Standing beside his grave, I tried not to think that his life had been sacrificed to the faults and violence of another; I tried not to think too hardly of that other, who at least had suffered in death.

The dear old Pilgrim herself! She was sold, at the end of this voyage, to a merchant in New Hampshire, who employed her on short voyages, and, after a few years, I read of her total loss at sea, by fire, off the coast of North Carolina.

Captain Faucon, who took out the Alert, and brought home the Pilgrim, spent many years in command of vessels in the Indian and Chinese seas, and was in our volunteer navy during the late war, commanding several large vessels in succession, on the blockade of the Carolinas, with the rank of lieutenant. He has now given up the sea, but still keeps it under his eye, from the piazza of his house on the most beautiful hill in the environs of Boston. I have the pleasure of meeting him often. Once, in speaking of the Alert's crew, in a company of gentlemen, I heard him say that that crew was exceptional: that he had passed all his life at sea, but whether before the mast or abaft, whether officer or master, he had never met such a crew, and never should expect to; and that the two officers of the Alert, long ago shipmasters, agreed with him that, for intelligence, knowledge of duty and willingness to perform it, pride in the ship, her appearance and sailing, and in absolute reliableness, they never had seen their equal. Especially he spoke of his favorite seaman, French John. John, after a few more years at sea, became a boatman, and kept his neat boat at the end of Granite Wharf, and was ready to take all, but delighted to take any of us of the old Alert's crew, to sail down the harbor. One day Captain Faucon went to the end of the wharf to board a vessel in the stream, and hailed for John. There was no response, and his boat was not there. He inquired of a boatman near, where John was. The time had come that comes to all! There was no loyal voice to respond to the familiar call, the hatches had closed over him, his boat was sold to another, and he had left not a trace behind. We could not find out even where he was buried.

Mr. Richard Brown, of Marblehead, our chief mate in the Alert, commanded many of our noblest ships in the European trade, a general favorite. A few years ago, while stepping on board his ship from the wharf, he fell from the plank into the hold and was killed. If he did not actually die at sea, at least he died as a sailor,—he died on board ship.

Our second mate, Evans, no one liked or cared for, and I know nothing of him, except that I once saw him in court, on trial for some alleged petty tyranny towards his men,—still a subaltern officer.

The third mate, Mr. Hatch, a nephew of one of the owners, though only a lad on board the ship, went out chief mate the next voyage, and rose soon to command some of the finest clippers in the California and India trade, under the new order of things,—a man of character, good judgment, and no little cultivation.

Of the other men before the mast in the Alert, I know nothing of peculiar interest. When visiting, with a party of ladies and gentlemen, one of our largest line-of-battle ships, we were escorted about the decks by a midshipman, who was explaining various matters on board, when one of the party came to me and told me that there was an old sailor there with a whistle round his neck, who looked at me and said of the officer, "he can't show him anything aboard a ship." I found him out, and, looking into his sunburnt face, covered with hair, and his little eyes drawn up into the smallest passages for light,—like a man who had peered into hundreds of northeasters,—there was old "Sails" of the Alert, clothed in all the honors of boatswain's-mate. We stood aside, out of the cun of the officers, and had a good talk over old times. I remember the contempt with which he turned on his heel to conceal his face, when the midshipman (who was a grown youth) could not tell the ladies the length of a fathom, and said it depended on circumstances. Notwithstanding his advice and consolation to "Chips," in the steerage of the Alert, and his story of his runaway wife and the flag-bottomed chairs (ante, p. 249), he confessed to me that he had tried marriage again, and had a little tenement just outside the gate of the yard.

Harry Bennett, the man who had the palsy, and was unfeelingly left on shore when the Alert sailed, came home in the Pilgrim, and I had the pleasure of helping to get him into the Massachusetts General Hospital. When he had been there about a week, I went to see him in his ward, and asked him how he got along. "Oh! first-rate usage, sir; not a hand's turn to do, and all your grub brought to you, sir." This is a sailor's paradise,—not a hand's turn to do, and all your grub brought to you. But an earthly paradise may pall. Bennett got tired of in-doors and stillness, and was soon out again, and set up a stall, covered with canvas, at the end of one of the bridges, where he could see all the passers-by, and turn a penny by cakes and ale. The stall in time disappeared, and I could learn nothing of his last end, if it has come.

Of the lads who, beside myself, composed the gig's crew, I know something of all but one. Our bright-eyed, quick-witted little cockswain, from the Boston public schools, Harry May, or Harry Bluff, as he was called, with all his songs and gibes, went the road to ruin as fast as the usual means could carry him. Nat, the "bucket-maker," grave and sober, left the seas, and, I believe, is a hack-driver in his native town, although I have not had the luck to see him since the Alert hauled into her berth at the North End.

One cold winter evening, a pull at the bell, and a woman in distress wished to see me. Her poor son George,—George Somerby,—"you remember him, sir; he was a boy in the Alert; he always talks of you,—he is dying in my poor house." I went with her, and in a small room, with the most scanty furniture, upon a mattress on the floor,—emaciated, ashy pale, with hollow voice and sunken eyes,—lay the boy George, whom we took out a small, bright boy of fourteen from a Boston public school, who fought himself into a position on board ship (ante, p. 231), and whom we brought home a tall, athletic youth, that might have been the pride and support of his widowed mother. There he lay, not over nineteen years of age, ruined by every vice a sailor's life absorbs. He took my hand in his wasted feeble fingers, and talked a little with his hollow, death-smitten voice. I was to leave town the next day for a fortnight's absence, and whom had they to see to them? The mother named her landlord,—she knew no one else able to do much for them. It was the name of a physician of wealth and high social position, well known in the city as the owner of many small tenements, and of whom hard things had been said as to his strictness in collecting what he thought his dues. Be that as it may, my memory associates him only with ready and active beneficence. His name has since been known the civilized world over, from his having been the victim of one of the most painful tragedies in the records of the criminal law. I tried the experiment of calling upon him; and, having drawn him away from the cheerful fire, sofa, and curtains of a luxurious parlor, I told him the simple tale of woe, of one of his tenants, unknown to him even by name. He did not hesitate; and I well remember how, in that biting, eager air, at a late hour, he drew his cloak about his thin and bent form, and walked off with me across the Common, and to the South End, nearly two miles of an exposed walk, to the scene of misery. He gave his full share, and more, of kindness and material aid; and, as George's mother told me, on my return, had with medical aid and stores, and a clergyman, made the boy's end as comfortable and hopeful as possible.

The Alert made two more voyages to the coast of California, successful, and without a mishap, as usual, and was sold by Messrs. Bryant and Sturgis, in 1843, to Mr. Thomas W. Williams, a merchant of New London, Connecticut, who employed her in the whale-trade in the Pacific. She was as lucky and prosperous there as in the merchant service. When I was at the Sandwich Islands in 1860, a man was introduced to me as having commanded the Alert on two cruises, and his friends told me that he was as proud of it as if he had commanded a frigate.

I am permitted to publish the following letter from the owner of the Alert, giving her later record and her historic end,—captured and burned by the rebel Alabama:—

New London, March 17, 1868.

Richard H. Dana, Esq.:

Dear Sir,—I am happy to acknowledge the receipt of your favor of the 14th inst., and to answer your inquiries about the good ship Alert. I bought her of Messrs. Bryant and Sturgis in the year 1843, for my firm of Williams and Haven, for a whaler, in which business she was successful until captured by the rebel steamer Alabama, September, 1862, making a period of more than nineteen years, during which she took and delivered at New London upwards of twenty-five thousand barrels of whale and sperm oil. She sailed last from this port, August 30, 1862, for Hurd's Island (the newly discovered land south of Kerguelen's), commanded by Edwin Church, and was captured and burned on the 9th of September following, only ten days out, near or close to the Azores, with thirty barrels of sperm oil on board, and while her boats were off in pursuit of whales.

The Alert was a favorite ship with all owners, officers, and men who had anything to do with her; and I may add almost all who heard her name asked if that was the ship the man went in who wrote the book called "Two Years before the Mast"; and thus we feel, with you, no doubt, a sort of sympathy at her loss, and that, too, in such a manner, and by wicked acts of our own countrymen.

My partner, Mr. Haven, sends me a note from the office this P. M., saying that he had just found the last log-book, and would send up this evening a copy of the last entry on it; and if there should be anything of importance I will enclose it to you, and if you have any further inquiries to put, I will, with great pleasure, endeavor to answer them.

Remaining very respectfully and truly yours,

THOMAS W. WILLIAMS.

P. S.—Since writing the above I have received the extract from the log-book, and enclose the same.

THE LAST ENTRY IN THE LOG-BOOK OF THE ALERT.

"September 9, 1862.

"Shortly after the ship came to the wind, with the main yard aback, we went alongside and were hoisted up, when we found we were prisoners of war, and our ship a prize to the Confederate steamer Alabama. We were then ordered to give up all nautical instruments and letters appertaining to any of us. Afterwards we were offered the privilege, as they called it, of joining the steamer or signing a parole of honor not to serve in the army or navy of the United States. Thank God no one accepted the former of these offers. We were all then ordered to get our things ready in haste, to go on shore,—the ship running off shore all the time. We were allowed four boats to go on shore in, and when we had got what things we could take in them, were ordered to get into the boats and pull for the shore,—the nearest land being about fourteen miles off,—which we reached in safety, and, shortly after, saw the ship in flames.

"So end all our bright prospects, blasted by a gang of miscreants, who certainly can have no regard for humanity so long as they continue to foster their so-called peculiar institution, which is now destroying our country."

I love to think that our noble ship, with her long record of good service and uniform success, attractive and beloved in her life, should have passed, at her death, into the lofty regions of international jurisprudence and debate, forming a part of the body of the "Alabama Claims"; that, like a true ship, committed to her element once for all at her launching, she perished at sea, and, without an extreme use of language, we may say, a victim in the cause of her country.

R. H. D., Jr.

BOSTON, May 6, 1869.

[1] Pronounced *Leese.*

9 789361 903069

Printed at Repro India Ltd.